European Political Facts of the Twentieth Century

European Political Facts of the Twentieth Century

Chris Cook

and

John Paxton

Fifth Edition

palgrave

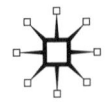
Published 2001 by
PALGRAVE
Houndmills, Basingstoke, Hampshire RG21 6XS and
175 Fifth Avenue, New York, N. Y. 10010
Companies and representatives throughout the world

PALGRAVE is the new global academic imprint of
St. Martin's Press LLC Scholarly and Reference Division and
Palgrave Publishers Ltd (formerly Macmillan Press Ltd).

ISBN 0–333–79203–3

This book is printed on paper suitable for recycling and
made from fully managed and sustained forest sources.

A catalogue record for this book is available
from the British Library.

Library of Congress Cataloging-in-Publication Data
Cook, Chris, 1945–
    European political facts of the twentieth century / Chris Cook and John
    Paxton.— 5th ed.
        p. cm.
    Rev. ed. of: European political facts, 1900–1996. 4th ed. 1998.
    Includes bibliographical references and index.
    ISBN 0–333–79203–3
        1. Europe—Politics and government—Handbooks, manuals, etc. 2.
    International agencies—Handbooks, manuals, etc. I. Paxton, John. II.
    Cook, Chris, 1945– European political facts, 1900–1996. III. Title.
    JN12 .C643 2000
    320.94'02'02—dc21
                                                                    00–055686

10 9   8   7   6   5   4   3   2   1
10 09 08 07 06 05 04 03 02 01

Printed and bound in Great Britain by
Antony Rowe Ltd, Chippenham, Wiltshire

To Tim Farmiloe
with affection

Contents

Preface

Almost 30 years have now elapsed since we started work on the first edition of this book which was published in 1973. During this period, the face of European politics has seen a dramatic transformation. In Eastern Europe communism has collapsed. The Soviet Union itself is no more. Such states as Czechoslovakia and Yugoslavia have split apart, while new nation states have arisen from the Baltic to the Balkans in their place. With the creation of the European Union, many of the democracies of Western Europe have been exploring ways of achieving ever closer political, economic and social co-operation. Against this background, there remains a clear and increasing need for readily accessible facts concerning the changing history of modern Europe over the last hundred years. Now, with the advent of a new century, the original *European Political Facts* volume has been revised and extended to encompass the whole of the twentieth century, from the earliest events of 1900 to the dramatic resignation of the Russian President, Boris Yeltsin, on 31 December 1999.

Our coverage once again is from the Atlantic to the Urals and in adopting this broad, outward-looking concept of Europe we have, naturally, continued to encounter considerable editorial difficulties. The general aim is comparability between countries. This was not always easy to achieve and in some cases impossible, particularly for comparisons between 'East' and 'West' Europe. This new edition has also expanded in size to accommodate new data, but space provides a natural limit to the information which can be presented for so many countries over so turbulent a century.

We are grateful to many people and organizations for their help and advice. In the first place we should like to acknowledge our debt to David Butler, who was a pathfinder with his original and highly successful *British Political Facts* (Macmillan) (now published as *Twentieth Century British Political Facts*).

Gratitude also goes to Sheila Fairfield and Dione Daffin for hours of work digging for facts; to Brian Hunter for tremendous help on Eastern European countries; and to Stephen Brooks, Harry Harmer and James Robinson.

We have once again to thank Penny White and Linda Hollingworth for excellent typing and sharp eyes for inconsistencies.

But some error and inconsistency can still appear in a work of this kind and the editors are solely responsible. We do ask readers to alert us if they spot errors, and constructive and informed criticism will be welcome for future reprints.

Chris Cook
John Paxton

1
International Organizations

THE UNITED NATIONS (UN)

The United Nations is an association of states which have pledged themselves, through signing the Charter, to maintain international peace and security and to co-operate in establishing political, economic and social conditions under which this task can be securely achieved. Nothing contained in the Charter authorizes the organization to intervene in matters which are essentially within the domestic jurisdiction of any state.

The United Nations Charter originated from proposals agreed upon at discussions held at Dumbarton Oaks (Washington, DC) between the USSR, US and UK from 21 Aug to 28 Sep, and between the US, UK and China from 29 Sep to 7 Oct 1944. These proposals were laid before the United Nations Conference on International Organization, held at San Francisco from 25 Apr to 26 Jun 1945, and (after amendments had been made to the original proposals) the Charter of the United Nations was signed on 26 Jun 1945 by the delegates of 50 countries. Ratification of all the signatures had been received by 31 Dec 1945.

The United Nations formally came into existence on 24 Oct 1945, with the deposit of the requisite number of ratifications of the Charter with the US Department of State. The official languages of the United Nations are Chinese, English, French, Russian, Spanish and Arabic.

The headquarters of the United Nations is in New York City, USA.

Membership. Membership is open to all peace-loving states whose admission will be effected by the General Assembly upon recommendation of the Security Council.

The Principal Organs of the United Nations are: 1. The General Assembly, 2. The Security Council, 3. The Economic and Social Council, 4. The Trusteeship Council, 5. The International Court of Justice, 6. The Secretariat.

1. The General Assembly consists of all the members of the United Nations. Each member has one vote. The General Assembly meets regularly once a year, commencing in September; the session normally lasts until mid-December and is resumed for some weeks in the new year if this is required. Special sessions may be convoked by the Secretary-General if requested by the Security Council, by a majority of the members of the United Nations or by one member concurred with by the majority of the members. The General Assembly elects its President for each session.

The first regular session was held in London from 10 Jan to 14 Feb and in New York from 23 Oct to 16 Dec 1946.

The work of the General Assembly is divided between six main committees, on each of which every member has the right to be represented by one delegate: I. Disarmament and International Security, II. Economic and Financial, III. Social, Humanitarian and Cultural, IV. Special Political and Decolonization, V. Administrative and Budgetary, VI. Legal.

In addition there is a General Committee charged with the task of co-ordinating the proceedings of the Assembly and its Committees; and a Credentials Committee which verifies the credentials of the delegates. The General Committee consists of 29 members, comprising the President of the General Assembly, its 21 Vice-Presidents and the Chairmen of the six main committees. The Credentials Committee consists of nine members, elected at the beginning of each session of the General Assembly. The Assembly has two standing committees – an Advisory Committee on Administrative and Budgetary Questions and a Committee on Contributions. The General Assembly establishes subsidiary and *ad hoc* bodies when necessary to deal with specific matters.

The General Assembly may discuss any matters within the scope of the Charter, and with the exception of any situation or dispute on the agenda of the Security Council, may make recommendations on any such questions or matters. For decisions on important questions a two-thirds majority is required, on other questions a simple majority of members present and voting. If the Security Council, because of lack of unanimity of the permanent members, fails to exercise its primary responsibility for the maintenance of international peace and security in any case where there appears to be a threat to the peace, breach of the peace or act of aggression, the General Assembly shall consider the matter immediately with a view to making appropriate recommendations to members for collective measures, including in the case of a breach of the peace or act of aggression the use of armed force when necessary, to maintain or restore international peace and security.

The General Assembly receives and considers reports from the other organs of the United Nations, including the Security Council. The Secretary-General makes an annual report to it on the work of the organization.

2. The Security Council consists of 15 members, each of which has one vote. There are 5 permanent and 10 non-permanent members elected for a 2-year term by a two-thirds majority of the General Assembly. Retiring members are not eligible for immediate re-election. Any other member of the United Nations will be invited to participate without vote in the discussion of questions specially affecting its interests.

The Security Council bears the primary responsibility for the maintenance of peace and security. It was also responsible for the functions of the United Nations in trust territories classed as 'strategic areas'. Decisions on procedural questions are made by an affirmative vote of nine members. On all other matters the affirmative vote of nine members must include the concurring votes of all permanent members (in practice, however, an abstention by a permanent member is not considered a veto), subject to the provision that when the Security Council is considering methods for the peaceful settlement of a dispute, parties to the dispute abstain from voting.

For the maintenance of international peace and security the Security Council can, in accordance with special agreements to be concluded, call on armed forces, assistance and facilities of the member states. It is assisted by a Military Staff Committee consisting of the Chiefs of Staff of the permanent members of the Security Council or their representatives.

The Presidency of the Security Council is held for one month in rotation by the member states in the English alphabetical order of their names.

The Security Council functions continuously. Its members are permanently represented at the seat of the organization, but it may meet in any place that will best facilitate its work.

A United Nations peacekeeping force was established in Europe in 1964 to prevent a recurrence of fighting in Cyprus between the Greek Cypriot and Turkish Cypriot communities.

The Council has three standing committees, of Experts on Rules of Procedure, on Council Meetings away from headquarters and on the Admission of New Members. In addition, from time to time, it establishes *ad hoc* committees and commissions such as the Truce Supervision Organization in Palestine.

Permanent Members: China, France, Russia, UK, USA.

3. The Economic and Social Council is responsible under the General Assembly for carrying out the functions of the United Nations with regard to international economic, social, cultural, educational, health and related matters.

The Economic and Social Council consists of 54 member states elected by a two-thirds majority of the General Assembly. Retiring members are eligible for immediate re-election. Each member has one vote. Decisions are made by a majority of the members present and voting.

The Council nominally held two sessions a year, from 1992 one, and special sessions may be held if required. The President is elected for one year and is eligible for immediate re-election.

The Economic and Social Council has the following commissions:

Regional Economic Commissions: ECE (Economic Commission for Europe); ESCAP (Economic Commission for Asia and the Pacific; Bangkok); ECLAC (Economic Commission for Latin America and the Caribbean; Santiago, Chile); ECA (Economic Commission for Africa; Addis Ababa); ESCWA (Economic Commission for Western Asia; Baghdad). These Commissions have been established to enable the nations of the major regions of the world to co-operate on common problems and also to produce economic information.

Nine functional commissions on: Crime and Criminal Justice; Social Development; Human Rights; Narcotic Drugs; Science and Technology for Development; Status of Women; Statistics; Sustainable Development; Population and Development.

The Economic and Social Council has the following standing committees: the Committee on Non-Governmental Organizations; the Committee for Programme and Co-ordination; the Committee on Natural Resources; the Committee for Development Planning; the Committee of Experts on the Transport of Dangerous Goods.

Other special bodies are the International Narcotics Control Board and the Administrative Committee on Co-ordination to ensure (1) the most effective implementation of the agreements entered into between the United Nations and the specialized agencies, and (2) co-ordination of activities.

4. The Trusteeship Council. The Charter provides for an international trusteeship system to safeguard the interests of the inhabitants of territories which are not yet fully self-governing and which may be placed thereunder by individual trusteeship agreements. These are called trust territories.

All the original 11 trust territories had become independent or had joined independent countries by 1996.

5. The International Court of Justice was created by an international treaty, the Statute of the Court, which forms an integral part of the United Nations Charter. All members of the United Nations are *ipso facto* parties to the Statute of the Court.

The Court is composed of independent judges, elected regardless of their nationality, who possess the qualifications required in their countries for appointment to the highest judicial offices, or are jurisconsults of recognized competence in international law. There are 15 judges, no 2 of whom may be nationals of the same state. They are elected by the Security Council and the General Assembly of the United Nations sitting independently. Candidates are chosen from a list of persons nominated by the national groups in the Permanent Court of Arbitration established by Hague Conventions of 1899 and 1907. In the case of members of the United Nations not represented in the Permanent Court of Arbitration, candidates are nominated by national groups appointed for the purpose by their governments. The judges are elected for a 9-year term and are eligible for immediate re-election. When engaged on business of the Court, they enjoy diplomatic privileges and immunities.

The Court elects its own President and Vice-Presidents for 3 years and remains permanently in session, except for judicial vacations. The full Court of 15 judges normally sits, but a quorum of 9 judges is sufficient to constitute the Court. In 1993 the Court formed a 70-member Chamber for Environmental Matters. It may form chambers of 3 or more judges for dealing with particular categories of cases, and forms annually a chamber of 5 judges to hear and determine, at the request of the parties, cases by summary procedures.

Competence and Jurisdiction. Only states may be parties in cases before the Court, which is open to the states party to its Statute. The conditions under which the Court will be open to other states are laid down by the Security Council. The Court exercises its jurisdiction in all cases which the parties refer to it and in all matters provided for in the Charter, or in treaties and conventions in force. Disputes concerning the jurisdiction of the Court are settled by the Court's own decision.

The Court may apply in its decision: (a) international conventions; (b) international custom; (c) the general principles of law recognized by civilized nations; and (d) as subsidiary means for the determination of the rules of law, judicial decisions and the teachings of highly qualified publicists. If the parties agree, the Court may decide a case *ex aequo et bono*. The Court may also give an advisory opinion on any legal question to any organ of the United Nations or its agencies.

Procedure. The official languages of the Court are French and English. At the request of any party the Court will authorize the use of another language by this party. All questions are decided by a majority of the judges present. If the votes are equal, the President has a casting vote. The judgment is final and without appeal, but a revision may be applied for within ten years from the date of the judgment on the ground of a new decisive factor. Unless otherwise decided by the Court, each party bears its own costs.

Judges. The judges of the Court are elected by the Security Council and the General Assembly.

'National' Judges. If there is no judge on the bench of the nationality of the parties to the dispute, each party has the right to choose a judge. Such judges shall take part in the decision on terms of complete equality with their colleagues.

The Court has its seat at The Hague, but may sit and exercise its functions elsewhere whenever it considers this desirable. The expenses of the Court are borne by the United Nations.

6. The Secretariat is composed of the Secretary-General, who is the chief administrative officer of the organization, and an international staff appointed by him under regulations established by the General Assembly. However, the Secretary-General, the High Commissioner for Refugees and the Managing Director of the Fund are appointed by the General Assembly.

The Secretary-General acts as chief administrative officer in all meetings of the General Assembly, the Security Council, the Economic and Social Council and the Trusteeship Council.

Secretaries-General:

Trygve Lie (Norway)	1 Feb 1946–10 Apr 1953
Dag Hammarskjöld (Sweden)	10 Apr 1953–17 Sep 1961
U Thant (Burma) [Acting Secretary-General 1961–2]	3 Nov 1961–31 Dec 1971
Kurt Waldheim (Austria)	1 Jan 1972–31 Dec 1981
Javier Perez de Cuellar (Peru)	1 Jan 1982–31 Dec 1991
Boutros Boutros-Ghali (Egypt)	1 Jan 1992–31 Dec 1996
Kofi Annan (Ghana)	1 Jan 1997–

The Secretary-General is assisted by Under-Secretaries-General and Assistant Secretaries-General.

Bibliography:

Baratta, J.P., *United Nations System* [Bibliography] Oxford and New Brunswick (NJ), 1994

THE LEAGUE OF NATIONS

The League of Nations formally came into existence on 10 Jan 1920, through the coming into force at that date of the Treaty of Versailles. The two official languages of the League were English and French. The seat of the League was Geneva, Switzerland.

The League of Nations was an association of states which had pledged themselves, through signing the Covenant (*i.e.* the constitution of the League) not to go to war before submitting their disputes with each other, or states not members of the League, to arbitration or enquiry and a delay of from three to nine months. Furthermore, any state violating this pledge was automatically in a state of outlawry with the other states, which were bound to sever all economic and political relations with the defaulting state.

Secretaries-General of the League:

Sir Eric Drummond [Earl of Perth] (Britain)	1919–1932
Joseph Avenol (France)	1933–1940

On Joseph Avenol's resignation, 26 Jul 1940, Sean Lester (Irish Republic) became Acting Secretary-General.

Membership. The following European states joined the League on the dates given below:

Albania[1]	16 Dec 1920
Belgium	10 Jan 1920
Bulgaria	16 Dec 1920
Czechoslovakia	10 Jan 1920
Denmark	8 Mar 1920
Estonia[1]	22 Sep 1921
Finland	16 Dec 1920
France	10 Jan 1920
Germany	8 Sep 1926
Greece	30 Mar 1920
Hungary	18 Sep 1922
Irish Free State	10 Sep 1923
Italy	10 Jan 1920
Latvia[1]	22 Sep 1921
Lithuania[1]	22 Sep 1921
Luxembourg	16 Dec 1920
Netherlands	9 Mar 1920
Norway	5 Mar 1920
Poland	10 Jan 1920

Portugal	8 Apr 1920
Romania	8 Apr 1920
Spain	10 Jan 1920
Sweden	9 Mar 1920
Switzerland	8 Mar 1920
Turkey	18 July 1932
USSR	18 Sep 1934
UK	10 Jan 1920
Yugoslavia	10 Feb 1920

[1] Made declarations putting the protection of their national minorities under League auspices as a condition of their entry into the League.

The following European states withdrew from the League: Spain on 8 Sep 1926, Germany on 21 Oct 1933, Italy on 11 Dec 1937, and Hungary on 11 Apr 1939, according to Art. 1, par. 3, of the Covenant the notice of withdrawal only came into force two years after it had been given. On 22 Mar 1928, Spain resolved to continue as a member of the League.

Austria ceased to be a member after her annexation by Germany in Mar 1938.

The League was formally dissolved at its final meeting on 8 Apr 1946, but in practice it had not met since 1939.

THE ORGANS OF THE LEAGUE

The Primary Organs of the League were: 1. The Council, 2. The Assembly, 3. The Secretariat, 4. The Permanent Court of International Justice (at The Hague).

1. The Council was originally composed of 4 permanent members (the British Empire, France, Italy and Japan) and 4 non-permanent members to be elected every year by a majority of the Assembly. The first non-permanent members, appointed by the Peace Conference and named in the Covenant before the first Assembly met, were Belgium, Brazil, Greece and Spain. With the approval of the majority of the Assembly, the Council was able to appoint new permanent and non-permanent members. At the Assembly of Sep 1926 Germany was admitted to the League and given a permanent seat on the Council. At the same time the number of non-permanent seats, already increased to 6 in 1922, was further increased to 9, the period of office to be 3 years. In order to institute the new system of rotation, 3 were elected for 1 year, 3 for 2 years, and 3 for 3 years, so that at all subsequent Assemblies 3 members retired instead of 9 at once. Furthermore, the rule was established that a retiring member was ineligible for re-election for 3 years unless specially declared re-eligible. The number of members elected after being declared re-eligible could not exceed 3. Hitherto the only states to secure a declaration of re-eligibility had been Poland and Spain. Both countries applied for re-eligibility in 1937, but neither of them obtained the necessary majority for re-election during the 18th Assembly, Sep 1937. China re-entered the Council in 1936 as a result of such a declaration. Owing to complaints that a number of members of the League were in practice unable to enter the Council, a 10th non-permanent seat was created for 3 years in 1933, and in 1936 this seat was continued in existence for another 3 years and an 11th non-permanent seat created for 3 years (*i.e.* until 1939). Any member of the League not represented on the Council was invited to send a representative to sit on it at any meetings at which matters especially affecting it were being discussed. A similar invitation could be extended to states not members of the League.

The Council met on the 3rd Monday in January, the 2nd Monday in May, and just before and after the Assembly in September.

2. The Assembly. Every member state of the League was entitled to be represented by a delegation to the Assembly composed of not more than three delegates and three substitute delegates, but it had only one vote. It met at the seat of the League (Geneva) on the second or, in certain circumstances, the first Monday in September. It could meet at other places than Geneva; extraordinary sessions could be called to deal with urgent matters.

The President was elected at the first meeting of the session, and held office for the duration of the session.

The Assembly divided itself into the following seven principal committees, on each of which every member state of the League had the right to be represented by one delegate:

   I. Juridical.
  II. Technical Organizations.
 III. Disarmament.
 IV. Budget and Staff.
  V. Social Questions.
 VI. Political Questions and admission of New Members.
VII. As an experiment, the General Committee of the 19th Assembly decided to set up a Seventh Committee to deal with questions of Health, Opium and Intellectual Co-operation.

The decisions of the Assembly had to be voted unanimously, except where the Covenant or the Peace Treaties provided otherwise. As a general principle decisions on questions of procedure were voted by majority, or in some cases by a two-thirds majority.

3. The Secretariat was a permanent organ composed of the Secretary-General and a number of officials selected from among citizens of all member states and from the United States of America. The Secretary-General, who took office in Jul 1933, was M. Joseph Avenol (France). The other officials were appointed by the Secretary-General with the approval of the Council.

The Under-Secretaries-General as from 1 Feb 1937 were:

> Sean Lester (Ireland) Deputy-Secretary-General
> F. Walters (UK)
> Vladimir Sokoline (USSR) as from 20 Feb 1937
> Podesta Costa (Argentine) as from Jan 1938

4. Permanent Court of International Justice. The Permanent Court at The Hague was created by an international treaty, the Statute of the Court, which was drafted in 1920 by a committee appointed by the Council of the League of Nations and revised in 1929 with amendments which came into force in 1936. The revised Statutes adopted at the 10th Assembly provided for 15 judges for the Court, and stipulated that the Court should remain permanently in Session except for such holidays as it may decide. The judges were elected jointly by the Council and the Assembly of the League for a term of 9 years.

On the dissolution of the League of Nations and the establishment of the United Nations Organization, the Court was superseded by the International Court of Justice.

The Secondary Organs of the League were:

(a) The Technical Organizations
    1. Economic and Financial
    2. Health
    3. Communications and Transit
(b) Advisory Committees
    1. Military, Naval and Air Commission
    2. Commission of Enquiry for European Union
    3. Mandates Commission
    4. Opium Committee
    5. Social Committee
    6. Committee of Experts on Slavery
(c) Committees on Intellectual Co-operation
(d) International Institutes
    1. Institute of Intellectual Co-operation (Paris)
    2. Institute of Private Law (Rome)
(e) Administrative Organization High Commissioner for Free City of Danzig

BANK FOR INTERNATIONAL SETTLEMENTS (BIS)

Founded in 1930, originally to settle the question of German First World War reparations, the BIS is the 'central banks' bank'. It aims to promote co-operation between central banks, to provide facilities for international financial operations and act as agent or trustee in international financial settlements. Its assets are owned by 32 central banks, and the headquarters are in Basle, Switzerland.

The Board of Directors consists of the governor of the central bank and one other appointee from Belgium, France, Germany, Italy, the UK and the USA. Governors of not more than nine central banks are eligible for election.

INTERNATIONAL LABOUR ORGANIZATION (ILO)

The ILO was constituted in 1919 as an autonomous organization of the League of Nations. Its aim is to improve labour conditions through international action. Membership of the League carried with it membership of the Organization. In 1946 the Organization was recognized as a specialized agency of the United Nations.

One of the ILO's principal functions is the formulation of international standards in the form of International Labour Conventions and Recommendations. Member countries are required to submit Conventions to their competent national authorities with a view to ratification. If a country ratifies a Convention it agrees to bring its laws into line with its terms and to report periodically how these regulations are being applied. More than 6000 ratifications of 176 Conventions had been deposited by mid-1995. Machinery is available to ascertain whether Conventions thus ratified are effectively applied.

Recommendations do not require ratification, but member states are obliged to consider them with a view to giving effect to their provisions by legislation or other action. By the end of 1995 the International Labour Conference had adopted 183 recommendations.

The ILO consists of the International Labour Conference, the Governing Body and the International Labour Office.

In 1960 the ILO established in Geneva the International Institute for Labour Studies. The Institute specializes in advanced education and research on social and labour policy. It brings together for group study experienced persons from all parts of the world – government administrators, trade-union officials, industrial experts, management, university and other specialists. The International Training Centre of the ILO, in Turin, was set up in 1965 to lead the training programmes implemented by the ILO as part of its technical co-operation activities. Member states and the UN system also call on its resources and experience. A UN Staff College was established on the Turin Campus in 1996.

INTERNATIONAL CONFEDERATION OF
FREE TRADE UNIONS (ICFTU)

The ICFTU was founded in London in Dec 1949. The amended constitution provides for co-operation with the UN and the ILO and for regional organizations to promote trade unionism, especially in developing countries.

The Congress of the Confederation meets every 4 years and elects the Executive Board of 50 members nominated on an area basis for a 4-year period; the Board meets at least once a year. There are joint committees with the International Trade Secretariat. In 1999 there was a membership of about 124m. from 188 affiliated organizations in 145 countries.

WORLD CONFEDERATION OF LABOUR (WCL)

The International Federation of Christian Trade Unions was established in 1920 as a mainly Catholic organization; it ceased to exist in 1940 through Fascist and Nazi suppression, most of its members being Italian or German. It was reconstituted in 1945 and renamed World Confederation of Labour in 1968. Its policy is based on the papal encyclicals *Rerum novarum* (1891) and *Quadragesimo anno* (1931), but it claims some Protestant members in Europe.

The Christian International is federative, leaving wide discretion to the autonomy of its constituent unions. Its governing body is Congress, which meets every 3 years. The General Council, meeting at least once a year, is composed according to the proportion of membership of Congress. Congress elects the Executive Committee of at least 12 members which appoints the Secretary-General.

A total membership of 11m. in about 90 countries is claimed. The largest group is the Confederation of Christian Trade Unions of Belgium with a membership of 1.2m.

ORGANIZATION FOR ECONOMIC CO-OPERATION
AND DEVELOPMENT (OECD)

On 30 Sep 1961 the Organization for European Economic Co-operation (OEEC) was replaced by the Organization for Economic Co-operation and Development. The change of title marks the Organization's altered status and functions: with the accession of Canada and the USA as full members it ceased to be a purely European body; while at the same time it added development aid to the list of its other activities. The member countries were (1996) Australia, Austria, Belgium, Canada, the Czech Republic, Denmark, Finland, France, Federal Republic of Germany, Greece, Iceland, Ireland, Italy, Japan, Luxembourg, Mexico, the Netherlands, New Zealand, Norway, Portugal, Spain, Sweden, Switzerland, Turkey, UK and USA. The EU Commission generally takes part in OECD work.

Objectives are to promote economic and social welfare throughout the OECD area by assisting its member governments in the formulation of policies designed to this end and by co-ordinating these policies; and to stimulate and harmonize its members' efforts in favour of developing countries.

The supreme body is the Council composed of one representative for each member country. It meets either at Heads of Delegations level (about twice a month) under the chairmanship of the Secretary-General, or at ministerial level (usually once a year) under the chairmanship of a minister of a country elected annually to assume these functions. Decisions and Recommendations are adopted by mutual agreement of all members of the Council.

The Council is assisted by an Executive Committee composed of 14 members of the Council designated annually by the latter. The major part of the Organization's work is, however, prepared and carried out in specialized committees, working parties and sub-groups, of which there exist over 200.

In 1990 the Centre for Co-operation with European Economies in Transition (CCET) was established to act as OECD's point of contact for Central and East European countries seeking guidance in moving towards a market economy.

Three autonomous or semi-autonomous bodies also belong to the Organization: the International Energy Agency (IEA); the Nuclear Energy Agency (NEA) and the Centre for Educational Research and Innovation (CERI). Each one of these bodies has its own governing committee.

The Council, the committees and the other bodies are serviced by an international Secretariat. The Council is chaired by a minister from each country elected in annual rotation.

All member countries have established permanent Delegations to OECD, each headed by an ambassador.

Secretaries-General:

Thorkil Kristensen (Denmark)	1961–1969
Emile van Lennep (Netherlands)	1969–1984
Jean-Claude Paye (France)	1984–1996
Donald Johnston (Canada)	1996–

Headquarters: 2 rue André Pascal, 75775 Paris Cedex 16, France.

NORTH ATLANTIC TREATY ORGANIZATION (NATO)

On 28 Apr 1948 the Canadian Secretary of State for External Affairs broached the idea of a 'security league' of the free nations, in extension of the Brussels Treaty of 17 Mar 1948. The United States Senate, on 11 Jun, recommended 'the association of the United States with such regional and other collective arrangements as are based on continuous self-help and mutual aid, and as affect its national security'. Detailed proposals were subsequently worked out between the Brussels Treaty powers, the USA and Canada.

On 4 Apr 1949 the foreign ministers of Belgium, Canada, Denmark, France, Iceland, Italy, Luxembourg, the Netherlands, Norway, Portugal, the UK and the USA met in Washington and signed a treaty, the first article of which read as follows:

> The parties undertake, as set forth in the Charter of the United Nations, to settle any international disputes in which they may be involved by peaceful means in such a manner that international peace and security and justice are not endangered, and to refrain in their international relations from the threat or use of force in any manner inconsistent with the purposes of the United Nations.

The Treaty came into force on 24 Aug 1949. Greece and Turkey acceded to the Treaty in 1952, the Federal Republic of Germany in 1955 (the reunified Germany in 1990), Spain in 1982, Czech Republic, Hungary and Poland in 1999. Total 19 members.

The Atlantic Alliance was established as a defensive political and military alliance of independent countries in accordance with the terms of the UN Charter. It provides common security for its members through co-operation and consultation in political, military and economic as well as scientific and other non-military fields. The Alliance also links the security of North America to that of Europe. NATO is the organization which enables the goals of the Alliance to be implemented. With the demise of the Warsaw Pact in 1991 and the end of the Cold War, the Atlantic Alliance has undertaken a fundamental transformation of its structures and policies, following the London (Jul 1990), Rome (Nov 1991) and Brussels (Jan 1994) Summits, to meet the new security challenges in Europe.

The initiatives taken at the Brussels Summit in Jan 1994 include endorsement of the concept of Combined Joint Task Forces (CJTFs) and other measures to support the development of a European Security and Defence Identity. CJTFs will provide separable military capabilities which could be employed either by NATO or, in some circumstances, by the Western European Union. They could also enable non-NATO member nations to participate in military operations.

The Brussels Summit reaffirmed that the Alliance remains open to new member states, as part of an evolutionary process; and it launched a major new initiative, which goes beyond dialogue and co-operation, called Partnership for Peace. The states participating in the NACC and other CSCE countries able and willing to contribute to this programme have been invited to join the NATO member states in this Partnership. The Partnership for Peace programme seeks to expand and intensify political and military co-operation throughout Europe. Depending on the capacity and desire of each participating state, Partners work towards transparency in defence budgeting, promoting democratic control of defence ministries, joint planning, joint military exercises, and creating an ability to operate with NATO forces in such fields as peacekeeping, search and rescue and humanitarian operations. Moreover, NATO will consult with any active Partner that perceives a direct threat to its territorial integrity, political independence, or security.

At a summit meeting held in Madrid in July 1997, three new countries (Czech Republic, Hungary and Poland) were invited to begin negotiations to join NATO. This was achieved in 1999.

A further summit meeting was held in Washington in April 1999, during the height of the conflict in Kosovo, when NATO countries conducted an air campaign to end the ethnic cleansing and repression of human rights perpetrated by the government of the Federal Republic of Yugoslavia. The conflict ended in late Jun 1999, following the withdrawal of Serb forces and the deployment of the NATO-led Kosovo Force (KFOR) tasked by the UN Security Council with the implementation of the Military–Technical Agreement concluded on 9 Jun.

The Washington Summit focused on the ongoing crisis in Kosovo and addressed issues relating to future stability in south-eastern Europe. Other decisions taken in Washington included the approval and publication of a revised Alliance Strategic Concept; adoption of a Membership Action Plan; endorsement of measures to further enhance the Partnership for Peace programme; and the launching of new initiatives designed to adapt the defence capabilities of NATO member countries to changing requirements and inject new momentum into efforts to limit the proliferation of weapons of mass destruction.

Twenty-five Central and Eastern European and other CSCE countries have joined Partnership for Peace: Albania, Armenia, Austria, Azerbaijan, Belarus, Bulgaria, the Czech Republic, Estonia, Finland, Georgia, Hungary, Kazakhstan, Kyrgyzstan, Latvia, Lithuania, Moldova, Poland, Romania, Russia, Slovakia, Slovenia, Sweden, Turkmenistan, Ukraine and Uzbekistan.

Headquarters: B-1110 Brussels, Belgium.

Secretaries-General:

Lord Ismay (UK)	1952–1957
Paul-Henri Spaak (Belgium)	1957–1961
Alberico Casardi (Acting)	1961 (Mar–Apr)
Dirk Stikker (Netherlands)	1961–1964
Manlio Brosio (Italy)	1964–1971
Joseph Luns (Netherlands)	1971–1984
Lord Carrington (UK)	1984–1988
Manfred Wörner (Germany)	1988–1995
Javier Solana Madariaga (Spain)	1995–1999
Lord Robertson (UK)	1999–

The Secretary-General takes the chair at all Council meetings, except at the opening and closing of Ministerial sessions, when he gives way to the Council President. The office of President is held annually by the Foreign Minister of one of the Treaty countries.

The Military Committee is composed of the Chiefs of Staff or their representatives of all the member countries except France, which in 1966 withdrew from the Military Committee while remaining a member of the Council. (Iceland, having no military establishment, may be represented by a civilian.) It meets at Chiefs of Staff level at least twice a year as required, but remains in permanent session at the level of military representatives and is assisted by an integrated international military staff. It provides general policy guidance of a military nature to the Council.

The area covered by the North Atlantic Treaty was divided among three commands: the Atlantic Ocean Command, the European Command and the Channel Command. These were replaced by two commands in Jul 1994: the European and the Atlantic.

The *Canada-US Regional Planning Group*, which covers the North American area, develops and recommends to the Military Committee plans for the defence of this area. It meets alternately in Washington and Ottawa.

Supreme Allied Commanders, Europe:

Dwight D. Eisenhower (US)	1950–1952
Matthew Ridgway (US)	1952–1953
Alfred M. Gruenther (US)	1953–1956
Lauris Norstad (US)	1956–1963

Lyman L. Lemnitzer (US)	1963–1969
Andrew J. Goodpaster (US)	1969–1974
Alexander Haig (US)	1974–1979
Bernard Rogers (US)	1979–1987
John R. Galvin (US)	1987–1992
John Shalikashvili (US)	1992–1993
George Joulvan (US)	1993–1997
Wesley Clark (US)	1997–

Bibliography:

Williams, P., *North Atlantic Treaty Organization (NATO)* [Bibliography] Oxford and New Brunswick (NJ), 1994

WESTERN EUROPEAN UNION (WEU)

On 17 Mar 1948 a 50-year treaty 'for collaboration in economic, social and cultural matters and for collective self-defence' was signed in Brussels by the Foreign Ministers of the UK, France, the Netherlands, Belgium and Luxembourg.

On 20 Dec 1950 the Western Union defence organization was merged with the North Atlantic Treaty command.

After the rejection by France of the European Defence Community on 30 Aug 1954 a conference was held in London from 28 Sep to 3 Oct 1954, attended by Belgium, Canada, France, Federal Republic of Germany, Italy, the Netherlands, Luxembourg, the UK and the USA, at which it was decided to invite the Federal Republic of Germany and Italy to accede to the Brussels Treaty, to end the occupation of Western Germany and to invite the latter to accede to the North Atlantic Treaty; the Federal Republic agreed that it would voluntarily limit its arms production, and provision was made for the setting-up of an agency to control the armaments of the seven Brussels Treaty powers; the UK undertook not to withdraw from the continent her four divisions and the Tactical Air Force assigned to the Supreme Allied Commander against the wishes of a majority, *i.e.* four, of the Brussels Treaty powers, except in the event of an acute overseas emergency. The Union was formally inaugurated on 6 May 1955. Owing to an overlap with both NATO and the Council of Europe the Union lost much of its role. The social and cultural activities were transferred to the Council of Europe in 1960.

Efforts were made to add a security dimension to the European Community's European Political Co-operation. Opposition came from Denmark, Greece and Ireland and this led the remaining EC countries, all WEU members, to reactivate the Union in 1984. Members committed themselves to harmonizing their views on defence and security and developing a European security identity, while bearing in mind the importance of transatlantic relations.

The European Union Maastricht Treaty designated the WEU as the future defence component of the European Union. WEU foreign ministers agreed in the Petersberg Declaration 1992 to assign forces to WEU command for 'peace-making' operations.

A Council of Ministers (foreign and defence) meets biannually in the capital of the presiding country; the presidency rotates biannually, and from 1999 the sequence of WEU presidencies has been harmonized with those of the EU Council of Ministers. A Permanent Council of the member states' permanent representatives meets weekly in Brussels. The Permanent Council is chaired by the Secretary-General and serviced by the Secretariat. A planning department has been established to draw up contingency plans in the areas of humanitarian relief, peacekeeping and crisis management and a military committee was established in 1998. The Assembly of the WEU is composed of 115 parliamentarians of member states and meets twice annually in Paris.

Membership (1999):

Belgium, France, Germany, Greece, Italy, Luxembourg, Netherlands, Portugal, Spain and the United Kingdom. In 1998 Austria, Denmark, Ireland, Finland and Sweden had observer status; the Czech Republic, Hungary, Iceland, Norway, Poland and Turkey were associate members; Bulgaria, Estonia, Latvia, Lithuania, Romania, Slovakia and Slovenia are associate partners.

Secretary-General: José Cutileiro (Portugal).
Headquarters: 4 rue de la Regence, B-1000 Brussels, Belgium.

COUNCIL OF EUROPE

In 1948 the 'Congress of Europe', bringing together at The Hague nearly 1000 influential Europeans from 26 countries, called for the creation of a united Europe, including a European Assembly. This proposal, examined first by the Ministerial Council of the Brussels Treaty Organization, then by a conference of ambassadors, was at the origin of the Council of Europe. The Statute of the Council was signed in London on 5 May 1949 and came into force 2 months later. The founder members were Belgium, Denmark, France, Ireland, Italy, Luxembourg, the Netherlands, Norway, Sweden and the UK. Turkey and Greece joined in 1949, Iceland in 1950, the Federal Republic of Germany in 1951 (having been an associate since 1950), Austria in 1956, Cyprus in 1961,

Switzerland in 1963, Malta in 1965, Portugal in 1976, Spain in 1977, Liechtenstein in 1978, San Marino in 1988, Finland in 1989, Hungary in 1990 and Czechoslovakia (after partitioning the Czech Republic and Slovakia rejoined in 1993) and Poland in 1991, Bulgaria in 1992, Estonia, Lithuania, Romania and Slovenia in 1993, Andorra in 1994 and Albania, Latvia, Macedonia, Moldova and the Ukraine in 1995.

Membership is limited to European states which 'accept the principles of the rule of law and of the enjoyment by all persons within (their) jurisdiction of human rights and fundamental freedoms'. The Statute provides for both withdrawal (Art. 7) and suspension (Arts 8 and 9). Greece withdrew from the Council in Dec 1969 and rejoined in Nov 1974.

Structure. Under the Statute two organs were set up: an inter-governmental *Committee of* (Foreign) *Ministers* with powers of decision and of recommendation to governments, and an inter-parliamentary deliberative body, the *Parliamentary Assembly* – both of which are served by the Secretariat. In addition, a large number of committees of experts have been established, two of them, the Council for Cultural Co-operation and the Committee on Legal Co-operation, having a measure of autonomy; on municipal matters the Committee of Ministers receives the recommendations from the European Local Authorities Conference. The Committee of Ministers meets usually twice a year, their deputies monthly.

The Parliamentary Assembly consists of 291 persons elected or appointed by their national parliaments; it meets 3 times a year. The work of the Assembly harmonizes relations between the 2 organs.

Under the European Convention of 1950 a special structure has been established for the protection of human rights. A European Commission investigates alleged violations of the Convention submitted to it either by states or, in some cases, by individuals. Its findings can then be examined by the European Court of Human Rights (set up in 1959), whose obligatory jurisdiction has been recognized by 20 states, or by the Committee of Ministers, empowered to take binding decisions by two-thirds majority vote. The European Court of Human Rights sits in chambers of 7 judges or exceptionally as a grand chamber of 17 judges. Litigants must exhaust legal processes in their own country before bringing cases before the Court.

For questions of national refugees and over-population, a Special Representative has been appointed, responsible to the governments collectively.

Aims and Achievements. Art. 1 of the Statute states that the Council's aim is 'to achieve a greater unity between its members for the purpose of safeguarding and realizing the ideals and principles which are their common heritage and facilitating their economic and social progress'; 'this aim shall be pursued . . .

by discussion of questions of common concern and by agreements and common action'. The only limitation is provided by Art. 1 (d), which excludes 'matters relating to national defence'.

It has been the task of the Assembly to propose action to bring European countries closer together, to keep under constant review the progress made and to voice the views of European public opinion on the main political and economic questions of the day. The Ministers' role is to translate the Assembly's recommendations into action, particularly as regards lowering the barriers between the European countries, harmonizing their legislation or introducing where possible common European laws, abolishing discrimination on grounds of nationality and undertaking certain tasks on a joint European basis.

In May 1966 the Committee of Ministers approved a programme designed to streamline the activities of the Council of Europe. It comprises projects for co-operation between member governments in economic, legal, social, public health, environmental and educational and scientific matters and is to be reviewed every year.

Some 152 conventions and agreements have been concluded, covering such matters as social security, patents, extradition, medical treatment, training of nurses, equivalence of degrees and diplomas, cultural affairs, protection of archaeological heritage, conservation of European wild life and natural habitat, innkeepers' liability, compulsory motor insurance, the protection of television broadcasts, adoption of children, transportation of animals and *au pair* replacement. A *Social Charter* sets out the social and economic rights which all member governments agree to guarantee to their citizens.

The official languages are English and French.

Secretaries-General:

Jacques Camille-Paris (France)	1949–1953
Leon Marchal (France)	1953–1957
Ludovico Benvenuti (Italy)	1957–1964
Peter Smithers (UK)	1964–1969
Lujo Toncic-Sorinj (Austria)	1969–1974
Georg Kahn-Ackermann (Federal Republic of Germany)	1974–1979
Franz Karasek (Austria)	1979–1984
Marcelino Oreja Aguirre (Spain)	1984–1989
Catherine Lalumière (France)	1989–1994
Daniel Tarschys (Sweden)	1994–

Headquarters: Palais de l'Europe, Strasbourg, France.

EUROPEAN UNION (EU)

In May 1950, Belgium, France, the Federal Republic of Germany, Italy, Luxembourg and the Netherlands started negotiations with the aim of ensuring continual peace by a merging of their essential interests. The negotiations culminated in the signing in 1951 of the Treaty of Paris creating the European Coal and Steel Community (ECSC). After it was found impossible to create European Communities covering Defence and Foreign Affairs, two more communities with the aims of gradually integrating the economies of the six nations and of moving towards closer political unity, the European Economic Community (EEC) and the European Atomic Energy Community (EAEC or Euratom) were created in 1957 by the signing of the Treaties of Rome.

On 30 Jun 1970 membership negotiations began between the Six and the United Kingdom, Denmark, Ireland and Norway. Earlier attempts were vetoed in 1963 and 1967. On 22 Jan 1972 those 4 countries signed a Treaty of Accession, although this was rejected by Norway in a referendum in Nov 1972. On 1 Jan 1973 the UK, Denmark and Ireland became full members. On 28 May 1979 the Greek Treaty of Accession was signed, and Greece joined the Community on 1 Jan 1981; Spain and Portugal on 1 Jan 1986, and Austria, Finland and Sweden on 1 Jan 1995. In a consultative referendum held on 24 Feb 1982, Greenlanders voted by 12 615 to 11 180 to withdraw from the European Community and this was achieved in 1985.

At 31 Dec 1999 13 countries had been accepted as candidates to join the EU. They were: Bulgaria, Cyprus, the Czech Republic, Estonia, Hungary, Latvia, Lithuania, Malta, Poland, Romania, Slovakia, Slovenia, Turkey.

Among the significant landmarks in the development of the European Union have been:

At the summit held at Maastricht 9–10 Dec 1991 the European Council reached agreement on the draft treaty on European Union concerning Political Union and Economic and Monetary Union. This came into effect in Nov 1993. Three 'pillars' formed the basis of the new treaty:

(i) The European Community with its established institutions and decision-making processes;
(ii) A Common Foreign and Security Policy with the Western European Union as the potential defence component of the EU;
(iii) Co-operation in justice and home affairs, with the Council of Ministers to co-ordinate policies on asylum, immigration, conditions of entry, cross-border crime, drug trafficking and terrorism.

The Treaty established a common European citizenship for nationals of all member states and introduced the principle of subsidiarity whereby decisions are taken at the most appropriate level: national, regional or local.

The UK obtained an opt-out from the third state of EMU which established a deadline of 1999 for the introduction of a single currency and did not commit itself to the objectives in the 1989 Social Charter. On 1 Jan 1999 qualifying member states irrevocably fixed their exchange rates against each other and against the euro. The European Central Bank took charge of the single monetary policy and the euro replaced the ECU. The euro became the legal tender of the participating states. Euro notes and coins will be introduced from 1 Jan 2002 and it is planned that they will circulate alongside national currencies for six months, after which time national currencies will be abolished.

On 17 Jan 1997 a new Treaty of Europe, the **Treaty of Amsterdam** was agreed by leaders of the member states of the EU. The Treaty had four main objectives:

(i) To place employment and citizens' rights at the heart of the Union;
(ii) To sweep away the last remaining obstacles to freedom of movement and to strengthen security;
(iii) To give Europe a stronger voice in world affairs;
(iv) To make the Union's institutional structure more efficient with a view to enlarging the Union.

The institutional arrangements of the Communities provide for an independent executive with powers of proposal (the Commission), various consultative bodies, and a decision-making body drawn from the governments (the Council). Until 1967 the three Communities were completely distinct, although they shared both an Assembly (later the European Parliament) and a Court of Justice: from that date the executives were merged in the European Commission, and the decision-taking bodies in the Council. The institutions and organs of the Communities are as follows:

The **Commission** consists of 20 members appointed by the member states to serve for 5 years. Austria, Belgium, Denmark, Finland, Greece, Ireland, Luxembourg, the Netherlands, Portugal, and Sweden all have one Commissioner each, whilst France, Germany, Italy, Spain and the UK have 2 each. The Commission acts independently of any country in the interests of the Community as a whole, with as its mandate the implementation and guardianship of the Treaties. In this it has the right of initiative (putting proposals to the Council for action); and execution (once the Council has decided); and can take the other institutions or individual countries before the Court of Justice should any of these renege upon their responsibilities.

Presidents of the High Authority of the European Coal and Steel Community:

1952	Jean Monnet
1955	René Mayer
1958	Paul Finet
1959	Piero Malvestiti
1963	Dino Del Bo

Presidents of the Commission of the European Economic Community:

1958	Walter Hallstein

Presidents of the Commission of the European Atomic Energy Community:

1958	Louis Armand
1959	Étienne Hirsch
1962	Pierre Chatenet

The Institutions of the three Communities were merged on 1 Jul 1967.
  Presidents of the Commission of the European Communities:

1967	Jean Rey
1970	Franco-Maria Malfatti
1972	Sicco Mansholt
1973	François-Xavier Ortoli
1977	Roy Jenkins
1981	Gaston Thorn
1985	Jacques Delors
1995	Jacques Santer
1999	Romano Prodi

The **Council of the European Union** consists of ministers from the 15 national governments and represents the national as opposed to the Community interests. It is the body which has the power of decision in the Community.

  Each member state has the following weighting attached to its vote in the Council, making a total of 87:

Austria	4	Italy	10
Belgium	5	Luxembourg	2
Denmark	3	Netherlands	5
Finland	3	Portugal	5
France	10	Spain	8
Germany	10	Sweden	4
Greece	5	United Kingdom	10
Ireland	3		

The qualified majority is 62, and a blocking minority 26.

The Presidency of the Council rotates every six months, in January and July, and is as follows for 1995–2002:

1995	France and Spain	1999	Germany and Finland
1996	Italy and Ireland	2000	Portugal and France
1997	Netherlands and Luxembourg	2001	Sweden and Belgium
1998	United Kingdom and Austria	2002	Spain and Denmark

In addition, the Heads of Government meet at least twice a year as the **European Council**.

The **European Parliament** consists of 626 members elected by all member states every five years (since 1979). The division of the seats (1999) was as follows:

Austria	21	Italy	87
Belgium	25	Luxembourg	6
Denmark	16	Netherlands	34
Finland	16	Portugal	25
France	87	Spain	61
Germany	99	Sweden	22
Greece	25	United Kingdom	87
Ireland	15		

The Parliament has a right to be consulted on a wide range of legislative proposals, and forms one arm of the Communities Budgetary Authority. Under the Single European Act it gained greater authority in legislation and can reject certain Council drafts at second reading. Under the Maastricht Treaty it gained the right of 'co-decision' with the Council of Ministers on a restricted range of domestic matters.

Presidents of the European Parliament:

Robert Schuman (France)	1958–1960
Hans Furler (Federal Republic of Germany)	1960–1962
Gaetano Martino (Italy)	1962–1964
Jean Duvieusart (Belgium)	1964–1965
Victor Leemans (Belgium)	1965–1966
Alain Poher (France)	1966–1969
Mario Scelba (Italy)	1969–1971
Walter Behrendt (Federal Republic of Germany)	1971–1973
Cornelius Berkhouwer (Netherlands)	1973–1975
Georges Spénale (France)	1975–1977
Emilio Colombo (Italy)	1977–1979
Simone Veil (France)	1979–1982
Pieter Dankert (Netherlands)	1982–1984
Pierre Pflimlin (France)	1984–1987
Lord Plumb (UK)	1987–1989
Enrico Barón Crespo (Spain)	1989–1991
Egon Klepsch (Germany)	1992–1994
Klaus Hänsch (Germany)	1994–1997
Jose Maria Gil-Robles Gil-Delgado (Spain)	1997–

The Court of Justice comprises 15 judges assisted by 9 advocates-general. A Court of First Instance also comprising 15 judges was established in 1989. The members of these Courts, which sit in Luxembourg, are appointed for 6 years by agreement between the governments of the member states.

The Court's role is to ensure that the European Treaties are interpreted and applied in accordance with the law. The Court can find that a member state has failed to fulfil an obligation under the Treaties. If the member state does not comply with the judgment, the Court may impose a lump-sum or penalty payment on it. The Court reviews the legality of measures taken by the institutions in actions brought to have such measures set aside, and it has power to judge that they are in breach of the Treaties for failing to act.

The Court also gives preliminary rulings, on application by a national court, on the interpretation or validity of points of Community law. If a legal action produces a disputed point of this kind, a national court may seek a ruling from the European Court; it *must* do so if there is no higher court of appeal in the member state concerned, in which case the judgment of the Court is binding.

The Court of First Instance deals with actions brought by individuals and businesses; appeals on points of law are only dealt with by the Court of Justice.

President: Gil Carlos Rodríguez Iglesias (Spain).

Address: Palais de la Cour de Justice, Kirchberg, Luxembourg.

The office of European Union **Ombudsman** was established in 1995.

Ombudsman: Jacob Söderman (Finland)

The **Economic and Social Committee** has an advisory role and consists of 222 representatives of employers, trade unions, consumers, etc. Membership is proportionally distributed among member states: 24 each for France, Germany, Italy and UK, 21 for Spain, 12 each for Austria, Belgium, Greece, the Netherlands, Portugal and Sweden, 9 each for Denmark, Finland and Ireland, 6 for Luxembourg.

The **Court of Auditors** was established by a Treaty of 22 Jul 1975 which took effect on 1 Jun 1977. It consists of 15 members and was raised to the status of a full EU institution by the 1993 Maastricht Treaty. It audits all income and current and past expenditure of the EU.

The **European Investment Bank** (EIB) was created in 1958 by the EEC Treaty to which its statute is annexed. Its governing body is the Board of Governors consisting of ministers designated by member states. Its main task is to contribute to the balanced development of the common market in the interest of the Community by financing projects; for developing less-developed regions; modernizing or converting undertakings; or developing new activities.

The **European Central Bank** (formerly the European Monetary Institute) based in Frankfurt, Germany was established in 1993 by the Maastricht Treaty. It came into operation in Jun 1998 and is responsible for administering the euro.

The **Schengen Agreement** was signed in 1990 by France, Federal Republic of Germany, Belgium, Luxembourg and the Netherlands. The Agreement committed the signatories to abolishing internal border controls. The United Kingdom and Ireland are the only EU member states which do not participate. Norway and Iceland are non-EU countries taking part.

Other bodies include:

The Committee of the Regions (Brussels)
European Monitoring Centre for Drugs (Lisbon)

European Medicines Evaluation Agency (London)

European Agency for Safety and Health at Work (Bilbao)

European Centre for the Development of Vocational Training (Thessalonika)

European Environment Agency (Copenhagen)

European University Institute (Florence)

European Police Office (Europol) (The Hague)

European Foundation for the Improvement of Living and Working Conditions (Dublin)

Office for Harmonization in the Internal Market (Alicante)

Bibliography:

Paxton, J., *European Communities* [Bibliography] Oxford and New Brunswick (NJ), 1992

EUROPEAN FREE TRADE ASSOCIATION (EFTA)

The Stockholm Convention establishing the Association entered into force on 3 May 1960. Founder members were Austria, Denmark, Norway, Portugal, Sweden, Switzerland and the UK. With the accession of Austria, Denmark, Finland, Portugal, Sweden and the UK to the EU, EFTA was reduced to four member countries by 1996: Iceland, Liechtenstein, Norway and Switzerland.

Free trade in industrial goods among members was achieved by 1996. Co-operation with the EU began in 1972 with the signing of free trade agreements and culminated in the establishment of a European Economic Area (EEA), encompassing the free movement of goods, services, capital and labour throughout EFTA and EU countries. The EEA Agreement was signed by all members of the EU and EFTA on 2 May 1992, but was rejected by Switzerland in a referendum on 6 Dec 1992. Entry into force took place on 1 Jan 1994.

Its main provisions are: free movement of products within the EEA from 1993 (special arrangements to cover food, energy, coal and steel); EFTA to assume EU rules on company law, consumer protection, education, the environment, research and development and social policy; EFTA to adopt EU competition rules on antitrust matters, abuse of a dominant position, public procurement, mergers and state aid; EFTA to create an EFTA Surveillance Authority and an EFTA Court; individuals to be free to live, work and offer services throughout the EEA, with mutual recognition of professional qualifications; capital movements to be free with some restrictions on investments; EFTA countries to maintain their own domestic agricultural policies if they wish.

Secretaries-General:

Frank Figgures (UK)	1960–1965
John Coulson (UK)	1965–1972
Bengt Rabaeus (Sweden)	1972–1975
Charles Muller (Switzerland)	1976–1981
Magnus Vahlquist (Sweden) (Acting)	1981 (Oct–Nov)
Per Kleppe (Norway)	1981–1988
Georg Reish (Austria)	1988–1994
Kjartan Johannsson (Iceland)	1994–

NORDIC COUNCIL

The Nordic Council was founded in 1952 as a meeting place for members of parliament and government representatives. The Nordic Council comprises Denmark, Sweden, Iceland, Norway and Finland, as well as the three autonomous territories of Åland, the Faroe Islands and Greenland. The Sami populations in Norway, Sweden and Finland enjoy observer status.

Nordic co-operation is founded on common cultural and political values, reinforced by bonds of affinity and kinship. National identities are strong in the Nordic region; nonetheless, a distinct Nordic identity exists in parallel, exerting considerable influence also over the actions of national governments. Nordic co-operation assumes many forms, and takes place at practically all levels of society.

While the Nordic Council is a parliamentary forum, the Nordic Council of Ministers, which was established in 1971, co-ordinates government activity. Nordic political co-operation is based on the consensus principle.

A common labour market was created in 1954. Equal treatment in matters of social security was assured in 1957. A passport union, designed to eliminate the need for passport controls at inter-Nordic borders, was introduced in 1957. In the following decades co-operation has expanded to include nearly every issue in the public domain.

All five members have strong ties with the European Union, either as members or as partners through the EEA (European Economic Area).

The Nordic Council is composed of 87 parliamentarians. The Nordic Council may adopt resolutions demanding government action. The Nordic Council of Ministers and individual national governments are answerable to the Council for their follow-up. The Nordic Council may also modify the budget of the Council of Ministers. The Plenary Assembly, which convenes once a year, is the highest body of the Nordic Council. Government representatives participate in the Plenary Assembly and have the right to submit proposals and take part in discussions (they do not, however, have the right to vote). The Council is co-ordinated and led by the Presidium, which in 1999 consisted of 13 members.

Secretaries-General:[1]

Emil Vindsetmoe	1 Jul 1971–30 Jun 1973
Helge Seip	1 Dec 1973– 1 Aug 1977
Gudmund Saxrud	18 Aug 1977–31 Aug 1982
Ilkka-Christian Björklund	1 Sep 1982–31 Jan 1987
Gerhard af Schultén	1 Feb 1987–31 Dec 1989
Jostein Osnes	1 Jan 1990–31 Aug 1994
Anders Wenström	5 Sep 1994–31 Jul 1996
Berglind Ásgeirsdóttir	Sep 1996– Sep 1999
Frida Nokken	Sep 1999–

[1] Before 1971 there was no central secretariat.

Headquarters: Store Strandstræde 18, P.O. Box 3043, DK-Copenhagen K, Denmark.

COMMONWEALTH OF INDEPENDENT STATES (CIS)

The Commonwealth of Independent States (CIS) is a multilateral grouping of independent states which proclaimed itself the successor to the Union of Soviet Socialist Republics (USSR) in some aspects of international law and affairs. The member states are the founders, Russia, Belarus and the Ukraine, and nine subsequent adherents: Armenia, Azerbaijan, Georgia, Kazakhstan, Kyrgyzstan, Moldova, Tajikistan, Turkmenistan and Uzbekistan. The common affairs of the CIS are conducted on a multilateral, interstate basis rather than by central institutions. It provides a framework for military, foreign policy and economic co-ordination.

Extended negotiations in the USSR in 1990 and 1991, under the direction of President Gorbachev, sought to establish a 'renewed federation' or, subsequently, to conclude a new union treaty that would embrace all the 15 constituent republics of the USSR at that date. According to a referendum conducted in Mar 1991, 76 per cent of the population (on an 80 per cent turnout) wished to maintain the USSR as a 'renewed federation of equal sovereign republics in which the human rights and freedoms of any nationality would be fully guaranteed'. In Sep 1991 the three Baltic republics, Estonia, Latvia and Lithuania, were nonetheless recognized as independent states by the USSR State Council, and subsequently by the international community. Most of the remaining republics reached agreement on the broad outlines of a new 'union of sovereign states' in Nov 1991, which would have retained a directly elected President and an all-union legislature, but which would have limited central authority to those powers specifically delegated to it by the members of the union.

A referendum in the Ukraine in Dec 1991, however, showed overwhelming support for full independence, and following this Russia, Belarus and the Ukraine concluded an agreement on 8 Dec 1991 establishing a Commonwealth of Independent States (CIS) with its headquarters in Minsk. The USSR, as a subject of international law and a geopolitical reality, was declared no longer in existence, and each of the three republics individually renounced the 1922 treaty through which the USSR had been established.

The CIS declared itself open to other former Soviet republics, as well as to states elsewhere that shared its objectives, and on 21 Dec 1991 in Alma Ata a further declaration was signed by representatives of the three original members and of eight other republics: Armenia, Azerbaijan, Kazakhstan, Kyrgyzstan, Moldova, Tajikistan, Turkmenistan and Uzbekistan. The declaration committed those who signed it to recognize the independence and sovereignty of other members, to respect human rights including those of national minorities, and to the observance of existing boundaries. Relations among the members of the CIS were to be conducted on an equal, multilateral basis, but it was agreed to endorse the principle of unitary control of strategic nuclear arms and the concept of a 'single economic space'. Members pledged themselves to discharge the obligations that arose from the international treaties and agreements to which the USSR had been a party. In a separate agreement the heads of member states agreed that Russia should take up the seat at the United Nations formerly occupied by the USSR, and a framework of inter-state and inter-government consultation was established. Following these developments, Mikhail Gorbachev resigned as USSR President on 25 Dec 1991 and on 26 Dec the USSR Supreme Soviet voted a formal end to the treaty of union that had been signed in 1992 and dissolved itself.

The 'supreme organ' of the CIS is a **Council of Heads of States**; associated with its work is a **Council of Heads of Government**. At a summit meeting of heads of all the states except Azerbaijan in Jul 1992, agreements were reached on the formation of a CIS peacekeeping force, the establishment of an economic arbitration court and a way to divide former Soviet assets abroad, and some progress was made towards the creation of economic co-ordinating structures. At their subsequent meeting in Jan 1993 Russia, Belarus, Armenia,

Kazakhstan, Kyrgyzstan, Turkmenistan and Uzbekistan agreed on a charter to establish a defence alliance, an economic co-ordination committee and an inter-state court. Three participants (Ukraine, Moldova and Tajikistan) agreed only to a declaration that any state would be free to sign the charter in future, and that an inter-state bank should be set up.

On 24 Sep 1993 Russia, Armenia, Azerbaijan, Belarus, Kazakhstan, Kyrgyzstan, Moldova, Tajikistan and Uzbekistan signed an agreement to form an economic union, with Ukraine and Turkmenistan as associated members. Georgia signed some provisions.

A summit meeting in Dec 1993 established a **Council of CIS Foreign Ministers**.

In Dec 1993 the **CIS Inter-State Bank** was set up to facilitate multilateral clearing of CIS inter-state transactions with a starting capital of 5000m. roubles.

The former USSR railway network is administered by the **CIS Railway Council** through operating authorities set up in 1991 in each member country.

Meeting in Jul 1992, representatives of the defence and foreign ministries of member states agreed on the creation of a peacekeeping force (white helmets) to be deployed in intra-CIS conflicts at the request of member states, and with the consent of the parties to the conflict. CIS members contribute to this force in proportion to the size of their armed forces; the commander is appointed on each occasion by the CIS heads of state.

In 1994 the CIS was accorded observer status in the UN.

On 29 Mar 1996 Belarus, Kazakhstan, Kyrgyzstan and Russia signed an agreement increasing their mutual economic and social integration by creating a 'Community of Integrated States'. Tajikistan signed in 1998.

On 2 Apr 1996 a Treaty was signed between Belarus and Russia providing for political, economic and military integration thus creating a 'Community of Russia and Belarus' later renamed 'Union of Belarus and Russia'.

Executive Secretary: Yuri Yarov.
Headquarters: 220000 Minsk, Kirova 17, Belarus.

THE WARSAW PACT

On 14 May 1955 the USSR, Albania, Bulgaria, Czechoslovakia, the German Democratic Republic, Hungary, Poland and Romania signed, in Warsaw, a 20-year treaty of friendship and collaboration, after the USSR had (on 7 May) annulled the 20-year treaties of alliance with the UK (1942) and France (1944).

The main provisions of the Treaty were as follows:

Article 4. In case of armed aggression in Europe against one or several States party to the pact by a State or group of States, each State member of the pact

... will afford to the State or States which are the object of such aggression immediate assistance ... These measures will cease as soon as the Security Council takes measures necessary for establishing and preserving international peace and security.

Article 5. The contracting Powers agree to set up a joint command of their armed forces to be allotted by agreement between the Powers, at the disposal of this command and used on the basis of jointly established principles. They will also take over agreed measures necessary to strengthen their defences.

Article 9. The present treaty is open to other States, irrespective of their social or Government regime, who declare their readiness to abide by the terms of the treaty in order to safeguard peace and security of the peoples.

Article 11. In the event of a system of collective security being set up in Europe and a pact to this effect being signed – to which each party to this treaty will direct its efforts – the present treaty will lapse from the day such a collective security treaty comes into force.

In 1988 (estimate) the armed forces of the Warsaw Pact countries totalled 3 090 000, compared with 2 213 593 NATO forces.

From 1962 Albania was no longer invited to the Warsaw Pact meetings but was not formally expelled. On 8 Jan 1990 Hungary announced that it would cease to participate in Warsaw Pact military activities and would leave the alliance at the end of 1991. East Germany formally withdrew from the Pact on 24 Sep 1990.

On 19 Nov 1990 the Warsaw Pact nations signed the Conventional Forces in Europe Treaty in Paris.

The Warsaw Pact was formally disbanded on 31 Mar 1991.

Commanders-in-Chief:

Marshal I.S. Konev (USSR)	1955–1960
Marshal A.A. Grechko (USSR)	1960–1967
Marshal I.I. Yakubovsky (USSR)	1967–1976
Marshal Viktor G. Kulikov (USSR)	1977–1991

COUNCIL FOR MUTUAL ECONOMIC ASSISTANCE (COMECON OR CMEA)

Membership. Founder members, in 1949, were USSR, Bulgaria, Czechoslovakia, Hungary, Poland and Romania. Later admissions were Albania (1949; ceased participation 1961), Cuba (1972), German Democratic Republic (1950), Mongolia (1962) and Vietnam (1978). From 1964 Yugoslavia enjoyed associated status with limited participation. Afghanistan, Angola, Ethiopia, Laos, Mozambique, Nicaragua and Yemen sent observers to some CMEA bodies.

The Charter consisted of a preamble and 17 articles.
Extracts from the Charter:

Article 1 *Aims and Principles*: '(1) The purpose of the Council is to facilitate, by uniting and coordinating the efforts of its member countries, the planned development of the national economy, acceleration of economic and technical progress in these countries, a rise in the level of industrialization in countries with less developed industries, uninterrupted growth of labour productivity and a steady advance of the welfare of the peoples. (2) The Council is based on the principles of the sovereign equality of all member countries.'

Article 2 *Membership* 'open to other countries which subscribe to the purposes and principles of the Council'.

Article 3 *Functions and Powers* to (a) 'organize all-round . . . cooperation of member countries in the most rational use of natural resources and acceleration of the development of their productive forces', (b) 'foster the improvement of the international socialist division of labour by coordinating national economic development plans, and the specialization and cooperation of production in member countries', (d) to 'assist . . . carrying out joint measures for the development of industry and agriculture . . . transport . . . principal capital investments . . . [and] trade'.

Article 4 *Recommendations and Decisions* '. . . shall be adopted only with the consent of the interested member countries'.

The supreme authority was the *Session* of all members held (usually annually) in members' capitals in rotation. All decisions were unanimous. The Executive Committee was made up of one representative from each member state of deputy premier rank. It met at least once every three months and had a *Bureau for Common Questions of Economic Planning*. The administrative organ was the *Secretariat*.

In 1988 the Secretariat and its subordinate committees and permanent commissions were reduced in size and reorganized. Decision-making on trade matters was delegated to enterprise level.

There were 6 Committees: for Co-operation in Planning; for Scientific and Technical Co-operation; for Co-operation in Engineering; for Co-operation in the Agro-Industrial Complex; for Electronics; and for Co-operation in Foreign Economic Relations. There were 11 Permanent Commissions.

The *International Bank for Economic Co-operation* was founded in 1963 with a capital of 300m. roubles and started operating on 1 Jan 1964. It undertook multilateral settlements in 'transferable roubles' (*i.e.* used for intra-COMECON clearing accounts only) and advanced credits to finance trading and other operations.

The *International Investments Bank* was founded in 1970 and went into operation on 1 Jan 1971 with a capital of 1071m. transferable roubles.

COMECON was founded in Jan 1949, partly in response to such Western initiatives as the Marshall Plan, and ostensibly to promote economic development through the joint utilization and co-ordination of resources. In its early years, however, member states were dominated by the Stalinist drive to autarky and the Council remained a façade, functioning merely as a registration agency for bilateral foreign trade and credit agreements. The mid-1950s brought the first attempts to reduce the parallelism in member states' economies, and the Council began to function as a discussion centre for long-term plan co-ordination, a process perhaps hastened by the signature of the Treaty of Rome in 1957.

In 1962 Khrushchev, with the support of the more industrialized members (Czechoslovakia, East Germany, Poland) attempted to convert COMECON from a trade organization into a supra-national authority under which member states' economies would be integrated according to the 'international socialist division of labour'.

Integration plans failed at this stage, partly owing to domestic developments in the USSR (dismissal of Khrushchev), and partly owing to the obstructionist attitude of Romania, who objected to the status of non-industrialized raw-material producer.

In the aftermath of the USSR's invasion of Czechoslovakia, renewed Soviet pressure in 1969 for integration encountered rather less intransigence. Romania refused to adhere to the International Investments Bank when it was first mooted in 1970, but joined eventually in 1971. Hungary and Poland propounded a view that a free trade area with preferential tariffs should be formed and individual currencies should ultimately be made convertible.

On 10 Jan 1990 COMECON agreed gradually to adopt a free-market approach to their trading policies, and in a final communiqué stressed the need for 'renewal of the whole system of mutual co-operation'. COMECON finally collapsed in 1991 after the revolutions in Eastern Europe. The 9 member states signed a protocol on 28 Jun 1991 providing for the Council to be dissolved in 90 days and this took place on 26 Sep 1991.

Secretaries:

Nikolai Faddeyev (USSR)	1949–1983
Vyacheslav Sychev (USSR)	1983–1991

Bibliography:

Brine, J., *COMECON: The Rise and Fall of an International Socialist Organization* [Bibliography] Oxford and New Brunswick (NJ), 1992

ORGANIZATION FOR SECURITY AND
CO-OPERATION IN EUROPE (OSCE)

Initiatives from both NATO and the Warsaw Pact culminated in the first summit Conference on Security and Co-operation in Europe (CSCE) attended by heads of state and government in Helsinki on 30 Jul–1 Aug 1975, which adopted a 'Final Act' laying down 10 principles concerning human rights, self-determination and the inter-relations of the participant states. Conferences followed in Belgrade (1977–1978), Madrid (1980–1983), Stockholm (1984–1986) and Vienna (1986–1989). At the Paris summit of 19–21 Nov 1990, the members of NATO and the Warsaw Pact signed a Treaty on the Reduction of Conventional Armed Forces in Europe (CFE) and a declaration that they were 'no longer adversaries' and did not intend to 'use force against the territorial integrity or political independence of any state'. All the 34 participants adopted the Confidence and Security-Building Measures (CSBMs), applying to the exchange of military information, verification of military installations, objection to unusual military activities etc., and signed the Charter of Paris.

On 1 Jan 1995 the CSCE changed its name to the Organization for Security and Co-operation in Europe (OSCE).

Members. In 1999 the 55 member nations were: Albania, Andorra, Armenia, Austria, Azerbaijan, Belarus, Belgium, Bosnia–Hercegovina, Bulgaria, Canada, Croatia, Cyprus, the Czech Republic, Denmark, Estonia, Finland, France, Georgia, Germany, Greece, Holy See, Hungary, Iceland, Ireland, Italy, Kazakhstan, Kyrgyzstan, Latvia, Liechtenstein, Lithuania, Luxembourg, Macedonia, Malta, Moldova, Monaco, Netherlands, Norway, Poland, Portugal, Romania, Russian Federation (succeeding USSR), San Marino, Slovak Republic, Slovenia, Spain, Sweden, Switzerland, Tajikistan, Turkey, Turkmenistan, Ukraine, UK, USA, Uzbekistan. Yugoslavia (Serbia and Montenegro) was suspended from activities in 1992.

The *Charter* sets out principles of human rights, democracy, and the rule of law to which all the signatories undertake to adhere, lays down the bases for East–West co-operation and other future action, and institutionalizes the OSCE.

Summits are the highest decision-making bodies. They are periodic meetings of Heads of State or Government of OSCE participating States that set priorities and provide orientation at the highest political level. During periods between summits, decision-making and governing power lies with the *Minis-*

terial Council, which is made up of the Foreign Ministers of the OSCE participating States (it meets at least once a year, but not when there is a summit). The Council's agent is the *Senior Council* which meets four times a year at the Secretariat in Prague.

The *Permanent Council* is the regular body for political consultation and decision-making on all issues pertinent to the OSCE and is responsible for the day-to-day business of the Organization. It meets weekly at the Hofburg Congress Centre in Vienna.

There is also a *Conflict Prevention Centre* in Vienna and an *Office for Democratic Institutions and Human Rights* in Warsaw. The Parliamentary Assembly is formally independent, but maintains close links with the OSCE process. Meetings take place annually in OSCE capitals in rotation. It has a secretariat in Copenhagen. The High Commissioner on National Minorities has the duty of early and impartial evaluation of ethnic conflicts and recommendation of action. There is an office in The Hague.

Secretary-General: Ján Kubiš (Slovakia).
Address: Kärtner Ring 5–7, A-1010 Vienna, Austria.

EUROPEAN BANK FOR RECONSTRUCTION AND DEVELOPMENT (EBRD, BERD)

A treaty to establish the EBRD was signed in May 1990; it was inaugurated on 15 Apr 1991. It had 41 original members: the European Commission, the European Investment Bank, all the EEC countries and all the countries of East Europe except Albania. Albania became a member in Oct 1991, and all the republics of the former USSR in Mar 1992, bringing membership to 60 in 1999.

Its founding capital was of ecu 10m., of which the USA contributed 10 per cent, the UK, France, Germany, Italy and Japan 8.5 per cent each, and the USSR 6 per cent. In 1999 the subscribed capital was ecu 20m. It was established to lend funds at market rates to Central and Eastern European companies and countries 'which are committed to, and applying, the principles of multi-party democracy and market economics'. Facilities were extended to the countries of the former USSR in 1992.

In 1991 the initial emphasis was placed on programmes to support the creation and strengthening of infrastructure; privatization, reform of the financial sector, including development of capital markets and privatization of commercial banks; development of productive competitive private sectors of small and medium-sized enterprises in industry, agriculture and services; restructuring industrial sectors to put them on a competitive basis; encouraging foreign investment and cleaning up the environment. By 1998 the Bank had approved 603 projects.

There is a Board of Governors with full management powers, and a 23-member Board of Directors which is involved in day-to-day operations.

President: Antonio Maria Costa (Italy).

Headquarters: 1 Exchange Square, London EC2A 2JN, England.

OTHER EUROPEAN ORGANIZATIONS

	founded
Economic Commission for Europe (ECE)	1947
Brussels Treaty Organization	1948
Danube Commission	1949
Inter-governmental Committee for European Migration	1952
European Conference of Ministers of Transport (ECMT)	1953
European Organization of Nuclear Research (CERN)	1954
European Civil Aviation Conference (CEAC)	1955
European Nuclear Energy Agency (ENEA)	1957
Benelux Economic Union	1958
European Conference of Postal and Telecommunications Administrations (CEPT)	1959
European Organization for the Safety of Air Navigation (EUROCONTROL)	1963
European Space Agency (ESA)	1975
Central European Initiative (CEI)	1989
Black Sea Economic Co-operation Group (BSEC)	1992
Council of Baltic Sea States	1992

2
Heads of State

ALBANIA

Declared independent 1912, invaded by Austria in 1916. Italian C.-in-C. in Albania proclaims independence again on 3 Jun 1917. A provisional republican government ruled until 1921, followed by government under a Council of Regents until Jan 1925, when Albania was proclaimed a Republic.

PRESIDENT

Ahmed Beg Zogu   31 Jan 1925–30 Aug 1928

Albania was proclaimed a monarchy on 1 Sep 1928 and the President became King Zog I.

KING

Zog I, m. Countess Geraldine Apponyi   1 Sep 1928–13 Apr 1949
                                                                 (formally deposed *in absentia*
                                                                                    2 Jan 1946)
Victor Emmanuel III of Italy (*see* Italy)   14 Apr 1939–30 Nov 1943
                                                          (reigned following Italian invasion until
                                                           Italian cabinet nullified his Albanian title)

Between 1 Dec 1943 and 1 Dec 1945 there were provisional governments with no head of state. The Republic was proclaimed 12 Jan 1946.

PRESIDENT

Omer Nishani   13 Jan 1946–24 Jul 1953
Haxhi Lleshi   24 Jul 1953–22 Nov 1982

Ramiz Alia	22 Nov 1982–8 Apr 1992
Sali Berisha	9 Apr 1992–24 Jul 1997
R. Mejdani	24 Jul 1997–

The President is a nominal head of state; power was held by the First Secretary of the Central Committee: Enver Hoxha, who died 11 Apr 1985, when Ramiz Alia became First Secretary.

ANDORRA

Under the 1993 Constitution, Andorra became an independent, democratic parliamentary co-principality with sovereignty vested in the people rather than the two co-princes, the President of France and the Bishop of Urgel. The co-princes remain heads of state but with limited powers.

ARMENIA

Independence from the USSR was declared on 30 Sep 1991.

PRESIDENT

L. Ter-Petrosyan	16 Oct 1991–3 Feb 1998
R. Kocharian	9 Apr 1998–

AUSTRIA

EMPEROR

Francis Joseph I, m. Elizabeth of Bavaria, succeeded his uncle	2 Dec 1848–21 Nov 1916
Karl, m. Zita of Bourbon-Parma, succeeded his great-uncle	21 Nov 1916–11 Nov 1918 (deposed)

The Republic was proclaimed on 12 Nov 1918.

PRESIDENT

X. Seits (President of the National Assembly and stood in for a head of state)	12 Nov 1918–9 Nov 1920
M. Hainisch	9 Dec 1920–4 Dec 1928
Dr W. Miklas	5 Dec 1928–13 Mar 1938

Austria was incorporated into the German Reich on 12 Mar 1938. For 1938–1945 *see* Germany. A provisional government was installed on liberation, 28 Apr 1945.

PRESIDENT

K. Renner	20 Dec 1945–31 Dec 1950
T. Körner	27 May 1951–4 Jan 1957
A. Schárf	5 May 1957–28 Feb 1965
F. Jonas	23 May 1965–23 Apr 1974 (died)
B. Kreisky	24 Apr 1974–8 Jul 1974 (interim)
R. Kirchschläger	8 Jul 1974–8 Jun 1986
K. Waldheim	8 Jun 1986–8 Jul 1992
T. Klestil	8 Jul 1992–

BELARUS

Belarus became independent in Aug 1991.

PRESIDENT

S. Shuskevich	Sep 1991–28 Jan 1994
M. Hryb	28 Jan 1994–10 Jul 1994
A. Lukashenka	11 Jul 1994–

BELGIUM

KING

Leopold II, m. Marie of Austria, succeeded his father	17 Dec 1865–17 Dec 1909
Albert I, m. Elizabeth of Bavaria, succeeded his uncle Leopold II	17 Dec 1909–17 Feb 1934
Leopold III, m. (i) Astrid of Sweden (ii) Mlle Lilian Baels, succeeded his father	23 Feb 1934–20 Sep 1944
Regency	21 Sep 1944–21 Jul 1950
Leopold III	22 Jul 1950–16 Jul 1951 (abdic.)
Baudouin, m. Fabiola de Mora y Aragón, succeeded his father	17 Jul 1951–31 Jul 1993
Albert II, m. Paola Ruffo di Calabria, succeeded his brother	9 Aug 1993–

BOSNIA–HERCEGOVINA

Bosnia–Hercegovina was recognized as an independent state by the USA and European Union in Apr 1992.

PRESIDENT

A. Izetbegovic	Dec 1990–13 Oct 1998
Z. Radisic	13 Oct 1998–15 Jul 1999
A. Jelavic	15 Jul 1999–

BULGARIA

KING

Ferdinand of Saxe-Coburg-Gotha (elected), m. (i) Marie Louise of Parma (ii) Eleonore of Reuss Köstritz	7 Jul 1887–4 Oct 1918 (abdic.)
Boris III, m. Giovanña of Savoy, succeeded his father	4 Oct 1918–28 Aug 1943
Simeon II, succeeded his father	28 Aug 1943–8 Sep 1946

On 8 Sep 1946 a plebiscite ended the monarchy and established a Republic, which was proclaimed on 15 Sep, but had no head of state until the new constitution came into force on 4 Dec 1947.

PRESIDENT (Chairman of the Presidium)

M. Netchev	9 Dec 1947–27 May 1950
G. Damianov	27 May 1950–27 Nov 1958
D. Ganev	30 Nov 1958–20 Apr 1964
G. Traikov	23 Apr 1964–7 Jul 1971
T. Zhivkov	7 Jul 1971–10 Nov 1989
P. Mladenov	10 Nov 1989–6 Jul 1990
Z. Zhelev	1 Aug 1990–23 Jan 1997
P. Stoyanov	23 Jan 1997–

CROATIA

Croatia declared its independence from Yugoslavia on 30 May 1991.

PRESIDENT

F. Tudjman	19 May 1990–10 Dec 1999
V. Pavletic (acting)	26 Nov 1999–

CYPRUS

From 1918 until 1959 Cyprus was a British dependency; for heads of state *see* United Kingdom. An independent Republic came into being on 16 Aug 1960, the President having been previously elected.

PRESIDENT

Archbishop Makarios[1]	14 Dec 1959–3 Aug 1977 (died)
Spyros Kyprianou	3 Aug 1977–28 Feb 1988
George Vassiliou	28 Feb 1988–28 Feb 1993
Glafcos Clerides	28 Feb 1993–

A Turkish Cypriot Federated State with Rauf Denktash as President was proclaimed 13 Feb 1975.

[1] Nicos Sampson assumed the Presidency on the temporary overthrow of Archbishop Makarios; he was succeeded by the President of the House of Representatives, Glafcos Clerides, on 23 Jul 1974 until 7 Dec 1974 when Archbishop Makarios reassumed the Presidency after his return to Cyprus.

CZECHOSLOVAKIA

An independent state was founded on 14 Nov 1918, formed from four provinces of the Austrian Empire: Bohemia, Moravia, Silesia, Slovakia. (Hungarian Slovakia and Ruthenia joined the Czechoslovak state in 1920.)

PRESIDENT

Tomas G. Masaryk	14 Nov 1918–13 Dec 1935
Edvard Beneš	18 Dec 1935–4 Oct 1938
Emil Hácha	1 Dec 1938–1 Jun 1945

Edvard Beneš continued as President of the Czech government in exile after Czechoslovakia was proclaimed a German protectorate on 16 Mar 1939. He returned to Prague in 1945. (Slovakia: *see* separate entry.)

PRESIDENT

Edvard Beneš	2 Jun 1945–7 Jun 1948
K. Gottwald	14 Jun 1948–14 Mar 1953

A. Zápotecký	21 Mar 1953–13 Nov 1957
A. Novotný	19 Nov 1957–22 Mar 1968
L. Svoboda	30 Mar 1968–27 May 1975
G. Husák	29 May 1975–10 Dec 1989
V. Havel	29 Dec 1989–31 Dec 1992

The Federation of Czechoslovakia was dissolved on 31 Dec 1992.

CZECH REPUBLIC

PRESIDENT

V. Havel	2 Feb 1993–

DENMARK

KING

Christian IX, m. Louise of Hesse-Kessel, formerly Prince Christian of Schleswig-Holstein-Sonderburg-Glücksburg, and appointed heir by the Treaty of London on 8 May 1852	15 Nov 1863–29 Jan 1906
Frederick VIII, m. Louise of Sweden-Norway, succeeded his father	29 Jan 1906–14 May 1912
Christian X, m. Alexandrine of Mecklenburg-Schwerin, succeeded his father Frederick VIII	14 May 1912–20 Apr 1947
Frederick IX, m. Ingrid of Sweden, succeeded his father	20 Apr 1947–14 Jan 1972

QUEEN

Margrethe II, m. Henri de Laborde de Morpezat, succeeded her father	14 Jan 1972–

ESTONIA

Proclaimed an independent state 24 Feb 1918. The constitution came into force on 20 Dec 1920, with a provisional government in power. On formation of the cabinet in 1923 the Prime Minister was given powers of head of state.

PRIME MINISTER AND HEAD OF STATE

I. Kukk	25 Nov 1923–15 Dec 1924
M. Jaakson	16 Dec 1924–14 Dec 1925
J. Teemant	15 Dec 1925–8 Dec 1927
M. Toenisson	9 Dec 1927–3 Dec 1928
A. Rei	4 Dec 1928–8 Jul 1929
O. Strandmann	9 Jul 1929–11 Feb 1931
C. Paets	12 Feb 1931–20 Feb 1932
J. Teemant	21 Feb 1932–31 Oct 1932
C. Paets	1 Nov 1932–26 Apr 1933

A new constitution, setting up the office of President, was adopted on 3 Oct 1934. Constantin Paets was appointed President.

The USSR incorporated Estonia as a member on 7 Aug 1940.

On 20 Aug 1991 Estonia declared an end to the transition period to independence from the USSR and this was recognized by the USSR on 6 Sep 1991.

CHAIRMAN OF THE SUPREME COUNCIL

A. Rüütel	8 May 1990–5 Oct 1992

PRESIDENT

L. Meri	5 Oct 1992–

FINLAND

Proclaimed independent on 6 Dec 1917, and a Regent installed. Republican constitution came into force on 14 Jun 1919.

PRESIDENT

K.J. Ståhlberg	1 Aug 1919–15 Feb 1925
L. Relander	16 Feb 1925–15 Feb 1931
P.E. Svinhufvud	16 Feb 1931–14 Feb 1937
K. Kallio	15 Feb 1937–30 Nov 1940
R. Ryti	19 Dec 1940–4 Aug 1944
C.G.E. Mannerheim	4 Aug 1944–9 Mar 1945
J. Paasikivi	9 Mar 1945–15 Feb 1956
U. Kekkonen	15 Feb 1956–26 Jan 1982
M. Koivisto	26 Jan 1982–1 Mar 1994
M. Ahtisaari	1 Mar 1994–

FRANCE

PRESIDENT OF THE REPUBLIC

E. Loubet	16 Feb 1899–18 Feb 1906
C.A. Fallières	18 Feb 1906–18 Feb 1913
R. Poincaré	18 Feb 1913–18 Feb 1920
P. Deschanel	18 Feb 1920–20 Sep 1920
A. Millerand	20 Sep 1920–11 Jun 1924
G. Doumergue	11 Jun 1924–13 Jun 1931
P. Doumer	13 Jun 1931–6 May 1932
A. Lebrun	10 May 1932–10 Jul 1940

Marshal Pétain on 11 Jul 1940 took over the powers of President and added them to his own as Prime Minister. He then appointed a Chief of State.

CHIEF OF STATE

Adm. Darlan	10 Feb 1941–16 Nov 1942
P. Laval	17 Nov 1942–12 May 1945 (left France)

A Government of National Unity was formed on 1 Dec 1945, with Gen. Charles de Gaulle as head of state. He resigned on 27 Jan 1946. A new constitution came into force on 24 Dec 1946 (Fourth Republic).

PRESIDENT OF THE REPUBLIC

V. Auriol	16 Jan 1947–23 Dec 1953
R. Coty	24 Dec 1953–5 Oct 1958

A new constitution came into force on 5 Oct 1958 (Fifth Republic).

PRESIDENT OF THE REPUBLIC

C. de Gaulle	8 Jan 1959–28 Apr 1969
A. Poher	28 Apr 1969–19 Jun 1969 (interim)
G. Pompidou	19 Jun 1969–2 Apr 1974
A. Poher	2 Apr 1974–24 May 1974 (interim)
V. Giscard d'Estaing	24 May 1974–21 May 1981
F. Mitterrand	21 May 1981–17 May 1995
J. Chirac	17 May 1995–

GEORGIA

Proclaimed an independent state 26 May 1918.

PRESIDENT

N. Jordania	26 May 1918–

Georgia was occupied by Soviet forces in 1921, and became a member of the USSR. Georgia became independent of the USSR on 9 Apr 1991.

PRESIDENT

Z. Gamsakhurdia	May 1991–6 Jan 1992
E. Shevardnadze, Chairman of State Council from 10 Mar 1992	6 Nov 1992–

GERMANY

The German Empire was established on 18 Jan 1871 with King Wilhelm of Prussia as Emperor. From then until 9 Nov 1918 the Kings of Prussia were Emperors of Germany.

EMPEROR

Wilhelm II, m. Augusta of Schleswig-Holstein, succeeded his father	15 Jun 1888–9 Nov 1918 (abdicated)

The Republic was proclaimed on the abdication of Kaiser Wilhelm II.

PRESIDENT

F. Ebert	11 Feb 1919–28 Feb 1925
P. von Hindenburg	26 Apr 1925–2 Aug 1934

CHANCELLOR AND FÜHRER

A. Hitler	2 Aug 1934–30 Apr 1945
C. Doenitz	30 Apr 1945–5 Jun 1945

All power was transferred to the Allied Control Council on the surrender of Germany at the end of World War II on 5 Jun 1945. The constitution of the Federal Republic of Germany came into force on 21 Sep 1949 and reunification with the German Democratic Republic occurred on 3 Oct 1990.

PRESIDENT

T. Heuss	13 Sep 1949–12 Sep 1959
H. Lübke	13 Sep 1959–30 Jun 1969
G. Heinemann	1 Jul 1969–30 Jun 1974
W. Scheel	1 Jul 1974–30 Jun 1979
K. Carstens	1 Jul 1979–30 Jun 1984
R. von Weizsäcker	1 Jul 1984–30 Jun 1994
R. Herzog	1 Jul 1994–30 Jun 1999
J. Rau	1 Jul 1999–

The constitution of the German Democratic Republic came into force on 7 Oct 1949; the Republic ceased to exist on 3 Oct 1990.

PRESIDENT

Wilhelm Pieck	11 Oct 1949–7 Sep 1960

The office of President was replaced by the Council of State on 12 Sep 1960.

CHAIRMAN OF THE COUNCIL OF STATE

Walter Ulbricht	12 Sep 1960–1 Aug 1973
Willi Stoph	3 Oct 1973–29 Oct 1976
E. Honecker	29 Oct 1976–18 Oct 1989
E. Krenz	24 Oct 1989–3 Dec 1989
M. Gerlach	6 Dec 1989–5 Apr 1990
S. Bergmann	5 Apr 1990–3 Oct 1990

GREECE

KING

Gëorgios of Schleswig-Holstein-Sonderburg-Glücksburg (elected) m. Olga of Russia	30 Mar 1863–18 Mar 1913
Konstantinos XII, m. Sophia of Prussia, succeeded his father	18 Mar 1913–11 Jun 1917 (abdic.)
Alexandros, succeeded on the expulsion of his father, Konstantinos	12 Jun 1917–25 Oct 1920
Konstantinos XII, recalled by plebiscite to succeed his son	5 Dec 1920–27 Sep 1922 (abdic.)

Gëorgios II, m. Elizabeth of Romania, succeeded his father	27 Sep 1922–18 Dec 1923 (expelled)

A Republic was established by plebiscite on 13 Apr 1924.

PROVISIONAL PRESIDENT

Adm. Konduriotis	20 Dec 1923–18 Mar 1926

DICTATOR

Gen. Pangalos	18 Mar 1926–22 Aug 1926

PROVISIONAL PRESIDENT (Reappointed)

Adm. Konduriotis	4 Dec 1926–14 Dec 1929

PRESIDENT

A. Zaimis	14 Dec 1929–3 Nov 1935

By a plebiscite on 3 Nov 1935 the Republic ended and the monarchy was restored.

KING

Gëorgios II, returned	25 Nov 1935–1 Apr 1947
Paul I, m. Frederika Louise of Brunswick, succeeded his brother	1 Apr 1947–6 Mar 1964
Konstantinos XIII, m. Anne-Marie of Denmark, succeeded his father	6 Mar 1964–1 Jun 1973

The King handed over his powers to a Regent on 13 Dec 1967 and left Greece. The monarchy was declared abolished on 1 Jun 1973.

PROVISIONAL PRESIDENT

G. Papadopoulos	1 Jun 1973–25 Nov 1973

PRESIDENT

P. Ghizikis	25 Nov 1973–14 Dec 1974
M. Stassinopoulos	18 Dec 1974–20 Jun 1975
K. Tsatsos	20 Jun 1975–12 May 1980
K. Karamanlis	15 May 1980–10 Mar 1985
C. Sartzetakis	29 Mar 1985–5 May 1990
K. Karamanlis	5 May 1990–10 Mar 1995
K. Stefanopoulos	10 Mar 1995–

HUNGARY

The Austrian Emperors ruled Hungary as Emperors until the Dual Monarchy on 12 Jun 1867, when they became separately Emperors of Austria and Kings of Hungary. The Emperor Karl renounced his power in the government of Hungary on 13 Nov 1918.

An independent Republic was proclaimed on 16 Nov 1918.

PROVISIONAL PRESIDENT

Count M. Károlyi   16 Nov 1918–22 Mar 1919

The Soviet Hungarian Republic was proclaimed by Béla Kun's government on 22 Mar 1919, and was followed by a counter-revolutionary régime under Admiral Horthy. In Jun 1920 Hungary was proclaimed a monarchy.

REGENT

Adm. M. von Nagybánya Horthy   1 Mar 1920–16 Oct 1945

A Regency Council was appointed after Horthy's resignation and ruled until the setting up of the Provisional National Government on 24 Dec 1945.

A new republican constitution came into force on 1 Feb 1946.

PRESIDENT

Z. Tildy   1 Feb 1946–30 Jul 1948
A. Szakasits   3 Aug 1948–24 Apr 1950
S. Rónai   8 May 1950–1 Aug 1952

CHAIRMAN OF THE PRESIDIUM

I.M. Dobi   1 Aug 1952–14 Apr 1967

CHAIRMAN OF THE PRESIDING COUNCIL

P. Losonczi   14 Apr 1967–25 Jun 1987
K. Nemeth   28 Jun 1987–29 Jun 1988
B.F. Straub   29 Jun 1988–18 Oct 1989
M. Szuros   18 Oct 1989–3 Aug 1990

PRESIDENT

A. Göncz   3 Aug 1990–

ICELAND

A sovereign state came into being on 1 Dec 1918, still acknowledging the Danish King as head.

KING

Christian X (*see* Denmark)   1 Dec 1918–24 May 1944

The link with the crown was ended and a Republic came into being on 17 Jun 1944.

PRESIDENT

Sveinn Björnssen	17 Jun 1944–25 Jan 1952
Ásgeir Ásgeirsson	1 Aug 1952–31 Jul 1968
Kristján Eldjárn	1 Aug 1968–31 Jul 1980
Vigdis Finnbogadóttir	1 Aug 1980–31 Jul 1996
Olafur Ragnar Grímsson	1 Aug 1996–

IRELAND

By the Irish Free State Agreement Act of 1922 Ireland obtained the status of a self-governing Dominion, still recognizing the British sovereign as head of state.

KING

George V (*see* United Kingdom)
Edward VIII (*see* United Kingdom)
George VI (*see* United Kingdom)

The constitution of the Irish Free State as an independent sovereign state came into force on 29 Dec 1937.

PRESIDENT

Dubhglas de hIde (Dr Douglas Hyde)	25 Jun 1938–24 Jun 1945
S.T. Ô Ceallaigh (S.T. O'Kelly)	25 Jun 1945–24 Jun 1959
Éamon de Valéra	25 Jun 1959–24 Jun 1973
Erskine Childers	25 Jun 1973–17 Nov 1974
Cearbhall Ó Dalaigh	3 Dec 1974–22 Oct 1976
Patrick Hillery	3 Dec 1976–3 Dec 1990
Mary Robinson	3 Dec 1990–12 Sep 1997
Mary McAleese	11 Nov 1997–

ITALY

KING

Victor Emmanual III, m. Elena of Montenegro, succeeded his father Umberto	29 Jul 1900–9 May 1946 (abdic.)
Umberto II, succeeded his father	9 May 1946–13 Jun 1946 (abdic.)

(On 30 Mar 1938 King Victor Emmanual gave unlimited powers to Benito Mussolini to hold in time of war and in the name of the King. Mussolini resigned these powers on 25 Jul 1943.)

A Republic was proclaimed on 18 Jun 1946.

PRESIDENT

L. Einaudi	10 May 1948–29 Apr 1955
G. Gronchi	29 Apr 1955–6 May 1962
A. Segni	6 May 1962–28 Dec 1964
G. Saragat	28 Dec 1964–29 Dec 1971
G. Leone	29 Dec 1971–15 Jun 1978
A. Fanfani	15 Jun 1978–8 Jul 1978
A. Pertini	9 Jul 1978–3 Jul 1985
F. Cossiga	3 Jul 1985–28 Apr 1992
O.L. Scalfaro	28 May 1992–18 May 1999
C.A. Ciampi	18 May 1999–

LATVIA

Proclaimed a sovereign state on 18 Nov 1918.

PRESIDENT

J. Tschakste	18 Nov 1918–8 Apr 1927
G. Zemgals	8 Apr 1927–8 Apr 1930
A. Kviesis	9 Apr 1930–11 Apr 1936
K. Ulmanis	12 Apr 1936–21 Jul 1940

The USSR agreed to accept Latvia on 6 Aug 1940. The USSR recognized the independence of Latvia on 10 Sep 1991.

CHAIRMAN OF THE SUPREME COUNCIL

A. Gorbunovs	–7 Jul 1993

PRESIDENT

G. Ulmanis	7 Jul 1993–8 Jul 1999
V. Vike-Freiberga	8 Jul 1999–

LIECHTENSTEIN

PRINCE

John II, succeeded his father	12 Nov 1858–11 Feb 1929
Francis I, succeeded his brother	11 Feb 1929–25 Aug 1938
Francis Joseph II, succeeded his great-uncle	26 Jul 1938–13 Nov 1989
Hans-Adam II,[1] succeeded his father	13 Nov 1989–

[1] Prince Hans-Adam II exercised the prerogatives to which the sovereign is entitled from 24 Aug 1984.

LITHUANIA

The Lithuanian State was founded in 1253 by Grand Duke Mindaugas and ruled by the Russian Empire 1795–1915.

Proclaimed an independent state 18 Feb 1918. On 21 Jul 1940 Lithuania voted to become a member of the USSR. The USSR recognized the independence of Lithuania on 10 Sept 1991.

PRESIDENT

A. Smetona	1 Apr 1919–19 Jun 1920
A. Stulginskis	21 Dec 1922–7 Jun 1926
K. Grinius	7 Jun 1926–17 Dec 1926
A. Smetona	19 Dec 1926–15 Jun 1940

1940–1941	Soviet occupation
1941–1944	Nazi occupation
1944–1990	Soviet occupation

A.M. Brazauskas	25 Feb 1993–25 Feb 1998
V. Adamkus	26 Feb 1998–

LUXEMBOURG

GRAND DUKE

Adolf William of Nassau	23 Nov 1890–17 Nov 1905
William, succeeded his father	17 Nov 1905–25 Feb 1912

GRAND DUCHESS

Marie-Adelaide, succeeded her father Grand Duke Willem	26 Jun 1912–15 Jan 1919 (abdic.)
Charlotte, m. Felix of Bourbon Parma, succeeded her sister	15 Jan 1919–12 Nov 1964 (abdic.)

GRAND DUKE

Jean, m. Joséphine Charlotte of Belgium, succeeded his mother	12 Nov 1964–

MACEDONIA (FORMER YUGOSLAVIA)

Independence from Yugoslavia was declared on 18 Sep 1991.

PRESIDENT

K. Gligorov	27 Jan 1991–19 Nov 1999
S. Klimovski (acting)	19 Nov 1999–

MALTA

A Republic was established on 13 Dec 1974 with a president.

PRESIDENT

Sir A. Marno	13 Dec 1974–27 Dec 1976
A. Buttigieg	27 Dec 1976–16 Feb 1982
A. Barbara	16 Feb 1982–15 Feb 1987
P. Xuereb (acting)	15 Feb 1987–4 Apr 1989
C. Tabone	4 Apr 1989–4 Apr 1994
U.M. Bonnici	4 Apr 1994–4 Apr 1999
G. de Marco	4 Apr 1999–

MOLDOVA

In Aug 1991 Moldova declared its independence from the USSR.

PRESIDENT

M. Snegur	8 Dec 1991–1 Dec 1996
P. Lucinschi	1 Dec 1996–

MONACO

PRINCE

Albert, m. (i) Lady Mary Douglas Hamilton, (ii) Alice, Dowager Duchess de Richelieu, succeeded his father	10 Sep 1889–26 Jun 1922
Louis II, succeeded his father	26 Jun 1922–9 May 1949
Rainier III, m. Miss Grace Kelly, succeeded his grandfather	9 May 1949–

MONTENEGRO

PRINCE-BISHOP

Nicholas I,[1] succeeded his uncle	Aug 1860–26 Nov 1918

[1] On 28 Aug 1910 Nicholas declared himself King.

THE NETHERLANDS

QUEEN

Wilhelmina, m. Henry of Mecklenburg-Schwerin, succeeded her father	23 Nov 1890–4 Sep 1948 (abdic.)
Juliana, m. Bernhard of Lippe-Besterfeld, succeeded her mother	4 Nov 1948–30 Apr 1980 (abdic.)
Beatrix, m. Claus von Amsberg, succeeded her mother	1 May 1980–

NORWAY

KING

Haakon VII, formerly Prince Carl of Denmark, m. Maud of Great Britain, elected to the throne	18 Nov 1905–21 Sep 1957
Olav V, m. Märtha of Sweden, succeeded his father	21 Sep 1957–17 Jan 1991
Harald V, m. Sonja Haraldsen, succeeded his father	17 Jan 1991–

POLAND

Independent state proclaimed on 5 Nov 1918.

PRESIDENT

J. Piłsudski	11 Nov 1918–9 Dec 1922
Gabriel Narutowicz	9 Dec 1922–16 Dec 1922 (assassinated)
S. Wojciechowski	20 Dec 1922–15 May 1926
I. Moscicki	1 Jun 1926–29 Mar 1939

On 29 Mar 1939 the German occupation of Poland began.

PRESIDENT, HEAD OF THE POLISH GOVERNMENT IN EXILE

W. Raczkiewicz	30 Sep 1939–28 Jun 1945

PRESIDENT

Boleslaw Bierut	28 Jun 1945–21 Jul 1952

On 22 Jul 1952 a new constitution replaced the office of President with a Council of State.

CHAIRMAN OF THE COUNCIL OF STATE

A. Zawadski	20 Nov 1952–7 Aug 1964
E. Ochab	12 Aug 1964–8 Apr 1968
M. Spychalski	10 Apr 1968–23 Dec 1970
J. Cyrankiewicz	23 Dec 1970–28 Mar 1972
H. Jabloński	28 Mar 1972–6 Nov 1985
Gen. W. Jaruzelski[1]	6 Nov 1985–22 Dec 1990

PRESIDENT

L. Walesa	22 Dec 1990–23 Dec 1995
A. Kwásniewski	23 Dec 1995–

[1] On 19 Jul 1989 Jaruzelski was elected President of Poland.

PORTUGAL

KING

Carlos I, m. Maria Amalia of Bourbon-Orleans, succeeded his father	19 Oct 1889–1 Feb 1908
Manuel II, succeeded his father	1 Feb 1908–5 Oct 1910 (deposed)

Republic proclaimed 5 Oct 1910.

PRESIDENT

T. Braga	5 Oct 1910–19 Jun 1911
–. Braachamp	19 Jun 1911–24 Aug 1911
M. de Arriga	24 Aug 1911–7 Aug 1915
B. Machado	7 Aug 1915–28 Apr 1918
S. Paes	28 Apr 1918–14 Dec 1918 (assassinated)
J. Antunes	16 Dec 1918–5 Oct 1919
A. de Almeida	5 Oct 1919–5 Oct 1923
M.T. Gomes	5 Oct 1923–11 Dec 1925
B.L. Machado Guimarâes	11 Dec 1925–1 Jun 1926

A provisional government was in power from 1 Jun 1926 until 29 Nov 1926.

Marshal A.O.F. Carmona	29 Nov 1926–18 Apr 1951
Marshal F.H.C. Lopes	22 Jul 1951–9 Aug 1958
Rear-Adm. A. de D.R. Tomás	9 Aug 1958–25 Apr 1974
Gen. Antonio de Spinola	15 May 1974–30 Sep 1974
Gen. Francisco da Costa Gomes	30 Sep 1974–27 Jun 1976
Gen. Antonio R. Eanes	14 Jul 1976–16 Feb 1986
M. Soares	16 Feb 1986–9 Mar 1996
J. Sampaio	9 Mar 1996–

ROMANIA

KING

Carol I, elected	14 Mar 1881–10 Oct 1914
Ferdinand I, m. Marie of Saxe-Coburg-Gotha, succeeded his uncle	11 Oct 1914–21 Jul 1927
Mihai (Michael) I, succeeded his grandfather since his father Carol had renounced his rights	21 Jul 1927–8 Jun 1930
Carol II, m. Helen of Greece, succeeded his son by act of parliament	8 Jun 1930–6 Sep 1940 (abdic.)
Mihai (Michael) I, proclaimed on abdication of his father	6 Sep 1940–30 Dec 1947 (abdic.)

As a result of a plebiscite a Republic was established and the King abdicated.

PRESIDENT OF THE PRESIDIUM

C.I. Parhon	13 Apr 1948–23 Jan 1952
P. Groza	2 Jun 1952–7 Jan 1958
I.G. Maurer	11 Jan 1958–21 Mar 1961
G. Gheorghiu-Dej	21 Mar 1961–19 Mar 1965
C. Stoica	22 Mar 1965–9 Dec 1967
N. Ceauçescu	9 Dec 1967–22 Dec 1989
I. Iliescu	3 Jan 1990–17 Nov 1996
E. Constantinescu	17 Nov 1996–

RUSSIA

TSAR

Nicholas II, m. Alexandra of Hesse-Darmstadt, succeeded his father	1 Nov 1894–16 Jul 1918 (murdered)

See USSR.

After the dissolution of the USSR in Dec 1991 Russia became a member of the Commonwealth of Independent States and was recognized as an independent state by the USA and the European Union in Jan 1992.

PRESIDENT

B. Yeltsin	10 Jul 1991–31 Dec 1999
V. Putin (acting)	31 Dec 1999–

SAN MARINO

No titular head of state; co-regents are annually elected.

SERBIA

Serbia became independent of Turkey by the Treaty of Berlin on 13 Jul 1878.

KING

Milan IV Obrenovitch (formerly Prince), created King	6 Mar 1882–6 Mar 1889 (abdic.)

Alexander I Obrenovitch, m. Draga Mascin	6 Mar 1889–10 Jun 1903 (murdered)
Provisional government	11 Jun 1903

See Yugoslavia.

SLOVAKIA

Slovakia was declared an independent country 14 Mar 1939.

PRESIDENT

J. Tiso	26 Oct 1939–1 Apr 1945

Slovakia was re-incorporated with Czechoslovakia in Apr 1945. The Czechoslovakian Federation was dissolved on 31 Dec 1992.

PRESIDENT

M. Kovac	2 Mar 1993–2 Mar 1998
R. Schuster	16 Jun 1999–

SLOVENIA

Independence from the Yugoslav Federation was declared on 25 Jun 1991.

PRESIDENT

M. Kučan	23 Dec 1992

SPAIN

KING

Alphonso XIII, m. Victoria Eugenie Battenberg, succeeded his father at his birth	17 May 1886–14 Apr 1931 (abdic.)

A Republic was proclaimed on 14 Apr 1931.

PRESIDENT

N.A. Zamora y Torres	10 Dec 1931–7 Apr 1936
M. Azaña	10 May 1936–4 Mar 1939

CHIEF OF THE SPANISH STATE

Gen. Francisco Franco	9 Aug 1939–20 Nov 1975

Prince Juan Carlos de Borbòn y Borbòn, grandson of Alphonso XIII, was sworn in as successor to the Chief of State in Jul 1969.

KING

Juan Carlos, I. m. Sophia of Greece	22 Nov 1975–

SWEDEN

KING

Gustaf V, m. Victoria of Baden, succeeded his father Oscar II	8 Dec 1907–29 Oct 1950
Gustaf IV Adolf, m. (i) Margaret Victoria of Connaught, (ii) Lady Louise Mountbatten, succeeded his father	29 Oct 1950–16 Sep 1973
Carl XVI Gustaf, m. Silva Renate Sommerlath, succeeded his grandfather	16 Sep 1973–

SWITZERLAND

PRESIDENTS (Elected for an annual term)

1900 Walter Hauser	1916 Camille Decoppet
1901 Ernest Brenner	1917 Edmond Schultess
1902 Josef Zemp	1918 F. Ludwig
1903 Adolf Deucher	1919 Gustave Ador
1904 Robert Comtesse	1920 Giuseppe Motta
1905 Marc Ruchet	1921 Edmund Schulthess
1906 Louis Forrer	1922 Robert Haab
1907 Eduard Müller	1923 Karl Scheurer
1908 Ernest Brenner	1924 Ernest Chuard
1909 Adolf Deucher	1925 Jean M. Musy
1910 Robert Comtesse	1926 Henri Häberlin
1911 Marc Ruchet	1927 Giuseppe Motta
1912 Louis Forrer	1928 Edmund Schulthess
1913 Eduard Müller	1929 Robert Haab
1914 Artur Hoffman	1930 Jean M. Musy
1915 Giuseppe Motta	1931 Henri Häberlin

1932 Giuseppe Motta

1933 Edmund Schulthess

1934 Marcel Pilet-Golaz

1935 Rudolf Minger

1936 Albert Meyer

1937 Giuseppe Motta

1938 Johannes Baumann

1939 Philipp Etter

1940 Marcel Pilet-Golaz

1941 Ernst Wetter

1942 Philipp Etter

1943 Enrico Celio

1944 Walter Stampfi

1945 Eduard von Steiger

1946 Karl Kobelt

1947 Philipp Etter

1948 Enrico Celio

1949 Ernst Nobs

1950 Max Petitpierre

1951 Eduard von Steiger

1952 Karl Kobelt

1953 Philipp Etter

1954 Rudolphe Rubattel

1955 Max Petitpierre

1956 Markus Feldmann

1957 Hans Streuli

1958 Thomas Holenstein

1959 Paul Chaudet

1960 Max Petitpierre

1961 Friedrich Trangott Wahlen

1962 Paul Chaudet

1963 Willy Spühler

1964 Ludwig von Moos

1965 Hanspeter Tschudi

1966 Hans Schattner

1967 Roger Bonvin

1968 Willy Spühler

1969 Ludwig von Moos

1970 Hanspeter Tschudi

1971 Rudolf Gnägi

1972 Nello Celio

1973 Roger Bonvin

1974 Ernst Brugger

1975 Pierre Graber

1976 Rudolf Gnägi

1977 Kurt Furgler

1978 Willi Ritschard

1979 Hans Hürlimann

1980 Georges-André Chevallaz

1981 Kurt Furgler

1982 Fritz Honegger

1983 Pierre Aubert

1984 Léon Schlumpf

1985 Kurt Furgler

1986 Alphons Egli

1987 Pierre Aubert

1988 Otto Stich

1989 Jean-Pascal Delamuraz

1990 Arnold Koller

1991 Flavio Cotti

1992 René Felber

1993 Adolf Ogi

1994 Otto Stich

1995 Kaspar Villiger

1996 Jean-Pascal Delamuraz

1997 Arnold Koller

1998 Flavio Cotti

1999 Ruth Dreifuss

TURKEY

SULTAN

Abd el Hamid II, succeeded his brother	30 Aug 1876–27 Apr 1909
Mohammed V, succeeded his brother	27 Apr 1909–3 Jul 1918
Mohammed VI, succeeded his brother	3 Jul 1918–1 Nov 1922

The office of Sultan was abolished on 1 Nov 1922 and only that of Caliph (held by the Sultans) retained, to be filled by election from the Osman princes.

CALIPH

Prince Abdul Medjid	17 Nov 1922–2 Mar 1924

A Republic was proclaimed on 29 Oct 1923.

PRESIDENT

M. Kemal Atatürk	29 Oct 1923–10 Nov 1938
I. Inönü	11 Nov 1938–21 May 1950
C. Bayar	22 May 1950–27 May 1960
C. Gursel	26 Oct 1961–27 Mar 1966
Cevdet Sunay	28 Mar 1966–28 May 1973
Fahri Korutürk	6 Apr 1973–6 Apr 1980
Ihsan Sabri Caglayangil	6 Apr 1980–12 Sep 1980
Gen. Kenan Evren	12 Sep 1980–9 Nov 1989
T. Özal	9 Nov 1989–17 Apr 1993
H. Cindoruk (acting)	17 Apr 1993–16 May 1993
S. Demirel	16 May 1993–

UKRAINE

Ukraine declared itself independent of the USSR, subject to a referendum, in Aug 1991. At the referendum held on 1 Dec 1991, 90 per cent of the electorate voted for independence.

PRESIDENT

L. Kravchuk	1 Dec 1991–19 Jul 1994
L. Kuchma	19 Jul 1994–

UNION OF SOVIET SOCIALIST REPUBLICS (USSR)

Constitution for the Federal Republic adopted on 10 Jul 1918, by a government which took office on 8 Nov 1917.

PRESIDENT OF THE COUNCIL OF PEOPLE'S COMMISSARS

V.I. Ulianov-Lenin	8 Nov 1917–29 Dec 1922

A new constitution of 30 Dec 1922 replaced this office by a Central Executive Committee with four chairmen.

A new constitution came into force on 5 Dec 1936 establishing the office of Chairman of the Presidium of the Supreme Soviet of the USSR, as head of state.

CHAIRMAN

M.I. Kalinin	5 Dec 1936–27 Jul 1946
N.M. Shvernik	19 Mar 1946–6 Mar 1953
Marshal K.E. Voroshilov	6 Mar 1953–7 May 1960
L.I. Brezhnev	7 May 1960–15 Jul 1964
A.I. Mikoyan	15 Jul 1964–9 Dec 1965
N.V. Podgorny	9 Dec 1965–16 Jun 1977
L.I. Brezhnev	16 Jun 1977–10 Nov 1982
Y.V. Andropov	16 Jun 1983–9 Feb 1984
K.U. Chernenko	11 Apr 1984–10 Mar 1985
A. Gromyko	14 Mar 1985–30 Sep 1988
M. Gorbachev[1]	1 Oct 1988–25 May 1989

Negotiations in 1990 and 1991 under President Gorbachev attempted to establish a 'renewed federation' and to conclude a new Union Treaty, but these failed and the Union was declared 'no longer in existence' in Dec 1991.

[1] On 25 May 1989 M. Gorbachev was elected President of the USSR by the newly constituted 2250-member Congress of People's Deputies.

UNITED KINGDOM

QUEEN

Victoria, m. Albert of Saxe-Coburg-Gotha, succeeded her uncle	20 Jun 1837–22 Jan 1901

KING

Edward VII, m. Alexandra of Schleswig-Holstein-Sonderburg-Glücksburg, succeeded his mother	22 Jan 1901–6 May 1910
George V, m. Victoria Mary of Teck, succeeded his father Edward VII	6 May 1910–20 Jan 1936
Edward VIII, succeeded his father	20 Jan 1936–10 Dec 1936 (abdic.)
George VI, m. Lady Elizabeth Bowes-Lyon, succeeded on the abdication of his brother	10 Dec 1936–6 Feb 1952

QUEEN

Elizabeth II, m. Philip of Greece, succeeded her father	6 Feb 1952–

VATICAN

SUPREME PONTIFF

Leo XIII	3 Mar 1878–20 Jul 1903
Pius X	9 Aug 1903–20 Aug 1914
Benedict XV	3 Sep 1914–22 Jan 1922
Pius XI	6 Mar 1922–13 Feb 1939
Pius XII	2 Mar 1939–9 Oct 1958
John XXIII	28 Oct 1958–3 Jun 1963
Paul VI	21 Jun 1963–6 Aug 1978
John Paul I	26 Aug 1978–28 Sep 1978
John Paul II	16 Oct 1978–

YUGOSLAVIA

The state was founded on 29 Dec 1918 as the Serb, Croat and Slovene State (Montenegro joined on 1 Mar 1921). The name was changed to Yugoslavia on 3 Oct 1929.

KING

Peter I, m. Zorka of Montenegro, elected king	2 Jun 1903–6 Aug 1921

Alexander I, m. Marie of Romania, succeeded his father	6 Aug 1921–9 Oct 1934 (assassinated)
Peter II, succeeded his father	9 Oct 1934–29 Nov 1945 (abdic.)

On 29 Nov 1945 King Peter abdicated and a Republic was proclaimed.

PRESIDENT OF THE PRESIDIUM

Dr I. Ribar	2 Dec 1945–13 Jan 1953

PRESIDENT OF THE REPUBLIC

Marshal J. Broz-Tito	14 Jan 1953–4 May 1980

HEAD OF THE COLLECTIVE PRESIDENCY

L. Kolisevski	4 May 1980–15 May 1980
C. Mijatović	15 May 1980–15 May 1981
S. Krajger	15 May 1981–15 May 1982
P. Stambolić	15 May 1982–15 May 1983
M. Spiljak	15 May 1983–15 May 1984
V. Djuranović	15 May 1984–15 May 1985
R. Vlajković	15 May 1985–15 May 1986
S. Hasani	15 May 1986–15 May 1987
L. Mojsov	15 May 1987–15 May 1988
R. Dizdarević	15 May 1988–15 May 1989
J. Drnovsek	15 May 1989–15 May 1990
B. Jovic	15 May 1990–15 May 1991
S. Mešić	15 May 1991–15 Jun 1992

FORMER YUGOSLAVIA (SERBIA AND MONTENEGRO)

Serbia and Montenegro announced on 22 Apr 1992 the formation of the Federal Republic of Yugoslavia, constituted by themselves, as the legal successor to the former Socialist Federal Republic of Yugoslavia.

FEDERAL PRESIDENT

D. Cosić	15 Jun 1992–1 Jun 1993
Z. Lilić	25 Jun 1993–25 Jun 1997
S. Bozović (acting)	25 Jun 1997–23 Jul 1997
S. Milošević	23 Jul 1997–

3
Parliaments

ALBANIA

From 1920 until the Italian invasion Albania had a parliamentary system of government with a single elected chamber, but neither under the Republic nor under the monarchy did this function effectively. Under the Republic formed in 1946 there has been one chamber, the People's Assembly, elected on universal suffrage of all over 18, and sitting for a 4-year term. The Assembly chose its Presidium and Council of Ministers. The Chairman of the Presidium was also the head of the state, and the Chairman of the Council of Ministers the Prime Minister. The Assembly, the Council and the Presidium operated on the Soviet pattern; the Assembly sat for short sessions, the Presidium more or less permanently, although the Assembly had to meet twice a year. The Assembly had one member for each 8000 voters. The Presidium had a chairman and three deputy chairmen, a secretary and 10 members. The initiation and passing of legislation, and the exercise of legislative and executive power was the same as in the Soviet Union.

Following anti-government demonstrations after Jul 1990, the political structure of Albania changed. In Dec 1990 a decree was adopted by the People's Assembly legalizing opposition parties (*see* p. 323). A new constitution was promulgated on 26 Apr 1991. The supreme legislative body is the single-chamber National Assembly of 155 deputies, 115 directly elected, 40 elected by proportional representation, for 4-year terms. Parliament elects the President for 5-year terms.

A draft new constitution, submitted to a referendum in Nov 1994, was rejected by 53.8 per cent of votes cast.

ARMENIA

Following the collapse of the Soviet Union, the Supreme Soviet in Armenia adopted a declaration of sovereignty in Aug 1990. It voted to unite Armenia with Nagorno-Karabakh and renamed Armenia the 'Republic of Armenia'. A popular vote in Sep 1991 resulted in a 99 per cent majority support for a fully independent status.

On 16 Oct 1991 Levon Ter-Petrosyan was elected the Republic's first President in a popular ballot by 83 per cent of votes cast against 5 opponents. He was re-elected in 1996.

A new constitution, followed by elections, was adopted in Jul 1995. Under it, the head of state is the President, elected for 5-year terms. Parliament consists of a 190-seat National Assembly (150 members directly elected by first-past-the-post, 40 by proportional election). The President nominates the government.

AUSTRIA

Prior to the collapse of the Habsburg Empire in 1918, the Austrian Parliament had been constituted under the terms of the 1867 *Ausgleich*.

The *Ausgleich* of June 1867 provided that the Reichsrat should be a parliament for the Austrian half of the new Dual Monarchy (Austria-Hungary). This was confirmed by the constitution of 21 Dec 1867 which provided for a bicameral legislature, the executive power being exercised by the Emperor through responsible ministers. He had power to appoint the ministers and all officials, to create peers, to summon and dissolve both houses. All his acts had to be countersigned by the ministers, but he had appointed them and they were his servants, not the servants of parliament. His assent was necessary before a bill became law, and he could refuse it even if the bill was passed by both houses.

The lower house sat for a 6-year term. Its members were originally chosen by the provincial Diets, but in 1868 a law provided for direct election of representatives from those provinces where the Diet refused to name any. On 2 Apr 1873 election superseded nomination by the Diets altogether, and the number of deputies was raised from 203 to 353. By 1896 there were 425. Voters were of 5 classes: large landowners, cities, chambers of commerce, rural communes and the general class. There was a constituency for each class in each district. The house was obliged to meet annually. It had power to legislate for the Austrian half of the Dual Monarchy, but the execution of the laws was left to the provincial Diets. Bills were passed through committees set up by 'bureaux' within the house; a joint committee was appointed by both houses to deal with the public debt.

The upper house had 81 nobles, princes and bishops, and 94 members nominated for life, with no limit to the number of new nominations. Both houses had the same rights and powers, except that the budget and bills on recruitment had to go first to the lower house.

The competence of both houses was limited by the extensive list of matters which came within the competence of the provincial Diets and might not be considered in the central parliament.

On 12 Nov 1918 the Austrian members of the Austro-Hungarian imperial Reichsrat, having constituted themselves the German National Assembly, declared that Austria was a Republic. The following January a Constituent Assembly was elected as supreme authority for the purpose of framing a new constitution which came into operation in Nov 1920. The Assembly had one chamber and was elected on universal adult suffrage. The new constitution provided for a bi-cameral federal legislature. The National Council was elected by proportional representation for four years, and could be adjourned only by its own decision. It could be summoned immediately on the request of at least a quarter of its members, or of the government. The Federal Council was elected by the Provincial Diets, having representatives from each province who sat for the length of term of their Diet. The Federal Council could initiate bills through the government; a bill passed by the National Council would be passed to the Federal Council and, if amended by them, reconsidered by the National Council and passable by a majority in that house. The Federal Council had no power to amend estimates.

The President was elected by both houses in joint session, for four years; his duties were mainly ceremonial and symbolic and all acts of government were the responsibility of ministers. The ministers were elected by the National Council on a motion submitted by its Principal Committee, and were not allowed to continue as Council members, if they were, or became, Council members while in office. Legislature and Executive were widely separate. The government suspended parliament in 1933 and in 1934 dissolved the Socialist Party; after strong reaction a new constitution, with socialist leanings, was brought in in 1935, but parliament worked with increasing difficulty until the integration with Germany in 1938, when it virtually ceased to operate.

A constitution similar to that of 1920 was restored in 1945. The state has now a Nationalrat with deputies elected on the original suffrage and a Bundesrat of deputies elected by the Provincial Diets. Bills must pass both houses. In 1999 the Nationalrat had 183 deputies and the Bundesrat 64; of the latter there may be no more than 12 members for any one Province, and no fewer than 3. Bundesrat members are not necessarily members of the Provincial Diets, but they must be eligible to be so; they are elected for varying terms, whereas Nationalrat members sit for 4 years, 2 regular sessions being convened each year in spring and autumn. An extraordinary session may be held if the government or one-third of the members of either house demand it.

Bills must pass both houses; they may be initiated by either house or by the government but must be presented in the National Council. There is provision also for the popular initiative; every proposal signed by 200000 Länder voters or half the voters in each of the three Länder must be submitted to the National Council. The National Council may also request a referendum on a bill which it has assented to. All bills go secondly to the Federal Council which may object to them within eight weeks; the bill becomes law if the National Council reaffirms it with half its members present.

AUSTRIA–HUNGARY (THE DUAL MONARCHY)

There was a deliberative body with two delegations, one from Austria and one from Hungary and each of 60 members of whom 20 were chosen by the upper house of each parliament and 40 by the lower. The body was re-elected annually. The proposals of both governments were put before both delegations at once, but they debated separately and only met in common session if they had failed three times to agree in their separate votes. The Hungarian delegation tended to have a unity which the Austrian did not; Hungarian delegates were chosen by majority votes in each house, with Magyars in the majority. Austrian delegates were chosen from the several provinces and did not necessarily have any common interest.

The body had little legislative power; it voted supplies and administered the laws made in the Austrian and Hungarian parliaments. The ministers for common affairs were not responsible to it or to any legislative body.

BELARUS

Belarus adopted a declaration of independence from the Soviet Union on 25 Aug 1991. The name 'Republic of Belarus' was adopted in Sep 1991.

A new constitution was adopted on 15 Mar 1994. It provides for a president who must be a citizen of at least 35 years of age, have resided for 10 years in Belarus and whose candidacy must be supported by the signature of 70 deputies or 100000 electors. Presidential elections were held on 23 Jun 1994. Alyaksandr Lukashenka was elected in the run-off on 11 Jul 1994.

BELGIUM

Belgium is a constitutional monarchy with two legislative chambers, the Chamber of Representatives and the Senate. The King shares legislative powers with the two chambers and exercises the executive power in conjunction with his ministers; he may not act alone. He appoints ministers from among members of parliament, and sanctions laws. The Chamber of Representatives consisted until 1995 of 212 members – the maximum was one for every 40000 inhabitants – elected on proportional representation for 4-year terms. Members had to be at least 25. The Senate members had to be at least 40 and were elected as follows: one member for every 200000 inhabitants, elected by the provincial councils by proportional representation; half the number of Chamber deputies elected by the same electorate. Since 1995 the federal parliament has consisted of a 150-member Chamber of Deputies (elected by proportional representation from 20 constituencies) and a Senate of 71 members. In practice, the Senate is now essentially a revising chamber. Traditionally the legislature possessed considerable control over the cabinet, since all legislation passes through a strong committee system in both houses. In the years between the two world wars particularly this provided stability when political life was disrupted by Fleming–Walloon or Catholic–Protestant differences.

In 1921 the length of service for members of the Senate was reduced from 8 years to 4, and the franchise was extended to all men over 21, together with women who were war-widows or war-sufferers. Before 1921 there was a system of plural votes on grounds of property or income. The franchise was extended to women in 1948.

Senate and Chamber meet annually in October (November until 1921) and must sit for at least 40 days. The government, through the King, has power to dissolve either Chamber separately or both Chambers at once. In the latter case a new election must take place within 40 days and a meeting of the Chambers within 2 months; no adjournment for longer than 1 month may be made without the consent of both Chambers.

Money bills originate in the Chamber of Representatives. There is also a strong subsidiary body – the Court of Accounts – with members appointed by the Chamber with authority to control all treasury work and all provision for revenue and expenditure. By an Act of 23 Dec 1946 a Council of State was also set up, with separate sections for legislation and administration on constitutional matters.

In the 1990s Belgium faced growing constitutional problems. In Feb 1992, legislation for the first stage of an eventual federal state was introduced in parliament. In Sep 1992, constitutional changes were made to devolve more power to the regions (*i.e.* to the parliaments of Dutch-speaking Flanders and French-speaking Wallonia). Meanwhile the royal power to accept or refuse prime-ministerial resignations was ended, as was the monarch's absolute right to dissolve parliament after a vote of no confidence. Further pressure for constitutional change grew after the child sex scandal of 1996 and continuing corruption revelations.

BOSNIA–HERCEGOVINA

Bosnia–Hercegovina seceded from the Yugoslav federation in Mar 1992, following a referendum which supported full independence. Bosnian independence was recognized by its admission to the United Nations in May 1992, but civil war continued (*see* p. 399). A provisional agreement for a new constitution was signed on 30 Jul 1993 by all three sides. This was overtaken by a new agreement between the Bosnian government and the Bosnian Croat leadership on 18 Mar 1994. A new Federation of Bosnia and Hercegovina was established in March. The new federal constitution provided for a balance of power between Muslims and Croats in a federation divided according to a cantonal system.

The constitution was formally adopted by a 123-member constituent Assembly on 30 Mar 1994. The basic principles of this Muslim–Croat federation were also upheld at the Dayton Peace Conference. There is a 3-member rotating Presidency, a Chamber of Representatives and a Chamber of Peoples.

BULGARIA

The constitution of 1879 was still in operation in 1918, after amendment in 1911. The legislature was a single chamber, the National Assembly (Sobranje). Members were elected by universal manhood suffrage; 1 member for every 20000 inhabitants. All literate men over 30 were eligible to sit, except for soldiers, clergy and those deprived of civil rights. The term was 4 years, but the Assembly could be dissolved at any time by the King, and elections held within 2 months. There was a second, but not permanent, chamber, the Grand Sobranje; this had twice the membership of the Sobranje but was elected only for special purposes. It sat to decide questions on territory, changes to the constitution or the succession to the throne. Both houses were elected on proportional representation. Laws passed by the National Assembly required the assent of the King, who might himself initiate legislation through his ministers. After 1911 the King might also make treaties with foreign powers without having the Assembly's consent; he might also issue regulations and take emergency measures in time of danger, although it was the cabinet who assumed responsibility for such measures. Cabinet members were chosen by the King. They were required to countersign royal acts and were responsible both to the King and to the Assembly.

In Oct 1937 an electoral law fixed the number of Sobranje members at 160 (it had previously had 227) and the size of constituencies to at least 20000 electors, comprising all men and all married women over 21.

A Republic was proclaimed in Sep 1946 and a new constitution drawn up in Dec 1947 which was replaced, but not significantly altered, by a new one in 1971; it provided for a parliament on the Russian model, except that there was only one Assembly, as before, consisting of deputies elected by secret, direct and universal suffrage of all inhabitants over 18, one deputy for every 30000

– later every 20 000 – inhabitants. The Assembly elected its Presidium of chairman, two deputy chairmen, secretary and 15 members; this was the most powerful organ of the state. There was also a Council of Ministers elected by the National Assembly. The relation of the three bodies to each other was on the Russian pattern.

In Jan 1990 the National Assembly instituted 21 constitutional reforms, including the abolition of the Communist Party's right to be the only governing party. This was followed in Apr 1990 by amendments which created an executive presidency, permitted free multi-party elections, and removed the words 'socialist' and 'communist' from the constitution.

A new constitution was adopted at Turnovo in Jul 1991. The President is directly elected for not more than two 5-year terms. Candidates for the presidency must be at least 40 years old and have lived for the last 5 years in Bulgaria. Presidential elections were held in 1992 and 1996.

The 240-member National Assembly is directly elected by proportional representation.

CROATIA

Following the secession from Yugoslavia, Croatia adopted a new constitution on 21 Dec 1990. The President is elected directly for a 5-year term. Parliament consists of the 127-member Sabor, elected by a combination of proportional representation and first-past-the-post methods, and an upper house, the 68-member Chamber of Counties, composed of representatives of counties elected by proportional representation, and 5 members nominated by the President. The role of the Chamber of Counties is mainly consultative.

CYPRUS

An independent Republic was set up in 1960 with a unicameral parliament, the House of Representatives. The House had 50 members, 35 Greek and 15 Turkish, who were directly elected within their respective communities. The communities also had their own Communal Chambers, to which certain domestic issues were reserved. The franchise was universal and the term for members 5 years. Greek members elected a Greek President of the House, Turkish members a Turkish Vice-President. The Prime Minister and Council of Ministers were appointed by the President of the Republic. In practice the offices of President and Prime Minister were combined.

In Dec 1963 the Turkish members ceased to attend parliament. On 13 Feb 1975 a Turkish Cypriot Federated State was formed, having its own legislative assembly and executive council.

CZECHOSLOVAKIA

The constitution of the Republic was put into operation in 1920. It provided for a 2-chamber parliament, the National Parliament, which consisted of a Chamber of Deputies and a Senate, elected on proportional representation by all citizens over 21. The Chamber was elected for 6 years and had 300 deputies; the Senate sat for 8 years and had 150 members. Legislation might be introduced by the government or by either of the chambers. Bills passed by the deputies were passed to the Senate for consideration. A bill rejected by the Senate could still become law if passed again with an absolute majority by the deputies. If the Senate rejected it by a three-quarters majority then it required a three-fifths majority to pass in the Chamber. A bill initiated in the Senate died if it was dismissed twice by an absolute majority in the Chamber. Bills relating to money and defence could only be initiated by the Deputies. The legislature had no strong control over the government; if the National Parliament rejected a government bill the government could still decide (unanimously) to put the bill to a referendum, provided it was not an amendment to the constitution.

The President (Dr Masaryk) was in fact elected for life, but the constitution provided that in future the President would be elected by the National Parliament for a seven-year term. His election would need the attendance of an absolute majority of the parliament and a three-fifths majority of votes. He was to be head of state, but the government would be responsible for the exercise of his powers. He could not declare war without parliamentary approval. He could dissolve both chambers, but not during the last six months of his presidency. He might return a bill to parliament with his observations on it, when it could only be carried if an absolute majority of all members adhered to it.

The parliament did not operate effectively after Czechoslovakia became a German Protectorate in 1939.

A new constitution of Jun 1948 provided for a single-chamber National Assembly with 300 members elected for 6 years. In 1953 a Presidium on the Soviet model was set up, with a Chairman (Prime Minister) and 10 deputies; later in the same year the number of deputies was reduced to 4 and the Presidium considerably reduced in power. In 1969 the state became a federation; the new Federal Assembly consisted of the Chamber of Nations, with 75 Czech and 75 Slovak delegates elected by the National Councils of the Czechs and Slovaks, and the Chamber of the People which had 200 deputies elected by national suffrage.

The Federal Assembly had overall responsibility for constitutional and foreign affairs, defence and the federal economy. Other matters fell to the National Councils; the Czech had 200 deputies and the Slovak 150. After 1971 all Deputies, federal and national, were elected for a 5-year term.

The Communist Party's monopoly of political power was abolished by the Federal Assembly on 30 Nov 1989 and independent parties were legalized. In Mar 1990 the Assembly passed election laws allowing for free multi-party elections with proportional representation. Assembly deputies were to be elected for 2-year terms. In Apr 1990 the state was renamed the Czech and Slovak Federative Republic. On 25 Nov 1992 the Czechoslovak Federal Parliament approved (by three votes) the creation of independent Czech and Slovak states from 1 Jan 1993. These states are now the Czech Republic and Slovakia.

CZECH REPUBLIC

The newly-independent Czech Republic came into existence on 1 Jan 1993. The constitution provides for a parliament comprising a 200-member House of Representatives, elected for 4-year terms by proportional representation, and an 81-member Senate elected for 6-year terms in single-member districts, 27 senators being elected every 2 years. All senators must be at least 40 years of age.

The President of the Republic is elected for a 5-year term by both Chambers of parliament. He or she must be at least 40 years of age. The President names the Prime Minister at the suggestion of the Speaker.

There is a Constitutional Court at Brno whose 15 members are nominated by the President and approved by the Senate for 10-year terms.

DENMARK

The constitutional Charter of 1915 provided that the legislative power should be held by the King and the Rigsdag (parliament) jointly, and that the executive power be held by the King and exercised through his ministers, although he could not declare war or sign a peace treaty without parliament's consent. There were two chambers: the Folketing (lower house) had 149 members, 117 of them elected by proportional representation and 31 additional seats divided among parties who had insufficient votes to win any. It sat for a 4-year term but might be dissolved by the King. There was no specific ruling that the ministers who formed the King's Council of State, and who were appointed and dismissed by him, were responsible to the Folketing in the parliamentary sense. The King normally presided over the Council of State; he had the right to object to its decisions and to re-introduce the matter at a future meeting. In his absence the Prime Minister presided. The Landsting had 78 members indirectly elected and sat for a term of 8 years; those members elected in the Landsting electoral districts sat for 4 years, when there was a further election for half of their number; members elected by the former Landsting sat for the whole 8 years; there were 56 members elected in the districts and 19 by the

Landsting. Parliament was obliged to meet annually in October. Ministers had access to both houses but could only vote in the chamber of which they were members.

The constitutional Charter of Jun 1953 abolished the Landsting. The Folketing remained with 179 members, 135 of them elected in the districts, and 40 additional seats. The Council of State continued to operate as a cabinet, ministers being individually and collectively responsible to the Folketing for their actions. The legislative power is still the joint prerogative of the Queen and the Folketing, and the executive power is still vested in the Queen acting through her ministers. The cabinet is only called the Council of State when the Queen is presiding.

Any member may initiate a bill. Bills are approved or not after 3 readings. If one-third of members request it, a bill that has been passed may be subject to a referendum. A bill that is to be subject to a referendum may be withdrawn within 5 weeks of its being passed. The referendum is held and its result acted upon in accordance with the Prime Minister's decision. Since 1978 the franchise, formerly of men and women over 21, has been extended to those over 18 years.

ESTONIA

The Constitutional Assembly of 1918 formulated a constitution which came into force in 1920. This provided for a republican state with a State Assembly elected by all citizens over 25, by proportional representation, and sitting for 3 years.

The Assembly had 100 members, and elected its own chairman and officers from among them. The Assembly appointed a government responsible to it and consisting of the head of state and his ministers. The executive prepared the budget and submitted it to the Assembly for approval. Bills passed in the Assembly might remain unpromulgated for 2 months if one-third of the Assembly demanded it; within that period a referendum could be demanded, or the bill's adoption recommended, by 25000 citizens entitled to vote.

A second constitution was framed in 1934 and a third in 1938, when the main changes were made. A President was to be popularly elected for a term of 6 years. Parliament had 2 chambers, the first having 80 members directly elected by the national electorate for a 5-year term. The second – the State Council – had 40 members all over 40 years of age and elected by organizations and public bodies. The Prime Minister, no longer head of state, was chosen by the President and formed his own cabinet which was responsible to parliament. He did not automatically resign on a vote of no confidence; it was the President's decision whether the cabinet should be dismissed or parliament dissolved.

After 1940 Estonia was a constituent Republic of the USSR. However, in Sep 1991, the independence of Estonia was recognized by the European Community, the United States and the USSR.

Following the declaration of independence from the Soviet Union of 20 Aug 1991, a draft constitution drawn up by a constitutional assembly was approved by 91 per cent of votes cast at a referendum on 28 Jun 1992. The constitution came into effect on 4 Jul 1992. It defined Estonia as a 'democratic state guided by the rule of law, where universally recognized norms of international law are an inseparable part of the legal system'. It provides for a 101-member National Assembly (Riigikogu) elected by proportional representation for 4-year terms. The National Assembly elects the head of State for 5-year periods.

FINLAND

The constitutional law of 1919 provided for a republican state with a President and a single-chamber parliament. The President is elected by direct popular vote for a 6-year term. He or she ratifies or withholds consent to new laws, dissolves the Diet and orders new elections and conducts foreign affairs. In all this he must act through his ministers, who are individually and collectively responsible to the Diet, and must take all his decisions in meetings of the cabinet. He has a strong veto power on legislation, and if he does not give the necessary approval within three months the bill dies. In this event, if the new Diet accepts the bill exactly as it was after new elections, it becomes valid without his assent.

Every citizen over 18 may vote and every citizen over 20 may be elected to the Diet, which has 200 members and is elected by proportional representation for a 4-year term (originally a 3-year term). The House meets annually for at least 120 days after which it determines the date of its own rising. The President, as embodying the supreme executive power, initiates legislation by introducing bills into the Diet; the Diet with the President has power to propose a new law or to repeal or amend an existing one. New bills are drafted by the Council of State (cabinet), and may be passed for opinion to the Supreme Court or Supreme Administrative Court. Bills adopted by the House are submitted to the President. The Council of State has no fixed size but consists of as many ministers as are necessary, and always includes a Chancellor of Justice and a deputy who have the right to assist at all sessions of the Council of State and of tribunals and public departments, with free access to their minutes. These may not be members of the Diet. There is a strong system of Diet committees which must be constituted within 5 days of the opening of a session. Standing committees are the Committees on Fundamental Laws, Laws, Foreign Affairs, Finance and a Bank Committee. The Grand Committee must also be established within the same period, having 45 members elected by the Diet.

No member of the government may be a committee member. The Grand Committee serves as a body to consider bills which have had their first reading and previously been passed to one of the specialist committees for opinion. The opinion of the Grand Committee is heard at the second reading.

FRANCE

The Third Republic kept the constitution of 1875 until it ended in 1940. This provided for 2 chambers, a Chamber of Deputies and a Senate. The Chamber of 533 members was elected for 4 years by manhood suffrage on proportional representation. The Senate had 314 members elected for 9 years, one-third retiring every 3. Both houses assembled annually in January, and were obliged to remain in session for at least 5 months of the 12. Bills could be presented in both houses either by the government or by private members, except financial bills which were solely the concern of the deputies. There was also a Council of State presided over by the Minister of Justice and other members all appointed by the President. It gave opinion on any question of administration put to it by the government.

The President was a symbolic head of state, theoretically with many powers but in practice not exercising them. He had the right to dissolve the Chamber, but did not use it after 1877; the suspensory veto over acts of parliament was never used. His role in lawmaking and the determination of policy was controlled by the cabinet.

The government's executive power lay with the ministers who were not necessarily members of either house and were chosen by the President in conjunction with the Prime Minister. They were responsible to both houses and were obliged to countersign (individually) every act of the President. Political dissension between many small parties made for weakness in the executive which had on several occasions to be offset by a grant of special powers made by parliament to the ministers. Special powers to proceed by decree for budgetary and taxation measures were granted in 1926; special powers were also granted in 1934, 1935, 1937 and 1938 and over a hundred decrees issued. Similarly ministers seldom felt strong enough to ask for a dissolution and election on the defeat of a measure; they normally resigned. Between 1870 and 1934 France had 88 ministries with an average life of less than 9 months.

The constitution for the Fourth Republic was submitted to the vote in 1946. The Senate was replaced by the Council of State as a purely advisory body, the Chamber by the National Assembly as the legislative body. The executive had limited power to dissolve parliament, and popular sovereignty was invested in the referendum. In 1954, by a constitutional amendment, the Council of the Republic had some power restored to it as a delaying body, with power to hold up National Assembly action in public matters for 108 days. It could also initiate bills and pass them to the National Assembly. The Assembly then had 627 members, 544 of them from Metropolitan France, elected all at the same time for a 5-year term. The position of the President was similar to that under the Third Republic, except that the President of the Council of Ministers (Prime Minister) had taken over some of his powers, principally the power to propose legislation to parliament and to issue edicts to supplement the law. The programme of the cabinet had to be approved by public vote by an absolute majority of the National Assembly before the Council of Ministers could be appointed. Once appointed they were responsible to the Assembly but not to the Council of the Republic. The Prime Minister in theory had considerable powers; he assured the execution of all national laws, directed the armed forces and appointed most civil and military officials. In practice, however, he spent much of his time trying to maintain a cohesive executive when no one party was ever strong enough to govern alone.

Under the Fifth Republic the President is head of the government as well as head of state. He can dissolve parliament, negotiate treaties and deal with emergencies without counter-signature. He appoints (rather than formally nominating) the Prime Minister. He is indirectly elected for a 7-year term, but there is no bar to re-election. He may submit matters to the Constitutional Council for opinion, ask parliament to reconsider bills, give ruling on proposals to submit bills to referendum. Before acting outright in an emergency he must consult both executive and legislature, but he is not bound to their advice. Nor is he bound to accept the resignation of the government if the National Assembly has caused it to resign.

The Constitutional Council is appointed for 9 years, one-third of its members retiring every 3 years. The National Assembly now has 577 members directly elected for 5 years (555 from Metropolitan France) and neither the Prime Minister nor any of the cabinet are allowed to hold seats in it. The Council of the Republic continues as the Senate, and all bills go to it. The Senate has 321 members (296 from Metropolitan France), indirectly elected for 9 years, one-third retiring every 3 years. Both houses sit for about 5 months of the year, one session beginning in October, and the second in April. Sessions are shorter than before, the number of private members' bills is considerably fewer – an average of 2000 a year under the Fourth Republic, 200 a year under the Fifth – and the programme of the National Assembly is determined by the government and not by the house.

GEORGIA

With the collapse of the Soviet Union, nationalist pressures in Georgia gathered strength. On 9 Apr 1991, following a 98.9 per cent popular vote in favour, the Supreme Soviet unanimously declared the Republic an independent state based on the treaty of independence of May 1918. In May 1991 an armed insurrection led to control falling to a military council. In presidential elections in 1992, Edward Shevardnadze became *de facto* head of state. Under the constitution of Aug 1995 Georgia became a presidential Republic with federal elements. The President (head of state) is directly elected by universal suffrage for a 5-year term. The president may not serve more than two 5-year terms. The 235-member parliament is elected by a system combining single-member districts with proportional representation based on party lists.

GERMANY

In the old German Empire, prior to its collapse, the imperial constitution of 16 Apr 1871 had provided for a bicameral parliament. The lower house, the Reichstag, was elected on universal manhood suffrage for 3-year terms (5 after 1888), by direct and secret election. The members were elected from districts which did not over-step state boundaries, but they represented the whole electorate and not their constituents. There was one member for every 100 000 inhabitants of the state or portion of 100 000. It had power to debate government policy and to vote the budget, although many expenses and sources of income were outside its control because of the method of their administration. Bills passed through committees which were set up by 'bureaux', 7 of which were created at the beginning of each session. Representation on the committees was according to party strength. The house could be dissolved by the upper house with the Emperor's consent.

The upper house or Bundesrat was composed of representatives of the member states and free cities. There were 58 members; Prussia sent 17, Bavaria 6, Saxony and Württemberg 4, Hesse and Baden 3, Mecklenburg-Schwerin and Brunswick 2 and the others 1 each. The members were solely responsible to their governments and not to the Reichstag, in which they might not sit. Its presidency was held by the Chancellor. In practice, bills were normally initiated in the Bundesrat by the Chancellor, worked through the permanent committees, of which there were 7, and presented to the Reichstag for assent; the consent of both houses was necessary before a bill became law, and the Reichstag had the right to question the Chancellor and debate Bundesrat policy, but no vote followed.

The Bundesrath might sit alone, the Reichstag could not. The Bundesrat's standing committees might sit when the house was not in session. Bundesrat members voted *en bloc* for their states, and all the votes could be cast by one representative. The members were appointed by their governments for no fixed term.

There was no responsible imperial ministry; only the Chancellor was answerable to the Reichstag.

Following the defeat of Germany, and the wartime upheavals, in Jan 1919 a National Assembly was elected by proportional representation, the franchise being of all over 20. This assembly elected the first President of the Republic in Feb 1919, and laid down that future presidents were to be elected by direct vote, for 7 years. A constitution was promulgated on 11 Aug 1919 by which a new federal Republic was provided with a bicameral federal parliament, to be responsible for defence, foreign relations, tax, customs and railways. The upper house (Reichsrat) had 55 members representing the component states and each member had an individual vote. All bills had to be approved by the Reichsrat before being introduced into the lower house (Reichstag). Members of the Reichstag were elected by proportional representation on a franchise of all over 20, for a 4-year term. There was a cabinet appointed by the President but requiring the confidence of the Reichstag.

The President initiated orders and decrees, although they had still to be countersigned, appointed all national officials, decided the sessions and dissolutions of the Reichstag and ordered referenda. Without consulting the government or the legislature he could, in time of danger, suspend the national authorities and appoint a national commissioner in their place, employ the armed forces and suspend certain fundamental rights. By 1932 his emergency powers had been used 233 times, the Reichstag having the right to repeal any measures taken when the emergency was over.

By the law of 14 Jul 1933 all political parties except the National Socialist German Workers' Party were declared illegal; the Reichstag did not operate normally from that date. Its meetings became shorter until they were limited to sessions of two or three days, and it met infrequently. It remained virtually dead until 1949.

Note: The constitution of 1919 provided for popular election of the President, but Paul von Hindenburg was the only President so elected. President Ebert was elected by the Constituent Assembly itself, and Adolf Hitler assumed the Presidency by incorporating it with his own office of Chancellor.

FEDERAL REPUBLIC OF GERMANY

A Constituent Assembly met in 1948 and devised a Basic Law which was approved by the parliaments of the separate states of the federation and came into force in 1949 as the first constitution of the Federal Republic. Parliament consists of the Federal Council (Bundesrat) which is composed of members of governments of the Länder.

The Bundesrat originally had 49 members and 22 non-voting members for Berlin. Since re-unification the Bundesrat has grown to 69 members. Elections for a new Bundestag take place in the last 3 months of its term, or in the case of its dissolution after not more than 60 days. The new house meets not more than 30 days after election. The President of the Bundestag may convene the house at any time and must do so if asked by one-third of its members or by the Federal President or Federal Chancellor. The Bundestag currently (1999) has 669 members.

Meetings are public, but the public may be excluded. Members of the Bundesrat or of the government have free access to the Bundestag meetings and committee meetings and must be heard at any time; the same is true of Bundestag members at meetings of the Bundesrat, and either house may demand the presence of any member of the Federal Government.

The governments of the 16 Länder appoint and recall those of their members who make up the Bundesrat, or they may appoint other members to represent them. Each Land has at least 3 votes; Länder with over 2m. inhabitants have 4, those with over 6m. have 5. Each Land has as many members as it has votes, and the votes may only be given as a block. The government has an obligation to keep the Bundesrat informed of the conduct of Federal affairs.

Bills are introduced in the Bundestag either by the government or by members of either house. Government bills go to the Bundesrat first, and the house must give an opinion within three weeks. A bill adopted in the Bundestag then goes to the Bundesrat, which may within two weeks demand a joint committee to consider it. Bills altering or adding to the constitution require Bundesrat approval before they may be passed; such bills need a two-thirds majority in both houses. For other bills the Bundesrat has a power of veto, but even then a veto adopted by a majority of Bundesrat votes may be rejected by a majority of Bundestag votes. There is provision for a state of legislative emergency for a bill which the Bundestag has rejected despite the government declaring it urgent, or a bill which has been put forward with a request for a vote of confidence.

The Federal Chancellor is elected by the Bundestag on the proposal of the Federal President. Ministers are appointed and dismissed by the President on the Chancellor's proposal. The Chancellor determines and assumes responsibility for general policy, and within that policy the ministers run their own departments on their own responsibility. The President is elected by indirect vote for a five-year term; immediate re-election is allowed once. His orders and instructions require countersignature by the Chancellor or by a minister.

Major constitutional implications followed the approach of German reunification. The two German states' economic and monetary systems were unified on 1 Jul 1990. On 31 Aug 1990 East and West Germany signed a treaty covering some political and social aspects of German unity, leaving others to be decided by an all-German parliament. On 20 Sep 1990 both states ratified unification terms by which East Germany would merge with the Federal Republic under Art. 23 of the West German Basic Law on 3 Oct 1990. The Basic Law was amended to prevent future claims on former German territory now under Polish or Soviet Union control. In December 1990 all-German elections were held for a single German parliament.

GERMAN DEMOCRATIC REPUBLIC

In 1948 the Soviet-occupied zone of Germany had a People's Council: this was converted into a People's Chamber in 1949 and on 7 Oct 1949 the Chamber enacted a constitution for the Democratic Republic. A new constitution was approved by referendum on 6 Apr 1968.

The Chamber had 500 deputies who were directly elected for 4 years. It assured the enforcement of its own laws and decisions and laid down the principles to which the Council of State, the Council of Ministers, the National Defence Council, the Supreme Court and the Procurator General should adhere. No one could limit the rights of the Chamber. It could hold plebiscites, declare a state of defence when necessary, and approve and terminate state treaties. In between its sessions it authorized the Council of State to fulfil all tasks resulting from the Chamber's laws and decisions. The Council was elected for 4 years. It dealt with bills to be submitted to the Chamber and submitted them for discussion by the Chamber's committees; it convened the Chamber either on request or on its own initiative; it issued decrees and decisions with the force of law; it had power to interpret existing law; it issued the writs for elections; its Chairman represented the Republic in international relations. The Council was formed to replace the office of President abolished in 1960. The Council was an organ of the Chamber and was responsible to it.

The Council of Ministers was also an organ of the Chamber and was elected by it. Its Chairman was proposed to the Chamber by the Chairman of the Council of State. It functioned collectively in the exercise of executive power; from within its ranks it appointed a Presidium; the Chairman of the Council was also the Chairman of the Presidium. The Chamber reached decisions by majority vote. Bills were presented by the deputies of the parties or mass organizations represented, by the committees of the Chamber, the Council of State, the Council of Ministers or by the Confederation of Free German Trade Unions. The bill's conformity with the constitution was examined by the Council of State; the bill was then discussed in committee and comments submitted to the Chamber in plenary session. Drafts of basic laws, prior to their being passed, were submitted to the electorate for discussion.

The Chamber could be dissolved before the end of its electoral term only on its own decision taken on a two-thirds majority. After the end of an electoral term the Council of Ministers and the Council of State continued their work until the new Chamber elected new Councils.

The German Democratic Republic ceased to exist following reunification in 1990. *See* Federal Republic of Germany (pp. 79–81).

GREECE

The constitution of 1864 was replaced by the 1911 constitution which continued in force until 1925 when it was replaced temporarily by a new one; this was abandoned in 1935 and the original reinstated, although some parts of the second constitution were substituted for some of the original clauses later in the year. The constitution of 1952 further amended that of 1911, and remained in force until 1968 when a new one was adopted after a referendum. In 1973 the Monarchy ended and a Republic came into being, with a President as head of state. The 1952 constitution was reintroduced in modified form in 1974, and a new one was promulgated in 1975. All constitutions except the 1925 have provided for a single-chamber parliament, the House of Representatives. This has been the sole or joint source of legislation except during periods of rule by military junta (1967–1973, 1973–1974).

The House had at least 150 members elected by direct universal suffrage for 4 years. It met annually in October for each regular session, which had to be for at least 3 months. It sat in public but the public could be excluded, if the majority of members so decided. It shared with the King or his Regent the legislative power and the right of proposing laws; this second right the King or the Regent exercised through his ministers. Their counter-signature was necessary for all his acts, and through them his executive power was exercised. If no minister consented to sign the decrees dismissing an entire ministry and appointing a new one, they could be signed by the President of the new ministry whom the King had appointed. He could suspend the work of a session once only; he could dissolve the House, but the decree of dissolution had to include the convocation of the electors within 45 days and of the new House within 3 months. He had no power to delay the operation of the law. A bill was at first accompanied by an explanatory report and sent to a committee of the House; it was brought in for discussion when the committee had reported, or when the time allowed for such report had elapsed. No proposal was considered accepted unless it had been discussed and voted on twice at separate sittings. A bill could be passed in one sitting provided the committee to which it was submitted had agreed, and provided fewer than 20 representatives objected before the close of the debate, Ministers had free access to debates and could demand a hearing at any time; they voted only if they were members. They were individually responsible to the House, and no order from the King could release them from their responsibility.

The 1925 Republican constitution provided for a Senate as well as a Chamber of Representatives, and a President. The President was elected for 5 years by both houses in joint session. The Chamber had between 200 and 300 directly elected members and the Senate 120 members indirectly elected. The ministers were responsible to both houses for the actions of the executive, *i.e.* the President. Bills could be introduced by members of both houses and by the government; the Senate had power to delay legislation but the Chamber could pass a bill by majority vote over the Senate's opposition after 3 months or earlier at a joint session if the Senate requested one. The budget was initiated in the Chamber and the Senate was obliged to pronounce on it within one month. The President required ministerial counter-signature for all his acts.

The unicameral parliament provided by other constitutions had members directly elected by universal adult suffrage, for 4 years. Under the monarchy there were at least 150 members, under the presidency, at least 200.

The House shares with the President the legislative power and the right to propose laws; this second right the President exercises through his ministers. Their counter-signature is necessary for all his acts, and through them his executive power is exercised. He has no power to delay the operation of the law. Ministers have free access to debates and may demand a hearing at any time; they vote only if they are members. They are individually responsible to the House.

HUNGARY

Prior to the collapse of the Habsburg monarchy in 1918, since 1867 a bicameral parliament had met in Budapest.

The Upper House had about 270 members and was composed of princes, nobility and bishops, and representatives from Croatia, Slavonia and Transylvania. From 1886, no titled magnate might sit unless he paid a land tax of 3000 florins; church officers were also admitted and life members appointed by the King.

The Lower House had 453 members including 40 for Croatia. They were elected by specific classes of voters on a property suffrage; voters must be aged 24 and over and Magyar-speaking. The term was 3 years (5 after 1886).

Bills passed through both houses in committees appointed by 'bureaux' or standing committees. Committee reports were considered either by the bureaux or by the whole House.

The first permanent parliament set up after the end of the Austro-Hungarian monarchy was the National Assembly of 1920. The head of the state was Admiral Horthy who held the title of Regent; he had power of suspensive veto over laws passed by the Assembly and power to dissolve the house provided a newly elected Assembly met within 90 days. When the Assembly ended in 1922 a law was passed by government decree (*i.e.* by the Regent's ministers) making the 200 seats in rural constituencies subject to open and not secret voting. Men over 24 who had completed the course at elementary school, and women over 30 with certain qualifications received the vote. The government's supporters were returned in strength, but the working of parliament became disorderly and difficult. In 1924 the government was granted extraordinary powers for a 2-year period of reconstruction.

In 1926 a second chamber was formed, comprising male members of the former reigning house, elected representatives of hereditary members of the former Upper House, about 50 members elected by town and county municipalities, about 31 members as religious representatives, about 40 members elected by institutions and organizations and some life members appointed by the head of the state. It ceased functioning after 1944. In 1937 the Regent was made no longer responsible to parliament. In 1938 the number of deputies in the Assembly was increased from 245 to 260. The Assembly proclaimed a Republic in 1946.

In 1949 a further – Communist – constitution was set up with parliament electing a Presidium on the Soviet model; the Presidium was in continual session and had power to dissolve government bodies and to annul legislation. The Assembly had 352 deputies, and after 1967 more than one candidate was allowed to stand for election in each constituency provided they supported the policies of the Patriotic Front and received 30 per cent of the votes cast at pre-election nominations. Members were elected for 4 years until 1975, when the term was changed to 5 years. The Assembly also elected a Council of Ministers with a chairman as Prime Minister. The relationship between Assembly, Council and Presidium was on the Soviet model.

Parliament approved a new constitution on 18 Oct 1989 dissolving the People's Republic, removing the right of any party to sole governing powers, and instituting parliamentary democracy. A Hungarian Republic was proclaimed on 23 Oct 1989.

Under the 1989 constitution, the single-chamber National Assembly has 386 members (176 victors in individual constituencies, 152 allotted by proportional representation and 58 from a national list). Members are elected for a 4-year term. The head of state is the President of the Republic.

ICELAND

The constitution in force in 1900 was based on the Charter of 1874. Executive power belonged to the King (who was King of both Denmark and Iceland as two separate sovereign states) and was exercised through ministers responsible to him and to parliament (the Althing). The legislative power rested conjointly with the Althing and the King. The Althing had 40 members, 34 of them elected by universal suffrage in constituencies and the remaining 6 elected for the whole country on proportional representation. The 34 sat for 6 years, the rest for 12. The Althing had an Upper House of 14 members – *i.e.* the 6 described above and 8 others elected by the whole Althing from among the 34. The remaining 26 members formed the Lower House. The Althing met every other year in July, and could not sit for longer than 4 weeks without royal sanction. Ministers had free access to both houses, but could only vote in the house of which they were members. Budget bills had to be introduced in the Lower House, but all other bills could be introduced in either. If the houses could not agree on a bill they assembled in common sitting and the decision was by a two-thirds majority except in the case of a budget bill, for which a simple majority was enough.

In the Charter of 1920 and its amendments of 1934 some alterations were made to the composition of the Althing: the number of members had not to exceed 49, of whom 38 were elected from the constituencies, each electing candidates by simple majority except for the capital which elected 6 on proportional representation. Not more than 11 supplementary seats were distributed among parties having insufficient seats in proportion to their electors. The Upper House was composed of one-third of Althing members elected by both houses in common sitting. The Althing met every year. The electoral law of 1984 provided for an Althing of 63 members, of whom 54 were elected in 8 constituencies by proportional representation, with 9 supplementary members chosen as before. The Republic was proclaimed in 1944 and a President elected to exercise executive power through the ministers. He serves for 4 years.

IRELAND

There are two houses in the Irish parliament, the House of Representatives (Dáil) and the Senate. The House had 166 members in 1999 elected by universal adult suffrage. The Senate had 60 members of whom 11 are nominated by the Prime Minister, 6 elected by the universities and 43 elected by a college from representatives of the public services and interests. The President is elected for a 7-year term and may be re-elected for consecutive terms. The constitution in force is that of 1937. The constitution formed by Dáil Eireann in 1919 was a temporary one, not intended as a permanent basis for a fully operating government. It provided for a chairman for the Dáil, a Prime Minister and other ministers; it defined the competence of the Dáil and made provision for audit and budgeting. The constitution of the Irish Free State in 1922 provided for a constitutional monarchy with responsible government by a cabinet of ministers. In order to restrict the power of the executive there was also provision for referendum and popular initiative, and for the direct election by the Dáil of ministers who were not Dáil members or members of the cabinet. All these measures, however, had lapsed or been removed within 5 years.

Note: The 1937 constitution did not declare a Republic. It provided instead for a continuation of the arrangements made at the abdication of Edward VIII, when the mention of the Crown was removed from the previous constitution and an ordinary statute (The Executive Authority (External Relations) Act) put in its place to provide an organ for the state in the conduct of its external affairs. In 1948 it was therefore possible to create the Republic by ordinary legislation and not by changing the constitution. The President appoints the Prime Minister on the nomination of the Dáil, and the other ministers on the nomination of the Prime Minister, with the previous approval of the Dáil. The Prime Minister holds office until he chooses to resign, in which case the government is deemed also to have resigned, until he loses majority support or until he himself secures dissolution by asking the President. Appointment to the government is distinct from appointment to a department. Members of the government may include members of the Senate (but in practice have rarely done so). There is also provision for ministers without portfolio.

Bills are proposed mainly by the government in planned legislative programmes. There is provision for private members' bills, but few are initiated. The Senate has power to delay legislation while the Dáil reconsiders its previous decision. Bills can be discussed at parliamentary party meetings either between their preparation and presentation to the House, or between presentation and second reading.

There may be no amendment to the constitution without a referendum, though this was possible before 1930. The referendum of May 1998 approved the 'Good Friday' peace agreement. Under this, Ireland would abandon the Republic's territorial claim to Northern Ireland. This claim was formally abandoned in December 1999.

ITALY

Italy is a Republic, with a President and a parliament consisting of a Chamber of Deputies and a Senate. The Chamber is elected for 5 years by direct and universal suffrage (changed in 1993) with one deputy for every 80 000 inhabitants. The Senate is elected for 5 years with at least 7 senators for each Region, except for the Valle d'Aosta which has only 1 and Molise with 2. The President can nominate 11 senators for life, and may himself become a senator for life upon retiring from the Presidency.

Parliament may be dissolved by the President. A cabinet need resign only on a motivated motion of censure.

A joint session of Chamber and Senate is needed to elect a President, with an additional three delegates from each Regional Council (one from the Valle d'Aosta). The presidential term is seven years.

The Republic was established in 1946, following a referendum on 2 Jun and the consequent abdication of King Umberto II on 13 Jun. The republican constitution came into force on 1 Jan 1948.

The constitution prior to 1948 was an expansion of the Statuto fondamentale del Regno of 1848. The executive power belonged to the sovereign and was exercised through responsible ministers; legislative power rested in King and parliament, which consisted of a Senate and a lower chamber. This latter was the Chamber of Deputies until 1938; it was elected by universal adult male suffrage for 5 years with one deputy for every 71 000 of the population. The King had power to dissolve it at any time provided he ordered new elections and convoked a new meeting within 4 months. In 1938 the Chamber was replaced by the Chamber of Fasci and Corporations which had first met in 1929. Membership of this consisted of the Duce and the members of the Grand Fascist Council, a third body whose approval was needed for all constitutional measures and which consisted of original members of the Fascist Party on its coming to power, who were appointed for an indefinite period, ministers and other dignitaries appointed for the duration of their terms of office and other members appointed for 3 years by the Duce. The Duce as Prime Minister was responsible to the King.

Suffrage in 1919 was by proportional representation. In 1923 this was replaced by a system of election in 15 constituencies, with two-thirds of seats allotted to whichever party gained at least 25 per cent of total votes. In 1925 there was a further alteration introducing single-member constituencies, by-elections and suffrage for all over 25. Parliament, however, did not function normally after the Fascist ministry took power in 1922, as the Fascists were the only effective party.

In 1993, against a background of political scandals, and as a result of the Apr 1993 referendum, the Italian parliament voted to revise the proportional representation system.

Under the new electoral system (first used in the Mar 1994 elections), three-quarters of the members of each house (472 deputies and 232 senators) are elected by a majority 'winner-takes-all' system. The remaining quarter of senators and deputies are still elected by the old proportional representation (PR) system. A party requires 4 per cent of the national proportional vote to be awarded any of the PR seats. Constituencies averaged 120 000 population for the Chamber of Deputies and 244000 for the Senate in 1999.

Attempts to create a new constitution finally collapsed in Jun 1998 after prolonged consideration.

LATVIA

A constitution came into force in 1922 and provided for a republican state with a single house of parliament (the Saeima). The house had 100 representatives directly elected on universal adult suffrage by proportional representation for a term of 3 years. The house elected the state President by absolute majority for a 3-year term. The President chose the Prime Minister, who appointed the cabinet. The cabinet was responsible to the house. The President had the right to dissolve parliament only after the proposal to dissolve it had been voted on and confirmed by the electorate. If he did not obtain this confirmation he was obliged to resign. In 1934 the parliament was disbanded and a government set up which combined executive and legislative power in the former Council of Ministers. This government was led by the former Prime Minister Karlis Ulmanis. He combined his office with that of President in 1936. From 1940 to 1991 Latvia was a constituent Republic of the USSR.

In May 1990 the Latvian Supreme Soviet declared that the Soviet occupation of Latvia on 17 Jun 1940 was illegal. It resolved to re-establish the 1922 Constitution. The declaration of independence of 21 Aug 1991 stated that Latvia was an independent, democratic Republic as set out in the 1922 constitution.

Under the constitution as re-instituted on 6 Jul 1993, the head of state is the President, elected by parliament. The single-chamber parliament of 100 deputies is elected by direct proportional election for a 4-year period. All citizens aged 18 or over have the vote. Political parties have to pass a 5 per cent threshold to secure representation in parliament. The referendum of 3 Oct 1998 liberalized the hitherto strict laws on citizenship.

LIECHTENSTEIN

The constitution of 1921 provided for a Diet of 15 members in one house, elected on universal suffrage and proportional representation. In 1988 this total was increased to 25. They sit for 4 years. The Prince convokes, closes and dissolves the Diet, and may adjourn it for 3 months provided the adjournment is announced before the full Diet. Convocation may be demanded by 400 citizens, and dissolution decided by plebiscite on the demand of 600. The Diet supervises the entire administration of the state. Bills may be initiated by the Diet, the Prince acting through the government, and the citizens (1000 or 3 communes). To be valid a law must be passed by an absolute majority of at least two-thirds of members. If the Diet rejects a bill submitted to it by popular initiative, it is obliged to submit the bill to a referendum, when it can be passed by the citizens even if the Diet disagrees. The government is appointed by the Prince with the approval of the Diet; he acts through them, but all his actions must be counter-signed and it is his ministers who are responsible.

LITHUANIA

A constitution was adopted in 1922 and provided for a single-chamber parliament elected for 3 years by universal suffrage and proportional representation. Elections for a new house had to take place before the expiration of the previous term. The President of the Republic was elected by parliament for 3 years and by absolute majority; he could run for 2 successive terms but no third term without a break. He appointed the Prime Minister, and confirmed the ministers chosen by him, and also appointed the State Comptrollers (with auditing powers), but all bodies appointed could only function with the confidence of the house. He had power to return a bill to the house for reconsideration within 21 days of the passage; but was then bound to accept it if it was passed again by an absolute majority. His power of delay could be cancelled by a declaration of urgency by the house. He presided at and took part in cabinet meetings.

Any amendment to the constitution could be brought forward by the house, the government, or 50000 citizens, but needed a three-fifths majority of the total number of deputies for adoption. After that a referendum could be demanded on it. Ministers had individual and collective responsibility.

In 1926 the democratic system was brought to an end by political confusion. Further constitutional changes were made in 1928 and 1938 on authoritarian lines. By 1938 a dictatorship had been established and the house was no longer operating normally. In 1940 Lithuania became a constituent Republic of the USSR.

The independence of Lithuania was recognized by the Soviet Union on 6 Sep 1991. Earlier, in a referendum of Feb 1991, over 90 per cent of those voting were in favour of independence. A draft constitution was published in Apr 1991. A referendum approved the new constitution in Oct 1992. Parliament (the *Seimas*) comprises 141 members. It is elected by a system partly proportional and partly constituency-based, with 70 seats allocated to parties according to their share of the vote (with a 4 per cent threshold except for ethnic parties). The 71 constituency seats require candidates to poll more than 50 per cent of the vote, otherwise there are run-off ballots.

LUXEMBOURG

The constitution of 1868 was amended in 1919, 1948 and 1956. It has seen 7 revisions since 1972, the last in 1998. In 1919 it was decided that sovereign power was vested in the people and that deputies to the single Chamber of Deputies were to be elected on universal suffrage by the list system of proportional representation. The Chamber of Deputies had 48 members in 1919. They were elected for a 6-year term, half of them being re-elected every 3 years. The head of state shared legislative power with the Chamber and exercised the executive power through the cabinet. The constitution allowed the sovereign to organize the government. The sovereign also chose the 15 members of the permanent Council of State who served for life. The Council discussed proposed legislation and was obliged to give an opinion on any matter referred to it by the sovereign or the representatives of the law. In 1956 the term of office for deputies was altered to 5 years. In 1999 the number of deputies was 60.

The Grand Duke names and dismisses the government, which must consist of at least 3 members who may not be members of the Chamber, and who are responsible collectively and individually.

Bills are passed after two readings with an interval of three months approved by an absolute majority.

MACEDONIA

The independence of Macedonia was proclaimed on 20 Nov 1992. It was admitted to the United Nations on 8 Apr 1993 under the name of 'Former Yugoslav Republic of Macedonia' a decision acceptable to Greece. On 20 Nov 1992 parliament had promulgated a new constitution which asserted Macedonia's independence. The President is directly elected for 5-year terms. Candidates must be citizens aged at least 40 years. The parliament is a 120-member single chamber Assembly (*Sobranie*), elected by universal suffrage for 4-year terms. The *Sobranie* has power to adopt and amend the constitution, enact laws and gives interpretations thereof, adopts the budget of the Republic, decides on war and peace and chooses the government. The Assembly may also call for a referendum.

MALTA

Malta received internal self-government in 1961, with Britain remaining responsible for internal affairs and defence. When Malta became independent in 1964, the independent state had a House of Representatives of 50 elected members. The President was the head of state of Malta. Under a constitutional amendment of Mar 1996, where more than 2 parties stood at a general election, if only 2 parties won seats the party with the most votes would be allocated extra seats.

MOLDOVA

With the collapse of the Soviet Union, Moldova declared itself an independent Republic in Aug 1991. A new constitution became effective on 27 Aug 1994. It defined Moldova as an independent, democratic and unitary state. However, in the predominantly Russian-speaking areas of Transdniestria a self-styled Republic was established in Sep 1991, and approved by a local referendum in Dec 1991. Under the Moldovan constitution, parliament has 104 seats and is elected for 4-year terms. There is a 4 per cent threshold for election; votes falling below this are redistributed to successful parties. The President is elected for 4-year terms. Elections were first held in independent Moldova in 1994 (see p. 258).

MONACO

The constitution of 1911 lasted until 1959; it provided for a National Council of 18 members elected for a 5-year term by 30 delegates of municipalities and 21 electors chosen by adult male suffrage. Legislative power was exercised by the Prince and the Council, executive power by a Minister of State and a 3-member Council of Government under the Prince.

In 1959 the Prince suspended this constitution and dissolved the National Council, which was then revived in 1962 as a directly elected body with a 5-year term. Executive power is still vested in the Prince, the Minister of State who represents him, and the Council. The Minister directs all administration and presides over the Council with the casting vote. The Council consists of 3 members named by the Prince (members for the Interior, Finance and Public Works). The Council takes its decisions after deliberation and prepares drafts and ordinances for the Prince's consideration. Legislative power is vested in the Prince and the National Council. The Assembly of the National Council chooses a Bureau with President and Vice-President. The Assembly sits for 2 sessions a year, each of 15 days at most; the Prince may convoke and dissolve it. He communicates with the assembly through the Minister of State, who, together with the councillors, may attend at his own wish and must attend when asked. The initiative rests with the Prince, but the National Council may submit draft proposals to him and ask him to initiate them. The National Council controls the budget, which is submitted to it by the Council, and has sole right to levy direct taxation.

THE NETHERLANDS

The parliament consists of 2 chambers. The Upper House has had 75 members since 1956, prior to which it had 50. They are elected by members of the Provincial States. The Second Chamber has had 150 deputies since 1956 (100 before that) and they are directly elected on universal suffrage and proportional representation. The Second Chamber shares legislative power with the sovereign, who has power to dissolve both chambers provided elections take place within 40 days and the new house or houses be convoked within 3 months.

The Upper House is elected for six years, and half the members retire every three years. The Lower House members are elected for four years.

Bills are proposed either by the Sovereign, acting through responsible ministers, or by a member of the Lower House. The Upper House has power only to approve or reject them without amendment; the houses must ultimately agree. Ministers and Secretaries of State attend sessions of both houses either at their own or parliament's wish, but they may not be members of either house. The constitution can only be revised if the bill for its revision is passed and confirmed again by a second parliament after the dissolution of the first.

The constitutional amendments of 1922 provided that the Upper House should be elected for 6 years and not for 9 as formerly. Until 1922 the right to declare war and to conclude and ratify treaties with foreign powers was a royal power, exercised in conjunction with the cabinet. Since then, the exercise of these powers has depended on previous parliamentary sanction. The constitution allows considerable royal initiative, but in practice the operation of the cabinet system has set this aside. There is also a Council of State of not more than 16 members which sits as an advisory body on all legislative matters and is consulted by the Crown, the government or parliament.

NORWAY

Norway's constitution dates from 1814; although there have been amendments since, the nature of the Storting (parliament) is virtually the same as then provided. The state is a constitutional monarchy; in default of male heirs the King proposes a successor to parliament which has the right to select another. The King also has power of veto which may be exercised twice; a bill which passes three parliaments formed by three elections becomes law without his assent.

Parliament assembles in October every year for a session of no fixed duration. Once the House is assembled it divides in two by electing one-quarter of its members to form the Lagting or Upper House; the remaining three-quarters forming the Odelsting or Lower House. There is a President nominated for each

House and for the joint House. Most questions are decided by the joint House, but legislation must be considered by both houses separately. If they disagree, then the bill must be decided by parliament as a whole and the decision taken on a two-thirds majority (of voters, not of total membership). The same majority is needed for constitutional amendments.

The executive is represented by the Crown acting through the Prime Minister and cabinet of 14 ministers. The ministers attend sessions of parliament and take part in discussions, but they do not vote. They do initiate bills.

There is a strong committee system through which all proposed legislation must pass before submission to the House. All bills are proposed in the Odelsting, and if accepted are sent to the Lagting. The Lagting may either approve a bill as it stands or reject it as it stands and give its reasons. If rejected it is returned to the Odelsting which will send it once more, either in an amended or original form, to the Lagting. If still rejected the joint session must take place to pass it.

The Crown has no power of dissolution, nor can it summon parliament to meet. The dates of meeting are decided by parliament itself. Election is direct, by all citizens over 20 and by proportional representation. The country is divided into 19 electoral districts. The 165 members are elected for a 3-year term.

OTTOMAN EMPIRE *See* TURKEY

POLAND

The constitution of the Republic came into operation in 1920. The legislature consisted of a Diet and a Senate. Diet members were elected on universal suffrage for a 5-year term. The Senate was elected on universal suffrage of all citizens over 30 and by proportional representation in the provincial districts. It sat also for 5 years. National minorities represented 20 per cent of Diet membership.

The Diet had the power of initiating legislation, and had to submit every bill it passed to the Senate. The Senate was obliged to refer a bill back within 30 days if it was suggesting amendments; otherwise the bill was promulgated. If the Diet accepted the Senate's amendments by a simple majority or rejected them by a majority of eleven-twentieths, the bill was passed in the form it left the Diet for the second time.

A President was elected by parliament as a whole for a term of seven years. His position was largely symbolic and his actions required the consent of parliament. He might dissolve the Diet if he had the consent of the Senate, but the Senate in so consenting determined its own dissolution. He exercised the executive power through a council of ministers responsible to the Diet.

There was also a Supreme Court of Control which made independent and judicious survey of the government's provincial administration. Its President was a minister, not a member of the Council of Ministers but responsible to the Diet.

The constitution could only be amended by a two-thirds majority of at least half the number of deputies and senators fixed by law. It might be revised once every 25 years by simple majority of a joint session.

The constitution of 1935 made radical changes in the office of President and the composition of the houses. The working of the original Diet was frequently disrupted by party differences; now there were to be no political parties in the Diet or the Senate. The Senate was to have one-third of its 96 senators nominated by the President of the Republic and the remaining two-thirds elected by colleges.

The President was chosen by referendum from two candidates, one elected by the two houses together and the other nominated by the retiring President. He could now exercise without counter-signature his right to nominate and dismiss the Prime Minister and the Inspector-General of the armed forces, to nominate judges and senators, and to dissolve the Diet and the Senate before the end of their term. If the Diet and the Senate demanded the dismissal of a minister or of the cabinet, the President might concur or dissolve the houses.

The next constitution was adopted in 1952. There was now one chamber which sat for 4 years and was elected by all citizens over 18. It elected, on the Russian pattern, a Council of Ministers with a chairman as Prime Minister, and a Council of State composed of a chairman, a secretary and 14 members, which sat in almost permanent session and exercised the power of a Presidium.

Round-table talks were held in Feb 1989 between Solidarity and the government. Fundamental changes to the constitution were proposed. These included a new office of State President, and the establishment of a new bicameral National Assembly with a newly-created Senate acting as the Upper House. The Senate would not have power to initiate legislation, but would have a power of veto over the Sejm.

Constitutional changes continued to be demanded by Solidarity after 1990. These constitutional reforms (known as the 'Small Constitution') took place in Aug 1992. Under them, the authority of the Republic was vested in the Sejm (Parliament) of 460 members, elected by proportional representation for 4 years by all citizens over 18. There was a 5 per cent threshold for parties and 8 per cent for coalitions, but seats were reserved for representatives of ethnic minorities even if their vote fell below 5 per cent. The Sejm elected a Council of State and a Council of Ministers. There was also an elected 100-member upper house, the Senate. The Senate had a power of veto which only a two-thirds majority of the Sejm could override. The head of state was the President. The Prime Minister was chosen by the President with the approval of the Sejm. At the referendum of May 1997 Poland voted for a new constitution with diminished powers for the President and increased powers for the Sejm.

PORTUGAL

By the republican constitution of 1911, legislative power was given to a Congress with a Chamber of Deputies and a Senate. There were 164 deputies elected for 3 years by male suffrage. The Senate had 71 members elected by electoral colleges formed from the Municipal Councils, and sat for 6 years with half the number retiring every 3 years. The Chamber of Deputies had priority in the discussion of financial bills, bills promoted by the government and of those relating to the armed forces. The Senate might amend or reject, but both houses had to agree, by joint session if necessary, before a bill could be promulgated by the President.

The President was elected by joint session of both houses for a four-year term. He had no power of veto but did have power of dissolution after consulting the cabinet. The cabinet was responsible for his acts. For the period of the first constitution the cabinet was extremely weak owing to differences between numerous small parties. Its power to advise dissolution was used frequently and both houses were dissolved for long periods.

The constitution of 1933 remained in force until 1974. It provided for a President directly elected by citizens with literacy or financial qualifications. The National Assembly was to have one chamber with 90 deputies elected for 4 years by direct suffrage. There was to be a Privy Council of 10 members to assist the President. In practice one party took over the National Assembly and retained control. In 1959 the constitution was amended to provide for indirect election of the President by an electoral college made up of members of the National Assembly and of the Corporative Chamber. On 25 Apr 1974 the government was overthrown and a Junta of National Salvation installed. The dissolution of the National Assembly and of the Council of State followed.

A new constitution was adopted in 1976 and revised in 1982. The President was now elected by popular vote for a 5-year term. He was to appoint the Prime Minister and, on the latter's recommendation, the other ministers. A new National Assembly was provided with 250 members, still elected by direct vote for a 4-year term. In 1982 the effective ruling junta was abolished and replaced by a Council of State and a Constitutional Tribunal. The role of the President was reduced. The National Assembly now (1999) has 230 members.

ROMANIA

The constitution of 1866 continued in force with amendments until 1923. It provided for a monarchy acting through responsible ministers, and a two-chamber parliament. The Chamber of Deputies was elected by three classes of electors whose franchise depended on property and educational qualifications. The Senate was elected by two classes with property qualifications higher than those required for electors to the Chamber. By the 1923 constitution the King's powers were defined as those of a constitutional monarch, sharing legislative power with the Chamber and the Senate. All three had the right of initiating measures.

The Chamber of Deputies was elected in universal suffrage by all over 21, by proportional representation and compulsory ballot. The Senate was composed of elected and *ex officio* members, some elected on a similar system to members of the Chamber, some by electoral colleges of local councillors with one senator for each Department (the largest local government unit), and some by members of Chambers of Commerce, institutes of agriculture and commerce, etc., and by the universities. The *ex officio* members included church officials, members of learned institutions, former political and parliamentary figures. All bills, initiated by either the chamber or the King, passed before a Legislative Council which gave help in drafting and co-ordinating measures. It was consulted in all cases except those concerning the budget. The King had power of suspensive veto.

A constitution was adopted in 1938 which introduced Senate members nominated by the King, equal in number to those elected. Senators sat for 9 years and deputies for 6, and the election of deputies was now by all citizens of 30 years and over engaged in manual work, agriculture, commerce, industry or intellectual work. Senators were elected by the same professions, but the age limit was 40. In 1939 the Principal Council and the Grand Council were instituted, to elect 8 representatives from each of three classes – agriculturists, free professions and workers. The Principal Council would have executive power and the Grand Council would be an advisory body. By that time the parliament had been in dissolution for over a year, having been dissolved in Dec 1937. In Dec 1947 the state became a Republic. A new constitution was passed in 1948 providing for one chamber, the Grand National Assembly, which was elected by all over 18 years, for 4 years with one deputy for every 40 000 inhabitants. This body sat in short sessions twice a year. It elected a Presidium which sat almost permanently and to which its legislative powers were delegated. The Presidium had a chairman, who was head of state, four vice-chairmen, a secretary and 22 members. There was also a Council of Ministers, but all ministerial policies were shaped by deliberative collegiate bodies of which the minister was chairman. The Council of Ministers and the Presidium (or Council of State) related to the Assembly as on the Russian pattern. In 1972 the National Assembly's term was changed from 4 years to 5.

Following the revolution of Dec 1989 and the fall of the Ceauçescu régime, the National Salvation Front assumed sweeping power pending the drafting of a new constitution. The leading role of the Communist Party was abolished by decree and multi-party elections were held.

The National Assembly drafted a new constitution in Nov 1991 which was approved by referendum on 8 Dec 1991. Under this constitution, the National Assembly consists of a 341-member Chamber of Deputies and a 143-member Senate. Both are elected for 4-year terms from 41 constituencies by modified proportional representation, the number of seats won in each constituency being determined by the proportion of the total vote. There is a 3 per cent threshold for admission to either house.

RUSSIA

Two legislative bodies existed in 1900 in Imperial Russia: the Senate (established by Peter the Great) and the Council of the Empire. Neither body was elected. The constitution of 1905 provided for a parliament (Duma) of 442 members, one from each province, elected by colleges of 5 classes. The Central Asian provinces returned 23 members to the first and second parliaments but were then disfranchised. In 1906 the Council of the Empire was attached to the Duma as an upper house with 196 members, 98 of them nominated by the Tsar and 98 elected by the clergy, the corporations of nobles and other academic, civic and commercial bodies. Both houses had the same powers. The Duma had limited competence. It might not consider the army or navy; all laws had to be proposed to a minister who would consider them and prepare his own draft, and ministers were responsible to the Tsar. A preliminary report of all measures had to be submitted to the Council of the Empire and the Tsar for approval. A majority vote of the Duma was submitted to the upper house, and in case of disagreement the Tsar could intervene. The Tsar might dissolve parliament and had power to enact measures when the house was not sitting. The revolution of 1917 swept away all this (*see* p. 103 for the Soviet era).

At the time of the collapse of the Soviet Union, the Russian constitution was a heavily amended version of the 1977 Soviet constitution (*see* Union of Soviet Socialist Republics). In Dec 1991 President Boris Yeltsin (elected on 12 Jun 1991) was given power by the Congress of People's Deputies to rule by decree. An attempt to cancel this power failed in Apr 1992. A referendum was held on 25 Apr 1993 to test support for the basic principles of a new constitution.

A constitutional conference opened in Jun 1993 but the situation remained fluid as the president and the Congress continued to disagree. The abrogation of the constitution and dissolution of the Congress of People's Deputies by Yeltsin, in Sep 1993, was followed by the announcement that a new constitution would be written and new parliamentary elections held before the end of 1993 (*see* p. 286) followed by a presidential election.

The referendum of 12 Dec 1993 approved the new Basic Law, replacing the 1978 constitution passed under Brezhnev. The new constitution greatly strengthens the powers of the President, who is elected for four years and can serve no more than two terms. The new powers as head of state include the right to pass decrees without reference to parliament (although they can be vetoed by a two-thirds majority); the right to declare a state of emergency (with parliamentary consent); the appointment of military commanders, diplomats and senior judges; the right to reject legislation passed by the lower house (the State Duma); and the right to call parliamentary elections. The President can be impeached after court decisions followed by a two-thirds majority in each house of parliament. There is no provision for a Vice-President.

Parliament consists of two chambers. The lower house, the State Duma, has 450 deputies, half elected by the 'first-past-the-post' system and the remainder by proportional representation from party lists. The Duma approves legislation but can only draft laws affecting the budget with government consent. The upper house, the Federation Council, has 178 representatives, 2 from each member state of the federation. The council cannot be dissolved by the President and approves Duma legislation.

Among the constitution's provisions, which mark a decisive break with the Communist past, are affirmation of the freedom of worship, speech and travel, as well as a free press. Private property is enshrined as an inalienable right and all mention of a state ideology vanished. Parliament can only make constitutional changes by a two-thirds majority in each house.

SLOVAKIA

Under the constitution adopted on 1 Sep 1992 for an independent Slovakia (which came into being on 1 Jan 1993), parliament is the National Council. This consists of 150 members elected by proportional representation for a 4-year term. The President, elected by universal adult suffrage for a 5-year term, is the head of state.

Citizenship belongs to all citizens of the former federal Slovak Republic; other residents of five years' standing may apply for citizenship. Slovakia grants dual citizenship to Czechs.

SLOVENIA

Slovenia declared its complete independence of former Yugoslavia on 8 Oct 1991. Its independence was recognized by Germany on 23 Dec 1991 and by the European Communities on 15 Jan 1992. Under the constitution enacted by the Assembly in Dec 1991, there is a bicameral parliament consisting of a 90-member National Assembly elected for 4-year terms by proportional representation with a 3 per cent threshold; and a 40-member State Council, elected for 5-year terms by interest groups. It has veto powers over the National Assembly.

SPAIN

Spain was a constitutional monarchy until the system was virtually set aside by the military *coup d'état* under General Primo de Rivera in 1923. The constitution had provided for legislative power being exercised by the parliament of two chambers and the King; both chambers were equal in authority, and ministers were responsible to them. Parliamentary life was frequently disrupted and always weakened by political confusion, and no single strong authority emerged.

The military and civil dictatorships which followed abolished the parliament temporarily, together with the post of Prime Minister and other Ministries except War and Foreign Affairs. In 1925 a civilian cabinet was restored, but the parliament was still in dissolution.

The constitution of 1931 provided a single-chamber parliament, Congress, and republican state under a President. The Congress was elected for 4 years by universal suffrage on proportional representation. Electors and deputies had to be over 23. Executive power was held by the head of state, through a Council of Ministers headed by a Prime Minister whom he appointed. There was a Council of the Realm of 16 members, of whom 10 were elected by the Cortes (parliament), and a National Council which was partly elected and partly appointed. The Cortes consisted of members of the government; national councillors; presidents of the supreme court of justice, the council of the realm, the supreme military tribunal, the court of exchequer and the national economic council; 150 representatives of trade unions; representatives of municipalities and provincial councils elected by their respective corporations; 100 deputies (2 from each province) elected by the heads of families; 30 representatives of universities, learned societies, chambers of commerce. Its function was to prepare and pass laws, working through commissions and through plenary session. The Commissions were arranged and appointed by the President of the Cortes in agreement with the government. President and government also arranged the agenda. Laws once passed were sent to the head of state who might within one month return them to the Cortes for fresh deliberation.

A new constitution came into force in 1978, establishing a parliamentary monarchy. The new Cortes was bicameral. The upper house or Senate had 208 senators, 4 each for the 47 peninsular provinces and others elected by the insular provinces, Ceuta and Melilla and the autonomous communities. The lower house or Congress of Deputies had 300–400 members, elected by proportional representation. (There were 350 in the 1996 general election.) Suffrage for both houses is universal and direct; the term of both houses is 4 years. Executive power is vested in the Prime Minister, who is elected by the Congress, and his cabinet.

SWEDEN

The constitution in force in 1900 was that of 1809, under which executive power lay with the King who exercised it through the Council of State with the Prime Minister at its head. All members of the Council of State were responsible for the acts of the government. The ministers prepared bills for the Diet, issued general directives and made higher appointments but did not as a rule take individual administrative decisions. This was done by central boards, whose organization depended on the appropriations granted by the Diet. The King in Council might ask the advice of the boards, but was not bound to follow it. All members of the Council of State were also members of parliament.

Until 1971 there were two chambers of the legislature, the Upper and Lower Houses. The Upper House had members elected by proportional representation, candidates being chosen on property or income qualifications. They sat for 8 years and were elected by members of county councils, the electors of Stockholm and 5 other large towns. The Lower House had 230 members elected by proportional representation. In 1921 women were given the franchise like men, at the age of 23. Also in 1921 the 2 houses gained the right to appoint their own Speakers, with an elected substitute to take his place if necessary. Formerly Speakers were appointed by the King. In the same year the King's prerogative of consulting a private committee on important questions of foreign relations was modified; a Foreign Affairs Committee was set up consisting of 16 members from each house and appointed by the parliament, and the King was bound to take its advice. All foreign agreements of importance were submitted to parliament for ratification.

Bills passed by the houses passed through a strong committee system which provided opinion on all except finance bills. If the houses disagreed on any bill, the matter would go to each house separately; the houses would then sit together and decide by majority. Both houses had equal powers in framing laws.

Since 1971 the Diet has consisted of one chamber. It has 349 members directly elected by universal suffrage for 3 years. All over 19 have the vote, and proportional representation is used in 29 constituencies from which 310 members are elected. The remaining 39 seats are distributed to parties receiving at least 4 per cent of votes.

In 1975 a new constitution made parliament the central organ of government, in which the King no longer had any powers but remained head of state.

SWITZERLAND

The constitution is that of 1874, and under it the highest authority is vested in the electorate. This consisted of all male citizens over 20 until 1971 when the franchise was extended to women. All Swiss citizens over 18 can now (1999) vote. The electorate has power through referenda to vote on amendments to or revision of the constitution. Referenda are also held on laws and international treaties if 50000 voters or 8 cantons request them, and the electorate can also initiate constitutional amendments if 100000 voters support the initiative. The legislature consists of 2 chambers, the Council of States and the National Council. The Council of States has 46 members chosen and paid by the 23 cantons; election procedures depend on which canton they represent. The National Council has 200 councillors directly elected for 4 years in proportion to the population of the cantons, with at least one member for each canton or half-canton. Members are paid not by the cantons but from federal funds.

Laws to be submitted to popular vote must have been agreed by both chambers. The chief executive authority lies with the Bundesrat or Federal Council. It has seven members elected from seven different cantons by a joint session of both chambers. It sits for a four-year term. The members must not hold any other office in the cantons or the Confederation. The President of the Federal Council is the President of the Confederation. He and his Vice-President are first magistrates of the state. They are elected by a Federal Assembly for one year only. The seven members of the Council act as ministers and heads of the seven administrative departments.

Bills can be introduced in parliament by a member, by either of the houses or by the Federal Council.

TURKEY

In the old Ottoman Empire, a constitution had been granted in 1876 and provided for a bicameral parliament. The Sultan had power to convoke and prorogue the parliament and might dissolve the Chamber of Deputies (lower house). He named and dismissed the ministers. The Senate members were nominated by the Sultan for life, and in number had not to exceed a third of the Chamber of Deputies. The Chamber had one deputy for each 50000 male inhabitants, elected secretly for a 4-year term. All Turkish men at least 30 years old having civil rights and speaking Turkish might sit. The Chamber presented to the Sultan a list of 9 candidates as President and Vice-President of the House, and he chose from it.

Laws were initiated by the government; ministers were chosen by the Sultan but responsible to the Chamber of Deputies except in an emergency when the

House was not sitting, when their decisions had the force of law without the Assembly's consent, providing the Sultan approved them. Laws had no force otherwise unless approved by both houses and the Sultan.

In Apr 1920 the Grand National Assembly declared itself the sole sovereign representative of the nation, and repudiated the authority of the Sultan and the old parliament at Constantinople. The Assembly consisted of one chamber and every citizen over 18 voted for its members, who had to be at least 30. Members sat for 2 years then (from 1924) for 4 years. The House sat annually and could not be in recess for more than 4 months of the year. Special sessions could be convened at the request of one-fifth of the members, the President of the Council or the President of the Republic. The Assembly was responsible for preparing, framing and passing laws, concluding conventions and treaties of peace, making declarations of war, examining and ratifying laws presented to it by the Commission on the Budget, coining money and administering punishment and pardon. A law passed by the Assembly was passed to the President of the Republic. He might return it for further consideration within 10 days, but the Assembly could override his objections and re-vote the law. On bills concerning the budget or the constitution there was no power of veto. The President was elected by the Assembly for its own term, and might be re-elected. All his acts required countersignature by the President of the Council and the minister concerned. The President appointed the President of the Council (Prime Minister) who in turn designated members of his council from among members of the Assembly. Within a week of his appointment he was obliged to offer a programme and ask for a vote of confidence. Ministers were collectively and individually responsible to the Assembly.

There was also a Council of State elected from among suitably qualified men by the Assembly. This gave advice on legislation. In 1934 the age for the franchise was altered to 23 and the age for deputies to 31.

In 1937 the principles of the Republican People's Party were incorporated into the constitution; from then on only this party was active in parliament, although there were independent members. Opposition parties came into being again in 1945. The Grand National Assembly was dissolved by the military *coup d'état* of 1960.

The Constitution of 1961 provided for a 7-year term for the President, who might not be re-elected. He was elected by joint session of 2 houses, the National Assembly and the Senate, which had 150 members directly elected, 15 nominated by the President and 18 life senators. Laws were only initiated by the Assembly and the Council of Ministers. Bills were debated first in the Assembly and then referred to the Senate. If the houses did not agree on the bill, the decision was made by a joint committee which prepared another draft for submission to the Assembly. The Assembly then accepted either this draft or the one previously passed to the Senate, or the one amended by the Senate. If the Senate had amended by absolute majority, the Assembly could only revert to its unamended draft, also by absolute majority. Any bill which the Assembly rejected but the Senate adopted was returned to the Assembly for review.

In Sep 1980 the Assembly was dissolved and power passed to a National Security Council. A new constitution was drafted and came into force in 1982. All who were members of parliament on 1 Jan 1980 were banned from political life for 5 years. The new Assembly was to have 400 members sitting for a 4-year term. A deputy could be expelled, and prevented from standing again for his new party, if he changed sides. The Assembly could also force the resignation of the Council of Ministers by a vote of no confidence. The President was to be elected by a two-thirds majority of the Assembly and would serve for 7-year terms. He would appoint the Prime Minister, who would then appoint a cabinet. Presidential decrees must be countersigned by the Prime Minister, who assumes responsibility for them. The President was to be advised by a 20-member State Consultative Council which he appointed himself.

The number of deputies was increased from 400 to 450 in Jun 1987 and further increased to 550 in constitutional changes in Jul 1995. Deputies are elected for 5-year terms by universal suffrage (all aged 18 or over) by proportional representation.

UKRAINE

With the collapse of the Soviet Union, the independence of Ukraine was declared on 5 Dec 1991 (having been preceded by a referendum on 1 Dec 1991 in which 90.3 per cent of votes were cast in favour of independence). Under the constitution adopted on 28 Jun 1996, the head of state is the President. A single-chamber 450-member parliament (the Supreme Council) is elected for 4-year terms by universal suffrage. Turnout must reach 50 per cent in an electoral district for the election in that area to be valid. The President nominates the Prime Minister, subject to the agreement of more than half the Supreme Council.

UNION OF SOVIET SOCIALIST REPUBLICS (USSR)

The Union of Soviet Socialist Republics was formally constituted on 6 Jul 1923. The central executive power was the Council of the Union together with the Council of Nationalities, the latter being composed of 5 representatives from each of the autonomous and allied republics and one representative from each of the autonomous regions. The supreme authority, however, lay with the Central Executive Committee which was elected by the Congress of Soviets of the Union. This was the source of all legislation and its decrees and resolutions were sovereign. Between its sessions authority was exercised by the Presidium, which was self-electing and nearly identical in membership with the Presidium of the Russian Socialist Federal Soviet Republic. The Central Executive Committee met infrequently and for short terms; the power of the Presidium was therefore considerable. By 1926 the Executive Committee numbered about 300 and met 3 times a year. The Presidium prepared the order of business and executed the resolutions passed, being itself in almost continuous session.

The Central Executive Committee also elected the Council of People's Commissars. Originally this had greater power than the Presidium and acted as a cabinet of ministers responsible for departments, but by 1923 its power as a body had been considerably weakened. The Presidium had power to ratify or to stay the executions of the Council's resolutions, to be a court of appeal for any Commissar against the Council as a whole, and to require quarterly reports of all proceedings and instructions of the Council.

A new constitution was formed on 5 Dec 1936 and remained in force until 1977. Under it there existed the Council (or 'Soviet') of the Union and the Soviet of Nationalities; their legislative rights were equal; they were elected for a term of 4 years, the Soviet of the Union by citizens of the USSR on the basis of one deputy for every 300000 inhabitants, the Soviet of Nationalities by citizens voting by Union and Autonomous Republics, Autonomous Regions and National Areas. The latter Soviet had 32 deputies from each Union Republic, 11 from each Autonomous Republic, 5 from each Autonomous Region and 1 from each National Area. The Council of Ministers (previously called People's Commissars) was appointed by the Supreme Soviet. It was the highest executive and administrative organ but had no legislative power. It executed laws already made and co-ordinated departmental administration. The Chairman of the Council was equivalent to a Prime Minister. It had two First Deputy Chairmen with no departmental responsibility, and 4 vice-chairmen of whom one had a departmental responsibility. It was itself responsible to the Supreme Soviet or to the Presidium when the Soviet was not in session.

The Presidium of the Supreme Soviet had 39 members including a chairman (the President of the USSR), 5 vice-chairmen (one from each union Republic) 21 members and a secretary. It was the practice to elect the chairmen of the Presidia of the Union Soviets from among the vice-chairmen. Members of the Council of Ministers could not be elected to the Presidium. The Presidium convened the sessions of the Supreme Soviet, dissolved it in the event of a deadlock and arranged new elections. It had the power to hold referenda and to rescind the decisions and orders of the Council of Ministers if they were not in accordance with the law and constitution. The Presidium itself was empowered to interpret the law and constitution. Ministers were appointed and removed by the Presidium, but normally at the instance of the Council of Ministers. The Presidium commanded the armed forces and had the power to declare war.

The constitution of 1977 defined the separation of powers between the central government and the constituent republics with their own Supreme Soviets, Councils of Ministers and Presidia. The Law on Elections to the Supreme Soviet of the USSR, 1978, laid down procedures for choosing candidates, who stood either as Communists or as 'non-party' candidates, and were elected by universal adult suffrage and direct ballot, following a preliminary selection conference.

On 13 Mar 1990 the Soviet Congress of People's Deputies repealed Art. 6 of the constitution, ending the Communist Party's monopoly of political power. It also strengthened the powers of the presidency, combining the posts of head of government and head of state. The President could be subject to a parliamentary veto and was prohibited from declaring a state of emergency in any of the Soviet republics without the agreement of local officials. Mikhail Gorbachev, the sole candidate, was elected President by the Congress on 15 Mar 1990. The President would be chosen by popular election in 1995. In Oct 1990 the Supreme Soviet passed a law giving political parties equivalent legal status to the Communist Party, opening the way for a multi-party democracy. At the same time the Communist Party's authority over Soviet institutions – including the armed forces, the KGB, and the official trade unions – was removed. The constitutional position was, however, complicated by 9 of the USSR's 15 constituent republics having declared by Jun 1990 that their own laws had precedence over those of central government. The attempted *coup* of Aug 1991 transformed the constitutional position once again and precipitated the collapse of the Soviet Union. The Soviet Union ceased to exist on 31 Dec 1991 after the formation of the Commonwealth of Independent States (*see* p. 29).

For Russia, *see* p. 97. See also entries for Armenia, Belarus, Moldova, Ukraine, etc.

UNITED KINGDOM

Parliament has 2 houses, the House of Lords and the House of Commons. The Commons are elected directly by universal adult suffrage for a 5-year term. In 1918 the franchise was widened extensively for men over 21 and now included women over 30; it was extended to women over 21 in 1928, and in 1970 the voting age was lowered to 18 years. The Lords was composed until 1999 of hereditary peers and peeresses, those on whom peerages had been conferred for life, 2 archbishops and 24 bishops. Most hereditary peers were removed in

1999 under the reforms of the Labour government but the exact future shape of the Lords had not yet been decided.

The executive power lies nominally with the Crown, but in fact is exercised through the cabinet of responsible ministers, headed by the Prime Minister who recommends the appointment of other ministers. Ministers are members of either house.

In 1918 the House of Lords was as it had been reorganized by the Parliament Act of 1911. Bills certified by the Speaker of the House of Commons as money bills were to receive the royal assent one month after being sent to the House of Lords, whether the Lords had approved them or not. Any other public bill (except for one extending the life of parliament) passed by the Commons in three successive sessions and rejected by the Lords was to receive the royal assent nevertheless, provided two years had elapsed between the second reading in the first session of the Commons and the third reading in the third session. The 1949 Parliament Act reduced the delaying powers of the upper house to two sessions and one year. In 1958 the parliamentary balance of the house was improved by the introduction of peerages given for life to men and women by the Sovereign on the advice of the Prime Minister. The right of most hereditary peers to vote was removed in 1999. Opposition party leaders are able to convey their own recommendations for peerages through the Prime Minister to the Queen.

Parliament sits from September or October to the same time of the following year, with a summer recess beginning in July. During adjournments the Speaker or the Lord Chancellor may give notice of an earlier meeting if it is in the national interest. All sessions end by prorogation, and all bills not passed by then lapse. Bills (including private members' bills) may originate in either House unless they deal with finance or representation, when they are introduced in the Commons. Until 1939 private members generally had precedence for bills and motions on some 22 days in each session, of which some 13 days would be Fridays and shorter than other working days. Since 1967 private members have had precedence on 20 Fridays in session. The United Kingdom has no written constitution.

After its election in 1997, the Labour government introduced certain devolved powers to a newly-created Scottish Parliament and Welsh Assembly (the establishment of these had earlier been approved by referenda).

YUGOSLAVIA

The Republic was established in 1945, with a President in place of the King. The constitution framed in 1953 provided for a parliament of 2 houses, the Federal Council and the Council of Producers, the latter being composed of one deputy for every 70 000 of the active population – that is, all engaged in production, transport and commerce. The houses sat separately except for joint sessions to elect officers, including the President of the Republic.

In 1963 a new Federal Assembly was established, with 5 chambers: Federal, Economic, Education and Culture, Social Welfare and Health, Organizational-Political. Each had 120 deputies and the Federal Chamber also had 70 members delegated by the six republics and 2 autonomous provinces; they sat as a Chamber of Nationalities. All members were elected for 4 years, half their number being renewed every 2 years; no one could be elected successively as a member of the same chamber or of the Federal Executive Council.

The Federal Chamber elected the Federal Executive Council from among its own members, to act as the Assembly's political executive organ; it consisted of a President, two Vice-Presidents and 14 members. The President of the Republic was elected by the Assembly in joint session of all its chambers.

In 1974 a new constitution set up a system of assemblies, based on workplace, employment or community, and at its apex a new bicameral legislature, the Assembly, consisting of the Federal Chamber and the Chamber of Republics and Provinces. The Federal Chamber had 30 delegates from self-managing organizations, communities and socio-political organizations from each Republic, and 20 from each Autonomous Province. The Chamber of Republics and Provinces had 12 from each Republican Assembly and 8 from each Provincial Assembly. The Federal Executive Council had a Chairman (Prime Minister), 14 members, 8 Federal Secretaries and 6 Chairmen of Federal Committees. The Republics were equally represented, with corresponding representation of the Autonomous Provinces. The Prime Minister was proposed by the President and elected by the Assembly, who also elected the other ministers at the proposal of the Prime Minister.

There was a State Presidency of 8 members elected every 5 years; the annual President was head of state. The suffrage was for all over 18 years (16, if employed).

Against a background of increasing demands for secession, in Dec 1989 a constitutional change gave the central government more power to deal with unrest. Constitutional changes in the constituent republics (especially Slovenia and Croatia) increased the likelihood that the country would fall apart.

Following the disintegration of Yugoslavia, and the emergence of the independent states of Slovenia, Croatia, Bosnia–Hercegovina and Macedonia, the two remaining constituents of Yugoslavia (Serbia and Montenegro) announced on 27 Apr 1992 the formation of a Federal Republic of Yugoslavia constituted by themselves as the legal successor to the former Socialist Federal Republic of Yugoslavia. Under the 1992 constitution, the head of state is the Federal President, elected by both chambers of the federal parliament.

The federal parliament consists of 2 chambers. The Chamber of the Republics has 40 members, 20 each elected from the assemblies of Montenegro and Serbia. Its assent is necessary to all legislation. The Chamber of Citizens has 138 members, elected by universal suffrage.

4
Ministers

ALBANIA

Turham Pasha was Prime Minister from 1918–1920. S. Delvin, 1920 and in Dec 1920 H. Prishtina was P.M. for a few days. P. Evangheli, Jul–Dec 1921; X. Ypi, Dec 1921–Dec 1922. A. Zogu (later King Zog) Dec 1922–Feb 1924; S. Verlaci, Feb 1924–Jun 1924; F. Noli, Jun–Dec 1924; K. Kotta, Dec 1924–Mar 1930.

Date of taking office	Prime Minister	Foreign Minister	Finance Minister
12 Jan 1933	P. Evangheli	X. Vila	A. Dibra

In Apr 1939 Italy invaded Albania and in Jun the office of Foreign Minister was abolished.

Date	Prime Minister	Foreign Minister	Finance Minister
12 Apr 1939	S. Verlazi	X. Dino	
3 Dec 1941	M. Kruja		
19 Jan 1943	E. Libohova		
13 Feb 1943	M. Bushati		
12 May 1943	E. Libohova		
2 Dec 1945	E. Hoxha	N. Miskane	
24 Mar 1946		E. Hoxha Gen. M. Shehu	
24 Jul 1953		B. Shtylla	T. Jakova
20 Jul 1954	Gen. M. Shehu		A. Kellezi
4 Jun 1956			A. Verli
18 Mar 1966		N. Nase	

ALBANIA (*continued*)

Date of taking office	Prime Minister	Foreign Minister	Finance Minister
29 Oct 1974			L. Gogo
13 Nov 1976			H. Toska
14 Jan 1982	A. Çarçani		Q. Mihali
1 Jul 1982		R. Malile	
17 Feb 1984			N. Gjyzari
17 Jul 1986			A. Nako
22 Feb 1991	F. Nano		
5 Jun 1991	Y. Bufi		
10 Dec 1991	V. Ahmeti		
13 Apr 1992	A. Meksi	A. Serreqi	G. Rulli
1994			P. Dishnica
1995			D. Vrioni
1996		T. Shehu	R. Bode
11 Mar 1997	B. Fino		
24 Jul 1997	F. Nano	P. Milo	A. Malaj
2 Oct 1998	P. Majko		
27 Oct 1999	I. Meta		

ARMENIA

Date of taking office	Prime Minister	Foreign Minister	Finance Minister
Aug 1990	V. Manukian		
1992	K. Harutunyan	R. Hovannisyan	
Nov 1992		A. Kirakosyan	
12 Feb 1993	H. Bagratian	V. Papazian	L. Barkhoudaryan
Nov 1996	A. Sarkissian		
21 Mar 1997	R. Kocharin		
Apr 1998	A. Darbinian		
Jun 1999	V. Sargsian		
Nov 1999	A. Sargsian	V. Oskanian	E. Sandoyan

AUSTRIA

MINISTERS FOR AUSTRIA

Date of taking office	Chancellor	Finance Minister
21 Dec 1899	H. von Wittek	A. von Jorkasch-Koch
19 Jan 1900	E. von Kœrber	E. Bohm von Bawerk
26 Oct 1904		M. Kosel
1 Jan 1905	P. Gautsch von Frankenthurn	
2 May 1906	K. von Hohenlohe-Waldenburg-Schillingsfürst	
2 Jun 1906	M.W. von Beck	W. von Korytowsky
14 Nov 1908	R. von Bienerth	A. von Jorkasch-Koch
10 Feb 1909		L. von Biliński
9 Jan 1911		R. Meyer
28 Jun 1911	P. Gautsch von Frankenthurn	
3 Nov 1911	K. von Stürgkh	
19 Nov 1911		Count von Zaleski
8 Oct 1913		A. Engel von Mainfelden
3 Nov 1915		K. von Leth
31 Oct 1916	E. von Kœrber	K. Marek
20 Dec 1916	H. von Clam-Martinitz	A.B. Spitzmüller
23 Jun 1917	E. Seidler von Feuchtenegg	Baron von Wimmer
25 Jul 1918	M. Hussarek von Heinlein	
27 Oct 1918	H. Lammasch	J. Redlich

MINISTERS FOR COMMON AFFAIRS

Date of taking office	Chancellor	Foreign Minister	Finance Minister
4 Jun 1882			B. von Kállay
16 May 1895	A. Golochowski	A. Golochowski	
14 Jul 1903			A. Golochowski
24 Jul 1903			S. Burián
24 Oct 1906	A. Lexa d'Aerenthal	A. Lexa d'Aerenthal	

AUSTRIA (*continued*)

Date of taking office	Chancellor	Foreign Minister	Finance Minister
17 Feb 1912	L. Berchthold	L. Berchthold	
20 Feb 1912			L. von Biliński
13 Jan 1915	S. Burián	S. Burián	
7 Feb 1915			E. von Kœrber
2 Dec 1916			K. von Hohenlohe-Waldenburg-Schillingsfürst
22 Dec 1916	O. Czernin	O. Czernin	S. Burián
16 Apr 1918			A.B. Spitzmüller
24 Oct 1918	J. Andrássy		
2 Nov 1918	L. von Flotow		
4 Nov 1918			Baron von Kuh-Chrobak
12 Nov 1918	K. Renner	K. Renner	R. Reisch
25 Jun 1920	M. Mayr	M. Mayr	F. Grimm
21 Jun 1921	J. Schober	Baron Hennet	A. Gurtler
31 May 1922	I. Seipel	A. Grunberger	V. Kienbock
17 Nov 1924	K. Ramek	H. Mataja	J. Ahrer
15 Jan 1926	I. Seipel	I. Seipel	V. Kienbock
3 May 1929	E. Streeruwitz		
26 Sep 1929	J. Schober	J. Schober	O. Juch
25 Sep 1930	M. Vaugoin		
3 Dec 1930	O. Ender		
20 Jun 1931	K. Buresch		
29 Jan 1932		K. Buresch	E. Weidenhoffer
20 May 1932	E. Dollfuss	E. Dollfuss	
10 May 1933			K. Buresch
30 Jul 1934	K. Schuschnigg	E. Berger-Waldenegg	
18 Oct 1935			L. Draxler
3 Nov 1936		G. Schmidt	H. Neumayer

AUSTRIA (*continued*)

Date of taking office	Chancellor	Foreign Minister	Finance Minister
13 Mar 1938	A. Seyss-Inquart	W. Wolf	
25 May 1938			M. Fischbock

Note: The cabinet was limited in size after the union with the German Third Reich. The Foreign Ministry was carried on in Berlin by the German Foreign Minister. The Seyss-Inquart cabinet was dissolved on the Allied occupation of Austria, and a provisional government under Dr K. Renner took office on 28 Apr 1945.

Date of taking office	Chancellor	Foreign Minister	Finance Minister
18 Dec 1945	L. Figl	L. Figl	G. Zimmerman
1 May 1946		K. Gruber	
7 Nov 1949			E. Margaretha
23 Jan 1952			R. Kamitz
2 Apr 1953	J. Raab		
25 Nov 1953		L. Figl	
16 Jul 1959		B. Kreisky	
9 Jun 1960		E. Heilingsetzer	
11 Apr 1961	A. Gorbach	B. Kreisky	J. Klaus
27 Mar 1963			F. Korinek
2 Apr 1964	J. Klaus		W. Schmitz
18 Apr 1966		L. Toncic-Sorinj	
18 Jan 1968		K. Waldheim	S. Koren
21 Apr 1970	B. Kreisky	R. Kirschlager	H. Androsch
25 Jun 1974		E. Bielka-Karttrev	
29 Oct 1976		W. Pahr	
14 Jan 1981			H. Salcher
24 May 1983	F. Sinowatz	E. Lane	
10 Sep 1984		L. Gratz	F. Vranitzky
9 Jun 1986	F. Vranitzky	P. Jankowitsch	F. Lacina
21 Jan 1987		A. Mock	
4 May 1995		W. Schüssel	
4 Jan 1996			V. Klima
28 Jan 1997	V. Klima		R. Edlinger

BELARUS

Belarus became independent in Aug 1991.

Date of taking office		Prime Minister	Foreign Minister	Finance Minister
	1991	V. Kebich		
Aug	1994	M. Chyhir	U. Syanko	
	1995	S. Ling	U. Latypov	N. Korbut

BELGIUM

Date of taking office	Prime Minister	Foreign Minister	Finance Minister
26 Mar 1894	J. de Burlet		P. de Smet de Nayer
26 Feb 1896	P. de Smet de Nayer	M. de Favereau	
24 Jan 1899	J. Vanden-peereboom		
5 Aug 1899	P. de Smet de Nayer		
2 May 1907	J. de Trooz	J. Davignon	J. Liebaert
9 Jan 1908	F. Schollaert		J. Renkin
Nov 1908			J. Liebaert
14 Jun 1911	M. Levie		
13 Jul 1911	Ch. de Broqueville		
27 Feb 1914			A. Burggraf van de Vyvere
21 Jan 1916		E. van Beyens	
30 Jul 1917		Ch. de Broqueville	
Jan 1918		P. Hyams	
3 Jun 1918	G. Cooreman		
21 Nov 1918	L. Delacroix		L. Delacroix
20 Nov 1920	H. Carton de Wiart	H. Jaspar	G. Theunis
14 Dec 1921	G. Theunis		
13 May 1925	M. van de Vijvere		
17 Jun 1925	Viscomte Poullet	E. Vandervelde	Baron Houtart
22 Nov 1927		P. Hyams	

BELGIUM (*continued*)

Date of taking office	Prime Minister	Foreign Minister	Finance Minister
24 Nov 1929	L. Delacroix		
6 Jun 1931	J. Renkin	P. Hyams	
19 Feb 1932			J. Renkin
23 Oct 1932	Ct de Brocqueville		H. Jaspar
12 Jun 1934		H. Jaspar	M. Sap
25 Mar 1935	P. van Zeeland	P. van Zeeland	M.L. Gérard
13 Jun 1936		P.H. Spaak	H. de Man
24 Nov 1937	P.E. Janson		
9 Mar 1938			M. Merlot (*ad interim*)
1 May 1938			E. Soudan
15 May 1938	P.H. Spaak		M.L. Gérard
3 Dec 1938			A. Jannsen
21 Jan 1939		P.E. Janson	
20 Feb 1939	H. Pierlot	E. Soudan	C. Gutt
18 Apr 1939		H. Pierlot	
4 Sep 1939		P.H. Spaak	
11 Feb 1945	A. van Acker		G. Eyskens
31 Mar 1946			F. de Vogel
19 Mar 1947	P.H. Spaak		G. Eyskens
10 Aug 1949	G. Eyskens	P. van Zeeland	H. Liebaert
8 Jun 1950	J. Duvieusart		J. van Houtte
15 Aug 1950	J. Pholien		
15 Jan 1952	J. van Houtte		Baron Janssen
12 Apr 1954	A. van Acker	P.H. Spaak	H. Liebaert
11 May 1957		V. Larock	
25 Jun 1958	G. Eyskens	P. Wigny	J. van Houtte
25 Apr 1961	T. Lefevre	P.H. Spaak	A. Dequae
28 Jul 1965	P. Harmel		G. Eyskens
20 Mar 1966	P. van den Boeynants	P. Harmel	R. Henrion
18 Jun 1968	G. Eyskens		Baron J. Snoy et d'Oppuers

BELGIUM (*continued*)

Date of taking office	Prime Minister	Foreign Minister	Finance Minister
20 Jan 1972			A. Vlerick
22 Jan 1973	E. Le Burton	R. van Elslande	W. de Clercq
25 Apr 1974	L. Tindemans		
3 Jun 1977		H. Simonet	G. Geens
20 Oct 1978	V. Boeynants		
3 Apr 1979	W. Martens		
18 May 1980		C.-F. Nothomb	R. Henrion
30 Jun 1980			P. Hatry
22 Oct 1980			M. Eyskens
6 Apr 1981	M. Eyskens		R. Vandeputte
17 Dec 1981	W. Martens	L. Tindemans	W. de Clercq
6 Jan 1985			F. Grootjans
28 Nov 1985			M. Eyskens
9 May 1988			P. Maystadt
29 Sep 1991		M. Eyskens	
7 Mar 1992	J.-L. Dehaene	W. Claes	
10 Oct 1994		F. Vandenbroucke	
22 Mar 1995		E. Derycke	
19 Jun 1998			J.J. Viseur
12 Jul 1999	G. Verhofstadt	L. Michel	D. Reynders

BOSNIA–HERCEGOVINA

Date of taking office	Prime Minister	Foreign Minister	Finance Minister
1990	J. Relivan		
Dec 1992	M. Akmandzić	H. Silajdžić	
25 Oct 1993	H. Silajdžić		
1995			B. Bilić
30 Jan 1996	H. Muratović	J. Prlic	M. Kikanović
3 Feb 1999	S. Mihajlović		
	H. Silajdžić		

BULGARIA

Date of taking office	Prime Minister	Foreign Minister	Finance Minister
18 Jan 1899	T. Ivantchov	T. Ivantchov	M. Tenev
28 Jan 1899	D. Grekov		
12 Oct 1899	T. Ivantchov		
23 Jan 1901	R. Petrov		
14 Mar 1901	P. Karavelov	S. Dánev	P. Karavelov
4 Jan 1902	S. Dánev		
15 May 1903	R. Petrov	R. Petrov	L. Payakov
14 Nov 1906	D. Pétkov	D. Stanciov	
16 Mar 1907	P.J. Gúdev		
29 Jan 1908	A. Málinov	S. Paprikov	J. Sallabechev
1910		A. Málinov	A. Liaptchev
20 Mar 1911	S. Dánev		
29 Mar 1911	J.E. Guéchov	J.E. Guéchov	T. Théodorov
4 Jul 1913	S. Dánev		
18 Jul 1913	V. Radoslavov	N. Ghenadiev	D. Tontchev
1914		V. Radoslavov	
16 Jun 1918	A. Málinov		
14 Oct 1919	A.S. Stamboliiski	A.S. Stamboliiski	R. Daskalov
11 Jan 1922			M. Turlakov
10 Feb 1923			P. Yanev

Note: Premier Stamboliiski was killed during the *coup d'état* of 9 Jun 1923.

Date	Prime Minister	Foreign Minister	Finance Minister
9 Jun 1923	A. Tsankov	K. Kaltov	P. Todorov
1 Jan 1925	A. Lyapchev	A. Burov	V. Mollov
12 Oct 1931	N. Mushanov	N. Mushanov	S. Stefanov
19 May 1934	K. Georgiev	K. Georgiev	P. Todorov *(coup d'état)*
24 May 1934		K. Batalov	
22 Jan 1935	Gen. P. Zlatev		M. Kalandarov *(coup d'état)*
21 Apr 1935	P.M. Toshev	G. Kyoseivanov	M. Ryaskov *(coup d'état)*

BULGARIA (*continued*)

Date of taking office	Prime Minister	Foreign Minister	Finance Minister
23 Nov 1935	G. Kyoseivanov		K. Gunev
1938			D. Bozhilov
16 Feb 1940	B. Filov	I. Popov	
11 Apr 1942		B. Filov	
9 Sep 1943	D. Bozhilov	S. Kirov	
10 Oct 1943		D. Shishmanov	
1 Jun 1944	I. Bagryanov	I. Bagryanov	D. Savov
12 Jun 1944		P. Draganov	
2 Sep 1944	K. Muraviev	P. Stainov	A. Girginov
9 Sep 1944	K. Georgiev		P. Stoyanov
31 Mar 1946		G. Kulishev	I. Stefanov
22 Nov 1946	G. Dimitrov	K. Georgiev	
11 Dec 1947		V. Kolarov	
21 Jul 1949	V. Kolarov		
6 Aug 1949		V. Poptomov	P. Kunin
8 Oct 1949			K. Lazarov
1 Feb 1950	V. Chervenkov		
27 May 1950		M. Neichev	
17 Apr 1956	A. Yugov		
18 Aug 1956		K. Lukanov	
19 Nov 1962	T. Zhivkov		
27 Nov 1962		I. Bashev	D. Popov
8 Jul 1971	S. Todorov		
16 Dec 1971		P. Mladenov	
16 Jun 1976			B. Beltchev
16 Jun 1981	G. Filipov		
21 Mar 1986	G. Atanasov		
20 Sep 1990	A. Loukanov	L. Gotsev	
20 Dec 1990	D. Popov	V. Valkov	I. Kostov
8 Nov 1991	F. Dimitov	S. Ganev	
30 Dec 1992	L. Berov	S. Daskalov	S. Aleksandrov
1993		S. Pashovski	

BULGARIA (*continued*)

Date of taking office	Prime Minister	Foreign Minister	Finance Minister
17 Oct 1994	R. Indzhova		
25 Jan 1995	Z. Videnov	G. Pirinski	D. Kostov
Dec 1996	G. Parvanov		
12 Feb 1997	S. Sofiyanski		
24 Apr 1997	I. Kostov		

CROATIA

Date of taking office	Prime Minister	Foreign Minister	Finance Minister
1991	J. Manolić		
1992	F. Gregurić	Z. Separović	
8 Sep 1992	H. Sarinić	Z. Škrabalo	Z. Jašić
23 Mar 1993	N. Valentić	M. Granić	B. Prka
4 Nov 1995	Z. Matesa		
14 Apr 1999			B. Skegro

CYPRUS

Cyprus was a British dependency until 1960, when it became an independent republic. Ministers were appointed in 1959, pending full independence.

Date of taking office	Prime Minister (or equivalent)	Foreign Minister	Finance Minister
5 Apr 1959	Archbishop Makarios	Archbishop Makarios	R. Theocarous

In 1960 President Makarios combined the powers of President and Prime Minister, and held both.

22 Aug 1960		S. Kyprianou	
1 Jul 1962			R. Solomides
15 Jun 1968			A. Patsalides
16 Jun 1972		L. Christophides	

CYPRUS (*continued*)

Date of taking office	Prime Minister (or equivalent)	Foreign Minister	Finance Minister
16 Jul 1974		D. Dimitrou	
8 Aug 1974		G. Clerides	
14 Jan 1975		L. Christophides	

On the death of President Makarios in 1977 the succeeding Presidents followed this practice regarding the post of Prime Minister. Cyprus has a presidential system of government. Executive power is exercised by the President of the Republic and legislative authority is exercised by the House of Representatives.

8 Mar 1978		N. Rolandis	
1 Nov 1979			A. Afxentiou
20 Apr 1982			S. Vassiliou
22 Sep 1983		G. Iacovou	
7 Jan 1985			C. Kittis
29 Jul 1986			C. Mavrellis
28 Feb 1988			G. Syrimis
28 Feb 1993		A. Michaelides	P. Economides
9 Apr 1994		I. Kasoulides	
7 Nov 1994			C. Christodoulou
19 Mar 1999			T.M. Klerides

The Turkish Federated State of Cyprus was proclaimed on 13 Feb 1975 with Rauf Denktash as President. A constituent Assembly was sworn in on 24 Feb 1975 and elections were held on 20 Jun 1976. A cabinet was appointed after N. Konuk had been appointed Prime Minister on 3 Jul 1976. The State declared itself independent on 15 Nov 1983 as the Turkish Republic of Northern Cyprus.

CZECHOSLOVAKIA

Date of taking office	Prime Minister	Foreign Minister	Finance Minister
14 Nov 1918	K. Kramař (provisional government)		
8 Jul 1919	V. Tusar	E. Beneš	K. Sontag
15 Sep 1920	J. Černý		M. Hanošek
26 Sep 1921	E. Beneš		A. Novák

CZECHOSLOVAKIA (*continued*)

Date of taking office	Prime Minister	Foreign Minister	Finance Minister
8 Oct 1922	A. Švehla		T. Becka
18 Mar 1926	J. Černý		K. Engliš
12 Oct 1926	A. Švehla		
13 Oct 1927	Mgr. J. Šrámek		
1 Feb 1929	J. Udrzal		B. Vlasek
8 Dec 1929			K. Engliš
16 Apr 1931			K. Trapl
29 Oct 1932	M. Malypetr		
18 Dec 1935		M. Hodža	
29 Feb 1936	M. Hodža	K. Krofta	E. Franke
21 Jul 1937			J. Kalfus
22 Sep 1938	Gen. J. Syrový		
4 Oct 1938		F. Chvalkovský	
30 Nov 1938	R. Beran		

Note: The Ministry of Foreign Affairs was dissolved by the Reich Protectorate, 18 Mar 1939.

27 Apr 1939	Gen. A. Elias		

Note: A government in exile was set up in London following the German invasion.

24 Jul 1940	Mgr. J. Šrámek	J. Masaryk	E. Outrata
27 Oct 1941			L. Feierabend
6 Nov 1945	Z. Fierlinger		V. Šrobár
2 Jul 1946	K. Gottwald		J. Dolansky
15 Jun 1948	A. Zápotocký	V. Clementis	
14 Mar 1950	V. Široký		
31 Jan 1953		V. David	
21 Mar 1953		V. Široký	J. Kabes
15 Sep 1953			J. Duris
22 Sep 1963	J. Lenárt		R. Dvořák
11 Nov 1965			B. Sucharda

CZECHOSLOVAKIA (*continued*)

Date of taking office	Prime Minister	Foreign Minister	Finance Minister
1 Apr 1968	O. Černík	J. Hajek	
19 Sep 1968		O. Černík	

Note: On 31 Dec 1968 Czechoslovakia became a federation, with separate governments for the Czech Socialist Republic and the Slovak Socialist Republic. Details below are for the central, federal, government:

Date of taking office	Prime Minister	Foreign Minister	Finance Minister
1 Jan 1969	O. Černík	J. Marko	B. Sucharda
3 Jan 1971	L. Štrougal		R. Rohliček
9 Dec 1971		B. Chňoupek	
14 Dec 1973			L. Lér
29 Nov 1985		J. Žák	
12 Oct 1988	L. Adamec	J. Johanes	J. Stejskal
10 Dec 1989	M. Čalfa	J. Dienstbier	V. Klaus
1 Jul 1992	J. Strasky		

The dissolution of the Czech and Slovak Federal Republic took place on 31 Dec 1992.

CZECH REPUBLIC

Date of taking office	Prime Minister	Foreign Minister	Finance Minister
26 Jan 1993	V. Klaus	J. Zieleniec	I. Kočàrník
30 Dec 1997	J. Tosovsky	J. Sedivy	I. Pilip
22 Jul 1998	M. Zeman	J. Kavan	P. Mertlík

DENMARK

Date of taking office	Prime Minister	Foreign Minister	Finance Minister
23 May 1897	K.E. Hørring	N.F. Ravn	K.E. Hørring
27 Apr 1900	H. de Sehested	H. de Sehested	H.W. Scharling
24 Jul 1901	J.H. Deuntzer	J.H. Deuntzer	C.F. Hage

DENMARK (*continued*)

Date of taking office	Prime Minister	Foreign Minister	Finance Minister
14 Jan 1905	J.C. Christensen	F.C.O. de Raben-Levetzau	V. Lassen
12 Oct 1908	N.T. Neergaard	C.W. de Ahlefeldt-Laurvigen	C. Brun
16 Aug 1909	L. von Holstein-Ledreborg		
28 Oct 1909	C.T. Zahle	E.J.C. de Scavenius	C.E.C. Brandes
5 Jul 1910	K. Berntsen	C.W. de Ahlefeldt-Laurvigen	N.T. Neergaard
21 Jun 1913	C.T. Zahle	E.J.C. de Scavenius	C.E.C. Brandes
4 May 1920	N. Neergard		N.T. Neergard
9 Oct 1922		C.M.T. Cold	
23 Apr 1924	T. Stauning	C.P.O.G. Moltke	C.V. Bramsnaes
29 Apr 1929		P. Munch	
			H.P. Hansen
4 Nov 1935			V. Buhl
		E.J.C. de Scavenius	
4 May 1942	V. Buhl		
16 Jul 1942			M. Andersen
9 Nov 1942	E. Scavenius		J. Koefoed
8 Nov 1945	K. Kristensen	G. Rasmussen	T. Kristensen
13 Nov 1947	H. Hedtoft		H.C. Hansen
30 Oct 1950	E. Erikson	O.B. Kraft	T. Kristensen
30 Sep 1953	H. Hedtoft	H.C. Hansen	V. Kampmann
29 Jan 1955	H.C. Hansen		
9 Oct 1958		J.O. Krag	
19 Feb 1960	V. Kampmann		
1 Mar 1960			K. Philip
5 Sep 1961			H.R. Knudsen
3 Sep 1962	J.O. Krag	P. Haekkerup	
9 Nov 1962			P. Hansen
24 Aug 1965			H. Grünbaum
28 Nov 1966		J.O. Krag	

DENMARK (*continued*)

Date of taking office	*Prime Minister*	*Foreign Minister*	*Finance Minister*
1 Oct 1967		H. Tabor	
1 Feb 1968	H.T.I. Baunsgard	P. Hartling	P. Moller
17 Mar 1971			E. Ninn-Hansen
9 Oct 1971	J.O. Krag	K.B. Andersen	H. Grünbaum
5 Oct 1972	A. Jørgensen		
19 Sep 1973	P. Hartling	O. Guldberg	A. Andersen
13 Feb 1975	A. Jørgensen	K.B. Andersen	K. Heinesen
30 Aug 1978		H. Christophersen	
26 Oct 1979		K. Olesen	S. Jakobsen
30 Dec 1981			K. Heinesen
10 Sep 1982	P. Schlüter	U. Ellemann-Jensen	H. Christophersen
23 Jul 1984			P. Simonsen
30 Oct 1989			H. Dyremose
25 Jan 1993	P. Nyrup Rasmussen	N. Helveg Petersen	M. Lykketoft

ESTONIA

Prime Ministers of Estonia 1918–1939

24 Feb 1918	K. Päts	4 Dec 1928	A. Rei
8 May 1919	O. Strandmann	9 Jul 1929	O. Strandmann
18 Nov 1919	J. Tõnisson	12 Feb 1931	K. Päts
26 Oct 1920	A. Piip	19 Feb 1932	J. Teemant
25 Jan 1921	K. Päts	19 Jul 1932	K. Einbund
21 Nov 1922	J. Kukk	7 Nov 1932	K. Päts
2 Aug 1923	K. Päts	18 May 1933	J. Tõnisson
26 Mar 1924	F. Akel	21 Oct 1933	K. Päts
16 Dec 1924	J. Jaakson	24 Apr 1938	K. Eeenpalu
15 Dec 1925	J. Teemant	12 Oct 1939	J. Uluots
9 Dec 1927	J. Tõnisson		

ESTONIA (*continued*)

Date of taking office	Prime Minister	Foreign Minister	Finance Minister
8 May 1990	E. Savisaar	L. Meri	R. Miller
30 Jan 1992	T. Vähi		
7 Apr 1992		J. Manitski	
21 Oct 1992	M. Laar	T. Velliste	M. Üürike
7 Jan 1994		J. Luik	
11 Jan 1994			H. Kranich
27 Jun 1994			A. Lipstok
8 Nov 1994	A. Tarand		
17 Apr 1995	T. Vähi	R. Sinijärv	M. Opmann
6 Nov 1995		S. Kallas	
Dec 1996		T.H. Ilves	
17 Mar 1997	M. Siimann		
14 Oct 1998		R. Mälk	
25 Mar 1999	M. Laar	T.H. Ilves	S. Kallas

FINLAND

Date of taking office	Prime Minister	Foreign Minister	Finance Minister
26 Nov 1918	L. Ingman	C. Enckell	
18 Apr 1919	K. Castren		
18 Aug 1919	J. Vennola		
15 Mar 1920	M. Erich	E.R.W. Holsti	M. Wartiowaara
1 Mar 1921	J. Vennola		R. Ryti
14 Nov 1922	K. Kallio	J. Vennola	
18 Jan 1924	A.K. Kajander	C. Enckell	H.M.J. Relander
22 Nov 1924	L. Ingman	H. Procopé	P. Pulkkinen
1 Jan 1926	K. Kallio	E.N. Setälä	K. Järvinen
13 Dec 1926	V. Tanner	V. Voionmaa	A. Ryoma
27 Dec 1928	O. Hantere	H. Procopé	H.M.J. Relander
16 Aug 1929	K. Kallio		T.H. Reinekka

FINLAND (*continued*)

Date of taking office	Prime Minister	Foreign Minister	Finance Minister
20 Mar 1931	J. Sunila	M. Yrsjö-Koskinen	K. Järvinen
14 Dec 1932	T.M. Kivimaki	A.V. Hackzell	H.M.J. Relander
12 Mar 1937	A.K. Kajander	E.R.W. Holsti	V. Tanner
16 Nov 1938		V. Voionmaa	
13 Dec 1938		E. Erkko	
2 Dec 1939	R. Ryti	V. Tanner	M. Pekkala
27 Mar 1940		R. Witting	
4 Jan 1941	J.W. Rangell		M. Pekkala and J. Koivosto (*Joint Ministry*)
May 1942			V. Tanner
4 Mar 1943	E. Linkomies	H. Ramsay	
8 Aug 1944	A. Hackzell	C. Enckell	M. Hiltonen
21 Sep 1944	U. Castren		
11 Nov 1944	J. Paasikivi		M. Helo
9 Apr 1945			S. Tuomioja
25 Mar 1946	M. Pekkala		R. Törngren
29 Jul 1948	K.A. Fagerholm		O. Hiltunen
18 Mar 1950	U. Kekkonen	A. Gartz	V.J. Sukselainen
17 Jan 1951			O. Hiltunen
20 Sep 1951		S. Tuomioja	V.J. Rantala
9 Jul 1953		R. Törngren	
16 Nov 1953	S. Tuomioja		T. Junnila
5 May 1954	R. Törngren	U. Kekkonen	V.J. Sukselainen
20 Oct 1954	U. Kekkonen	J. Virolainen	P. Tervo
17 Feb 1956	K.A. Fagerholm	R. Törngren	A. Simonen
27 May 1957	V.J. Sukselainen	J. Virolainen	N. Meinander
2 Jul 1957			M. Miettunen
29 Nov 1957	R. von Feiandt	P.J. Hynninen	L. Hietanen
26 Apr 1958	R. Kuuskoski		M.I.O. Nurmela
29 Aug 1958	K.A. Fagerholm	J. Virolainen	P. Hetemäki
13 Jan 1959	V.J. Sukselainen	R. Törngren	W. Sarjala
19 Jun 1959		A. Karjalainen	

FINLAND (*continued*)

Date of taking office	Prime Minister	Foreign Minister	Finance Minister
14 Jul 1961	M. Miettunen		
13 Apr 1962	A. Karjalainen		
18 Dec 1963	R.R. Lehto	J. Hallama	E.J. Rekola
12 Sep 1964	J. Virolainen	A. Karjalainen	E. Kaitila
27 May 1966	K.R. Paasio		M. Koivisto
29 Dec 1967			E. Raunio
22 Mar 1968	M. Koivisto		
14 May 1968	T. Aura	V. Leskinen	P. Hetemäki
15 Jul 1970	A. Karjalainen		C.O. Tallgren
29 Oct 1971	T. Aura	O. Mattila	P. Hetemäki
25 Feb 1972	K.R. Paasio	K. Sorsa	M. Koivisto
4 Sep 1972	K. Sorsa	A. Karjalainen	J. Virolainen
			E. Niskanen
13 Jun 1975	K. Liinamaa	O.J. Mattila	H. Tuominen
			T. Varjas
30 Nov 1975	M. Miettunen	K. Sorsa	P. Paavela
			V. Luukka
29 Sep 1976		E. Korhonen	E. Rekola
			J. Loikkanen
17 May 1977	K. Sorsa	P. Väyrynen	P. Paavela
			E. Rekola
25 May 1979	M. Koivisto		A. Pekkala
			P. Työläjärvi
28 May 1981			M. Forsman replaced P. Työläjärvi as 2nd
12 Feb 1982	K. Sorsa		
17 Feb 1982		P. Stenbäck	
1 Sep 1982			J. Laine replaced M. Forsman as 2nd
6 May 1983		P. Väyrynen	P. Vennamo replaced J. Laine as 2nd

FINLAND (*continued*)

Date of taking office	Prime Minister	Foreign Minister	Finance Minister
30 Apr 1987	H. Holkeri	K. Sorsa	E. Liikanen
1 Feb 1989		P. Paasio	
3 Jun 1990			M. Louekoski
26 Apr 1991	E. Aho	P. Väyrynen	I. Viinanen
1993		H. Haavisto	
13 Apr 1995	P. Lipponen	T. Halonen	S. Niinistö

FRANCE

Date of taking office	Prime Minister	Foreign Minister	Finance Minister
27 Jun 1898	E.H. Brisson	T. Delcassé	P.L. Peytral
1 Nov 1898	C. Dupuy		
22 Jun 1899	P.M. Waldeck-Rousseau		J. Caillaux
7 Jun 1902	E. Combes		M. Rouvier
24 Jan 1905	M. Rouvier		
13 Mar 1906	F. Sarrien	L. Bourgeois	R. Poincaré
23 Oct 1906	G. Clemenceau	S. Pichon	J. Caillaux
24 Jul 1909	A. Briand		G. Cochery
3 Nov 1910			L.L. Klotz
4 Mar 1911	A.E.E. Monis	J. Cruppi	J. Caillaux
27 Jun 1911	J. Caillaux	J. de Selves	L.L. Klotz
14 Jan 1912	R. Poincaré	R. Poincaré	
18 Jan 1913	A. Briand	C. Jonnart	
24 Mar 1913	L. Barthou	S. Pichon	C. Dumont
8 Dec 1913	G. Doumergue	G. Doumergue	J. Caillaux
9 Jun 1914	R. Viviani	L. Bourgeois	E. Clementel
3 Aug 1914		T. Delcassé	A. Ribot
4 Aug 1914		G. Doumergue	
27 Aug 1914		T. Delcassé	
12 Oct 1915		R. Viviani	
29 Oct 1915	A. Briand	A. Briand	

FRANCE (*continued*)

Date of taking office	Prime Minister	Foreign Minister	Finance Minister
20 Mar 1917	A. Ribot	A. Ribot	J. Thierry
12 Sep 1917	P. Painlevé		L.L. Klotz
17 Nov 1917	G. Clemenceau	S. Pichon	
20 Jan 1920	A. Millerand	A. Millerand	F. Marsal
20 Oct 1920	M. Leygues		
16 Jan 1921	A. Briand	A. Briand	P. Doumer
15 Jan 1922	R. Poincaré	R. Poincaré	M. de Lasteyrie
9 Jun 1924	F. Marsal		
14 Jun 1924	E. Herriot	E. Herriot	E. Clementel
10 Apr 1925	M. Painlevé		
23 Nov 1925	A. Briand		
23 Aug 1926	R. Poincaré	A. Briand	R. Poincaré
11 Nov 1928			H. Cheron
27 Jul 1929	A. Briand		
2 Nov 1929	A. Tardieu	A. Briand	P. Reynaud
13 Dec 1930	M. Steeg		
27 Jan 1931	P. Laval	A. Briand	P.-E. Flandin
14 Jan 1932		P. Laval	
20 Feb 1932	A. Tardieu	A. Tardieu	
3 Jun 1932	E. Herriot	E. Herriot	M. Germain-Martin
18 Dec 1932	J. Paul-Boncour	J. Paul-Boncour	H. Cheron
31 Jan 1933	E. Daladier		G. Bonnet
26 Oct 1933	A. Sarraut		
26 Nov 1933	C. Chautemps		
30 Jan 1934	E. Daladier	E. Daladier	R. Piétri
4 Feb 1934			P. Marchandeau
9 Feb 1934	G. Doumergue	L. Barthou	M. Germain-Martin
13 Oct 1934		P. Laval	
8 Nov 1934	P.-E. Flandin		
1 Jun 1935	F. Bouisson		J. Caillaux
7 Jun 1935	P. Laval		
24 Jan 1936	A. Sarraut	P.-E. Flandin	

FRANCE (*continued*)

Date of taking office	Prime Minister	Foreign Minister	Finance Minister
5 Jun 1936	L. Blum	Y. Delbos	V. Auriol
22 Jun 1937	C. Chautemps		G. Bonnet
18 Jan 1938			P. Marchandeau
13 Mar 1938	L. Blum	J. Paul-Boncour	L. Blum
10 Apr 1938	E. Daladier	G. Bonnet	P. Marchandeau
2 Nov 1938			P. Reynaud
21 Mar 1940	P. Reynaud	P. Reynaud	L. Lamoureux
18 May 1940		E. Daladier	
5 Jun 1940		P. Reynaud	Y. Bouthilier
16 Jun 1940	Marshal P. Pétain	P. Baudouin	
24 Oct 1940		P. Laval	
14 Dec 1940		P.-E. Flandin	
10 Feb 1941		Adm. F. Darlan	
18 Apr 1942	P. Laval	P. Laval	P. Cathala
10 Sep 1944	Gen. C. de Gaulle	G. Bidault	R. Pleven
29 Jan 1946	F. Gouin		A. Philip
24 Jun 1946	G. Bidault		R. Schuman
16 Dec 1946	L. Blum	L. Blum	A. Philip
22 Jan 1947	P. Ramadier	G. Bidault	R. Schuman
24 Nov 1947	R. Schuman		R. Mayer
26 Jul 1948	A. Marie	R. Schuman	P. Reynaud
5 Sep 1948	R. Schuman		C. Pineau
12 Sep 1948	H. Queuille		H. Queuille
12 Jan 1949			M. Petsche
28 Oct 1949	G. Bidault		
2 Jul 1950	H. Queuille		
12 Jul 1950	R. Pleven		
10 Mar 1951	H. Queuille		
11 Aug 1951	R. Pleven		R. Mayer
20 Jan 1952	E. Faure		E. Faure
8 Mar 1952	A. Pinay		A. Pinay
8 Jan 1953	R. Mayer	G. Bidault	M. Borgès-Mauoury

FRANCE (*continued*)

Date of taking office	Prime Minister	Foreign Minister	Finance Minister
28 Jun 1953	J. Laniel		E. Faure
19 Jun 1954	P. Mendès-France	P. Mendès-France	E. Faure
23 Feb 1955	E. Faure	A. Pinay	P. Pflimlin
31 Jan 1956	G. Mollet	C. Pineau	P. Ramadier
5 Nov 1957	F. Gaillard		P. Pflimlin
14 May 1958	P. Pflimlin		
1 Jun 1958	C. de Gaulle		
8 Jan 1959	M. Debré	M. Couve de Murville	A. Pinay
May 1959			M. Baumgartner
15 Apr 1962	G. Pompidou		V. Giscard d'Estaing
9 Jan 1966			M. Debré
12 Jul 1968	M. Couve de Murville	M. Debré	F. Ortoli
22 Jun 1969	J. Chaban-Delmas	M. Schumann	V. Giscard d'Estaing
6 Jul 1972	P. Messmer		
5 Apr 1973		M. Jobert	V. Giscard d'Estaing
27 May 1974	J. Chirac		
28 May 1974		J. Sauvagnargues	J.-P. Fourcade
17 Aug 1976	R. Barre	L. de Guiringaud	R. Barre
30 Mar 1977			R. Boulin
5 Apr 1978			R. Monory
30 Nov 1978		J. François-Poncet	
21 May 1981	P. Mauroy		
22 May 1981		C. Cheysson	J. Delors
17 Jul 1984	L. Fabius		
19 Jul 1984			P. Bérégovoy
7 Dec 1984		R. Dumas	
20 Mar 1986	J. Chirac	J.B. Raimond	E. Balladur
23 Jun 1988	M. Rocard	R. Dumas	P. Bérégovoy
15 May 1991	E. Cresson		

FRANCE (*continued*)

Date of taking office	Prime Minister	Foreign Minister	Finance Minister
2 Apr 1992	P. Bérégovoy		M. Sapin
29 Mar 1993	E. Balladur	A. Juppé	E. Alphandery
18 May 1995	A. Juppé	H. de Charette	A. Madelin
7 Nov 1995			J. Arthuis
4 Jun 1997	L. Jospin	H. Védrine	D. Strauss-Kahn
2 Nov 1999			C. Sautter

GEORGIA

Date of taking office	Prime Minister	Foreign Minister	Finance Minister
6 Jan 1992	T. Sigua		
6 Aug 1993	E. Shevardnadze (acting)		
20 Aug 1993	O. Patsatsia	A. Chikvaidze	D. Iakobidze
8 Dec 1995	N. Lekishvili		
15 Dec 1995		I. Menagarishvili	
14 May 1998			M. Chkuaseli
7 Aug 1998	V. Lortkipanidze		
19 Nov 1998			D. Onoprishvili

GERMANY

Date of taking office	Chancellor	Foreign Minister	Finance Minister
26 Oct 1894	Prince von Hohenlohe-Schillingsfürst		
20 Oct 1897		B. von Bülow	
17 Oct 1900	B. von Bülow	Baron von	
17 Jan 1906		Richthofen H. von Tschirschky und Bögendorff	
7 Oct 1907		W. von Schoen	
27 Jun 1909	T. Bethmann-Hollweg		

GERMANY (*continued*)

Date of taking office	Chancellor	Foreign Minister	Finance Minister
28 Jun 1910		A. von Kiderlen-Wächter	
11 Jan 1913		G. von Jagow	
25 Nov 1916		A. Zimmermann	
14 Jul 1917	G. Michaelis		
7 Aug 1917		R. von Kühlmann	
25 Oct 1917	G. von Herling		
9 Aug 1918		P. von Hintze	
4 Oct 1918	Prince Max of Baden	W. Solf	
9 Nov 1918[1]	F. Ebert		
20 Dec 1918		U. von Brockdorff-Rantzau	
13 Feb 1919	P. Scheidemann	U. von Brockdorff-Rantzau	E. Schiffer
21 Jun 1919	G. Bauer	H. Müller	M. Erzberger
28 Mar 1920	H. Müller	A. Köster	J. Wirth
25 Jun 1920	K. Fehrenbach	W. Simons	
10 May 1921	J. Wirth		A. Hermes
23 May 1921		F. Rosen	
31 Jan 1922		W. Rathenau	
22 Nov 1922	W. Cuno	F. von Rosenberg	
13 Aug 1923	G. Stresemann	G. Stresemann	R. Hilferding
30 Nov 1923	W. Marx		H. Luther
15 Jan 1925	H. Luther		O. von Schleiben
19 Jan 1926			P. Reinhold
17 May 1926	W. Marx		H. Kohler
28 Jun 1928	H. Müller		R. Hilferding
3 Nov 1929		J. Curtius	
1 Apr 1930	H. Brüning		P. Moldenhauer
26 Jun 1930			H.R. Dietrich
9 Oct 1931		H. Brüning	

Note: The Brüning government was dismissed on 30 May 1932.

GERMANY (*continued*)

Date of taking office	Chancellor	Foreign Minister	Finance Minister
2 June 1932	F. von Papen	K. von Neurath	L.E. Schwerin von Krosigk
4 Nov 1932	K. von Schleicher		
30 Jan 1933	A. Hitler		
5 Feb 1938		J. von Ribbentrop	
30 Apr 1945	C. Doenitz		

Note: Admiral Doenitz surrendered his powers to the allied occupation forces on 5 June 1945.

[1] This government, which was formed after the revolution of Nov 1918, contained only socialists. In theory all were considered equal but the senior members were F. Ebert and H. Haase.

FEDERAL REPUBLIC OF GERMANY[1]

Date of taking office	Chancellor	Foreign Minister	Finance Minister
20 Sep 1949	K. Adenauer		F. Schäffer
13 Mar 1951		K. Adenauer	
6 Jun 1955		H. von Brentano	
24 Oct 1957			F. Etzel
14 Nov 1961		G. Schröder	H. Starke
11 Dec 1962			R. Dahlgrün
17 Oct 1963	L. Erhard		
1 Dec 1966	K. Kiesinger	W. Brandt	F.J. Strauss
21 Oct 1969	W. Brandt	W. Scheel	A. Möller
13 May 1971			K. Schiller
7 Jul 1972			H. Schmidt
16 May 1974	H. Schmidt	H.-D. Genscher	H. Apel
16 Feb 1978			H. Matthöfer
28 Apr 1982			M. Lahnstein
1 Oct 1982	H. Kohl		
4 Oct 1982			G. Stoltenberg
21 Apr 1989			T. Waigel

FEDERAL REPUBLIC OF GERMANY[1] (*continued*)

Date of *taking office*	*Chancellor*	*Foreign Minister*	*Finance Minister*
18 May 1992		K. Kinkel	
27 Oct 1998	G. Schröder	J. Fischer	O. Lafontaine
12 Apr 1999			H. Eichel

[1] Following the reunification of Germany on 3 Oct 1990 elections were held on 2 Dec 1990.

GERMAN DEMOCRATIC REPUBLIC

Date of *taking office*	*Chairman*	*Foreign Minister*	*Finance Minister*
15 Nov 1950	O. Grotewohl	G. Dertinger	H. Loch
15 Jan 1953		A. Ackermann	
1 Oct 1953		L. Bolz	
24 Nov 1955			W. Rumpf
24 Sep 1964	W. Stoph		
24 Jun 1965		O. Winzer	
13 Jul 1967			S. Bohm
3 Oct 1973	H. Sindermann		
20 Jan 1975		O. Fischer	
3 Nov 1976	W. Stoph		
4 Jun 1980			Dr W. Schmieder
26 Jun 1981			H. Höfner
13 Nov 1989	H. Modrow		
12 Apr 1990	L. de Maizière	M. Meckel	W. Romberg

The German Democratic Republic ceased to exist on 3 Oct 1990.

GREECE

Date of *taking office*	*Prime Minister*	*Foreign Minister*	*Finance Minister*
14 Apr 1899	G.N. Theotókis	A. Românos	A.N. Simópoulos
12 Nov 1901	A. Zaïmis	A. Zaïmis	P. Negris

GREECE (*continued*)

Date of taking office	Prime Minister	Foreign Minister	Finance Minister
2 Dec 1902	T. Delyannis		
11 Jul 1903	D.G. Rhallis	D.G. Rhallis	D.G. Rhallis
1 Dec 1903	G.N. Theotókis		
24 Dec 1904	T. Delyannis		
26 Jun 1905	D.G. Rhallis		
21 Dec 1905	G.N. Theotókis	A.G. Skouzès	A.N. Simópoulos
5 Jul 1908	D.G. Rhallis	G. Baltazzi	D. Gunaris
28 Aug 1909	K. Mavromichalis	K. Mavromichalis	–. Evtaxias
7 Feb 1910	S. Dragoumis		
19 Oct 1910	E. Venizelos	J. Gryparis	L. Koromilas
1912		L. Koromilas	A.N. Diomidis
1913		D. Panàs	
1914		E. Venizelos	
7 Mar 1915	D. Gunaris		
15 Oct 1915	A. Zaïmis		
4 Nov 1915	S. Skuludis	S. Skuludis	S. Dragoumis
8 Apr 1916			D.G. Rhallis
21 Jun 1916	A. Zaïmis	A. Zaïmis	
16 Sep 1916	N. Kalojeropulos		
8 Oct 1916	S. Lambrós		
26 Apr 1917	A. Zaïmis	A. Zaïmis	
27 Jun 1917	E. Venizelos	N. Politis	M. Negropontis
1 Apr 1921	D. Gounaris	J. Baltazzi	M. Protopapadakis
26 Nov 1922	Col. Gonotas	A. Alexandris	M. Kofinas
11 Mar 1924	A. Papanastasiou	A. Papanastasiou	A. Papanastasiou
7 Oct 1924	A. Michalako-poulos	A. Michalako-poulos	C. Gotsis
25 Oct 1925	T. Rangalos	L.R. Canacaris	T. Rangalos
4 Dec 1926	A. Zaïmis	A. Michalako-poulos	C. Gotsis
19 Jul 1928	E. Venizelos	A. Karapanos	G. Maris
23 Dec 1930		A. Michalako-poulos	
23 Apr 1932			K. Varvaressos
26 May 1932	A. Papanastasiou	A. Papanastasiou	

GREECE (*continued*)

Date of taking office	Prime Minister	Foreign Minister	Finance Minister
5 Jun 1932	E. Venizelos	A. Michalako- poulos	
3 Nov 1932	P. Tsaldaris	J. Rhallis	P. Tsaldaris
13 Jan 1933	E. Venizelos	A. Michalako poulos	M. Kaphantaris
6 Mar 1933	Gen. Othonais (*ad interim*)		
10 Mar 1933	P. Tsaldaris	D. Maximos	S. Loverdos
5 Mar 1935		P. Tsaldaris	G. Pesmazoglou
9 Oct 1935	Gen. Kondylis	J. Theotokis	Gen. Kondylis
30 Nov 1935	C. Demerdjis	C. Demerdjis	M. Mandjavinos
15 Mar 1936			G. Mantzarinos
21 Jan 1937	J. Metaxas	J. Metaxas	P. Rediadis
11 Feb 1937			M. Apostolides
29 Jan 1941	A. Korizis		
21 Apr 1941	E. Tsouderos	E. Tsouderos	E. Tsouderos
30 Sep 1941			K. Varvaressos
13 Apr 1944	S. Venizelis	S. Venizelis	M. Manzadones
26 Apr 1944	G. Papandreou	G. Papandreou	
8 Jun 1944			P. Kanellopoulos
31 Aug 1944			A. Svolos
3 Jan 1945	Gen. Plastiras	J. Sophianopoulos	G. Sideris
8 Apr 1945	Adm. Voulgaris		G. Mantzarinos
11 Aug 1945		I. Politis	
17 Oct 1945	Archp Danaskires		
1 Nov 1945	P. Kanellopoulos	P. Kanellopoulos	Prof. Cassimatis
21 Nov 1945	T. Sofoulis	J. Sophianopoulos	M. Mylonas
29 Jan 1946		C. Rendis	
4 Apr 1946	M. Poulitsas	C. Tsaldaris	S. Stephanopoulos
17 Apr 1946	C. Tsaldaris		D. Helmis
27 Jan 1947	D. Maximos		
29 Aug 1947	C. Tsaldaris		
7 Sep 1947	T. Sofoulis		
30 Jun 1949	A. Diomedes		
6 Jan 1950	J. Theotokis	P. Pipinelis	G. Mantzarinos

GREECE (*continued*)

Date of taking office	Prime Minister	Foreign Minister	Finance Minister
23 Mar 1950	S. Venizelis	S. Venizelis	M. Zaimis
15 Apr 1950	Gen. Plastiras	Gen. Plastiras	K. Kartalis
13 Sep 1950	S. Venizelis	S. Venizelis	S. Castopoulos
2 Feb 1951			G. Mavros
8 Aug 1951		I. Politis	
27 Oct 1951	Gen. Plastiras	S. Venizelis	C. Evelpidis
19 Nov 1952	A. Papagos	S. Stephanopoulos	C. Papyannis
15 Dec 1954			D. Eftaxias
6 Oct 1955	C. Karamanlis	S. Theotokis	A. Apostolides
29 Feb 1956			C. Thiraios
27 May 1956		G. Averoff	
5 Mar 1958	M. Georgako-loulos	G. Pesmajogiou	M. Mestikopoulos
17 May 1958	C. Karamanlis	E. Averoff	C. Papaconstantinou
4 Nov 1961			S. Theotokis
19 Jun 1963	P. Pipinelis	P. Pipinelis	
8 Nov 1963	G. Papandreou	S. Venizelis	C. Mitsotakis
30 Dec 1963	I. Paraskevo-poulos	C. Xanthopoulos-Palamos	
18 Feb 1964	G. Papandreou	S. Kostopoulos	C. Mitsotakis
20 Jul 1965	G. Athanasiadis-Novas	G. Melas	S. Allamanis
20 Aug 1965	E. Tsirimokos	E. Tsirimokos	
17 Sep 1965	S. Stephanopoulos		G. Melas
11 Apr 1966		S. Stephanopoulos	
11 May 1966		I. Toumboas	
22 Dec 1966	I. Paraskevo-poulos	E. Economou-Gouras	P. Stergiotis
3 Apr 1967	P. Kanellopoulos	P. Kanellopoulos	C. Papaconstantinou
21 Apr 1967	C. Kollios	P. Economou-Gouras	A. Adroutsopoulos
2 Nov 1967		C. Kollios	
20 Nov 1967		P. Pipinelis	
13 Dec 1967	G. Papadopoulos		

GREECE (*continued*)

Date of taking office	Prime Minister	Foreign Minister	Finance Minister
1 Jan 1970		G. Papadopoulos	
26 Aug 1971			I. Koulis
8 Oct 1973	S. Markezinis	C. Xanthopoulos-Palamos	
25 Nov 1973	A. Androutso-poulos	S. Tetenes	A. Androutsopoulos
8 Jul 1974		K. Kypreos (provisional)	
24 Jul 1974	K. Karamanlis		
26 Jul 1974		G. Mavros	I. Pesmazoglou

On 8 Oct 1974 a caretaker government was formed, K. Karamanlis and G. Mavros retaining their posts, other ministers replaced by non-political persons. On 15 Oct 1974 D. Bitsios replaced G. Mavros.

Date of taking office	Prime Minister	Foreign Minister	Finance Minister
21 Nov 1974	K. Karamanlis	D. Bitsios	E. Devletoglou
28 Nov 1977		P. Papaligouras	I. Boutos
10 May 1978		G. Rallis	A. Kanellopoulos
9 May 1980	G. Rallis	K. Mitsotakis	M. Evert
21 Oct 1981	A. Papandreou	I. Charalambopoulos	E. Drettakis
2 Jun 1989	Tz. Tzannetakis	G. Papoulias	A. Samaras
13 Feb 1990	X. Zolotas	A. Samaras	G. Agapitos
Oct 1990	C. Mitsotakis		Y. Paleokrassas
24 Aug 1992		M. Papakonstandinou	S. Manos
10 Oct 1993	A. Papandreou	K. Papoulias	G. Gennimatas
8 Aug 1994			A. Papadopoulos
20 Mar 1996	C. Simitis	T. Pangalos	
22 Jun 1999		G. Papandreou	Y. Papantoniou

HUNGARY

Date of taking office	Prime Minister	Foreign Minister	Finance Minister
15 Jan 1895			L. von Lukács
25 Feb 1899	K. von Szell		

HUNGARY (*continued*)

Date of taking office	Prime Minister	Foreign Minister	Finance Minister
27 Jun 1903	K. Khuen-Héderváry		
3 Nov 1903	S. von Tisza		
18 Nov 1905	G. Fejérváry-von-Komlos-Keresztes		G. Fejérváry-von-Komlos-Keresztes
8 Apr 1906	A. Wekerle		A. Wekerle
17 Jan 1910	K. Khuen-Héderváry		L. von Lukács
22 Jan 1912	L. von Lukács		J. Teleszky
10 Jan 1913	S. von Tisza		
15 Jun 1917	M. von Esterhazy		G. Graz
20 Aug 1917	A. Wekerle		
16 Sep 1917			A. Wekerle
11 Feb 1918			A. Popovics
30 Oct 1918	J. von Hadik		
31 Oct 1918	M. von Károlyi		M. von Károlyi
14 Mar 1920	A. Simonyi-Semadam	Ct P. Teleki	Baron F. Korányi
14 Apr 1921	Ct I. Bethlen	Ct D. Banffy	M. Hegedüs
1 Jan 1922			T. Kállay
17 Jun 1922		G. Daruvary	
1 Jun 1924		T. Scitovsky	J. Bud
1 Nov 1925		L. Valkó	
5 Sep 1928			A. Wekerle
1 Oct 1929	Ct J. Károlyi	Ct J. Károlyi	
22 Aug 1931	G. Károlyi	L. Valkó	Ct J. Károlyi
1 Dec 1931			Baron F. Korányi
1 Oct 1932	G. Gömbös	K. Kánya	B. Imrédy
8 Jan 1935			T. Fabinyi
12 Oct 1936	K. Dáranyi		
9 Mar 1938			L. Reményi-Schneller
13 May 1938	B. Imrédy		
28 Nov 1938		B. Imrédy	

HUNGARY (*continued*)

Date of taking office	Prime Minister	Foreign Minister	Finance Minister
10 Dec 1938		Ct S. Csáky	
16 Feb 1939	Ct P. Teleki		
15 Feb 1941		L. Bárdossy	
5 Apr 1941	L. Bárdossy		
10 Mar 1942	I. Kállay		
23 Mar 1944	D. Sztójay	D. Sztójay	
29 Aug 1944	Gen. Lakatos	Fd-Marshal Henvey	
16 Oct 1944	F. Szálasi	Baron Keményi	
21 Dec 1944	Gen. B. Miklos	J. Gyöngyösy	I. Vásáry
10 Jul 1945			M. Ottványi
15 Nov 1945	Z. Tildy		F. Gordon
5 Feb 1946	F. Nagy		L. Dinnyés
13 Mar 1947			M. Nyárády
31 May 1947	L. Dinnyés	M. Mihalyti	
23 Sep 1947		E. Molnár	
5 Aug 1948		L. Rajk	
9 Dec 1948	I. Dobi		E. Gerö
10 Jun 1949		G. Kállai	I. Kossa
24 Feb 1950			K. Olt
13 May 1951		K. Kiss	
14 Aug 1952	M. Rákosi		
16 Nov 1952		E. Molnár	
4 Jul 1953	I. Nagy	J. Bodoczky	
18 Apr 1955	A. Hegedüs		
30 Jul 1956		I. Horváth	
24 Oct 1956	I. Nagy		
4 Nov 1956	J. Kádár		I. Kossa
9 May 1957			I. Antos
27 Jan 1958	F. Münnich		
16 Feb 1958		E. Sík	
16 Jan 1960			R. Nyers
13 Sep 1961	J. Kádár	J. Péter	
27 Nov 1963			M. Timar

HUNGARY (*continued*)

Date of taking office	Prime Minister	Foreign Minister	Finance Minister
28 Jun 1965	G. Kállai		
14 Apr 1967	J. Fock		P. Vályi
13 May 1971			L. Faluvégi
14 Dec 1973		F. Puja	
15 May 1975	G. Lázár		
27 Jun 1980			I. Hetényi
8 Jul 1983		P. Várkonyi	
30 Dec 1986			P. Medgyessy
25 Jun 1987	K. Grósz		
16 Dec 1987			M. Villányi
24 Nov 1988	M. Németh		
10 May 1989		G. Horn	L. Békesi
22 May 1990	J. Antall	G. Jeszensky	F. Rabár
22 May 1991			M. Kupa
24 Feb 1993			I. Szabó
27 Dec 1993	P. Boross		
15 Jul 1994	G. Horn	L. Kovacs	L. Békesi
28 Feb 1995			L. Bokros
1 Mar 1996			P. Medgyessy
6 Jul 1998	V. Orbán		
8 Jul 1998		J. Martonyi	Z. Járai

ICELAND

Date of taking office	Prime Minister	Foreign Minister	Finance Minister
25 Feb 1920	J. Magnusson		N. Gudmundsson
15 Mar 1922	S. Egers		M. Jonsson
22 Mar 1924	J. Magnusson		J. Thorlaksson
28 Feb 1927	T. Thorhallsson		N.J. Kristjansson
20 Oct 1931			E. Arnarson

ICELAND (*continued*)

Date of taking office	Prime Minister	Foreign Minister	Finance Minister
3 Jun 1932	A. Asgeirsson		A. Asgeirsson
29 Jul 1934	H. Jonasson		E. Jonsson
17 Apr 1939			J. Moller
18 Nov 1941		O. Thors	
1942		S. Stefansson	
16 May 1942	O. Thors		
16 Dec 1942	B. Thordarson	V. Thor	B. Olafsson
1 Oct 1944	O. Thors	O. Thors	P. Magnusson
4 Feb 1947	S.J. Stefansson	B. Benediktsson	J.T. Josefsson
14 Mar 1950	S. Steinthorsson		E. Jonsson
13 Sep 1953	O. Thors	K. Gudmundsson	
24 Jul 1956	H. Jonasson	G.I. Gudmundsson	
20 Dec 1958	E. Jonsson		G.I. Gudmundsson
20 Nov 1959	O. Thors		G. Thorodssen
14 Nov 1963	B. Benediktsson		
1 Sep 1965		E. Jonsson	
10 Jul 1970	J. Hafstein		
10 Oct 1970			M. Jonsson
14 Jul 1971	Ó. Jóhannesson	E. Ágústsson	H. Sigursson
29 Aug 1974	G. Hallgrímsson	E. Ágústsson	M.A. Mathiesen
31 Aug 1978	Ó. Jóhannesson	B. Groendal	T. Arnasson
15 Oct 1979	B. Groendal		S. Björgvinsson
8 Feb 1980	G. Thoroddsen	Ó. Jóhannesson	R. Arnalds
26 May 1983	S. Hermannsson	G. Hallgrímsson	A. Gudmundsson
16 Oct 1985			Th. Pálsson
24 Jan 1986		M.Á. Mathiesen	
8 Jul 1987	Th. Pálsson	S. Hermannsson	J.B. Hannibalsson
28 Sep 1988	S. Hermannsson	J.B. Hannibalsson	Ó.R. Grímsson
30 Apr 1991	D. Oddsson		F. Sophusson
23 Apr 1995		H. Ásgrímsson	
28 May 1999			G.H. Haarde

IRELAND

Date of taking office	Prime Minister	Foreign Minister	Finance Minister
16 Jan 1922	Provisional government: Finance and General Minister Michael Collins, Foreign Affairs Minister Gavan Duffy.		
6 Dec 1922	W. Cosgrave	D. Fitzgerald	W. Cosgrave
		P. MacGilligan	E. Blythe
9 Mar 1932	E. de Valera	E. de Valera	S. MacEntee
27 Sep 1939			S.T. O'Kelly
9 Jun 1944			F. Aiken
18 Dec 1948	J.A. Costello	S. MacBride	P. MacGilligan
30 May 1951	E. de Valera	F. Aiken	A. MacEntee
2 Jun 1954	J.A. Costello	L. Cosgrave	G. Sweetman
20 Mar 1957	E. de Valera	F. Aiken	J. Ryan
23 Jun 1959	S. Lemass		
21 Apr 1965			J. Lynch
9 Nov 1966	J. Lynch		
10 Nov 1966			C. Haughey
2 Jul 1969		P. Hillery	
8 May 1970			G. Colley
14 Mar 1973	L. Cosgrave	G. FitzGerald	R. Ryan
5 Jul 1977	J. Lynch	M. O'Kennedy	G. Golley
11 Dec 1979	C. Haughey	B. Lenihan	M. O'Kennedy
16 Dec 1980			E. FitzGerald
30 Jun 1981	G. FitzGerald	J. Dooge	J. Bruton
9 Mar 1982	C. Haughey	G. Collins	R. MacSharry
14 Dec 1982	G. FitzGerald	P. Barry	A. Dukes
13 Feb 1986			J. Bruton
10 Mar 1987	C. Haughey	B. Lenihan	R. McSharry
24 Nov 1988			A. Reynolds
12 Jul 1989		G. Collins	
11 Feb 1992	A. Reynolds	D. Andrews	B. Ahern
12 Jan 1993		D. Spring	
15 Dec 1994	J. Bruton		R. Quinn
26 Jun 1997	B. Ahern	R. Burke	C. McCreevy
8 Oct 1997		D. Andrews	

ITALY

Date of taking office	Prime Minister	Foreign Minister	Finance Minister
29 Jun 1898	L. Pelloux	F.N. Canevaro	P. Carcano
14 May 1899		E. Visconti-Venosta	P. Carmine
24 Jun 1900	G. Saracco		B. Chimirri
14 Feb 1901	G. Zanardelli	G. Prinetti	L. Wollemborg
23 Jun 1903		C. Morin	
3 Aug 1903			P. Carcano
3 Nov 1903	G. Giolitti	T. Tittoni	P. Rosano
10 Nov 1903			L. Luzatti
24 Nov 1904			A. Majorana
27 Mar 1905	A. Fortis		
27 Dec 1905		Marquis de San Giuliano	G. Baccelli
8 Feb 1906	S. de Sonnino	F. de Guicciardini	A. Salandra
9 May 1906	G. Giolitti	T. Tittoni	M. Massimini
1906			P. Lacava
10 Dec 1909	S. de Sonnino	F. de Guicciardini	E. Arlotta
30 Mar 1910	L. Luzzatti	Marquis de San Giuliano	L. Facta
27 Mar 1911	G. Giolitti		
21 Mar 1914	A. Salandra		L. Rava
5 Nov 1914		S. de Sonnino	E. Daneo
19 Jun 1916	P. Boselli		F. Meda
30 Oct 1917	V.E. Orlando		
21 Jun 1919	F. Nitti	V. Scialoja	G. de Nava
15 Jun 1920	G. Giolitti	Ct Sforza	F. Tedesco
25 Feb 1922	L. Facta	Dr C. Schauzer	G. Bertone
30 Oct 1922	B. Mussolini	B. Mussolini	A. de Stefani
30 Aug 1925			Ct G. Volpi
1 Jan 1929			A. Mosconi
12 Sep 1929		D. Grandi	
20 Jul 1932		B. Mussolini	G. Jung
24 Jan 1935			Ct P. Thaon de Reval

ITALY (*continued*)

Date of taking office	Prime Minister	Foreign Minister	Finance Minister
9 June 1936		Ct G.C. de Cortellezzo	
6 Feb 1943		B. Mussolini	Baron G. Acerbo
25 Jul 1943	Marshal Badoglio	Baron Guariglea	D. Bartolini
9 Jun 1944	I. Bonomi		M. Siglienti
10 Dec 1944		A. de Gasperi	M. Presenti
19 Jun 1945	F. Parri		M. Scoccimaro
4 Dec 1945	A. de Gasperi		
17 Oct 1946		P. Nenni	
30 May 1947		Ct Sforza	G. Pella
23 May 1948			E. Vanoni
16 Jul 1953		A. de Gasperi	
17 Aug 1953	G. Pella	G. Pella	
18 Jan 1954	A. Fanfani	A. Piccione	A. Zoli
10 Feb 1954	M. Scelba		R. Tremelloni
18 Sep 1954		G. Martino	
6 Jul 1955	A. Segni		G. Andreotti
20 May 1957	A. Zoli	G. Pella	
19 Jun 1958	A. Fanfani	A. Fanfani	L. Preti
16 Feb 1959	A. Segni		P.E. Taviani
25 Mar 1960	F. Tambroni	A. Segni	G. Trabucchi
26 Jul 1960	A. Fanfani		
29 May 1962		A. Piccione	
21 Jun 1963	G. Leone		M. Martinelli
4 Dec 1963	A. Moro	G. Saragat	R. Tremelloni
6 Mar 1965		A. Fanfani	
23 Feb 1966			L. Preti
24 Jun 1968	G. Leone	G. Medici	M.F. Aggradi
12 Dec 1968	M. Rumor	P. Nenni	O. Reale
5 Aug 1969		A. Moro	G. Bosco
27 Mar 1970			L. Preti
6 Aug 1970	E. Colombo		
15 Feb 1972	G. Andreotti		G. Pella

ITALY (*continued*)

Date of taking office	Prime Minister	Foreign Minister	Finance Minister
26 Jun 1972		G. Medici	A. Valsecchi
8 Jul 1973	M. Rumor	A. Moro	E. Colombo
15 Mar 1974			M. Tanassi
23 Nov 1974	A. Moro	M. Rumor	B. Visentini
12 Feb 1976			G. Stammati
30 Jul 1976	G. Andreotti	A. Forlani	F.M. Pandolfi
13 Mar 1978			F.M. Malfatti
5 Aug 1979	F. Cossiga	M.F. Malfatti	M. Reviglio
14 Jan 1980		A. Ruffini	
4 Apr 1980		E. Colombo	
19 Oct 1980	A. Forlani		F. Reviglio
28 Jun 1981	G. Spadolini		S. Formica
11 Dec 1982	A. Fanfani		F. Forte
4 Aug 1983	B. Craxi	G. Andreotti	B. Visentini
18 Apr 1987	A. Fanfani		G. Guarino
29 Jul 1987	G. Goria		A. Gava
13 Apr 1988	C. de Mita		E. Colombo
23 Jul 1989	G. Andreotti	G. de Michelis	R. Formica
28 Jun 1992	G. Amato		
29 Apr 1993	C. Ciampi	B. Andreatta	F. Gallo
11 May 1994	S. Berlusconi	A. Martino	G. Tremonti
17 Jan 1995	L. Dini	S. Agnelli	A. Fantozzi
17 May 1997	R. Prodi	L. Dini	V. Visco
22 Oct 1998	M. D'Alema		

LATVIA

Date of taking office	Prime Minister	Foreign Minister
18 Nov 1918	K. Ulmanis	Z.A. Meierovics
10 May 1919	A. Niedra	
14 Jul 1919	K. Ulmanis	

LATVIA (*continued*)

Date of taking office	Prime Minister	Foreign Minister	Finance Minister
19 Jun 1921	Z.A. Meierovics		
27 Jan 1923	J. Pauļuks		
28 Jun 1923	Z.A. Meierovics		
27 Jan 1924	V. Zāmuēls	L. Sēja	
19 Dec 1924	H. Celmiņš		
Aug 1925		H. Celmiņš	
24 Dec 1925	K. Ulmanis	H. Albāts	
7 May 1926	A. Alberings	K. Ulmanis	
19 Dec 1926	M. Skujenieks	F. Cielēns	
24 Jan 1928	P. Juraševskis	A. Balodis	
1 Dec 1928	H. Celmiņš		
9 Apr 1930		H. Celmiņš	
27 Mar 1931	K. Ulmanis		
6 Dec 1931	M. Skujenieks		
9 Dec 1931		K. Zariņš	
24 Mar 1933	A. Bļodnieks	V. Salnais	
17 Mar 1934	K. Ulmanis		

Independence was again achieved in Sep 1991.

7 May 1990	I. Godmanis		
14 May 1990			E. Siliņš
22 May 1990		J. Jurkāns	
10 Nov 1992		G. Andrejevs	
3 Aug 1993	V. Birkavs		U. Osis
7 Jun 1994		V. Birkavs	
15 Sep 1994	M. Gailis		A. Piebalgs
25 May 1995			I. Sāmīte
21 Dec 1995	A. Šķēle		A.G. Kreituss
17 Jan 1997			V. Meļņiks
1999	V. Krištopans		I. Godmanis
Aug 1999	A. Šķēle	I. Berziņš	E. Krastiņš

LITHUANIA

Prime Ministers of Lithuania 1918–1939

Nov 1918	A. Voldemaras	3 Feb 1925	V. Petrulis
27 Dec 1918	M. Sleževičius	25 Sep 1925	L. Bistras
12 Mar 1919	P. Dovydaitis	15 Jun 1926	M. Sleževičius
12 Apr 1919	M. Sleževičius	18 Dec 1926	A. Voldemaras
7 Oct 1919	E. Galvanauskas	23 Sep 1929	J. Tūbelis
19 Jun 1920	K. Grinius	24 Mar 1938	V. Mironas
12 Feb 1923	E. Galvanauskas	28 Mar 1939	J. Černius
18 Jun 1924	A. Tumenas	21 Nov 1939	A. Merkys

Date of taking office	Prime Minister	Foreign Minister	Finance Minister
17 Mar 1990	K.D. Prunskienė	A. Saudargas	R. Sikorskis
10 Jan 1991	A. Šimėnas		
13 Jan 1991	G. Vagnorius		E.J. Kunevičienė
21 Jul 1992	A.A. Abišala		A. Misevičius
12 Dec 1992	B. Lubys		
10 Mar 1993	A. Šleževičius	P. Gylys	E. Vilkelis
10 Feb 1995			R. Šarkinas
23 Feb 1996	L.M. Stankevičius		A. Križinauskas
4 Dec 1996	G. Vagnorius	A. Saudargas	R. Matiliauskas
19 Feb 1997			A. Šemeta
19 May 1999	R. Paksas		J. Lionginas
3 Nov 1999	A. Kubilius		

LUXEMBOURG

Date of taking office	Prime Minister	Foreign Minister	Finance Minister
23 Nov 1890	Separated from the Netherlands; at that date the following ministers were in office:		
	P. Eyschen	P. Eyschen	M. Mongenast
1915	H. Loutsch	H. Loutsch	E. Reiffen

LUXEMBOURG (*continued*)

Date of taking office	Prime Minister	Foreign Minister	Finance Minister
1 Apr 1921	E. Reuter		A. Neyens
1 Mar 1925	P. Pruom		A. Schmit
1 Jul 1926	J. Bech		M. Clemang
1 Aug 1926			P. Dupong
5 Nov 1937	P. Dupong	J. Bech	

Note: On 15 Aug 1940 the government was declared void by the German forces of occupation. A government in exile continued in London.

29 Dec 1953	J. Bech	J. Bech	P. Werner
1 Jan 1958	P. Frieden		
25 Feb 1959	P. Werner	E. Schauss	
15 Jul 1964		P. Werner	
23 Dec 1967		P. Gregoire	
29 Jan 1969		G. Thorn	
18 Jun 1974	G. Thorn	G. Thorn	R. Vouel
19 Jul 1976			J.F. Poos
16 Jul 1979	P. Werner		J. Santer
21 Nov 1980		C. Flesch	
20 Jul 1984	J. Santer	J.F. Poos	
14 Jul 1989			J.-C. Juncker
20 Jan 1995	J.-C. Juncker		
7 Aug 1999		L. Polfer	

REPUBLIC OF MACEDONIA

Date of taking office	Prime Minister	Foreign Minister	Finance Minister
20 Mar 1991	N. Kljusev	D. Maleski	M. Tosevski
4 Sep 1992	B. Crvenkovski		D. Hajredini
6 Jul 1993		S. Crvenkovski	
20 Dec 1994			J. Miljovski
23 Feb 1996		L. Frckoski	T. Fiti

REPUBLIC OF MACEDONIA (*continued*)

Date of taking office	Prime Minister	Foreign Minister	Finance Minister
30 May 1997		B. Handziski	
30 Nov 1998	Lj. Georgievski	A. Dimitrov	B. Stojmenov
27 Dec 1999			N. Guevski

MALTA

Date of taking office	Prime Minister	Foreign Minister	Finance Minister
4 Nov 1947	Dr P. Boffa		
1 Jan 1950			A. Colombo
26 Sep 1950	E. Mizzi		F. Azzopardi
20 Dec 1950	B. Olivier		
11 Mar 1995	D. Mintoff		D. Mintoff

Note: D. Mintoff resigned in Apr 1958 and the constitution was suspended.

5 Mar 1962	B. Olivier		G. Felice
21 Jun 1971	D. Mintoff	D. Mintoff	J. Abela
9 Jul 1981			J. Cassar
20 Dec 1981		A.S. Trigona	L. Spiteri
22 Dec 1985	C. Mifsud Bonnici		W. Abela
12 May 1987	E. Fenech Adami	V. Tabone	G. Bonello Du Puis
1989		E. Fenech Adami	
1990		G. De Marco	
1992			J. Dalli
28 Oct 1996	A. Sant	G. Vella	L. Spiteri
12 May 1987	E. Fenech Adami	V. Tabone	G. Bonello Du Puis
17 Mar 1989		E. Fenech Adami	
3 May 1990		G. de Marco	
25 Feb 1992			J. Dalli
28 Oct 1996	A. Sant	G. Vella	L. Spiteri
27 Mar 1997			L. Brincat

MALTA (*continued*)

Date of taking office	Prime Minister	Foreign Minister	Finance Minister
7 Sep 1998	E. Fenech Adami	G. de Marco	J. Dalli
25 Mar 1999		J. Borg	

MOLDOVA

Date of taking office	Prime Minister	Foreign Minister	Finance Minister
1 Jul 1992	A. Sangheli	I. Botnaru	K. Vasylivana
Nov 1993		M. Popov	V. Chitan
1993	V. Muravschi		
1996	I. Ciubuc		
Mar 1999	I. Sturza	N. Tabacaru	A. Arapu
Dec 1999	D. Braghis		M. Manole

MONTENEGRO

Date of taking office	Prime Minister	Foreign Minister	Finance Minister

Ministerial government was established in 1907.

Date of taking office	Prime Minister	Foreign Minister	Finance Minister
17 Apr 1907	L. Tomanovitch	L. Tomanovitch	D. Voukotitch
14 Sep 1910			P. Yergovitch
23 Aug 1911		D. Grégovitch	
1912	M. Martinovitch	M. Martinovitch	D. Drlievitch
8 May 1913	J. Voukotitch	P. Plamenatz	R. Popovitch
1915			–. Mouchkovitch
May 1916	A. Radovitch	A. Radovitch	A. Radovitch
Jan 1917	M. Tomanovitch	M. Tomanovitch	M. Tomanovitch
13 Jun 1917	E. Popovitch	E. Popovitch	E. Popovitch

THE NETHERLANDS

Date of taking office	*Prime Minister*	*Foreign Minister*	*Finance Minister*
26 Jul 1897	N.G. Pierson	W.H. de Beaufort	N.G. Pierson
27 Jul 1901	A. Kuyper	R. Melvil	J.J.I. Harte van Tecklenburg
9 Mar 1905		A.G. Ellis	
22 Apr 1905		W.M. van Weede van Beerencamp	
14 Aug 1905	T.H. de Meester	D.A.W. van Tets van Goudriaan	T.H. de Meester
12 Feb 1908	T. Heemskerk	R. de Marees van Svinderen	M.J.C.M. Kolkman
29 Aug 1913	P.W.A.C. van der Lynden	P.W.A.C. van der Lynden	A.E.J. Bertling
27 Sep 1913		J. Loudon	
24 Oct 1914			M.W.F. Treb
8 Feb 1916			A. van Gijn
22 Feb 1917			M.W.F. Treub
9 Sep 1918	C.J.M.R. de Beerenbroeck	H.A. van Karnebeek	S. de Vries
28 Jul 1921			D.J. de Geer
11 Aug 1923			H. Colijn
31 Jul 1925	H. Colijn		
8 Mar 1926	D.J. de Geer		D.J. de Geer
30 Mar 1927		F.B. van Blokland	
10 Aug 1929	C.J.M.R. de Beerenbroeck		
24 May 1933	H. Colijn	A.C.D. de Graeff	P.J. Oud
23 Jun 1937		H. Colijn	J.A. de Wilde
14 Sep 1937		J.A.N. Patijn	
21 May 1939			H. Colijn
10 Aug 1939	D.J. de Geer	E.N. van Kleffens	D.J. de Geer
4 Sep 1940	P.S. Gerbrandy		J.I.M. Welter
23 Nov 1941			J.W. Albarda

THE NETHERLANDS (*continued*)

Date of taking office	Prime Minister	Foreign Minister	Finance Minister
15 Sep 1942			J. van den Broek
24 Feb 1945			G.W.M. Huysmans
23 Jun 1945	W. Schermerhorn		P. Lieftinck
26 Feb 1946		J.H. van Royen	
13 Jul 1946	L.J.M. Beel	C.G.W.H. Baron van Boetzelaer van Ooterhuit	
7 Aug 1948	W. Drees	D.U. Stikker	
1 Sep 1952		J.W. Beyen J.M.A.H. Luns *Joint Ministry*	J.A. van der Kieft
12 Oct 1956			H.J. Hofstra
22 Dec 1958	L. Beel	J.M.A.H. Luns	J. Zijlstra
19 May 1959	J.E. de Quay		
24 Jul 1963	V.G.M. Marijunen		J.H. Witteveen
12 Apr 1965	J. Cals		A. Vondeling
22 Nov 1966	J. Zijlstra		J. Zijlstra
3 Apr 1967	P.J.S. de Jong		H.J. Witteveen
6 Jul 1971	B.W. Biescheuval	W.K.N. Schmelzer	R.J. Nelissen
11 May 1973	J. den Uyl	M. van der Stoel	W.F. Duisenberg
19 Dec 1977	A. van Agt	C. van der Klaauw	F. Andriessen
4 Mar 1980			A. van der Stee
11 Sep 1981		M. van der Stoel	
29 May 1982		A. van Agt	
4 Nov 1982	R. Lubbers	H. van den Broek	H. Ruding
7 Nov 1989			W. Kok
22 Aug 1994	W. Kok	H.A.F.M.O. van Mierlo	G. Zalm
3 Aug 1998		J. van Aartsen	

NORWAY

Date of taking office	Prime Minister	Foreign Minister	Finance Minister

Norway became independent of Sweden on 7 Jun 1905. At that date the following ministers were in office:

Since			
11 Mar 1905	P.C.H.K. Michelsen	J.G. Lövland	P.C.H.K. Michelsen
1906			A. Berge
28 Oct 1907	J.G. Lövland		J.M. Helvorsen
1908	G. Knudsen	W. Christopherson	G. Knudsen
1 Feb 1910	W. Konow	J. Irgens	A. Berge
19 Feb 1912	J. Brathé		W. Konow
31 Jan 1913	G. Knudsen	N. Ihlen	A.T. Omhalt
21 Jun 1920	O.B. Halvorsen	C.F. Michelet	E.H. Bull
22 Jun 1921	O.A. Blehr	A.C. Raested	O.A. Blehr
5 Mar 1923	O.B. Halvorsen	C.F. Michelet	A. Berge
1 May 1923	A. Berge		
7 Jul 1924	J.L. Mowinckel	J.L. Mowinckel	A. Holmboe
4 Mar 1926	I. Lykke	I. Lykke	F.L. Konow
13 Feb 1928	J.L. Mowinckel	J.L. Mowinckel	P. Lund
12 May 1931	N. Kolstad	B. Bradland	F. Sundby
15 Mar 1932	J. Hundseid		
27 Feb 1933	J.L. Mowinckel	J.L. Mowinckel	P. Lund
14 Nov 1934			G. Jan
19 Mar 1935	J. Nygaardsvold	H. Kont	A. Indreboe
			K. Bergsvik
30 Jun 1939			O.F. Torp
21 Feb 1941		T.H. Lie	

Note: The government in exile continued in London.

1 Mar 1942			P. Hartmann
24 Jun 1945	E. Gerhardsen		G. Jahn
1 Nov 1945			E. Brofoss
1 Nov 1947			O. Meisdalshagen
16 Nov 1951	O.F. Torp		T. Bratteli

NORWAY (*continued*)

Date of taking office	Prime Minister	Foreign Minister	Finance Minister
21 Jan 1955	E. Gerhardsen		M. Lid
1 Mar 1957			T. Bratteli
23 Apr 1960			P.J. Bjerve
23 Jan 1963			A. Cappelen
27 Aug 1963	J. Lyng	E. Wikborg	D. Vårvik
24 Sep 1963	E. Gerhardsen	H. Lange	A. Cappelen
12 Oct 1965	P. Borten	J. Lyng	O. Myrvoll
22 May 1970		S. Stray	
13 Mar 1971	T. Bratteli	A. Cappelen	R. Christiansen
7 Oct 1972	L. Korvald		
18 Oct 1972		D. Vårvik	J. Norbom
16 Oct 1973	T. Bratteli	K. Frydenlund	P. Kleppe
9 Jan 1976	O. Nordli		
5 Oct 1979			U. Sand
4 Feb 1981	G.H. Brundtland		
14 Oct 1981	K.I. Willoch	S. Stray	R. Presthus
25 Apr 1986			A. Skauge
9 May 1986	G.H. Brundtland	K. Frydenlund	G. Berge
9 Mar 1987		T. Stoltenberg	
16 Oct 1989	J.P. Syse	K.M. Bondevik	A. Skauge
3 Nov 1990	G.H. Brundtland	T. Stoltenberg	S. Johnsen
2 Apr 1993		J.J. Holst	
24 Jan 1994		B.T. Godal	
25 Oct 1996	T. Jagland		J. Stoltenberg
17 Oct 1997	K.M. Bondevik	K. Volleback	G. Restad

POLAND

Date of taking office	Prime Minister	Foreign Minister	Finance Minister
19 Jan 1919	I. Paderewski, provisional government.		
14 Dec 1919	L. Skulski	S. Patek	W. Grabski
24 Jun 1920	W. Grabski		

POLAND (*continued*)

Date of taking office	Prime Minister	Foreign Minister	Finance Minister
24 Jul 1920	W. Witos	Prince Sapieha	J.K. Steczkowski
23 Sep 1921	A. Ponikowski	K. Skirmunt	J. Michalski
28 Jun 1922	M. Sliwinski		
31 Jul 1922	M. Nowacki		
16 Dec 1922	W. Sikorski	Ct A. Skrzyński	W. Grabski
28 May 1923	W. Witos		
19 Dec 1923	W. Grabski	Ct M. Zamoyski Ct A. Skrzyński	
29 Nov 1925	Ct A. Skrzyński		J. Zdziechowski
9 Jun 1926	K. Bartel		
2 Oct 1926	J. Piłsudski	A. Zaleski	G. Czechowicz
18 Oct 1928	K. Bartel		M. Grodyński
14 Apr 1929	K. Świtalski		
29 Dec 1929	K. Bartel		
1 Apr 1930	W. Sławek		I. Matuszewski
25 Aug 1930	J. Piłsudski		
4 Dec 1930	W. Sławek		
29 Dec 1930	K. Bartel		
27 May 1931	A. Prystor		J. Piłsudski
7 Sep 1932			Z. Zawadzki
2 Nov 1932		J. Beck	
10 May 1933	J. Jedrzejewicz		
13 May 1934	L. Kozłowski		
28 Mar 1935	W. Sławek		
12 Oct 1935	M. Kosciałkowski-Zyndram		E. Kwiatkowski
16 May 1936	F.S. Składkowski		
20 Sep 1939	W. Sikorski	A. Zaleski	A. Koc

Note: The government in exile continued in Paris and later in London.

1 Jan 1941			H. Strasburger
28 Aug 1941		Ct E. Raczyński	
14 Jul 1943	S. Mikołajczyk	T. Romer	L. Grosfeld

POLAND (*continued*)

Date of taking office	Prime Minister	Foreign Minister	Finance Minister
30 Nov 1944	T. Arciszewski	A. Tarnowski	J. Kwapiński
28 June 1945	E. Osobka-Morawski	W. Rzymowski	K. Dabrowski
6 Feb 1947	J. Cyrankiewicz	Z. Modzelewski	
17 Mar 1951		S. Skrzeszewski	
20 Nov 1952	B. Bierut		
19 Mar 1954	J. Cyrankiewicz		
27 Apr 1956		A. Rapacki	
27 Jan 1957			T. Dietrich
16 Nov 1960			J. Albrecht
15 Jul 1968			S. Majewski
22 Dec 1968		S. Jędrychowski	
28 Jun 1969			J. Trendota
23 Dec 1970	P. Jaroszewicz		
22 Dec 1971		S. Olszowski	S. Jędrychowski
21 Nov 1974			H. Kisiel
2 Dec 1976		E. Wojtaszek	
18 Feb 1980	E. Babiuch		
24 Aug 1980	J. Pińkowski	J. Czyrek	M. Krzak
11 Feb 1981	Gen. W. Jaruzelski		
21 Jul 1982		S. Olszowski	
8 Oct 1982			S. Nieckadaz
6 Nov 1985	Z. Messner	M. Orzechowski	B. Samojlik
13 Oct 1988	M. Rakowski	T. Olechowski	A. Wroblewski
12 Sep 1989	T. Mazowiecki	K. Skubiszewski	L. Balcerowicz
4 Jan 1991	J.K. Bielecki		
Dec 1991	J. Olszewski		K. Lutkowski
Feb 1992			A. Olechowski
11 Jul 1992	H. Suchocka		J. Osiatyński
26 Oct 1993	W. Pawlak	A. Olechowski	M. Borowski
9 Feb 1994			H. Chmielak
28 Apr 1994			G. Kołodko

POLAND (*continued*)

Date of taking office	Prime Minister	Foreign Minister	Finance Minister
7 Mar 1995	J. Oleksy	W. Bartoszewski	
Dec 1995		D. Rosati	
7 Feb 1996	W. Cimoszewicz		
5 Feb 1997			M. Belka
31 Oct 1997	J. Buzek	B. Geremek	L. Balcerowicz

PORTUGAL

Date of taking office	Prime Minister	Foreign Minister	Finance Minister
7 Feb 1897	J. Luiciano de Castro	H. de Barros Gomes	F. Ressano Garcia
18 Aug 1898		Veiga Beirao	M.A. d'Espregueira
25 Jun 1900	E.R. Hintze Ribeiro	J. Arroyo	A. Andrade
1901		F. Mattoso	F. Mattoso
28 Feb 1903		W. de Lima	A.T. de Souza
20 Oct 1904	J. Luiciano de Castro	E. Villaça	M.A. d'Espregueira
20 Mar 1906	E.R. Hintze Ribeiro		
19 May 1906	J.F. Franco	L. Magalhães	E.D. Schröter
2 May 1907		L. Monteiro	F.A. Miranda de Carvalho
5 Feb 1908	F.J. Ferreira de Amaral	W. de Lima	M.A. d'Espregueira
19 Jul 1908	A.A. de Campos Henriques		
2 Apr 1909	S. Tellez		
15 May 1909	W. de Lima	C. di Roma du Bocage	P. Azevedo
22 Dec 1909	F.A. de Veiga Beirâo		
26 Jun 1910	A.T. de Souza		
5 Oct 1910	T. Braga	B. Machado	J. Belvas

PORTUGAL (*continued*)

Date of taking office	Prime Minister	Foreign Minister	Finance Minister
2 Sep 1911	J.P. Chagas		
11 Nov 1911	A. de Vasconcellos	A. de Vasconcellos	S. Pais
16 Jun 1912	D. Leite		V. Ferreira
9 Jan 1913	O. Costa	A. Macieira	O. Costa
8 Feb 1914	B. Machado Guimarães	F. Andrade	A. do Santos Lucas
7 Dec 1914	V.H. de Azevudo		
28 Jan 1915	J.P. Continho de Castro	A.L. Vieira Soares	V. Guimarães
14 Feb 1915	J.P. Chagas		
19 May 1915	A. Costa		
20 Jun 1915	J.P. de Castro		
30 Nov 1915	A. Costa		
16 Mar 1916	A.J. d'Almeida	A.L. Vieira Soares	A. Costa
15 Apr 1917	A. Costa		
8 Dec 1917	S. Pais		
12 Mar 1920	A.N. Bapista	X. da Silva	P. Lopes
2 Mar 1921	B. Machado	D. Pereira	A.M. da Silva
9 Feb 1922	A.M. da Silva	M. Barbosa-Magalhaes	M. Puero
1 Jan 1923		D. Pereira	V. Guimarães
18 Dec 1923	A. de Castro		A. de Castro
15 Feb 1925	V. Guimarães	P. Martins	V. Guimarães
18 Dec 1925	A.M. da Silva	V. Borges	A.M. Guedes
9 Jul 1926	A.O. de F. Carmona	A.M. de B. Rodrigues	J.J.S. de Cordes
10 Nov 1928	J.V. de Freitas	M.C.Q. Meireles	A. de O. Salazar
20 Jan 1930	D. de Oliveira	F.A. Branco	
5 Jul 1932	A. de O. Salazar	C. de S. Mendes	
11 Apr 1933		J.C. da Mata	
23 Oct 1934		A. de M. Guimarães	
18 Jan 1936		A.R. Monteiro A. de O. Salazar	

PORTUGAL (*continued*)

Date of taking office	Prime Minister	Foreign Minister	Finance Minister
28 Aug 1940			J.P. da C.L. Lumbrales
4 Feb 1947		J.C. da Mata	
1 Aug 1950		P.A.V. Cunha	A.A. de Oliveira
8 Jul 1955			A.M.P. Barbosa
13 Aug 1958		M.G.N.D. Matias	
3 May 1961		A.M.G.F. Nogueira	
13 Jun 1965			U.C. de A. Cortes
17 Aug 1968			J.A.D. Rosas
26 Sep 1968	M.J. das N.A. Caetano		
1 Apr 1969		M.J. das N.A. Caetano	
14 Jan 1970		R.M. de M. d'E. Patricio	
11 Aug 1972			M.A.C.A. Dias

The Caetano government was overthrown by the armed forces on 25 Apr 1974.

Date of taking office	Prime Minister	Foreign Minister	Finance Minister
16 May 1974	A. da P. Carlos	M. Soares	J. da S. Lopes
17 Jul 1974	V. dos S. Gonçalves		
25 Mar 1975		E.A. de M. Antunes	J.J. Fragoso
8 Aug 1975		M. Ruivo	
29 Aug 1975	J.B.P. de Azevedo		
19 Sep 1975		E.A. de M. Antunes	F.S. Zenha
16 Jul 1976	M. Soares		
23 Jul 1976		J.M. Ferreira	H.M. Carreira
10 Oct 1977		M. Soares	
28 Aug 1978	A.J.N. da Costa	C.G. Gago	J. da S. Lopes
25 Oct 1978	C.A.M. Pinto		
22 Nov 1978		J. de F. Cruz	M.J. Nunes
19 Jul 1979	M. de L. Pintassilgo		
1 Aug 1979			A.S. Franco
29 Dec 1979	F.L. Sá Carneiro		

PORTUGAL (*continued*)

Date of taking office	Prime Minister	Foreign Minister	Finance Minister
3 Jan 1980		D.F. do Amaral	A.A. Cavaco e Silva
4 Dec 1980	D.F. do Amaral (interim)		
22 Dec 1980	F.J.P. Pinto Balsemão		
9 Jan 1981		A.G. Pereira	J.A.M. Leitão
4 Sep 1981			J.F. Salgueiro
4 Jun 1982		V.G. Pereira	

F.J.P. Pinto Balsemão resigned on 19 Dec 1982. Dr Pereira Crespo was appointed Prime Minister on 27 Dec 1982, but his nominated ministry was not accepted. Pinto Balsemão was recalled on 23 Jan 1983 to lead a caretaker government, with the Foreign and Finance Ministers who were in office at his resignation, pending elections.

9 Jun 1983	Dr M. Soares	J. Gama	E. Lopes
6 Nov 1985	A.C. Silva	P.P. de Miranda	M. Cadilhe
17 Aug 1987		J. de D. Pinteiro	
5 Jan 1990			M. Beleza
1992		J.D. Barroso	J.B. de Macedo
1993			E.A. Catrogo
30 Oct 1995	A. Guterres	J. Gama	A.S. Franco

ROMANIA

Date of taking office	Prime Minister	Foreign Minister	Finance Minister
11 Apr 1899	G.C. Cantacuzène	J. Lahovari	G. Manu
7 Jul 1900	P.P. Carp	A. Marghiloman	P.P. Carp
14 Feb 1901	D. Stourdza	D. Stourdza	G.D. Pallade
1902		J.C. Brătianu	E. Costinescu
4 Jan 1905	G. Cantacuzène	J. Lahovari	T. Ionescu
25 Mar 1907	D. Stourdza	D. Stourdza	E. Costinescu
Mar 1909	J.C. Brătianu	A.G. Djuvara	

ROMANIA (*continued*)

Date of taking office	Prime Minister	Foreign Minister	Finance Minister
10 Jan 1911	P.P. Carp	T. Majorescu	P.P. Carp
10 Apr 1912	T. Majorescu		A. Marghiloman
16 Jan 1914	J.C. Brătianu	E. Porumbaru	E. Costinescu
9 Feb 1918	A. Averescu		
19 Mar 1918	A. Marghiloman	C. Arion	M. Saulescu
16 Mar 1920	A. Averescu	D. Zamsirescu	C. Argetoianu
21 Jun 1920		T. Ionescu	N. Titulescu
19 Jan 1922	I. Brătianu	I. Duca	V. Brătianu
30 Mar 1926	Gen. A. Averescu	M. Mitilineu	I. Lapedatu
27 Mar 1927			Gen. A. Averescu
24 Nov 1927	V. Brătianu	N. Titulescu	V. Brătianu
11 Nov 1928	J. Maniu	G. Mironescu	M. Popovici
Jun 1930			M. Manoilescu
19 Apr 1931	N. Iorga	C. Argetoianu	C. Argetoianu
		Prince D. Ghica	Prince D. Ghica
6 Jun 1932	A. Vaida-Voevod	G. Mironescu	
11 Aug 1932		A. Vaida-Voevod	G. Mironescu
8 Oct 1932		N. Titulescu	
19 Oct 1932	J. Maniu		V. Madgearu
14 Jan 1933	A. Vaida-Voevod		
14 Nov 1933	I. Duca		D. Brătianu
29 Dec 1933	C. Angelescu		
3 Jan 1934	G. Tatarescu		
5 Jan 1935			V. Slăvescu
4 Feb 1935			V. Antonescu
30 Aug 1936		V. Antonescu	M. Cancicov
28 Dec 1937	O. Goga	I. Micescu	E. Savu
11 Feb 1938	M. Cristea	G. Tatarescu	M. Cancicov
30 Mar 1938		N. Petrescu-Comnen	
21 Dec 1938		G. Gafencu	
1 Feb 1939			M. Constantinescu
6 Mar 1939	M. Calinescu		
21 Sep 1939	Gen. Argeseanu		

ROMANIA (*continued*)

Date of taking office	Prime Minister	Foreign Minister	Finance Minister
28 Sep 1939	C. Argetoianu		
24 Nov 1939	G. Tatarescu		
2 Jun 1940		I. Gigurtu	
4 Jul 1940	I. Gigurtu	M. Manoilescu	E. Savu
3 Sep 1940	I. Antonescu		
15 Sep 1940		M. Sturdza	G. Cretzianu
1 Dec 1940		I. Antonescu	
27 Jan 1941			N. Stoenescu
16 Oct 1942			A. Neagu
24 Aug 1944	C. Sănătescu	G. Niculescu-Buzeşti	G. Potopeaunu
2 Dec 1944	N. Radescu	C. Vişoianu	M. Romniceanu
6 Mar 1945	P. Groza	G. Tatarescu	D. Alimănişteanu
29 Nov 1946			A. Alexandrini
7 Nov 1947		A. Pauker	V. Luca
9 Mar 1952			D. Petrescu
2 Jun 1952	G. Gheorghiu-Dej		
5 Jul 1952		S. Bughici	
2 Oct 1955	C. Stoica	G. Preoteasa	M. Manescu
14 Jul 1957		I.G. Maurer	
11 Jan 1958		A. Bunaciu	
21 Mar 1961	I.G. Maurer	C. Manescu	A. Vijoli
13 Jul 1968			V. Pirvu
19 Aug 1969			F. Dŭmitrescu
18 Oct 1972		G. Macovescu	
29 Mar 1974	M. Manescu		
7 Mar 1978			P. Niculescu
23 Mar 1978		S. Andrei	
30 Mar 1979	I. Verdeţ		
26 Mar 1981			P. Gigea
21 May 1982	G. Dăscălescu		
11 Nov 1985		I. Vaduva	A. Babe
26 Aug 1986		I. Totu	G. Paraschiv
5 Dec 1987			I. Patan

ROMANIA (*continued*)

Date of taking office	Prime Minister	Foreign Minister	Finance Minister
3 Nov 1989		I. Stoian	
24 Dec 1989	P. Roman	S. Celac	T. Stolojan
28 Jun 1990		A. Năstase	E. Dijmărescu
1 Oct 1991	T. Stolojan		G. Danielescu
4 Nov 1992	N. Văcăroiu	T. Mele Şcanu	F. Georgescu
12 Dec 1996	V. Ciorbea	A. Severin	M. Ciumara
7 Feb 1998		A.G. Plesu	D. Daianu
15 Apr 1998	R. Vasile		D.T. Remes
(Dismissed Dec 1999)			

RUSSIA

Date of taking office	Prime Minister	Foreign Minister	Finance Minister
16 Jun 1895	J.N. Durnovo		
Sep 1896		N.P. Shishkin Count Muraviev	
22 Jun 1900		Count Lamsdorff	
29 Aug 1903	S.J. Witte		
31 Aug 1903			E.D. Pleske
10 Apr 1904			W.N. Kokovtsov
30 Oct 1905			I.P. Shipov
8 May 1906	I.L. Goremykin	A.P. Isvolsky	W.N. Kokovtsov
23 Jul 1906	P.A. Stolypin		
28 Sep 1910		S. Sazonov	
23 Sep 1911	W.N. Kokovtsov		
11 Nov 1914	I.L. Goremykin		P.L. Bark
2 Feb 1916	B.W. Stürmer		
23 Nov 1916	A.F. Trepov	N.N. Pokrovsky	
9 Jan 1917	N.D. Golitsin	P.N. Milyukov	M.I. Tereshchenko
14 Mar 1917	G.J. Lvov		
8 May 1917		M.I. Tereschchenko	
18 May 1917			A.I. Shingaryov

RUSSIA (*continued*)

Date of taking office	Prime Minister	Foreign Minister	Finance Minister
21 Jul 1917	A.F. Kerensky		
6 Aug 1917			N.V. Nekrasov
27 Sep 1917			M.W. Bernatsky

See USSR p. 181.

RUSSIAN FEDERATION

Date of taking office	Prime Minister	Foreign Minister	Finance Minister
1992	B. Yeltsin (acting)		
15 Jun 1992	Y. Gaidar		
14 Dec 1992	V. Chernomyrdin		
Jan 1996		Y. Primakov	
Mar 1998	S. Kiriyenko		M. Zadornov
Aug 1998	Y. Primakov		
Sep 1998		I. Ivanov	
12 May 1999	S. Stepashin		
9 Aug 1999	V. Putin		

SERBIA

Date of taking office	Prime Minister	Foreign Minister	Finance Minister
23 Oct 1897	V. Djordjević	V. Djordjević	S.D. Prjović
1898			M. Popović
1899			V. Petrović
12 Jul 1900	A.S. Jovanović	A.S. Jovanović	M. Popović
20 Mar 1901	M. Vujić	M. Vujić	
20 Oct 1902	P. Velimirović	V. Antonić	M. Radovanović
18 Nov 1902	D. Cinzar-Marković		
11 Jun 1903	J. Avakumović		
11 Feb 1904	S. Grujić	A. Nikolić	
10 Dec 1904	N. Pašić		

SERBIA (*continued*)

Date of taking office	*Prime Minister*	*Foreign Minister*	*Finance Minister*
28 May 1905	L. Stojanović	J. Zujović	Dr –. Markovitch
7 Mar 1906	S. Grujić		
28 Apr 1906	N.P. Pašić	N.P. Pašić	L. Patchou
7 Jul 1908	P. Velimirović	M.G. Milanović	M. Popović
24 Feb 1909	S. Novaković		
11 Oct 1909	N.P. Pašić		S.M. Protić
25 Jun 1911	M.G. Milanović		
2 Jul 1912	M. Trifković		
12 Sep 1912 until 1919	N.P. Pašić	N.P. Pašić	L. Patchou

SLOVAKIA

Date of taking office	*Prime Minister*	*Foreign Minister*	*Finance Minister*
1 Mar 1993	V. Mečiar		J. Tóth
16 Mar 1994	J. Moravcik		
13 Dec 1994	V. Mečiar	J. Schenk	S. Kozlík
Oct 1998	M. Dzurinda	E. Kukan	B. Schmögnerová

SLOVENIA

Date of taking office	*Prime Minister*	*Foreign Minister*	*Finance Minister*
10 Jan 1992			M. Gaspari
22 Apr 1992	J. Drnovšek		
25 Jan 1993		L. Peterle	
27 Jan 1995		Z. Thaler	
20 Jul 1996		D. Kračun	
28 Feb 1997		Z. Thaler	
25 Sep 1997		B. Frlec	

SPAIN

Date of taking office	Prime Minister	Foreign Minister	Finance Minister
4 Mar 1899	F. Silvela	F. Silvela	R.F. Villaverde
23 Oct 1900	M. de Azcárraga y Palmero	M. Aguilar de Campo	M.A. Salazar
26 Feb 1901	P.M. Sagasta		
6 Mar 1901		Duc de Almodóvar del Rio	A. Urzaiz
6 Dec 1902	F. Silvela		
20 Jul 1903	R.F. Villaverde		
8 Dec 1903	A. Maura y Montomar		
16 Dec 1904	M. de Azcárraga y Palmero		
27 Jan 1905	R.F. Villaverde		
23 Jun 1905	E. Montero Rios	P. Gullon	J. de Echegaray
20 Dec 1905	S. Moret		
6 Jul 1906	J. Lopez Dominguez		J. Navarro Reverter
25 Jan 1907	A. Maura y Montomar	M.A. Salazar	G.J. de Osma
1908			A. Gonzales-Besada
22 Oct 1909	S. Moret	J. Perez Caballero	J. Alvarado
9 Feb 1910	J. Canalejas	G. Prieto	E. Cobian
12 Nov 1912	A. Figueroa y Torres		J. Navarro Reverter
27 Oct 1913	E. Dato	Marquis de Lima	Count de Bugallal
10 Dec 1915	A. Figueroa y Torres	A. Gimeno	S. Alba
19 Apr 1917	M. Garcia-Prieto	J. Alvarado	
11 Jun 1917	E. Dato		
4 Nov 1917	M. Garcia-Prieto		
23 Mar 1918	A. Maura	E. Dato	A. Gonzales-Besada
9 Nov 1918	M. Garcia-Prieto		
5 May 1920	E. Dato	Marquis de Lima	D. Pascual
13 Mar 1921	M. Allendesalazar		M. Arguelles
8 Mar 1922	S. Guerra	F. Prida	M. Bergamin

SPAIN (*continued*)

Date of taking office	Prime Minister	Foreign Minister	Finance Minister
7 Dec 1922	Marquis de Alhucemas	S. Alba	J.M. Pedregal
3 Dec 1925	P. de Rivera	M. Yanguas	M. Calvo-Sotelo
27 Feb 1927		P. de Rivera	
1 Jan 1930	Gen. Berenguer	Duke of Alba	M. Arguelles
1 Apr 1931	A. Zamora	A. Lervoux	I. Prieto
16 Dec 1931	M. Azana y Diaz	L.Z. Escolano	J.C. Romeu
1 Mar 1933	A.L. Garcia	L.P. Romero	M.M. Ramon
4 Oct 1934		J.J.R. Garcia	
19 Feb 1936	M. Azana y Diaz	A. Barcia y Trelles	G.F. Lopez

A military rebellion under General Francisco Franco forced the civil war of 1936–1939. With the surrender of Madrid in Mar 1939 the Loyalist government fled to France and a corporate state was set up under Franco's dictatorship.

4 Sep 1936	F.L. Caballero	J.A. del Vaijo	J. Negrin
17 May 1937	J. Negrin	J. Giralt	
1 Feb 1938	F. Franco	Count de Jornada	M. Amado
10 Aug 1939		J.B. Atienza	J.L. Lopez
17 Oct 1940		R.S. Suner	
20 May 1941			J.B. Burin
3 Sep 1942		F. Gomez-Jordana	
11 Aug 1944		J.F. de Lequerica	
21 Jul 1945		A.M. Artajo	
1 Mar 1952		F. Gomez y de Llano	
1 Feb 1957		F.M. Castialla y Maiz	M. Navarro Rubio
1 Jul 1965			J.J. Espinoza
29 Oct 1969		G.L. Bravo de Costro	A.M. Luque
9 Jun 1973	Adm. L. Carrero Blanco		
11 Jun 1973		L. Lopez Rodo	A. Barrerra de Irimo
2 Jan 1974	C. Arias Navarro		
4 Jan 1974		P. Cortina Mauri	

SPAIN (*continued*)

Date of taking office	Prime Minister	Foreign Minister	Finance Minister
31 Oct 1974			R. Cabello de Alba y Grac
13 Dec 1975		J.M. de Areilza y Martines Rodas	J.M. Villar Mir
5 Jul 1976	A. Suarez Gonzalez		
8 Jul 1976		M. Oreja Aguirre	E. Carriles Galarraga
5 Jul 1977			F.F. Ordonez
6 Apr 1979			J.G. Anoveros
8 Sep 1980		J.P. Perez-Llorca	
26 Feb 1981	L. Calvo Sotelo y Bustelo		
2 Dec 1982	F. Gonzalez Marquez		
3 Dec 1982		F. Moran	M. Boyer
5 Jul 1985		F. Fernandez Ordonez	C. Solchaga
1994		J. Solana Madariaga	
Jul 1995		C. Westendorp	P. Solbes Mira
5 May 1996	J.M. Aznar Lopez	A. Matutes Juan	R. de Rato y Figaredo

SWEDEN

Date of taking office	Prime Minister	Foreign Minister	Finance Minister
12 Oct 1889	J.G.N.S. Åkerhielm	C. Lewenhaupt	E. Bull
1890			F. von Essen
24 Feb 1891	E.G. Boström		
1895			E.G. Boström
1896		L.W.A. Douglas	R. Wersäll
1899		C.H.T.A. de Lagerheim	H.H. Wachtmeister

SWEDEN (*continued*)

Date of taking office	Prime Minister	Foreign Minister	Finance Minister
12 Sep 1900	F.W. von Otter		
5 Jul 1902	E.G. Boström		E.F.W. Meyer
13 Apr 1905	J.O. Ramstedt		
2 Aug 1905	C. Lundeberg		
7 Nov 1905	K. Staaff	E.B. Trolle	J.E. Biesèrt
29 May 1906	S.A.A. Lindman		C.J.G. Swartz
11 Jun 1909		A.F. von Taube	
7 Oct 1911	K. Staaff	J.J.A. Ehrensvärd	A.T. von Adelswärd
17 Dec 1914	H. von Hammarskjöld	K.A. Wallenberg	A.F. Vennersten
29 May 1917	K. Swartz	S.A.A. Lindman	M. Carleson
19 Oct 1917	N. Edén	J. Hellner	R.W. Thorsson
10 Mar 1920	H. Branting	Baron Palmstierna	F.W. Thorsson
23 Feb 1921	O.F. von Sydow	Count H. Wrangel	K.J. Beskow
13 Oct 1921	H. Branting	H. Branting	F.W. Thorsson
9 Apr 1923	E. Trygger	Baron Marcks von Wurtemburg	K.J. Beskow
24 Jan 1925	R. Sandler	O. Unden	F.W. Thorsson
8 May 1925			E. Wigforss
7 Jun 1926	C.G. Ekman	E. Lofgren	E. Lyberg
2 Oct 1928	Adm. Lindman	E. Trygger	N. Wohlin A. Dahl
7 Jun 1930	C.G. Ekman	S.G.F. Ramel	F.T. Hamrin
7 Aug 1932	F.T. Hamrin		
24 Sep 1932	P.A. Hansson	R.J. Sandler	E. Wigforss
19 Jun 1936	M. Pehrsson	M. Westman	V.S. Ljungdahl
27 Sep 1936	P.A. Hansson	R.J. Sandler	E. Wigforss
12 Dec 1939		C. Gunther	
31 Jul 1945		O. Unden	
10 Oct 1946	T. Erlander		
30 Jun 1949			D. Hall
20 Oct 1949			P.E. Sköld
25 Sep 1955			G. Strang

SWEDEN (*continued*)

Date of taking office	Prime Minister	Foreign Minister	Finance Minister
19 Sep 1962		T. Nilsson	
14 Oct 1969	O. Palme		
29 Jun 1971		K. Wickmann	
31 Oct 1973		S. Andersson	
7 Oct 1976	T. Fälldin		
8 Oct 1976		K. Söder	I. Mundebo
13 Oct 1978	O. Ullsten		
18 Oct 1978		H. Blix	
11 Oct 1979	T. Fälldin		
12 Oct 1979		O. Ullsten	G. Bohman (Economic Affairs)
			I. Mundebo (Budget)
31 Jul 1980			I. Mundebo (Economic Affairs)
			R. Wirtén (Budget)
22 May 1981			R. Wirtén (Economic Affairs and Budget)
8 Oct 1982	O. Palme	L. Bodstrom	K.-O. Feldt
17 Oct 1985		S. Andersson	
12 Mar 1986	I. Carlsson		
27 Feb 1990		L. Hjelm-Wallén	A. Larsson
3 Oct 1991	C. Bildt	M. af Ugglas	A. Wibble
7 Oct 1994	I. Carlsson	L. Hjelm-Wallén	G. Persson
22 Mar 1996	G. Persson		E. Åsbrink
7 Oct 1998		A. Lindh	
12 Apr 1999			B. Ringholm

SWITZERLAND

The Federal Council has an active Vice-President elected for one year, and seven members each responsible for a department, elected for four years.

	Vice-President	Foreign Affairs	Finance Minister
1935	A. Meyer	G. Motta	A. Meyer
1936	G. Motta		

SWITZERLAND (*continued*)

	Vice-President	*Foreign Affairs*	*Finance Minister*
1937	J. Baumann		
1938	P. Etter		
1939	M. Pilet-Golaz		E. Wetter
1940	H. Obrecht	M. Pilet-Golaz	
1941	P. Etter		
1942	E. Celio		
1943	W. Stampfli		
1944	M. Pilet-Golaz		E. Nobs
1945	K. Koblet	M. Petitpierre	
1946	P. Etter		
1947	E. Celio		
1948	E. Nobs		
1949	M. Petitpierre		
1950	E. von Steiger		
1951	K. Koblet		
1952	P. Etter		M. Weber
1953	R. Rubattel		
1954	J. Escher		H. Streuli
1955	M. Feldmann		
1956	H. Streuli		
1957	T. Holenstein		
1958	P. Chaudet		
1959	G. Lepovi		
1960	F. Traugott Wahlen		J. Bourgknecht
1961	P. Chaudet		
1962	J. Bourgknecht	F. Traugott Wahlen	
1963	L. van Moos		R. Bonvin
1964	H.P. Schudi		
1965	H. Schaffner		
1966	R. Bonvin	W. Spuhler	
1967	W. Spuhler		
1968	L. van Moos		N. Celio

SWITZERLAND (*continued*)

	Vice-President	Foreign Affairs	Finance Minister
1969	H.P. Schudi		
1970	R. Gnägi	P. Graber	
1971	N. Celio		
1972	R. Bonvin		
1973	E. Brugger		G.-A. Chevellaz
1974	P. Graber		
1975	R. Gnägi		
1976	K. Furgler		
1977	W. Ritschard		
1978	H. Hürlimann	P. Aubert	
1979	G.-A. Chevallaz		
1980	K. Furgler		W. Ritschard
1981	F. Honegger		
1982	P. Aubert		
1983	G.-A. Chevallaz		
1984	L. Schlumpf		O. Stich
1985	K. Furgler		
1986	A. Egli		
1987	P. Aubert		
1988	O. Stich		
1989	J.-P. Delamuraz	R. Felber	
1990	A. Koller		
1991	R. Felber		
1992	A. Ogi	F. Cotti	
1993	O. Stich		
1994	K. Villiger		
1995	J.-P. Delamuraz		K. Villiger
1996	A. Koller		
1997	F. Cotti		
1998	R. Dreifuss		
1999	A. Ogi	J. Deiss	

TURKEY

Date of taking office	Prime Minister	Foreign Minister	Finance Minister
Nov 1895	Halil Rifat	A. Tewfik	Sabri Rey
1897			A. Nazif
1898			A. Tewfik
1899			Rechad Bey
13 Nov 1901	Said Pasha		
16 Jan 1903	M. Ferid		A. Nazif
1906			Zia Pasha
22 Jul 1908	Said Pasha		
7 Aug 1908	M. Kamil		
31 Mar 1909	A. Tewfik		
May 1909	H. Hilmi	Rifaat Pasha	Djavid Bey
12 Jan 1910	I. Hakki		
4 Oct 1911	Said Pasha	Assim Bey	Nail Bey
22 Jul 1912	G. Ahmed Mukhtar		
30 Oct 1912	M. Kâmil	Gabriel Effendi	Abdurrahman Bey
23 Jan 1913	M. Sevket		
15 Jun 1913	Said Halim	Said Halim	Rifaat Bey
4 Feb 1917	M. Talât	A. Nessimi	Djavid Bey
Oct 1918	A. Izzet		
Nov 1918	A. Tewfik		
5 Apr 1920	(Grand Vizier) Damad Ferid Pasha	Damad Ferid Pasha	Reshai Bey
21 Oct 1920	(Grand Vizier) Tewfik Pasha	Sefa Bey	Abdullah Bey
		Izzet Pasha	Nuzhet Bey
20 Jan 1921	New constitution established a Council of Commissioners instead of a cabinet.		
1 Feb 1923	(President) Reouf Bey	Ismet Pasha	Abdul Halik Bey
30 Oct 1923	Ismet Pasha		
4 Mar 1925		Tewfik Rustu Bey	
			Hassan Bey
			Abdul Halik Bey

TURKEY (*continued*)

Date of taking office	Prime Minister	Foreign Minister	Finance Minister
2 Nov 1927			S. Saracoglu
28 Sep 1930			Abdul Halik Bey
1 May 1931			Fuad Agrali
1 Mar 1935	Ismet Inönü		
13 Oct 1937	J. Bayar		
12 Nov 1938		S. Saracoglu	
27 Jan 1939	R. Saydam		
11 Mar 1943	S. Saracoglu	N. Menemencioglu	
15 Jun 1944		S. Saracoglu	
14 Sep 1944		H. Saka	N.E. Sumer
7 Aug 1946	R. Peker		H. Nazmikismir
9 Sep 1947	H. Saka	N. Sadak	
11 Jun 1948			S. Adalan
16 Jan 1949	S. Gunaltay		I. Aksal
22 May 1950	A. Menderes	F. Koprulu	H. Ayan
10 Mar 1951			H. Polatkan
15 Apr 1955		A. Menderes	
9 Dec 1955		F. Koprulu	N. Okmen
20 Jun 1956		E. Menderes	
30 Nov 1956			H. Polatkan
25 Nov 1957		F.R. Zorlu	
28 May 1960	C. Gursel	S. Sarpa	E. Alican
24 Dec 1960			K. Kurdas
20 Nov 1961	I. Inönü		S. Inan
25 Jun 1962		F.C. Erkin	F. Melen
21 Feb 1965	S.H. Urguplu	H. Isik	I. Gursan
27 Oct 1965	S. Demirel	I.S. Çağlayangil	
12 Nov 1966			C. Bilgehan
3 Nov 1969			M. Erez
1 Mar 1971	N. Erim	O. Olcay	S.N. Ergin
22 May 1972	F. Melen	U.H. Bayülken	S. Özbek
15 Apr 1973	N. Talû	U.H. Bayülken	S.T. Müftüoglu

TURKEY (*continued*)

Date of taking office	Prime Minister	Foreign Minister	Finance Minister
25 Jan 1974	B. Ecevit	T. Gunes	D. Baykal
17 Nov 1974	S. Irmak	M. Esenbel	B. Gürsoy
31 Mar 1975	S. Demirel	I.S. Çağlayangil	Y. Ergenekon
21 Jun 1977	B. Ecevit	G. Okçün	B. Üstünel
21 Jul 1977	S. Demirel	I.S. Çağlayangil	C. Bilgehan
5 Jan 1978	B. Ecevit	G. Okçün	Z. Müezzinoğlu
12 Nov 1979	S. Demirel	H. Erkmen	I. Sezgin

The government was overthrown on 12 Sep 1980 and its powers taken over by a National Security Council of the armed forces.

21 Sep 1980	B. Ülüsü	I. Turkmen	K. Erdem
14 Jul 1982			A.B. Kafaoğlu
13 Dec 1983	T. Özal	V. Halefoğlu	V. Arikan
26 Oct 1984			A.K. Alptemoçin
22 Dec 1987		M. Yilmaz	
31 Mar 1989			E. Pakdemirli
9 Nov 1989	Y. Akbulut		
22 Feb 1990		A. Bozer	
29 Mar 1990			A. Kahveci
12 Oct 1990		A.K. Alptemoçin	
23 Jun 1991	M. Yilmaz	S. Giray	
20 Nov 1991	S. Demirel		S. Oral
21 Nov 1991		H. Çetin	
25 Jun 1993	T. Çiller		I. Attila
27 Jul 1994		M. Soysal	
12 Dec 1994		M. Karayalçin	
27 Mar 1995		E. İnönü	
5 Oct 1995		C. Kirca	
30 Oct 1995		D. Baykal	
6 Mar 1996	M. Yilmaz	E. Gönensay	
7 Mar 1996			L. Kayalar
28 Jun 1996	N. Erbakan	T. Çiller	A. Şener

TURKEY (*continued*)

Date of taking office	Prime Minister	Foreign Minister	Finance Minister
20 Jun 1997	M. Yilmaz	I. Cem	Z. Temizel
7 Jan 1999	B. Ecevit		
3 May 1999			S. Oral

UKRAINE

Date of taking office	Prime Minister	Foreign Minister	Finance Minister
1992	V. Fokin	V.A. Kravtev	
13 Oct 1992	L. Kuchma	A. Zlenko	
22 Sep 1993	Y. Zvyahisky (until 27 Sep 1993 then vacant)		
16 Jun 1994	V. Masol		
1 Mar 1995	Y. Marchuk	H. Udovenko	P. Hermanchuk
27 May 1996	P. Lazarenko	G. Udovenko	V. Koronevsky
16 Jul 1997	V. Pustovoitenko	B. Tarasyuk	I. Mityukov
22 Dec 1999	V. Yushchenko		

UNITED KINGDOM

Date of taking office	Prime Minister	Foreign Minister	Chancellor of the Exchequer
25 Jun 1895	Lord Salisbury	Lord Salisbury	M. Hicks-Beach
1 Nov 1900		Lord Lansdowne	
12 Jul 1902	A.J. Balfour		
Aug 1902			C.T. Ritchie
5 Oct 1903			J.A. Chamberlain
10 Dec 1905	H. Campbell-Bannerman	E. Grey	H.H. Asquith
6 Apr 1908	H.H. Asquith		D. Lloyd-George
26 May 1915			R. McKenna

UNITED KINGDOM (*continued*)

Date of taking office	Prime Minister	Foreign Minister	Chancellor of the Exchequer
6 Dec 1916	D. Lloyd-George		
10 Dec 1916		A.J. Balfour	A. Bonar Law
10 Jan 1919			A. Chamberlain
23 Oct 1919		Lord Curzon	
1 Apr 1921			Sir R. Horne
23 Oct 1922	A. Bonar Law		
24 Oct 1922			S. Baldwin
22 May 1923	S. Baldwin		
27 Aug 1923			N. Chamberlain
22 Jan 1924	J.R. MacDonald	J.R. MacDonald	P. Snowden
4 Nov 1924	S. Baldwin		
6 Nov 1924		Sir A. Chamberlain	W. Churchill
5 Jun 1929	J.R. MacDonald		
7 Jun 1929		A. Henderson	P. Snowden
25 Aug 1931		Marquis of Reading	
5 Nov 1931		Sir J. Simon	N. Chamberlain
7 Jun 1935	S. Baldwin	Sir S. Hoare	
22 Dec 1935		A. Eden	
28 May 1937	N. Chamberlain		Sir J. Simon
21 Feb 1938		Viscount Halifax	
10 May 1940	W. Churchill		
12 May 1940			Sir K. Wood
22 Dec 1940		A. Eden	
24 Sep 1943			Sir J. Anderson
26 Jul 1945	C. Attlee		
27 Jul 1945		E. Bevin	H. Dalton
13 Nov 1947			Sir S. Cripps
19 Oct 1950			H. Gaitskell
9 Mar 1951		H. Morrison	
26 Oct 1951	Sir W. Churchill	Sir A. Eden	R. Butler
6 Apr 1955	Sir A. Eden		

UNITED KINGDOM (*continued*)

Date of taking office	Prime Minister	Foreign Minister	Chancellor of the Exchequer
7 Apr 1955		H. Macmillan	
20 Dec 1955		S. Lloyd	H. Macmillan
10 Jan 1957	H. Macmillan		
13 Jan 1957			P. Thorneycroft
6 Jan 1958			D. Heathcoat Amory
27 Jul 1960		Lord Home	S. Lloyd
13 Jul 1962			R. Maudling
18 Oct 1963	Sir A. Douglas-Home		
20 Oct 1963		R. Butler	
16 Oct 1964	H. Wilson	P. Gordon Walker	J. Callaghan
22 Jan 1965		M. Stewart	
11 Aug 1966		G. Brown	
30 Nov 1967			R. Jenkins
16 Mar 1968		M. Stewart	
19 Jun 1970	E. Heath		
20 Jun 1970		Sir A. Douglas-Home	I. Macleod
25 Jul 1970			A. Barber
4 Mar 1974	H. Wilson	J. Callaghan	D. Healey
5 Apr 1976	J. Callaghan		
8 Apr 1976		A. Crosland	
21 Feb 1977		D. Owen	
4 May 1979	M. Thatcher		
5 May 1979		Lord Carrington	Sir G. Howe
5 Apr 1982		F. Pym	
12 Jun 1983		Sir G. Howe	N. Lawson
24 Jul 1989		J. Major	
26 Oct 1989			J. Major
28 Oct 1989		D. Hurd	

UNITED KINGDOM (*continued*)

Date of taking office	Prime Minister	Foreign Minister	Chancellor of the Exchequer
28 Nov 1990	J. Major		
29 Nov 1990			N. Lamont
27 May 1993			K. Clarke
5 Jul 1995		M. Rifkind	
2 May 1997	A. Blair	R. Cook	G. Brown

USSR

Date of taking office	Prime Minister	Foreign Minister	Finance Minister
8 Nov 1917	V.I. Lenin	G.V. Chicherin	N.N. Krestinskii
1 Dec 1922			G.Y. Sokolnikov
1 Jan 1924	A.I. Rykov		
1 Mar 1926			N.P. Bryukhanov
21 Jul 1930		M.M. Litvinov	
1 Jan 1931	V.M. Molotov		G.F. Grinko
1 Aug 1937			V.Y. Chubar
19 Jan 1938			A.G. Zverev
3 May 1939		V.M. Molotov	
7 May 1941	J.V. Stalin		

Ministers were called People's Commissars until 1946.

17 Feb 1948			A.N. Kosygin
28 Dec 1948			A.G. Zverev
4 Mar 1949		A.Y. Vyshinski	
6 Mar 1953	G.M. Malenkov	V.M. Molotov	
8 Feb 1955	N.A. Bulganin		
1 Jun 1956		D.T. Shepilov	
15 Feb 1957		A.A. Gromyko	

USSR (*continued*)

Date of taking office	Prime Minister	Foreign Minister	Finance Minister
31 Mar 1958	N.S. Khrushchev		
16 May 1960			V.F. Garbuzov
15 Oct 1964	A.N. Kosygin		
23 Oct 1980	N.A. Tikhonov		
2 Jul 1985		E. Shevardnadze	
27 Sep 1985	N.I. Ryzhkov		
12 Nov 1985			B.I. Grostev
17 Jul 1989			V.S. Pavlov
15 Jan 1991		A. Bessmertnykh	
14 Jan 1991	V.S. Pavlov		
25 Aug 1991	I. Silayev		

The USSR collapsed on 25 Dec 1991.

YUGOSLAVIA

Date of taking office	Prime Minister	Foreign Minister	Finance Minister
12 Feb 1921	S. Protić	M. Trumbić	V. Janković
24 Dec 1921	N. Pasić	M. Ničić	K. Kumanudi
3 Dec 1922			M. Stojadinović
8 Apr 1926	N. Uzunović		N. Uzunović
1 Feb 1927		N. Perić	B. Narković
23 Feb 1928	V. Vukitčević	V. Marinković	
6 Jan 1929	Gen. P. Zivković		S. Svrljuga
4 Apr 1932	V. Marinković		M. Djordjević
11 Jul 1932	M. Serškić	B. Jevtić	
27 Jan 1934	N. Uzunović		
Dec 1934	B. Jevtić		
24 Jun 1935	M. Stojadinović	M. Stojadinović	D. Letica
5 Feb 1939	D. Cvetković	A.C. Marković	V. Juričić

YUGOSLAVIA (*continued*)

Date of taking office	Prime Minister	Foreign Minister	Finance Minister
26 Aug 1939			J. Šutej
27 Mar 1941	Gen. D. Simović	M. Ninčić	

In 1941 the Axis powers occupied Yugoslavia. A government-in-exile was established in London in Jun 1941 and eventually moved to Cairo.

11 Jan 1942	S. Jovanović		
Jun 1943	M. Trifimović		
10 Aug 1943	B. Purić		I. Cicin-Sain
7 Mar 1945	Marshal J.B. Tito	I. Subasić	S. Zejević
2 Feb 1946		S. Simić	
6 May 1948			D. Radosavljević
31 Aug 1948		E. Kardelj	
1 Nov 1951			M. Popović
14 Jan 1953		K. Popović	R. Nedelković
1 Jan 1954			N. Bozinović
1 Jan 1957			A. Humo
1 Jan 1959			N. Minčov
1 Jan 1963			K. Gligorov
29 Jun 1963	P. Stambolić		
23 Apr 1965		M. Nikezić	
18 May 1967	M. Spiljak		J. Smole
28 Apr 1969		M. Tepavac	
17 May 1969	M. Ribičić		
30 Jul 1971	D. Bijedić		
1 Nov 1972		J. Petrić	
5 Dec 1972		M. Minić	
17 May 1974			M. Cemović
14 Feb 1977	V. Djuranović		
16 May 1978		J. Vrhovec	P. Kostić
16 May 1982	M. Planinć	L. Mojsov	J. Florijanić
12 Mar 1989	A. Marković	B. Lončar	B. Žekan

FORMER YUGOSLAVIA

Date of taking office	Prime Minister	Foreign Minister	Finance Minister
14 Jul 1992	M. Panić		
Feb 1993	R. Kontić	M. Milutinović	J. Žebić
19 May 1998	M. Bulatović	Z. Jovanović	D. Pesić

5
Elections

ALBANIA

In Mar 1920 the Lushnjë congress elected a National Assembly and a Senate. Political parties began to emerge: a group known as 'liberals' and one known as 'conservatives'.

Elections were held on 4 Feb 1921 to a National Assembly of 77 deputies and a Senate of 18 (6 of whom were appointed). Alternative governments were formed by the conservative feudalistic Progressive Party and the People's Party which itself split into a right-wing faction headed by A. Zogu and a liberal faction (becoming a Democratic party) headed by Bishop Fan Noli.

At the elections of Dec 1923, 40 Progressive and 35 People's Party candidates were returned, together with 20 independents. Fan Noli left the People's Party to form an opposition and seized power on 17 Jun 1924. His government itself split into Radical and National Democrats, and Zogu seized power again in Dec 1924.

By a new constitution of Feb 1925 a bicameral National Assembly was set up with deputies elected every three years and a partly-elected Senate. The President was to be elected by the National Assembly for a seven-year period. In the 1925 elections opposition groups were not permitted to stand and complete victory went to the Zogists. Zogu became President.

By a new constitution of 1 Sep 1928 the Senate was abolished and a National Assembly of 56 set up. Political parties were forbidden and elections were indirect and on a limited suffrage. Government-nominated candidates were presented to the electors for approval. Albania became a monarchy and Zogu its king under the name Zog I. The elections of 1932 and 1937 were held under these conditions.

Note: Some parties are referred to by initials. *See* Chapter 6, 'Political Parties', for full names.

On 2 Dec 1945 elections were held for a new People's Assembly. There were 82 candidates standing on the single Democratic Front list for 82 seats; 89.9 per cent of the electorate voted, and 93.16 per cent of votes cast were for the Democratic Front.

At the elections of 28 May 1950 the electorate was 541 241, the turnout 99.43 per cent of whom 98.18 per cent voted for the 121 deputies (1 per 10 000). Turnout in subsequent elections up to 1970 (30 May 1954; 1 Jun 1958; 3 Jun 1962; 11 Jul 1966; 20 Sep 1970) was never less than 99 per cent and reached (it was claimed) 100 per cent in 1970. One deputy represented 8000 electors. Elections were held every 4 years. In subsequent elections, in Oct 1974, Nov 1978 and Nov 1982, there was 100 per cent turnout for the 250 candidates of the Democratic Front.

In elections held on 1 Feb 1987, it was reported that 1 830 652 valid votes were cast for 250 candidates, a turnout of 100 per cent. There was one invalid vote.

1991 (Mar–Apr)	Albania Party of Labour (Communists)	169
	Democratic Party	75
	Omonia (minority Greek)	5
	National Veterans' Committee	1
	Others (Agrarian Party, Ecology Party, Republican Party)	–
		250

1992 (Mar)

	Seats	%
Democratic Party	92	68
Socialist Party (ex-communists)	38	22
Social Democratic Party	7	4
Omonia (minority Greek)	2	3
Republican Party	1	3

1996 (May/Jun)

The elections of 26 May and 2 Jun 1996 resulted in the Democratic Party claiming 122 seats and 87 per cent of the vote. However the opposition, led by the Socialists, withdrew because of alleged intimidation.

1997 (Jun/Jul)

The elections of 29 Jun and 6 Jul 1997, held against a background of virtual anarchy, resulted in a Socialist victory. They secured 100 seats in the 155-seat assembly. The Democratic Party of President Berisha won 29. In third place was the Social Democratic Party of Albania with 8 seats. The results were disputed by nearly all the participants.

ARMENIA

For elections 1918–1921, *see* note on p. 311.

Elections in Armenia since independence in 1991 have consisted of the presidential election of 16 Oct 1991 (won by Levon Ter-Petrosyan of the Pan-Armenian National Movement with 87 per cent of the votes cast), the general elections of 1995 and 1999, and presidential elections in 1996. In the 1995 general election, 40 of the 190 seats were filled by proportional representation. The elections were dominated by the Republican bloc (a coalition of the Pan-Armenian National Movement and 5 other parties) which secured 119 of the 190 seats.

At the presidential election in 1996, President Ter-Petrosyan won 51.75 per cent of the votes cast, Vazgen Manukyan 41.29 per cent and the Communist Sergei Badalyan 6.34 per cent.

In the parliamentary elections of 30 May 1999, the Unity Bloc (Miasnutiun) was the easy winner (with 55 seats and 41.2 per cent of the vote). In second place was the Communist Party of Armenia (HKK) with 11 seats (12.1 per cent). The Right and Accord Bloc won 6 seats (8 per cent of the vote) and the Armenian Revolutionary Federation (Dashnak) 9 seats (7.7 per cent).

AUSTRIA

Voting procedures. Direct secret proportional elections in multi-member constituencies. Tyrol and Vorarlberg provinces had compulsory voting by law from 1919, Styria from 1949. Universal adult suffrage for all over 20 (over 21 in 1930 and 1945).

The calculation of aggregate voting figures for the former Austria–Hungary is almost impossible before the elections of 1907, when universal male suffrage was introduced. The results for the last two elections before the dissolution of the Habsburg Monarchy were dominated by the Christian Social Party. The three largest parties on each occasion are given below:

	Party	Seats	% votes
1907 (14 May)	Christian Social Party	94	52.3
	Social Democrats	28	21.0
	German People's Party	15	6.6

1911 (13 Jun)	Christian Social Party	70	45.5
	Social Democrats	33	25.4
	German Freedom Party	15	5.1

Since 1919, elections have been held as follows:

	Electorate	Valid votes	Votes per party		Seats	% of electorate	% of votes
1919	3554242	2973454	SDP	1211814	69	34.1	40.7
			CSP	1068382	63	30.0	36.0
			Grossdeutsche Partei	545938	24	15.4	18.4
1920	3752212	2980328	CSP	1245531	85	33.2	41.8
			SDP	1072709	69	28.6	36.0
			GdVP	514127	28	13.7	17.2
1923	3849484	3312606	CSP	1490876	82	38.7	45.0
			SDP	1311870	68	34.1	39.6
			GdVP	422600	15	11.0	12.8
1927	4119626	3641526	CSP ⎱ GdVP ⎰	1756761[1]	73 / 12	42.6	41.4 / 6.8
			SDP	1539635	71	37.4	42.3
1930	4121282	3687082	SDP	1516913	72	36.8	41.1
			CSP	1314468	66	31.9	35.6
			NWbLb	427962	19	10.4	11.6
1945	3449605	3217354	ÖVP	1602227	85	46.4	49.8
			SPÖ	1434898	76	41.6	44.6
			KPÖ	174257	4	5.0	5.4
1949	4391815	4193733	ÖVP	1846581	77	42.0	44.0
			SPÖ	1623524	67	37.0	38.7
			FPÖ ⎱ WdU ⎰	489213[1]	16	11.1	11.7
1953	4586870	4318688	SPÖ	1818517	73	39.6	42.1
			ÖVP	1781777	74	38.8	41.2
			FPÖ ⎱ WdU ⎰	472866[1]	14	10.3	10.9
1956	4614464	4351908	ÖVP	1999989	82	43.3	46.1
			SPÖ	1873292	74	40.6	43.0

[1] Two-party front.

Electorate	Valid votes	Votes per party		Seats	% of electorate	% of votes
		FPÖ ⎫ WdU ⎭	283749[1]	6	6.1	6.5
1959 4696633	4362856	SPÖ	1953935	78	41.6	44.8
		ÖVP	1928043	79	41.0	44.2
		FPÖ	336110	8	7.1	7.7
1962 4805351	4456131	ÖVP	2024501	81	42.1	45.4
		SPÖ	1960685	76	40.8	44.0
		FPÖ	313895	8	6.5	7.0
1966 4886534	4531864	ÖVP	2191128	85	44.8	48.4
		SPÖ	1928922	74	39.5	42.6
		FPÖ	242599	6	5.0	5.3
1970 5045841	4588961	ÖVP	2051012	79	40.6	44.7
		SPÖ	2221981	81	44.0	48.4
		FPÖ	253425	5	5.0	5.5
1971 4984448	4556990	ÖVP	1964713	80	39.4	43.1
		SPÖ	2280168	93	45.7	50.0
		FPÖ	248473	10	5.0	5.5
1975 5019168	4610533	SPÖ	2324309	93	46.3	50.4
		ÖVP	1980474	80	39.4	42.9
		FPÖ	249317	10	4.9	5.4
		KPÖ	54971	–	1.1	1.2
		Others	1462	–	–	–
1979 5186676	4728239	SPÖ	2412778	95	46.5	51.0
		ÖVP	1981286	77	38.1	41.9
		FPÖ	286644	11	5.5	6.1
		KPÖ	45270	–	0.9	1.0
		Others	2261	–	–	–
1983 5316438	4750773	SPÖ	2270997	90	42.7	47.8
		ÖVP	2052714	81	38.7	43.2
		FPÖ	236320	12	4.4	5.0
		VGÖ	89694	–	1.7	1.9
		ALÖ	60150	–	1.1	1.3
		KPÖ	31408	–	0.6	0.7
		Others	9490	–	0.2	0.2

The results of the elections since 1986 have been:

	Party	Seats	% of votes
1986	SPÖ	80	43.1
	ÖVP	77	41.3
	FPÖ	18	9.7
	KPÖ	–	0.7
	Greens	8	4.8
	Others	–	0.3
1990	SPÖ	81	42.8
	ÖVP	60	32.1
	FPÖ	33	16.6
	Greens	9	4.8
	Others	–	3.7
1994	SPÖ	65	34.9
	ÖVP	52	27.7
	FPÖ	42	22.5
	Greens (GAL)	13	7.3
	Liberal Forum	11	6.0
	Others	–	1.6
1995	SPÖ	71	38.2
	ÖVP	53	28.3
	FPÖ	40	21.9
	Liberal Forum	9	4.8
	Greens (GAL)	10	5.5
	Others	–	1.4
1999	Social Democrats (SPÖ)	65	33.1
	Freedom Party (FPÖ)	52	26.9
	People's Party (ÖVP)	52	26.9
	Greens	14	7.4
	Liberal Forum	–	3.6
	Others	–	2.1

BELARUS

Following independence, a new constitution was adopted in Mar 1994. In the second round of presidential elections on 10 Jul 1994 Alyaksandr Lukashenka easily defeated Vyacheslav Kebich (85 per cent to 15 per cent). The legislative elections of May 1995 failed to fill sufficient seats in the Supreme Council to form a quorum. The party affiliation of those elected was frequently unclear. Fresh elections were held in 141 seats in Nov and a third phase in Dec. Of 198 elected deputies on this occasion, 95 were without party affiliation. Of the 260-seat Supreme Council, the Party of Communists of Belarus led with 42 seats, the Agrarian Party had 33. No other party reached double figures.

BELGIUM

Voting procedures. Proportional representation in single-member constituencies. Vote for all males over 25 for the Chamber of Representatives and over 30 for the Senate, until the constitutional revision of 1920–1921 set the electoral age at 21. Women received the right to vote in 1948.

Between 1900 and 1918, elections were held on the following occasions for the Chamber of Representatives:

27 May 1900	24 May 1908
25 May 1902	22 May 1910
29 May 1904	2 Jun 1912
27 May 1906	24 May 1914

Only the elections of 1900 and 1912 were general elections for which meaningful figures can be produced. Both elections were dominated by the Catholic Party (86 seats out of 152 with 48.5 per cent of the vote in 1900 and 101 seats out of 186 in 1912 with 51.1 per cent of the vote).

	Votes per party		*Seats*	*% of votes*
1919	Catholics	645462	71	36.62
	Socialists	645075	70	36.60
	Liberals	310853	34	17.64
1921	Catholics	715041	69	37.01
	Socialists	672445	68	34.80
	Liberals	343929	33	17.80
1925	Socialists	820116	78	39.43
	Catholics	751058	75	36.11
	Liberals	304467	23	14.64

	Votes per party		Seats	% of votes
1929	Socialists	803 347	70	36.02
	Catholics	788 914	71	35.37
	Liberals	369 114	28	16.55
1932	Catholics	899 887	79	38.55
	Socialists	866 817	73	37.11
	Liberals	333 567	24	14.28
1936	Socialists	758 485	70	32.10
	Catholics	653 717	61	27.67
	Liberals	292 972	23	12.40
	Rexists	271 491	21	11.49
1939	Catholics	764 843	73	32.73
	Socialists	705 969	64	30.18
	Liberals	401 991	33	17.19
1946	Catholics	1 006 293	92	42.53
	Socialists	746 738	69	31.56
	Communists	300 099	23	12.68
	Liberals	211 143	17	8.92
1949	Catholics	2 190 898	105	43.56
	Socialists	1 496 539	66	29.75
	Liberals	767 180	29	15.25
1950	Catholics	2 356 608	108	47.68
	Socialists	1 705 781	77	34.51
	Liberals	556 102	20	11.25
1954	Catholics	2 123 408	95	41.14
	Socialists	1 927 015	86	37.34
	Liberals	626 983	25	12.15
1958	Catholics	2 465 549	104	46.50
	Socialists	1 897 646	84	35.79
	Liberals	585 999	21	11.05
1961	Catholics	2 182 642	96	41.46
	Socialists	1 933 424	84	36.73
	Liberals	649 376	20	12.33
1965	Catholics	1 785 211	77	34.45
	Socialists	1 465 503	64	28.28
	Liberals	1 119 991	48	21.61

	Votes per party		*Seats*	*% of votes*
1968	Catholics	1643785	69	31.8
	Socialists	1449172	59	28.0
	Liberals	1080894	47	20.9
1971	Catholics	1587195	67	30.1
	Socialists	1438626	61	27.2
	Liberals	865657	34	16.4
1974	Catholics	1699233	72	32.3
	Socialists	1401288	59	26.7
	Liberals	798896	30	15.2
	FDF/Rassemblement	575616	25	11.0
	Volksunie	536195	22	10.2
	Communists	169668	4	3.2
	Others	75758	–	1.4
1977	Catholics	1459997	56	26.2
	Socialists/PSC	543608	24	9.7
	PSB ⎱	1473329	35	13.4
	BSP ⎰		27	13.0
	PVV	475912	17	8.5
	PRLW ⎱	328571	14 ⎱	7.0
	PL ⎰	63041	2 ⎰	
	Volksunie	559634	20	10.0
	FDF	237280	10	4.7
	RW	158559	5	2.4
	Communists	151421	2	2.7
	Vlaams Blok ⎱		– ⎱	
	RAD-UDRT ⎰	122878	– ⎰	2.2
	Others ⎰		– ⎰	
1978	Catholics (CVP)	1446056	57	26.1
	Socialists (PSC)	560565	25	10.1
	PSB	719926	32	13.0
	BSP	684465	26	12.4
	PVV	571520	22	10.3
	PRLW	287942 ⎱	14	
	PL	42156 ⎰	1	6.0

Votes per party		Seats	% of votes
Volksunie	388 368	14	7.0
FDF	235 152	11	4.2
RW	158 563	4	2.9
Communists	180 088	4	3.2
Vlaams Blok ⎫		1	
RAD-UDRT ⎬	258 405	1	4.7
Others ⎭			
1981 CVP	1 165 155	43	19.3
PSC	430 712	18	7.1
PS	765 055	35	12.7
SP	744 586	26	12.4
PRL	516 291	24	8.6
PVV	776 882	28	12.9
VU	588 430	20	9.8
FDF			
RW	253 703	8	4.2
Communists	138 992	2	2.3
UDRT	163 725	3	2.7
Ecology	289 901	4	4.8
Vlaams Blok	66 424	1	1.1
Others	123 250		2.1
1985 CVP	1 291 595	49	21.3
PS	834 488	35	13.8
SP	883 065	32	14.6
PRL	619 392	24	10.2
PVV	650 604	22	10.7
PSC	482 559	20	8.0
VU	477 408	16	7.9
Ecolo	152 481	5	2.5 ⎫
Agalev	226 998	4	3.7 ⎭
FDF	72 361	3	1.2 ⎫
PW	9 294		0.2 ⎭
Vlaams Blok	85 330	1	1.4
Others	278 840	1	4.6

	Votes per party		Seats	*% of votes*
1987	CVP	1 194 687	43	19.5
	PS	961 429	40	15.7
	SP	913 975	32	14.9
	PVV	709 137	25	11.6
	PRL	577 897	23	9.4
	PSC	491 839	19	8.0
	VU	494 229	16	8.1
	Agalev	275 307	6	4.5
	Ecolo	157 985	3	2.6
	FDF	71 340	3	1.2
	Vlaams Blok	116 410	2	1.9
	Others	176 977	–	2.9

		Seats	*% votes*
1991 (24 Nov)	Christian Peoples Party (CVP)	39	16.7
	Socialist Party (PS)	35	13.6
	Socialist Party (SP)	28	12.0
	PVV (later renamed VLD)	26	11.9
	Liberal Reform Party (PRL)	20	8.2
	Social Christian Party (PSC)	18	7.8
	Vlaams Blok (VB)	12	6.6
	Ecolo	10	5.1
	Agalev	7	4.9
	Others	7	7.3
1995 (21 May)	Christian Peoples Party (CVP)	29	17.2
	Social Christian Party (PSC)	12	7.7
	Flemish Liberals & Democrats (VLD)	21	13.1
	Liberal Reform Party (PRL-FDF)	18	10.3
	Socialist Party (SP)	20	12.6
	Socialist Party (PS)	21	11.9
	Vlaams Blok (VB)	11	7.8
	Volksunie (VU)	5	4.7
	National Front (FN)	2	2.3

	Agalev	5	4.4
	Ecolo	6	4.0
1999 (Jun)	Flemish Liberals and Democrats (VLD)	23	14.3
	Christian Social Party (CVP)	22	14.1
	Liberal Reform Party – Democratic Front	18	10.1
	Socialist Party (SP)	14	9.6
	Socialist Party (PS)	19	10.1
	Vlaams Blok (VB)	15	9.9
	Social Christian Party (PSC)	10	5.9
	Volksunie (VU)	8	5.6
	National Front (FN)	1	1.5
	Agalev (Flemish Environmentalists)	9	7.0
	Ecolo	11	7.3
	Others	–	4.6

BOSNIA–HERCEGOVINA

The elections of Nov–Dec 1990 had the following outcome:

Party of Democratic Action	86
Serbian Democratic Party	72
Croat Democratic Union	44
League of Communists*/Socialist Alliance	20*
Alliance of Reform Forces	13
Others	5
	240

* Later renamed Socialist Democratic Party.

As agreed at the Dayton Peace Conference, nationwide elections were to take place in Bosnia–Hercegovina in Sep 1996. The outcome (for the presidential contest) was:

Candidate	Party	Votes
A Izetbegovic	Muslim/Democratic Party of Action	729 034
M Krajisnik	Serb/Serb Democratic Party	690 373
K Zubak	Croat/Croatian Democratic Union	342 007
M Ivanic	Serb/Socialist Party	305 803

Candidate	Party	Votes
H Silajdzic	Muslim/Party for Bosnia–Hercegovina	123 784
I Komsic	United List	38 261

The second elections since the 1995 Dayton Peace Accord were held on 12 and 13 September 1998. These were for the national presidency, for the Serb Republic and for the 42-seat All-Bosnian House of Representatives. Parties with 4 seats or more in the House of Representatives were:

Party	Seats	% vote
Coalition for a Single and Democratic Bosnia–Hercegovina (KCD)	17	40.0
Croatian Democratic Union of Bosnia–Hercegovina (HDZ)	6	14.0
Serb Democratic Party (SDS)	4	10.0
Social Democratic Party of Bosnia–Hercegovina (SDP)	4	10.0
Sloga	4	10.0

BULGARIA

By 1900 Bulgaria was a constitutional monarchy with an electoral system established by the 1879 Turnovo constitution. The legislature was the unicameral National Assembly, *Narodno Sŭbranie*, of deputies each representing 10 000 electors, elected by universal suffrage at 21 years for 3- (later 4-) year terms. To pass any constitutional amendment a Grand National Assembly, *Veliko Narodno Sŭbranie*, was elected of twice the usual number of deputies. Elections were on the proportional representation system.

		Votes per party	*Seats*
1923 (23 Apr)	Agrarians	569 000	212
	Communists	204 000	16
	Social Democrats	28 000	2
	Middle class and traditional parties	275 000	15
1923 (18 Nov)	Democratic *entente* in a bloc with		202⎫
	Social Democrats	638 675	29⎭
	Left-wing-Agrarians in a bloc with		31⎫
	Communists	217 607	8⎭
	Right-wing-Agrarians	42 737	19
	National Liberals	36 507	7

By an electoral law of 1927 proportional representation (abolished in 1923) was restored in a system favourable to the government party, Democratic *entente*, enabling it to win 168 of the 273 seats with 39 per cent of the votes in the election of 29 May 1927:

	Votes per party	*Seats*
Democratic *entente*	504 703	168
'Iron bloc' of Agrarians,		42
Social Democrats and		10
Artisans	285 758	4
Workers (*i.e.* Communists)	29 210	4
National Liberals		14
Democrats		12
Macedonians		11
Radicals		2

A new proportional representation system was introduced for the elections of 21 Jun 1931, the results of which were:

	Votes per party	*Seats*
Agrarians		69
'Popular bloc' of Democrats		43
Kyorchev Liberals and		32
Radicals	590 000	8
Democratic *entente* in a		
bloc with		63
Smilov Liberals	417 000	15
Workers (*i.e.* Communists)	166 000	33
Macedonians		8
Social Democrats		5

The government was taken over on 19 May 1934 in a *coup d'état* by a group of army officers in alliance with a group of intellectuals associated with the journal *Zveno*. Tsar Boris overthrew this government in turn on 22 Jan 1935 and set up a royal dictatorship.

By an electoral law of 1937 the number of deputies was reduced to 160, political parties were banned and unmarried women disfranchised.

At the election of Mar 1938 Agrarians and Social Democrats stood in opposition to the government in the Bulgarian version of the Popular Front called the 'Constitutional bloc', and won 63 seats. At the elections of 30 Jan 1940 opposition candidates (including 9 Communists) won 20 seats.

On 9 Sep 1944 at the beginning of the Soviet occupation a 'Fatherland Front' government of Communists and anti-fascists was set up.

18 Nov 45 (Opposition boycotted election)	Fatherland Front, 88.2% (85.6% of electorate voted)

A referendum was held on 8 Sep 1946 at which 92.7 per cent of the electorate voted, 3 801 160 for a Republic, and 197 176 to retain the monarchy. 119 168 votes were invalid. A People's Republic was proclaimed on 15 Sep 1946.

The elections of 27 Oct 1946 were for a 'Grand' National Assembly as was necessary to carry out constitutional change. The Communists and their allies stood in a Fatherland Front bloc; the opposition parties campaigned as the 'United opposition'.

		Votes per party	*Seats*
1946	Fatherland Front	2 980 000	366
	Communists	2 260 000	277
	Obbov Agrarians		67
	Neikov Social Democrats		9
	Zveno group		8
	Radicals		4
	United opposition	1 300 000	99
	Agrarians		89
	Social Democrats		9
	Independent		1

On 4 Dec 1947 the 'Dimitrov' constitution was promulgated. The National Assembly was elected for 4-year terms by all citizens of 18 and over. Each deputy represented 20 000 electors. The President was to be elected by the National Assembly.

Before the elections of 1949 the Social Democrats merged with the Communists and the *Zveno* group dissolved. 99.8 per cent of votes cast were for the single Fatherland Front list of Communist or Agrarian candidates.

	Electorate	Votes per party	% of Votes
1953	5 017 667 (99.48% voted)	Fatherland Front (465 deputies elected)	99.8
1957	5 218 602 (99.77% voted) (Votes = 5 206 428)	Fatherland Front 5 204 027 (number of deputies reduced to 253)	99.95
1962	5 485 607 (99.71% voted) (Votes = 5 466 517)	Fatherland Front (321 deputies elected)	99.9
1966	5 774 251 (99.63% voted) (Votes = 5 752 817)	Fatherland Front 5 744 072 (number of candidates = 416)	99.85
1971	(99.85% voted)	Fatherland Front	99.9

A new constitution was promulgated on 18 May 1971 by which the number of deputies was fixed at 400 and their term of service altered to 5 years.

In elections in May 1976, of an electorate of 6 378 348, some 6 375 092 voted (99.99 per cent). Of these, 6 369 762 (99.92 per cent) voted for the Fatherland Front, returning 272 members for the Bulgarian Communist Party, 100 for the Bulgarian Agrarian Party and 28 non-party members.

In elections in Jun 1981, of the total electorate some 6 524 086 (99.96 per cent) cast their votes. Of these 6 519 674 (99.93 per cent) were for the Fatherland Front. The members returned comprised 271 Bulgarian Communist Party, 99 Agrarian Union and 30 non-party.

In elections in Jun 1986, of the total registered electorate of 6 650 739 some 6 645 645 (99.92 per cent) cast their votes. The members returned comprised 276 Bulgarian Communist Party, 99 Agrarian Union and 25 non-party.

Following the fall of the former Communist régime, the first free elections for 58 years were held on 10 and 17 Jun 1990 for the 400-seat Grand National Assembly. Turnout on the first round of voting exceeded 80 per cent. The result was:

Bulgarian Socialist Party (BSP)	211
Union of Democratic Forces (UDF)*	144
Movement for Rights and Freedom (MRF)**	23
Agrarian Party	16
Independents	2
Others	4
	400

* A 16-party opposition alliance.
** The party of the ethnic Turkish minority.

Three other elections were held in the 1990s:

	Party	Seats	% votes
1991 (Oct)	Union of Democratic Forces (UDF)	110	34.4
	Bulgarian Socialist Party	106	33.1
	Movement for Rights and Freedom	24	7.6
	United Bulgarian Agrarian Party	–	3.8
	Others (Independents, smaller parties etc.)	–	21.1
1994 (18 Dec)	Bulgarian Socialist Party (BSP) (former Communists)	125	43.5
	Union of Democratic Forces (UDF)	69	24.2
	Popular Union (Agrarian Party and Democratic Party)	18	6.3
	Movement for Rights and Freedom (Turkish)	15	5.5
	Bulgarian Business Bloc*	13	4.8
1997 (19 Apr)	Union of Democratic Forces (UDF)	137	52.6
	Democratic Left (including Bulgarian Socialist Party)	58	22.1
	Union for National Salvation	19	7.6
	Euro-Left Coalition	14	5.5
	Bulgarian Business Bloc	12	4.9
	Others	–	7.3

* Other parties fell below 4 per cent threshold.

CROATIA

Elections were held in independent Croatia for the Sabor (Assembly) on 2 Aug 1992. The outcome was a landslide victory for the Croatian Democratic Union of Franjo Tudjman.

	Seats	% votes
Croatian Democratic Union	85	41.5
Croatian Social Liberal Party	14	18.3
Social Democratic Party/Party of Democratic Reform of Croatia	11	5.8
Croatian People's Party	6	6.9

	Seats	% votes
Dalmatian Action } Istrian Democratic Assembly } Rijeka Democratic Alliance }	6	na
Serbian People's Party	3	na
Others (including Independents)	13	na
	138	

In January 1993 a proportional representation system was introduced.

		Seats	% vote
1995 (29 Aug)	Croatian Democratic Union	75	44.8
	Peasant Party Coalition	16	18.4
	Croatian Social Liberal Party	12	11.6
	Social Democratic Party	10	na
	Croat Right-Wing Party	4	na
	Others	3	na

Electorate 3.6m. Turnout 66 per cent.

The last elections of the century, originally planned for Dec 1999 were postponed until 3 Jan 2000 as a result of the illness (and subsequent death) of Croatian President Tudjman. They resulted in the victory of a centre–left coalition and the defeat of the ruling Croatian Democratic Union.

CYPRUS (GREEK)

		Seats	% vote
1991	Democratic Rally (Disy)	20	35.8
	Akel (Communists)	18	30.6
	Democratic Party (Diko)	11	19.5
	EDEK (Socialists)	7	10.9
1996 (26 May)	Democratic Rally	20	34.5
	Akel	19	33.0
	Democratic Party	10	16.4
	EDEK (Socialists)	5	8.1
	Others	2	7.9

CYPRUS (TURKISH)

Elections held on 6 May 1990 produced a victory for the National Unity Party, with 34 of the 50 seats. The Democratic Struggle Party (comprising Republican Turkish Party, Communal Liberal Party and New Dawn) won 14 seats. Further elections were held in Dec 1993. In 1996, the Democratic Party had 16 seats in the Assembly, National Unity Party 15, the Republican Turkish Party 13, Communal Liberal Party 5 and the National Birth Party 1.

CZECHOSLOVAKIA

A National Assembly was set up on 14 Nov 1918 of 260 delegates of the following party composition:

Agrarians	54
Social Democrats	50
Slovaks	50
National Democrats	44
National Socialists	28
Catholics	28
Progressive Liberals	6

Representatives of the German minority refused to take part.

A constitution was promulgated on 29 Feb 1920 providing for a bicameral National Assembly, *Národni Shromáždĕni* to be elected by direct universal suffrage on the proportional representation method. The Chamber of Deputies of 300 members was to be elected for 6 years by citizens over 21; the Senate for 8 years by voters over 26, and to have 150 senators. The head of state was to be a President elected by both chambers for 7 years.

Elections to the Chamber of Deputies were held on 18 Apr 1920 and to the Senate on 25 Apr 1920. The electorate was 6 917 956 (for the Chamber of Deputies; the Senate electorate was a proportion of this which remained more or less constant throughout later elections. At this election it was 5 804 134). Turnout was 89.9 per cent. Valid votes cast for the Chamber of Deputies: 6 130 318.

Pre-war Czechoslovak politics was dominated by the problem of national minorities, and the official classification of voting figures in the 1920 election reflects this preoccupation: Czechoslovak parties polled 4 255 623 votes (68.64 per cent of votes cast) and gained 199 seats in the Chamber of Deputies, and gained 102 seats in the Senate with 70.07 per cent of votes cast. German parties:

72; 1586060 (25.58 per cent) and 37; 26.09 per cent. Hungarian-German parties: 9; 247901 (4 per cent) and 2; 1.93 per cent. Hungarian parties: 1; 30734 (0.5 per cent) and 1; 0.77 per cent.

Seats gained and proportion of votes polled by individual, successful parties were:

Chamber of Deputies:		*Seats*	*% of votes*
Czechoslovak parties	Social Democrats	74	25.65
	Populist Catholics	33	11.29
	Agrarians	28	9.74
	National Socialists	24	8.08
	National Democrats	19	6.25
	Slovak National Agrarians	12	3.90
	Professional Middle Class	6	1.98
	Working People (Progressive Socialists)	3	0.95

Chamber of Deputies:		*Seats*	*% of votes*
German parties	German Social Democrats	31	11.12
	German Electoral Union	15	5.30
	Union of German Peasants	11	3.90
	German Christian Social Party	10	3.44
	German Democratic Liberals	5	1.78
Hungarian-German parties	Hungarian-German Christian Socialists	5	2.25
	Hungarian-German Social Democrats	4	1.75
Hungarian parties	Hungarian Agrarians	1	0.43

Senate		*Seats*	*% of votes*
Czechoslovak parties	Social Democrats	41	28.07
	Populist Catholics	18	11.91
	Agrarians	14	10.15
	National Socialists	10	7.15
	National Democrats	10	6.78
	Slovak National Agrarians	6	3.47
	Professional Middle Class	3	2.06

	German Social Democrats	16	11.35
	German Electoral Union	8	5.75
German parties	Union of German Peasants	6	4.03
	German Christian Social Party	4	2.70
	German Democratic Liberals	3	2.26
Hungarian-German	Hungarian-German Christian Socialists	2	1.93
Hungarian	Hungarian Agrarians	1	0.77

At the elections of 15 Nov 1925 all 300 seats in the Chamber of Deputies and all 150 in the Senate were filled by election. The electorate was 7 855 822, the turnout was 91.4 per cent and 7 105 276 votes were cast.

	Chamber of Deputies			Senate		
	Votes	*% of votes*	*Seats*	*Votes*	*% of votes*	*Seats*
(Czechoslovak parties):						
Agrarians	970 489	13.66	45	841 647	13.81	23
Populist Catholics	691 238	9.73	31	618 033	10.14	16
Social Democrats	630 894	8.88	29	537 470	8.82	14
National Socialists	609 195	8.57	28	516 250	8.47	14
Professional Middle Class	285 928	4.02	13	257 171	4.22	6
National Democrats	284 628	4.01	13	256 360	4.20	7
German Social Democrats	411 040	5.79	17	363 310	6.84	12
German Christian Social Party	314 440	4.43	13	289 055	4.74	7
German Nationalists	240 879	3.39	10	214 589	3.52	5
Nazis	168 278	2.37	7	139 945	2.30	3
Union of German Peasants	571 198	8.04	24	505 597	8.29	12
Hlinka's Populist Slovak Catholics	489 027	6.88	23	417 206	6.84	12
Sub-Carpathian Russian Agrarians	35 674	0.50	1			
Polish People's and Workers' Union	29 884	0.42	1			
Hungarian Christian Social Party	98 383	1.39	4	85 777	1.41	2
Communists	933 711	13.14	41	774 454	12.70	20

At the elections of 27 Oct 1929 the electorate was 8 183 462, the turnout 91.6 per cent and 7 385 084 votes cast.

	Chamber of Deputies			Senate		
	Votes	*% of votes*	*Seats*	*Votes*	*% of votes*	*Seats*
(Czechoslovak parties):						
Agrarians	1 105 429	14.97	46	978 291	15.17	24
Social Democrats	963 312	13.05	39	841 331	13.04	20
National Socialists	767 571	10.39	32	666 607	10.33	16
Populist Catholics	623 522	8.44	25	559 700	8.68	13
National Democrats	359 533	4.87	15	325 023	5.04	8
Professional Middle Class	291 238	3.94	12	274 085	4.25	6
Anti-Electoral Scrutiny	70 857	0.96	3	51 617	0.80	1
German Social Democrats	506 750	5.76	19	446 940	6.93	11
German Electoral Coalition	396 383	5.37	16	359 002	5.57	9
German Christian Social Party	348 097	4.71	14	313 544	4.86	8
Nazis	204 096	2.77	8	171 181	2.65	4
German Nationalist and Sudeten German Union	189 071	2.56	7			
Hlinka's Populist Slovak Catholics	425 052	5.76	19	377 498	5.85	9
Hungarian Christian Socialists	257 231	3.48	9	233 772	3.62	6
Polish and Jewish Union	104 539	1.42	4			
Communists	753 444	10.20	30	644 896	10.00	15

At the elections of 19 May 1935 the electorate was 8 957 572, turnout was 92.8 per cent and 8 231 412 votes were cast.

	Chamber of Deputies			Senate		
	Votes	*% of votes*	*Seats*	*Votes*	*% of votes*	*Seats*
(Czechoslovak parties):						
Agrarians	1 176 593	13.29	45	1 042 924	14.33	23
Social Democrats	1 034 774	12.57	38	910 252	12.51	20
National Socialists	755 880	9.18	18	672 126	9.24	14
Populist Catholics	615 877	7.48	22	557 684	7.66	11
Artisans and Tradesmen	448 047	5.44	17	393 732	5.41	8
Fascists	167 433	2.04	6			
National Union	456 353	5.55	17	410 095	5.64	9
Sudeten Germans	1 249 531	15.18	44	1 092 255	15.01	23
German Social Democrats	299 942	3.64	11	271 097	3.73	6
German Christian Social Party	162 781	1.98	6	155 234	2.13	3
Union of German Peasants	142 399	1.73	5			

	Chamber of Deputies			Senate		
	Votes	*% of votes*	*Seats*	*Votes*	*% of votes*	*Seats*
Autonomous bloc (Hlinka's Slovaks, Poles and Hungarians)	564 273	6.86	22	495 166	6.80	11
Hungarian-German Christian Social bloc	291 831	3.55	9	259 832	3.57	6
Communists	849 509	10.32	30	740 696	10.18	16

With the dismemberment and annexation of Czechoslovakia by Germany in 1938 all political parties were proscribed and two puppet organizations set up: the Party of National Unity and the Party of Labour.

On 3 Apr 1945 Beneš established a provisional government at Košice with a cabinet of 7 Communists, 3 Slovak Democrats, 3 Populist Catholics, 3 National Socialists and 2 Social Democrats. This organized an indirect election in Sep and Oct 1945 of a provisional National Assembly which met on 28 Oct 1945. Four parties were recognized in the Czech lands (Communists, Agrarians, National Socialists, Social Democrats) and allotted 40 deputies each, 2 in Slovakia (Populist Catholics and Slovak Democrats) 50 each, 32 seats went to the Trade Union organization and 8 to outstanding individuals in the cultural sphere, making 300 in all.

At the elections of 26 May 1946 to a Constituent Assembly 8 official parties were allowed to stand: no independents, no fascist parties and (at Soviet insistence) no Agrarians. The electorate was 7 583 784 (all citizens over 18) of whom 7 138 694 voted.

Votes per party		Seats
Communists	2 695 915	114
National Socialists	1 298 917	55
Populist Catholics	1 110 920	47
Slovak Democrats	988 275	43
Social Democrats	905 654	36
Slovak Freedom	67 575	3
Slovak Labour	49 983	2

Elections were held on 30 May 1948 in which the electorate of 7 998 035 was invited to vote for a single list of National Front candidates. 7 419 253 votes were cast, 6 424 734 for the National Front.

President Beneš resigned and was succeeded by K. Gottwald.

A new constitution of 9 Jun 1948 provided for a single-chamber National Assembly, *Národni Shromáždĕni*, of 368 deputies elected by universal suffrage of citizens over 18 for a 6-year period. The President was to be elected by the National Assembly for 7 years.

An electoral law of May 1954 permitted only one candidate to stand per constituency; all candidates had to be nominated by the National Front.

At the elections of 28 Nov 1954 the electorate was 8 783 816, votes cast numbered 8 711 718 (99.18 per cent), of which 8 494 102 (97.89 per cent) were for the National Front. At the elections of 12 Jun 1960, 9 085 432 votes were cast (99.68 per cent of the electorate), of which 9 059 838 (99.86 per cent of votes cast) went to the National Front.

On 11 Jul 1960 a new constitution made Czechoslovakia a 'Socialist' instead of a 'People's' Republic, and fixed the number of National Assembly deputies at 300. The President was henceforth to be elected for a 5-year term, the National Assembly for 4.

At the elections of 14 Jun 1964, 9 418 349 votes were cast (99.98 per cent of the electorate), 9 412 309 for the National Front (99.99 per cent of votes cast).

Czechoslovakia became a Federal Republic of the Czech lands and Slovakia as of 1 Jan 1969. Each federative Republic elected a National Council. The Federal Assembly consisted of 2 chambers: the Chamber of the People of 200 deputies, and the Chamber of the Nations composed of 75 Czech and 75 Slovak deputies. Elections were held every 5 years, to coincide with Communist Party congresses.

The elections due in 1968 were postponed until 26–27 Nov 1971. In 1968 a new electoral law had permitted more than one candidate to stand for each seat, but this was annulled in the 1971 elections in which the number of candidates was once again equivalent to the number of seats. The electorate was 10 253 769 of whom 99.45 per cent voted. Votes for candidates: Federal Assembly Chamber of the People, 99.81 per cent; Federal Assembly Chamber of the Nations, 99.77 per cent; Czech National Council, 99.78 per cent; Slovak National Council, 99.94 per cent.

In elections in Oct 1976, of the 10 649 261 voters, 99.7 per cent cast their votes. Of these, 10 605 672 (99.97 per cent) voted for National Front candidates.

In elections in Jun 1981, of the 10 789 574 voters, 99.51 per cent cast their votes. Of these, 10 725 609 (99.9 per cent) voted for the National Front.

In elections in May 1986, of the 10 950 675 registered voters, 99.39 per cent reportedly cast their votes. All 200 candidates of the Communist National Front were elected.

With the fall of the Communist régime in the 'Velvet Revolution' of 1989, free elections subsequently took place on 8–9 Jun 1990. On a turnout of 96 per cent of Czechoslovakia's 11.2 million eligible voters, the main results were:

	Seats	% of votes
Civic Forum/Public Against Violence*	170	46.3
Communists	47	13.6
Christian Democratic Union**	40	11.6
Others (inc. separatist Slovak National Party)	43	28.5
	300	

* Public Against Violence was the sister-party of Civic Forum in Slovakia.
** A conservative coalition of the People's Party and the Czech and Slovak Christian Democratic Parties.

Note: Prior to the division of Czechoslovakia from 1 Jan 1993, elections to the Czech National Council took place in Jun 1992. The elections were dominated by the Civic Democratic Party–Christian Democratic Party coalition (76 seats, 29.7 per cent of votes cast), followed by the Left Bloc (35 seats, 14 per cent of the vote). The Czechoslovak Social Democratic Party and the Liberal Social Union each took 16 seats with 6.5 per cent of the vote.

CZECH REPUBLIC

The first elections to the Czech Republic, after the separation of Slovakia, were held on 2 Jun 1996. The second were held in 1998.

	Seats	% votes
1996 (Jun)		
Civic Democratic Party	68	29.6
Civic Democratic Alliance	13	6.4
CDU–CPP	18	8.1
Czech Social Democratic Party	61	26.4
Communist Party of Bohemia and Moravia	22	10.3
Association for the Republican Party of Czechoslovakia	18	8.0
1998 (Jun)		
CSSD (Social Democrats)	74	32.3
ODS (Civic Democratic Party)	63	27.7
US (Freedom Union)	19	8.6
KDU-CSL (Christian Democrats)	20	9.0
KSCM (Communist Party)	24	11.0
Others*	–	11.4

* The racist right-wing Republican Party failed to surmount the 5% hurdle for parliamentary representation.

DENMARK

By 1918, the capital had direct proportional elections, the provinces had direct elections in single-member constituencies with some additional seats allotted in proportion to the vote. From 1920, direct proportional elections in multi-member seats. Suffrage of men and women over 29, except those working as servants and farm helpers without their own household. Age reduced to 25 at the third election of 1920, to 23 in 1953 and to 21 in 1961. From 1915–1953 there was a second chamber, the Landsting. For this there was indirect election, electors being selected by city or parish, voters having one vote per elector allocated. Voters were all men and women over 35. Electors in turn elected 53 (first 2 elections of the period) of the 66 Landsting members, and 55 of them in the last 10 elections.

The main feature of Danish elections from 1900 was the rise of the Social Democrats. Elections were held in 1901, 1903, 1906, 1909, 1910, 1913 and 1915. For this last election no meaningful figures can be obtained. The Liberals dominated each election in terms of seats, but the Social Democrats rose steadily.

	Liberals	*Social Democrats*
1901	76 (39.4)	14 (19.3)
1903	73 (46.1)	16 (21.6)
1906	56 (31.1)	24 (25.4)
1909	48 (30.0)	24 (29.0)
1910	57 (34.1)	24 (28.3)
1913	44 (28.6)	32 (29.6)

		*Votes per party**	*Seats*	*% of votes*
1918	Liberals	269005	44	29.4
	Soc. Dem.	262796	39	29.4
	Rad. Lib.	192478	33	21.0
	Con.	167865	22	18.3
1920(1)	Liberals	350563	48	34.2
	Soc. Dem.	300345	42	29.3
	Con.	201499	28	19.7
	Rad. Lib.	122160	17	11.9

* Only 4 largest parties listed in early elections.

	Votes per party		*Seats*	*% of votes*
1920(2)	Liberals	343 351	51	36.1
	Soc. Dem.	285 166	42	29.9
	Con.	180 293	26	18.9
	Rad. Lib.	110 931	16	11.6
1920(3)	Liberals	411 661	51	34.0
	Soc. Dem.	389 653	48	32.2
	Con.	216 733	27	17.9
	Rad. Lib.	147 120	18	12.1
1924	Soc. Dem.	469 949	55	36.6
	Liberals	362 682	44	28.3
	Con.	242 955	28	18.9
	Rad. Lib.	166 476	20	13.0
1926	Soc. Dem.	497 160	53	37.2
	Liberals	378 137	46	28.3
	Con.	275 793	30	20.6
	Rad. Lib.	150 931	16	11.3
1929	Soc. Dem.	593 191	61	41.8
	Liberals	402 121	43	28.3
	Con.	233 935	24	16.5
	Rad. Lab.	151 746	16	10.7
1932	Soc. Dem.	660 839	62	42.7
	Liberals	381 862	38	24.7
	Con.	289 531	27	18.7
	Rad. Lib.	145 221	14	9.4
1935	Soc. Dem.	759 102	68	46.1
	Liberals	292 247	28	17.8
	Con.	293 393	26	17.8
	Rad. Lib.	151 507	14	9.2
1939	Soc. Dem.	729 619	64	42.9
	Liberals	309 355	30	18.2
	Con.	301 625	26	17.8
	Rad. Lib.	161 834	14	9.5

		Votes per party		*Seats*	*% of votes*
1943	Soc. Dem.		894632	66	44.5
	Con.		421523	31	21.0
	Liberals		376850	28	18.7
1945	Soc. Dem.		671755	48	32.8
	Liberals		479158	38	23.4
	Con.		373688	26	18.2
1947	Soc. Dem.		834089	57	40.0
	Liberals		574895	49	27.6
	Con.		259324	17	12.4
1950	Soc. Dem.		813224	59	39.6
	Liberals		438188	32	21.3
	Con.		365236	27	17.8
1953(1)	Soc. Dem.		836507	61	40.4
	Liberals		456896	33	22.1
	Con.		358509	26	17.3
1953(2)	Soc. Dem.		894913	74	41.3
	Liberals		499656	42	23.1
	Con.		364960	30	16.8
1957	Soc. Dem.		910170	70	39.4
	Liberals		578932	45	25.1
	Con.		383843	30	16.6
1960	Soc. Dem.		1023794	76	42.1
	Liberals		512041	38	21.1
	Con.		435764	32	17.9
1964	Soc. Dem.		1103667	76	41.9
	Liberals		547770	38	20.8
	Con.		527798	36	20.1
1966	Soc. Dem.		1068911	69	38.2
	Liberals		539028	35	19.3
	Con.		522027	34	18.7
1968	Soc. Dem.		974833	62	34.1
	Liberals		530167	34	18.6
	Cons.		581051	37	20.4

	Votes per party		*Seats*	*% of votes*
1971	Soc. Dem.	1074777	70	37.3
	Liberals	450904	30	15.6
	Cons.	481335	31	16.7
1973	Soc. Dem.	783145	46	25.6
	Soc. People's Party	183522	11	6.0
	Com.	110715	6	3.6
	Left Soc.	44843		1.5
	Lib. Dem.	374283	22	12.3
	Rad. Lib.	343117	20	11.2
	Chr. People's Party	123573	7	4.0
	Con.	279391	16	9.2
	Centre Dem.	236784	14	7.8
	Pro. Party	414212	24	13.6
	STP	54067		1.8
1975	Soc. Dem.	913155	53	30.0
	Soc. People's Party	150963	9	4.9
	Com.	127837	7	4.2
	Left Soc.	63579	4	2.1
	Lib. Dem.	711298	42	23.3
	Rad. Lib.	216553	13	7.1
	Chr. People's Party	162734	9	5.3
	Con.	168164	10	5.5
	Centre Dem.	66316	4	2.2
	Pro. Party	414212	24	13.6
	STP	54067	–	1.8
1977	Soc. Dem.	1150355	65	37.0
	Soc. People's Party	120357	7	3.9
	Com.	114022	7	3.7
	Left Soc.	83667	5	2.7
	Lib. Dem.	371728	21	12.0
	Rad. Lib.	113330	6	3.6
	Chr. People's Party	106082	6	3.4
	Con.	263262	15	8.5

	Votes per party		Seats	% of votes
	Centre Dem.	200347	11	6.4
	Pro. Party	453782	26	14.6
	STP	102149	6	3.3
	Pensioners Party	26889		0.9
1979	Soc. Dem.	1213456	68	38.3
	Lib. Dem.	396484	22	12.5
	Con.	395653	22	12.5
	Pro. Party	349243	20	11.0
	Soc. People's Party	187284	11	5.9
	Rad. Lib.	172365	10	5.4
	Left Soc.	116047	6	3.7
	Centre Dem.	102132	6	3.2
	Chr. People's Party	82133	5	2.6
	STP	83238	5	2.6
	Com.	58901		1.9
	Com. Workers Party	13070		0.4
1981	Soc. Dem.	1027376	59	32.9
	Con. People's Party	450970	26	14.4
	Soc. People's Party	353167	21	11.3
	Lib.	353435	20	11.3
	Pro. Party	278454	16	8.9
	Centre Dem.	258720	15	8.3
	Rad. Lib.	159933	9	5.1
	Left Soc.	82106	5	2.6
	Chr. People's Party	72020	4	2.3
	Others	85744	–	2.7
1984	Soc. Dem.	1062602	56	31.4
	Con. People's Party	788225	42	23.3
	Soc. People's Party	387115	21	11.4
	Venstre (Lib.)	405722	22	12.0
	Rad. Lib.	184634	10	5.5
	Centre Dem.	154557	8	4.6

	Votes per party		Seats	% of votes
	Pro. Party	120631	6	3.6
	Chr. People's Party	91633	5	2.7
	Others	191604	5	5.6
1987	Soc. Dem.	985906	54	29.3
	Con. People's Party	700886	38	20.8
	Soc. People's Party	490176	27	14.6
	Venstre (Lib.)	354291	19	10.5
	Rad. Lib.	209086	11	6.2
	Centre Dem.	161070	9	4.8
	Pro. Party	160461	9	4.8
	Chr. People's Party	79664	4	2.4
	Others	221017	4	6.6
1988	Soc. Dem.		55	29.9
	Con. People's Party		35	19.3
	Soc. People's Party		24	13.0
	Venstre (Lib.)		22	11.8
	Pro. Party		16	9.0
	Rad. Lib.		10	5.6
	Centre Dem.		9	4.7
	Chr. People's Party		4	2.0
	Others		–	4.6
1990	Soc. Dem.		69	37.4
	Con. People's Party		30	16.0
	Lib.		29	15.8
	Soc. People's Party		15	8.3
	Pro. Party		12	6.4
	Centre Dem.		9	5.1
	Rad. Lib.		7	3.5
	Chr. People's Party		4	2.3
	Others		–	5.2
			179*	100.0

* Total of 179 includes 4 from Greenland and the Faroes.

		Seats	% votes
1994	Soc. Dem.	62	34.6
	Lib.	42	23.3
	Con. People's Party	27	15.0
	Soc. People's Party	13	7.3
	Pro. Party	11	6.4
	Soc. Lib. (formerly Rad. Lib.)	9	4.6
	Red–Green Alliance	6	3.2
	Centre Dem.	5	2.8
	Others	1	2.8
		175	100.0

		Votes	Seats	% votes
1998 (11 Mar)	Social Democrats (SDP)	1 223 600	63	35.9
	Liberals	817 900	42	24.0
	Conservative People's Party	304 000	16	8.9
	Socialist People's Party	257 400	13	7.6
	Danish People's Party	252 400	13	7.4
	Centre Democrats	146 800	8	4.3
	Social Liberals	131 300	7	3.9
	Red–Green Alliance	91 900	5	2.7
	Others*	180 700	8	5.3

* Excluding Greenland and Faroe Islands.

ESTONIA

Elections for a Constituent Assembly were held 7 and 8 Apr 1919, and a coalition government formed headed by the Social Democratic Party. A constitution was adopted on 15 Jun 1920 which provided for a single-chamber parliament (*Riigikogu*) of 100 deputies elected every 3 years by proportional representation. Elections were held in 1920, 1923, 1926, 1929 and 1932. The system favoured the proliferation of political parties. There were also national minority parties: Swedish, German and Russian. The Communist Party was outlawed in Feb 1925 after an abortive *coup*. The fascist ex-servicemen's organization Vaps began to gain influence at a time of increasing dissatisfaction with government instability (between 1919 and 1933 there were 20 coalition governments) and instigated a referendum to amend the constitution in Oct 1933.

The amendment was approved by 416 879 votes (56.3 per cent of the electorate), but the President (K. Päts) on 12 Mar 1934 assumed direct control under emergency powers and presented a third constitution to the people in Feb 1936. This was approved by a majority of 76.1 per cent and came into force on 1 Jan 1938. It provided for a new two-chamber parliament: a 40-strong National Council of appointed specialists, and an 80-strong Chamber of Deputies elected every 5 years on the single-member constituency system. The President was to be directly elected every 6 years.

At the elections of 24 Apr 1938 the poll was a record 90 per cent. Päts was elected President. Fifty-five members of the pro-Päts Patriotic League were elected. Social Democrats and extreme left-wing groups were in opposition.

Elections were held in independent Estonia on 5 March 1995, with 1265 candidates from 16 parties.

	Seats	*% votes*
Coalition Party/Rural Union	41	32.2
Reform Party/Liberals	19	16.2
Centre Party	16	14.2
Fatherland Alliance	8	7.9
Moderate Party	6	6.0
Our Home is Estonia (Russian)	6	5.9
Right Wing	5	5.0

The results of parliamentary elections on 7 Mar 1999 were:

	Seats	*% votes*
Estonian Centre Party	28	23.4
Pro Patria Union	18	16.1
Estonian Reform Party	18	15.9
Mõõdukad	17	15.2
Estonian Coalition Party	7	7.6
Country People's Party	7	7.3
Estonian United People's Party	6	6.1

Electorate 857 270. Turnout 57.4 per cent.

EUROPEAN UNION

The European Parliament, which acquired its present name in 1962, originated as the Common Assembly of the ECSC (*see* p. 21). Its members were originally appointed from the membership of national parliaments. Direct elections were first held in 1979 and subsequently in 1984, 1989, 1994 and 1999. In 1994 the size of the Parliament increased to 567 seats (from 518). On 1 Jan 1995 it further increased to 626 seats with the accession of Austria, Finland and Sweden. In 1999 Britain abandoned its previous 'first-past-the-post' system of electing MEPs. Full figures for each election can be found in the EU Handbooks and also in the *Times Guide to the European Parliament* (published after each election).

Following the Jun 1999 European elections, the size of the various political groupings in the European Parliament was:

Party	Seats
European People's Party (Centre Right)	224
Party of European Socialists	180
European Liberal, Democratic and Reform (Liberals)	42
Greens	38
European United Left/Nordic Green Left	35
Group Union for Europe (Centre Right)	17
European Radical Alliance (left wing)	14
Independents for a Europe of Nations (anti-EU)	21
Non-attached	18
Uncertain	37

The outcome of voting in Britain for the European Parliament from 1979 to 1994 was as follows:

	UK seats won, 1979–1994			
	1979	*1984*	*1989*	*1994*
Conservative	60	45	32	18
Labour	17	32	45	62
Liberals (Lib Dems)	0	0	0	2
Scottish Nationalist	1	1	1	2
Democratic Unionist	1	1	1	1
Official Unionist	1	1	1	1
Social Democratic and Labour	1	1	1	1

The result in Jun 1999 (under a regional list system) was:*

Party	Seats	% votes
Conservative	36	35.8
Labour	29	28.0
Liberal Democrat	10	12.7
UK Independence	3	7.0
Green	2	6.3
Nationalist	4	4.5
Others	–	5.7

* Excluding Northern Ireland.

FEDERAL REPUBLIC OF GERMANY

From 1949, direct elections for 60 per cent of the seats in the Bundestag, the others filled by election from lists. From 1953, each voter votes (1) for a candidate in his constituency and (2) for a party list. Seats are distributed proportionally to the second vote. Suffrage since 1949 is for men and women over 21. For elections prior to 1949, *see* p. 231.

		Votes per party	Seats	% of votes
1949	CDU/CSU	7 359 100	139	31.0
	SPD	6 935 000	131	29.2
	FDP	2 829 900	52	11.9
1953	CDU/CSU	12 444 000	244	45.2
	SPD	7 994 900	151	28.8
	FDP	2 629 200	48	9.5
1957	CDU/CSU	15 008 400	270	50.2
	SPD	9 495 600	169	31.8
	FDP	2 307 100	41	7.7
1961	CDU/CSU	14 298 400	242	45.4
	SPD	11 427 400	190	36.2
	FDP	4 028 800	67	12.8
1965	CDU/CSU	15 524 100	245	47.6
	SPD	12 813 200	202	39.3
	FDP	3 096 800	49	9.5

	Votes per party		*Seats*	*% of votes*
1969	CDU/CSU	15 195 187	242	46.1
	SPD	14 065 716	224	42.7
	FDP	1 903 422	30	5.8
1972	CDU/CSU	16 806 020	225	44.9
	SPD	17 175 169	230	45.8
	FDP	3 129 982	41	7.6
1976	SPD	16 099 019	214	42.6
	CDU	14 367 302	190	38.0
	CSU	4 027 403	53	10.6
	FDP	2 995 085	39	7.9
	NPD	122 428	–	0.3
	DKP	118 488	–	0.3
	Others	92 571	–	0.4
1980	CDU	12 992 334	174	34.2
	CSU	3 908 036	52	10.3
	SPD	16 262 096	218	42.9
	FDP	4 030 608	53	10.6
	Die Grünen	568 265	–	1.5
	Others	181 713	–	0.4
1983	SPD	14 866 210	193	38.2
	CDU	14 856 835	191	38.2
	CSU	4 140 351	53	10.6
	FDP	2 705 795	34	6.9
	Die Grünen	2 164 988	27	5.6
	Others	203 391	–	0.4
1987	SPD	14 025 763	186	37.0
	CDU	13 045 745	174	34.5
	CSU	3 715 827	49	9.8
	FDP	3 440 911	46	9.1
	Die Grünen	3 126 256	42	8.3
	NPD	227 054	–	0.6
	Others	285 763	–	0.7

Following German reunification in Oct 1990, the first elections for the all-German parliament were held on 2 Dec 1990. The outcome was:

Votes per party		Seats	% of votes
CDU	17 051 128	268	36.7
CSU*	3 301 239	51	7.1
FDP	5 123 936	79	11.0
(Coalition		401	54.8)
SPD	15 539 977	239	33.5
PDS	1 129 290	17	2.4
Alliance 90/Greens	558 552	8	1.2
Die Grünen	1 788 214	–	3.9
Republicans	985 557	–	2.1
Others**	966 165	–	2.1
Turnout 77.8% (West Germany, 78.5%, East Germany, 74.5%)	636		

* DSU in Germany.
** 16 parties in all.

		Votes*	Seats	% of votes
1994 (16 Oct)	SPD	17 141 000	252	36.4
	CDU	16 089 000	244	34.2
	CSU	3 427 000	50	7.3
	Alliance 90/Greens	3 423 000	49	7.3
	FDP	3 258 000	47	6.9
	PDS	2 067 000	30	4.4
	Republican Party	875 000	–	1.9
	Others	823 000	–	1.7
			672	100.0

* Rounded to nearest '000.

		Votes cast*	Seats	% votes
1998 (27 Sep)	SPD	20 179 000	298	40.9
	CDU/CSU	17 329 000	245	35.2
	FDP	3 080 000	44	6.2
	Die Grünen/Alliance 90	3 300 000	47	6.7
	PDS (Communists)	2 514 000	35	5.1
	Others	2 898 000	–	6.0

*Rounded to nearest '000.

FINLAND

Voting procedures. Direct proportional elections from multi-member constituencies. Suffrage for all adults over 24 until 1945, and then over 21. In 1919, part of the population disenfranchised by the civil war.

		Votes per party	Seats	% of votes
1919	SSP	365 046	80	38.0
	MI	189 297	42	19.7
	KK	151 018	28	15.7
	KE	123 090	26	12.8
	RK	116 582	22	12.1
1922	SSP	216 861	53	25.1
	MI	175 401	45	20.3
	KK	157 116	35	18.1
	RK	107 414	25	12.4
	KE	79 676	15	9.2
1924	SSP	255 068	60	29.0
	MI	177 982	44	20.3
	KK	166 880	38	19.0
	RK	105 733	23	12.0
	KE	79 937	17	9.0
1927	SSP	257 572	60	28.3
	MI	205 313	52	22.5
	KK	161 450	34	17.7

	Votes per party		Seats	% of votes
	RK	111005	24	12.2
	KE	61613	10	6.8
1929	SSP	260254	59	27.4
	MI	248762	60	26.1
	KK	138008	28	14.5
	RK	108886	23	11.4
	KE	53301	7	5.6
1930	SSP	386026	66	34.2
	MI	308280	59	27.3
	KK	203958	42	18.1
	RK	113318	20	10.0
	KE	65830	11	5.8
1933	SSP	413551	78	37.3
	MI	249758	53	22.6
	RK	131440	21	11.2
	KK	121619	20	10.4
	IK	97891	14	8.3
1939	SSP	515980	85	39.8
	MI	296529	56	22.9
	KK	176215	25	13.6
	RK	124720	18	9.6
1945	SSP	425948	50	25.1
	SKDI	398618	49	23.5
	MI	362662	49	21.3
	KK	255394	28	15.0
1948	MI	455635	56	24.2
	SSP	494719	54	26.3
	SKDI	375820	38	20.0
	KK	320366	33	17.1
1951	SSP	480754	53	26.5
	MI	421613	51	23.2
	SKDI	391362	43	21.6
	KK	264044	28	14.6
1954	SSP	527094	54	26.2
	MI	483958	53	24.1

		Votes per party	Seats	% of votes
	SKDI	433528	43	21.6
	KK	257025	24	12.8
1958	SKDI	450506	50	23.2
	SSP	450212	48	23.2
	MI	448364	48	23.1
	KK	297094	29	15.3
1962	MI	528409	53	23.0
	SKDI	507124	47	22.0
	SSP	448930	38	19.5
	KK	346638	32	15.0
1966	MI	503047	49	21.2
	SKDI	502635	41	21.2
	SSP	645339	55	27.2
	KK	326928	26	13.8
1970	MI	434150	37	17.1
	SKDI	420556	36	16.6
	SSP	594185	51	23.4
	KK	457582	37	18.0
1972	MI	423039	35	16.4
	SKDI	438757	37	17.0
	SSP	664724	55	25.8
	KK	453434	34	17.6
1975	SSDP	695394	54	24.9
	SKDL	528026	40	18.9
	KP	488930	39	17.5
	KK	512213	35	18.4
	SFP	141381	10	5.0
	LKP	121722	9	4.4
	SKL	92108	9	3.3
	Others	214364	4	7.6
1979	SSDP	691256	52	23.9
	KK	626108	47	21.7
	KP	501012	36	21.0

	Votes per party		Seats	% of votes
	SKDL	516276	35	17.9
	SFP	122450	10	4.6
	LKP	106609	4	4.2
	SKL	137850	9	4.8
	Others	180744	7	1.7
1983	SSDP	795813	57	26.7
	KK	658975	44	22.1
	KP	525091	38	17.6
	SKDL	400483	26	13.5
	SMP	288435	17	9.7
	SFP	137189	10	4.6
	SKL	90374	3	3.0
	Others	79506	5	2.7
1987	SSDP	694666	56	24.1
	KK	665477	53	23.1
	KP	507384	40	17.6
	SKDL	269678	16	9.4
	SFP	153141	12	5.3
	SMP	181557	9	6.3
	SKL	74011	5	2.6
	Others	331606	9	11.4
1991	SSDP		48	22.1
	Centre Party (KESK)		55	24.8
	National Coalition Party (KK)		40	19.3
	Left-Wing Alliance (VL)		19	10.1
	Swedish People's Party (SFP)		12	5.5
	Greens		10	6.8
	Finnish Christian Union		8	3.1
	Rural Party (SMP)		7	4.8
	Others		1	3.5
1995	SSDP		63	28.3
	Centre Party		44	19.8
	National Coalition Party		39	17.9
	Left-Wing Alliance		22	11.2

Votes per party	Seats	% of votes
Swedish People's Party	12	5.1
Greens	9	6.5
Finnish Christian League	7	3.0
Progressive Finnish Party	2	2.8
Minor Parties and Others	2	5.3

	Votes per party	Seats	% of votes
1999 (21 Mar)	Social Democratic Party (SDP)	51	22.9
	Centre Party	48	22.4
	National Coalition Party	46	21.0
	Left-Wing League	20	10.9
	Greens	11	7.3
	Swedish People's Party (in Finland)	11	5.1
	Finnish Christian League	10	4.2
	Others	3	6.2

FRANCE

Voting procedures. From 1919–1927, mixed proportional and majority representation. From 1927–1945 the system was as in 1852. In 1945 proportional representation was restored as the sole system; this lasted until 1951 when mixed representation returned. Universal male suffrage until 1945, when women received the vote.

	Votes per party		Seats	% of votes
1902	Left Rep.	2 501 000	180	29.7
	Cons.	2 383 000	147	28.3
	Ind. Rad.	1 414 000	123	16.8
	Rad. Soc.	853 000	75	10.1
1906	Rad. Soc.	2 515 000	241	28.5
	Cons.	2 572 000	109	29.2
	Lib. Popular Action	1 238 000	69	14.0
	Soc.	877 000	53	10.0

		Votes per party		*Seats*	*% of votes*
1910	Rad. Soc.	1 727 000		121	20.4
	Cons.	1 602 000		112	19.0
	Rep. U.	1 472 000		103	7.4
	Soc.	1 111 000		78	13.1
1914	Rad. Soc.	1 530 000		140	18.1
	Soc.	1 413 000		103	16.8
	Rep. U.	1 588 000		96	18.8
	Ind. Rad.	1 400 000		96	16.6
1919	Rep. U.	1 820 000		201	22.3
	Rad. Soc.	1 420 000		106	17.4
	Rep. (left)	889 000		79	10.9
	Soc.	1 615 000		67	20.1
1924	Rep. U.	3 191 000		204	35.5
	Rad. Soc.	1 613 000		162	17.9
	Soc.	1 814 000		104	20.2
1928	Rep. U.	2 082 000		182	22.0
	Rad. Ind. ⎫ Rep. (left) ⎭	2 196 000		126	23.2
	Soc.	1 709 000		99	18.0
1932	Rad. Soc.	1 837 000		157	19.2
	Soc.	1 964 000		129	20.5
	Rep. U.	1 233 000		76	12.9
	Rep. (left)	1 300 000		72	13.6
	Rad. Ind.	956 000		62	10.0
1936	Centre party	2 536 000 ⎫	222		25.8
	Right-wing	1 666 000 ⎭			16.9
	Soc.	1 955 000		149	19.9
	Rad. Soc.	1 423 000		109	14.5
	Communist	1 502 000		72	15.3
1945	Communist ⎫ Progressive ⎭	5 005 000		148	26.1
	Soc.	4 561 000		134	23.8
	Chr. Dem.	4 780 000		141	24.9

		Votes per party		*Seats*	*% of votes*
1946(1)	Chr. Dem.	5 589 000		160	28.1
	Communist ⎫ Progressive ⎬	5 119 000		146	25.7
	Soc.	4 188 000		115	21.1
1946(2)	Communist ⎫ Progressive ⎬	5 489 000		166	28.6
	Chr. Dem.	5 058 000		158	26.3
	Soc.	3 432 000		90	17.9
	Moderates	2 566 000		70	13.4
1951	Gaulliste	4 125 000		107	21.6
	Com. and Prog.	5 057 000		97	26.4
	Soc.	2 745 000		94	14.3
	Moderates	2 657 000		87	13.9
	Chr. Dem.	2 370 000		82	12.4
1956	Com. and Prog.	5 514 000		147	25.8
	Moderates	3 258 000		95	15.2
	Soc.	3 247 000		88	15.2
	Rep. Front ⎫ Radicals ⎪	1 996 000 ⎫			9.3

	Right ⎬
	  Centre ⎪
	  Radicals ⎭
		838 000 ⎭		73	3.9

	Chr. Dem.	2 366 000		71	11.1
1958	Gaulliste	4 165 000		198	20.4
	Moderates	4 502 000		133	22.1
	Chr. Dem.	2 273 000		57	11.1
	Soc.	3 194 000		44	15.7
	Com. and Prog.	3 908 000		10	19.2
1962	Gaulliste	5 847 000		234	31.9
	Soc.	2 320 000		64	12.6
	Com. and Prog.	3 992 000		41	21.7
	Moderates	1 743 000		37	9.6
	Chr. Dem.	1 635 000		37	8.9

	Votes per party		*Seats*	*% of votes*
1967	Gaulliste	8 454 000	232	37.7
	Dem. Soc. Fed.	4 207 000	116	18.8
	Com. and Prog.	5 030 000	72	22.4
1968	Gaulliste	10 201 024	349	46.1
	Communist	4 435 357	33	20.0
	FGDS	3 654 003	57	16.5
	Moderates	2 700 864	31	12.2
1973	Communists	4 438 834	73	20.6
	PSU, extreme left	85 678		0.3
	Socialists	4 722 886	102	21.9
	Other Left	823 084		3.8
	Reformers	1 325 058	34	6.1
	URP UDR	6 730 147	183	31.3
	Ind Rep.	1 658 060	55	7.7
	CDP	841 576	30	3.9
	Various	706 942		3.2
	Others	139 236	13	0.6
1977	RPR	6 651 756	154	26.1
	UDF	5 907 603	124	23.2
	Communists	4 744 868	86	18.6
	Socialists	7 212 916 ⎱		28.3
	Left Radicals	595 478 ⎰	103	2.3
	Other Parties (inc.	357 418 ⎱		1.2
	Presidential Majority)	305 763 ⎰	14	1.2
1981	Socialists + Left Radicals	9 198 332	285	
	RPR	4 191 482	85	
	UDF	3 481 849	65	
	Communists	1 303 587	44	
	Other Right-wing	408 861	8	
	Other Left-wing	112 481	4	
	Extreme Left	3 517	–	
1986	Communists	2 740 972	35	9.8
	Socialists	8 702 137	206	31.0

	Votes per party		Seats	% of votes
RPR		3 142 373	76	11.2
UDF		2 330 072	53	8.3
UDF/RPR joint		6 017 207	147	21.5
Various Right		1 094 336	14	3.9
National Front		2 705 838	35	9.6
Others		1 304 245	9	4.7

		Seats	% votes 1st ballot	% votes 2nd ballot
1988	Socialists	276	37.5	48.7
	UDF* ⎱	129	18.5	21.2
	RPR* ⎰	127	19.2	23.1
	Communists (PCF)	27	11.3	3.4
	Various Right-wing	16	2.9	2.6
	National Front	1	9.7	1.1
	Others	–	0.9	–
1993	RPR (Gaullists)	247	20.4	28.3
	UDF (allied to RPR)	213	19.1	25.8
	Socialist Party	70	17.6	28.2
	National Front	–	12.4	5.7
	PCF (Communists)	23	9.2	4.6
	Greens	–	4.0	–
	Ecology	–	3.6	–
	Right-wing parties	24	4.7	–

* Contested elections jointly as URC (Union du Rassemblement et du Centre).

		Seats	% vote (1st ballot)
1997 (25 May/1 Jun)	Socialist Party (PS)	241	23.4
	Rally for the Republic (RPR)	134	15.7
	Union for French Democracy (UDF)	108	14.2
	French Communist Party (PCF)	38	9.9
	National Front (FN)	1	14.9
	Greens	7	6.8
	Radical Socialist Party	12	1.4

		Seats	% vote (1st ballot)
Others (right)		14	6.6
	Others (left)	21	2.8
	Independents	1	1.4
	Others	–	2.6
		577	

GEORGIA

For elections 1918–1921, *see* note on p. 310. After the declaration of independence in 1991, direct elections to the presidency were held on 26 May. These were won by Zviad Gamsakhurdia with 86.5 per cent of the votes cast. Presidential as well as parliamentary elections were subsequently held on 5 Nov 1995. Eduard Shevardnadze was elected president with 1 589 909 votes (74.9 per cent of the 2 121 510 votes cast). The parliamentary elections were dominated by the Citizen's Union of Georgia (107 seats), followed by the National Democratic Party of Georgia (34 seats) and the All-Georgian Union of Revival (31 seats).

GERMANY

Between 1900 and 1914 elections were held on three occasions in the German Empire (1903, 1907 and 1912). The Centre Party won most seats in 1903 and 1907, but the steadily growing Social Democrats emerged as the largest party in 1912. The figures below are for the top four parties in each of these elections.

	Votes per party		Seats	% of votes
1903	Centre Party	1 875 300	100	19.8
	Social Democrats	3 010 800	81	31.7
	German Conservatives	948 500	54	10.0
	National Liberals	1 317 400	51	13.9
1907	Centre Party	2 179 800	105	19.4
	German Conservatives	1 060 200	60	9.4
	National Liberals	1 630 600	54	14.5
	Social Democrats	3 259 000	43	29.0
1912	Social Democrats	4 250 400	110	34.8
	Centre Party	1 996 800	91	16.4
	National Liberals	1 662 700	45	13.6
	German Conservatives	1 126 300	43	9.2

From 1918–1933, direct proportional elections by list system with a uniform quota of 60 000 votes for 1 representative. Suffrage for all men and women over 20. From 1933 to 1945 there were 3 elections, but these are not recognized as free elections and no figures are given.

		Votes per party	Seats	% of votes
1919	SPD	11 509 100	163	37.9
	BVP	5 980 200	91	19.7
	DDP	5 641 800	75	18.6
	DNVP	3 121 500	44	10.3
1920	SPD	6 104 400	102	21.6
	BVP	5 083 600	85	17.8
	USPD	5 046 800	84	18.0
	DVP	3 929 400	65	14.0
1924	SPD	6 008 900	100	20.5
	DNVP	5 696 500	95	19.5
	BVP	4 861 100	81	16.6
	KPD	3 693 300	62	12.6
1924	SPD	7 881 000	131	26.0
	DNVP	6 205 800	103	20.5
	BVP	5 252 900	88	17.3
	DVP	3 049 100	51	10.7
1928	SPD	9 153 000	153	29.8
	BVP	4 657 800	78	15.2
	DNVP	4 381 600	73	14.2
	KPD	3 264 800	54	10.6
1930	SPD	8 577 700	143	24.5
	NSDAP	6 409 600	107	18.3
	BVP	5 187 000	87	14.8
	KPD	4 592 100	77	13.1
1932	NSDAP	13 745 800	230	37.4
	SPD	7 959 700	133	21.6
	BVP	5 782 000	97	15.7
	KPD	5 282 600	89	14.6

		Votes per party	*Seats*	*% of votes*
1932	NSDAP	11 737 000	196	33.1
	SPD	7 248 000	121	20.4
	KPD	5 980 200	100	16.9
	BVP	5 325 200	90	15.0
	DNVP	2 959 000	52	8.8
1933	NSDAP	17 277 200	288	43.9
	SPD	7 181 600	120	18.3
	BVP	5 498 500	92	13.9
	KPD	4 848 100	81	12.3
	DNVP	3 136 800	52	8.0

GERMAN DEMOCRATIC REPUBLIC

Electors voted at 18 and could be candidates at 21. Elections to the People's Chamber (*Volkskammer*) were 'universal, equal, direct and secret' and were held every 4 years. East Berlin had its own Assembly (*Ostberliner Abgeordenetenhaus*) of 200 and did not elect to the *Volkskammer*. However, it nominated 66 representatives thereto without voting rights.

There were 434 seats in the *Volkskammer* (500 in all when the East Berlin nominees were added). The parties were represented in pre-arranged proportions. Since 1967 more candidates were allowed to stand than there were seats. All candidates who received more than 50 per cent of the votes were considered elected; those in excess of the number of seats were placed on a reserve list in order of votes gained. As well as to parties, seats were allotted to social and cultural organizations, *e.g.* to trade unions.

The *Volkskammer* evolved through a series of People's Congresses dominated by the USSR and East German Communists which claimed to speak for all Germany. At the *Länder* elections of Oct 1946 the SED failed to gain 50 per cent of the vote and elections thereafter were conducted on the Soviet single-list model.

	Electorate	*Valid votes*	*Seats*	
1949	13 533 071	12 887 234	SED	90
			CDU	45
			LDPD	45
			NDPD	15
			DBP	15
			Others	130

These elections resulted in the 3rd People's Congress of 1525 delegates, which elected from among its members a German People's Council of 330 on 3 May 1949. On 7 Oct 1949 the formation of a go-it-alone German Democratic Republic was announced and the People's Council became the Provisional *Volkskammer* of 400 representatives. West Germany declared the GDR illegal in that it was not founded upon free elections.

An Upper Chamber of representatives of provinces (*Länderkammer*) was formed in 1949 but abolished in 1958. The term 'Provisional' was dropped from the title of the *Volkskammer* after that Chamber had been confirmed by the 1950 elections.

	Electorate	*Valid votes*	*Seats*	
1950	12 331 905	12 139 932	SED	100
			CDU	60
			LDPD	60
			NDPD	30
			Others	150
1954	12 085 380	11 892 849	SED	102
			CDU	47
			LDPD	46
			NDPD	45
			DBD	45
			Others	115
1958	11 839 217	11 707 715	SED	102
			CDU	47
			LDPD	46
			NDPD	45
			DBD	45
			Others	115

At the 1963 elections the electorate was 11 621 158 (valid votes, 11 533 859); 1967, 11 341 729 (11 208 816); 1971, 11 401 090 (11 227 535). The distribution of seats in all 3 elections was the same: SED, 128; CDU, 52; LDPD, 52; NDPD, 52; DBP, 52; others 164.

In elections held on 17 Oct 1976, of the total electorate of 11 425 194 some 11 262 948 (98.58 per cent) cast their vote. Of the valid votes, 99.85 per cent were cast for the National Front list.

In elections held on 14 Jun 1981, of the total electorate of 12 356 263 some 12 255 006 (99.21 per cent) cast their vote. Of the valid votes, 99.86 per cent were cast for the National Front list.

In the elections of 8 Jun 1986, 99.94 per cent of those eligible to vote duly voted for the National Front, once again the only party allowed to contest the elections.

After the fall of the Honecker régime and the end of the Communist era, the first free elections in East Germany were held in Mar 1990. The outcome was:

Party	Seats	% of votes
Alliance for Germany	193	48.1
⎰Christian Democrats	164	40.9
⎱Social Union	25	6.3
⎰Democratic Awakening	4	0.9
Social Democrats	87	21.8
Party of Democratic Socialism*	65	16.3
Alliance of Free Democrats	21	5.3
Alliance '90 (inc. New Forum)	12	2.9
Democratic Farmers	9	2.2
Greens/Ind. Women	8	1.9
Others	5	1.5

Of the eligible electorate of 12.1 million, 93.2% voted.
* Formerly the Communists.

For the results of the first all-German elections of 2 Dec 1990, *see under* Federal Republic of Germany, p. 221.

GREECE

Voting procedures. Party list system in electoral departments. Direct election, majority vote. Universal male suffrage. From 1926, proportional representation until 1928, and then again for the election of Sep 1932 and the elections of Jan 1936, Mar 1946, Mar 1950, Sep 1951 and May 1958 onwards. Vote extended to women in 1955.

		Votes per party	Seats	% of votes
1926	Liberals	303 140	102	31.6
	Populists	194 243	60	20.3
	Freedom Party	151 044	51	15.8

	Votes per party		*Seats*	*% of votes*
1928	Liberals	477502	178	46.9
	Pro-Liberals	74976	25	2.5
	Workers and Agrarian	68278	20	6.7
	Populists	243543	19	23.9
1932	Liberals	391521	98	33.4
	Populists	395974	95	33.8
	Progressives	97836	15	8.4
1933	Populists	434550	118	38.1
	Liberals	379968	80	33.3
1935	Populists ⎱ Nat. Radical ⎰	669434	287	65.0
	Royalists	152285	7	14.8
1936	Liberals	474651	126	37.3
	Populists	281597	72	22.1
	Populists and Rad.	253384	60	19.9
1946	Nationalist (union of Populists, Nat. Lib., Reformist and others)	610995	206	55.1
	Nat. Pol. Union (Venizelos Liberals, Soc. Dem., Nat. United Party and others)	213721	68	19.3
	Liberals	159525	48	14.4
1950	Populists	317512	62	18.8
	Liberals	291083	56	17.2
	Nat. Prog. Union	277739	45	16.4
	Papandreou Party (ex-Soc. Dem.)	180185	35	10.7
1951	Hellene Party	624316	114	36.5
	Nat. Prog. Union	401379	74	23.5
	Liberals	325390	57	19.0

	Votes per party		Seats	% of votes
1952	Hellenes	783 541	247	49.2
	Nat. Prog. Union ⎫ Liberals ⎬	544 834	51	34.2
1956	Nat. Rad. Union	1 594 112	165	47.4
	Dem. Union	1 620 007	132	48.2
	(Populists, Liberals,			
	Nat. Prog. Union,			
	Agrarians and Centre)			
1958	Nat. Rad. Union	1 583 885	171	41.2
	United Democratic Left	939 902	79	24.4
	Liberals	795 445	36	20.7
1961	Nat. Rad. Union	2 347 824	176	50.8
	Centre Union ⎫ Progressives ⎬	1 555 442	100	33.7
	Un. Dem. Left	675 867	24	14.6
	(under title Pandemocratic			
	Agrarian Front)			
1963	Centre Union	1 962 079	138	42.0
	Nat. Rad. Union	1 837 377	132	39.4
	Un. Dem. Left	669 267	28	14.3
1964	Centre Union	2 424 477	171	52.7
	Nat. Rad. Union ⎫ Progressives ⎬	1 621 546	108	35.3
	Un. Dem. Left	542 865	21	11.8

Note: On 21 Apr 1967 dictatorial power was seized by right-wing army colonels, aiming to forestall the expected electoral victory of the Centre Union under George Papandreou. Democracy was restored in 1974 when Constantine Karamanlis returned from exile in Paris to head a government of National Unity.

	Votes per party		Seats	% of votes
1974	New Democracy	2 670 804	220	54.4
	Panhellenic Socialist			
	Union	666 806	12	13.6

	Votes per party		Seats	% of votes
	Centre Union	1002908	60	20.4
	Communists/United Left	464331	8	9.4
	National Democratic			
	Union	54162	–	1.1
	Others	53345	–	1.1
1977	New Democracy	2146687	172	41.8
	Panhellenic Socialist			
	Movement	1299196	93	25.3
	Democratic Centre Union	613113	15	11.9
	Communist Party (KKE)	480188	11	9.4
	Left-wing and Progressive			
	Alliance	139762	2	2.7
	Others	405411	7	7.9
1981	Panhellenic Socialist			
	Movement	2725395	172	48.1
	New Democracy	2033774	115	35.9
	Communists (KKE			
	exterior)	619296	13	10.9
	Progressive Party	95697	–	1.7
	KKE (interior)	77465	–	1.4
	Others	119314	–	2.0
1985	PASOK	2916450	161	45.8
	New Democracy	2599949	126	40.9
	KKE – Exterior	629578	12	9.9
	KKE – Interior	117050	1	1.8
	Others	102072		1.6
1989 (Jun)	New Democracy		145	44.3
	PASOK		125	39.2
	Left Coalition		28	13.1
	Inds & Others		2	3.5
1989 (Nov)	New Democracy		148	46.2
	PASOK		128	40.7
	Left Coalition		21	11.0

	Votes per party	Seats	% of votes
	Ecologists	1	0.6
	Others	2	1.5
1990 (Apr)	New Democracy	150	46.9
	PASOK	123	38.6
	Left Coalition	19	10.2
	Ecologists	1	0.8
	Others	7	3.5
1993 (Oct)	PASOK	170	46.9
	New Democracy	111	39.3
	Political Spring	10	4.9
	Communist Party	9	4.5
	Others	–	3.1
1996 (Sep)	Panhellenic Socialist Movement (PASOK)	162	41.5
	New Democracy (ND)	108	38.2
	Communist Party (KKE)	11	5.6
	Coalition of the Left and Progress	10	5.1
	Democratic Social Movement (DHKKI)	9	4.4
	Others (including Political Spring)	–	5.2

HUNGARY

Before its extensive territorial reduction in 1918 the kingdom of Hungary formed part of the Austro-Hungarian empire. It had no codified written constitution. There was a bicameral parliament (*Országház*), but only 6 per cent of the population possessed the vote.

Towards the close of the war M. Károlyi's Party of Independence emerged on the political scene, standing for independence from Austria and unilateral withdrawal from hostilities. At a time of popular unrest Károlyi was appointed Prime Minister on 31 Oct 1918, leading a coalition government of Party of Independence, Radicals and Social Democrats. On 13 Nov 1918 King Charles IV renounced participation in affairs of state, and on 16 Nov 1918 Hungary was proclaimed a Republic with Károlyi as provisional President (he became President on 11 Jan 1919). Parliament was dissolved and replaced by a provisional unicameral National Assembly.

This government resigned on 22 May 1919 in protest at Allied territorial demands, and was succeeded by a Soviet Republic of Communists and Social Democrats led by Béla Kun. Elections to the Soviets were held on 17 Apr 1919. The Communist régime was short-lived and harassed by hostilities with foreign invaders and native anti-Communist forces. Kun resigned on 1 Aug 1919, and Romania occupied Budapest until M. Horthy entered on 16 Nov 1919 at the head of an anti-Communist army.

At Allied insistence an election with universal secret suffrage was held on 25 Jan 1920. The Christian Nationalists (government party) gained 77 seats, the Smallholders 49. The Social Democrats refused to take part.

This government annulled all Károlyi's and Kun's legislation and re-established the former constitution. The link with Austria was dissolved. On 23 Mar 1920 Hungary was proclaimed a kingdom again; Horthy had been chosen as regent on 1 Mar 1920.

This government decreed a new electoral system. The upper house (House of Magnates) was re-established. Secret ballot was abolished except in towns (20 per cent of constituencies were urban). Some 1.5 m. lost the vote. Educational, property and residence qualifications were introduced. Men voted at 24, women at 30. Candidates had to be nominated by 10 000 electors. The National Assembly was to consist of 245 deputies.

On 7 Mar and 29 Oct 1921 Charles IV made unsuccessful attempts to regain the throne.

At the elections of 28 May and 2 Jun 1922 Smallholders and Christian Nationalists combined to form the Party of National Unity, which gained 143 seats. The opposition parties gained 78 (including 25 Social Democrats).

An electoral law of 11 Nov 1926 gave definitive form to the House of Magnates, which was to consist of nominated members of the nobility and upper middle class, and other dignitaries. A small proportion of members were elected for ten-year terms.

1926   Party of National Unity, 171; Christian Social Union, 35; Social Democrats, 14; others, 25.

1931   Party of National Unity, 155; Christian Social Union, 32; Social Democrats 14; Independent Smallholders, 11; Independents, 21; others, 12.

1935   Party of National Unity, 170; Independent Smallholders, 23; Christian Social Union, 14; Social Democrats, 11.

By an electoral law of Dec 1938 residential and educational qualifications were made stricter, and male voting age raised from 24 to 26. In order to vote, women over 30 had to be self-supporting or the wives of electors. The number of deputies was raised to 260. 135 single-member constituencies were formed, election requirement being a simple majority over 40 per cent. Multi-member constituencies elected the remainder on a proportional representation scheme.

Secret ballot was introduced in May 1939, and many Jews were disenfranchised.

1939   Party of Hungarian Life (formerly Party of National Unity) in alliance, 186; Christian Union, 3; Arrow Cross (fascists), 29; Independent Smallholders, 14; National Social Front Union, 5; Citizens' Freedom Party, 5; Social Democrats, 5; Racialists, 4; National Front, 3; Christian National Social Front, 3; People's Will, 1; Independents, 2.

During the war an Independence Front began to take shape of Social Democrats, crypto-Communists, Smallholders, National Peasants and Legitimists.

With the Soviet invasion a provisional government was set up at Debrecen on 21 Dec 1944, which ultimately consisted of 127 Communists, 123 Smallholders, 94 Social Democrats, 63 Trade Unionists, 39 National Peasants, 22 Democrats and 30 independents.

By an electoral law of 19 Sep 1945 universal secret suffrage at 20 was introduced.

		Votes	*Seats*
1945	Smallholders	2 688 161	245
	Social Democrats	821 566	69
	Communists	800 257	70
	National Peasants	322 988	23
	Democrats	78 522	2
			409

1947 Electorate: 5 407 893. Voted: 4 996 100 (93 per cent). Seats 411.

Government bloc	*Votes*	*Seats*
Communists	1 082 497	100
Smallholders	757 821	68
Social Democrats	732 178	67
National Peasants	435 170	36
		271

Opposition	Votes	Seats
Popular Democrats	805 450	60
Hungarian Independence Party	718 193	49
Independent Democrats	256 396	18
Radicals	93 270	6
Christian Women's Union	67 792	4
Citizen Democrats	48 055	3
		140

During the next 2 years the opposition parties were eliminated or amalgamated into the People's Front. The Social Democrats merged into the Communists in Jun 1948. At the election of 15 May 1949 candidates were presented on a single list, the People's Front. Electorate: 6 053 972. Voted: 5 730 519 (94.6 per cent). For the People's Front: 5 478 515 (95.6 per cent).

A new constitution of Soviet type was promulgated on 18 Aug 1949. Hungary was proclaimed a 'People's Republic'. Voting age was lowered to 18. The National Assembly was to be elected every 4 years by universal secret suffrage.

At the election of 17 May 1953 there was a single list of People's Front. Electorate: 6 501 869. Voted: 6 370 519 (98 per cent). Votes for People's Front: 6 256 653 (98.2 per cent).

On 27 Oct 1956 there was a major reorganization of the government in response to armed insurrection: Independent Smallholders and National Peasants were co-opted in. Revolutionary councils sprang up demanding a free general election. On 30 Oct 1956 I. Nagy proclaimed the restoration of multi-party government. On 3 Nov 1956 the government was reorganized as a coalition of Communists, Smallholders, National Peasants and Social Democrats.

This government was overthrown by armed Soviet intervention and a 'Revolutionary Worker-Peasant government' set up under J. Kádár.

At the election of 16 Nov 1958, 6 493 680 voted (98.4 per cent of electorate). For People's Patriotic Front: 6 431 832 (99.6 per cent). There were 338 candidates for 338 seats.

At the election of 24 Feb 1963 the electorate was 7 114 855. Voted: 6 915 644 (97.2 per cent). Voted for the single list of People's Patriotic Front 6 813 058 (98.9 per cent). 340 deputies elected.

On 11 Nov 1966 an electoral law brought an end to the strict rigidity of the one seat – one candidate system by replacing the 20 multi-seat mega-constituencies by 349 single-member constituencies. All candidates remained nominees of the People's Patriotic Front, but it became possible for more than one candidate to contest a single seat.

In the election of 19 Mar 1967 this happened in 9 constituencies. None of the 9 challengers was elected. 7 131 151 votes were cast (99.7 per cent of the electorate) and 98.8 per cent of these were for the People's Patriotic Front candidates.

In Oct 1970 another electoral law liberalized the position further by introducing the participation of the ordinary citizenry in the nomination of candidates. In the election of 25 Apr 1970, 49 seats were contested by more than one candidate. Electorate: 7 432 420. Voted: 7 334 918 (98.7 per cent). Voted for the People's Patriotic Front: 7 258 121 (98.9 per cent). Elected: 352 deputies.

In elections held on 15 Jun 1975, 7 527 169 votes were cast (97.6 per cent of a total electorate of 7 760 464). Of these, 99.6 per cent of votes were cast for official candidates.

In elections held in Jun 1980, only 15 of the 352 seats were contested by more than 1 candidate. Of the 7.7 million who voted, 99.3 per cent of votes cast were for the official People's Patriotic Front.

In elections held in Jun 1985, 873 candidates were put forward for the 352 seats elected on a territorial basis (35 additional members were elected unopposed on a national list). The electorate was 7.7m., of whom 93.9 per cent voted in the first round and 83 per cent in the second round. Of the candidates, 795 were proposed by the Patriotic People's Front, 78 direct from the floor of nomination meetings (of these 78, 43 were elected). A total of 244 members were elected for the first time.

The first free elections in Hungary since the fall of the Communist régime were held on 25 Mar and 8 Apr 1990. The results of the elections for the 386 elected deputies were:

	No. of seats	% of votes
Hungarian Democratic Forum	165	42.74
Alliance of Free Democrats	92	23.83
Independent Smallholders' Party	43	11.13
Hungarian Socialist Party	33	8.54
Federation of Young Democrats	21	5.44
Christian Democratic People's Party	21	5.44
Independents	6	1.55
Joint candidates	4	1.03
Agrarian Alliance	1	0.25

Parliamentary elections were held in two rounds on 8 and 29 May 1994.

	No. of seats	% of votes
Hungarian Socialist Party	209	54.1
Alliance of Free Democrats	70	18.1
Hungarian Democratic Forum	37	9.6
Independent Smallholders' Party	26	6.7
Christian Democratic People's Party	22	5.7
Federation of Young Democrats	20	5.2
Agrarian Alliance	1	0.3
Liberal Bloc	1	0.3
	386	

		Total seats	% regional party list
1998 (10, 24 May)	FIDESZ/Hungarian Civic Party (MPP)	147**	29.5
	Socialist Party (MSzP)	134	32.9
	Independent Smallholders' Party (FKGP)	48	13.2
	Hungarian Democratic Forum (MDF)	18	3.1
	Alliance of Free Democrats	24	7.6
	Hungarian Justice and Life Party	14	5.5
	Others	1	8.2
		386*	

* Of which 304 regional party list.
** In order to gain a majority of seats in parliament, FIDESZ-MPP formed a coalition with the Hungarian Democratic Forum (MDF) with which it had allied itself in the elections, and with the rural Independent Smallholders' Party (FKGP) giving it an overall majority of 19.

ICELAND

Voting procedures. From 1915–1920, the Althing had 40 members directly elected, 6 proportionally and 34 by majority. Majority elections were in 25 constituencies, 9 of them 2-member, the rest single. Suffrage for the election of 34 members, all men and women property-holders over 25; for the 6, all those over 35. From 1920 onwards the Althing had additional members, including some elected by direct proportional election in Reykjavik. From 1934, suffrage extended to all men and women over 21 'in charge of their own finances and properties'.

	Votes per party		*Seats*	*% of votes*
1916	Home Rule Party	5 333	12	40.0
	Hardline Independence	2 097	7	15.7
	Farmers Party	1 173	5	8.8
	Others	4 745	10	36.5
1923	Citizens Party	16 272	21	53.6
	Progressives	8 062	13	26.6
	Soc. Dem.	4 912	1	16.2
1927	Progressives	9 532	17	29.8
	Liberals ⎫ Conservatives ⎭	15 474	13	42.0
	Soc. Dem.	6 097	4	19.1
1931	Progressives	13 844	12	35.9
	Independence	16 891	21	43.8
1933	Independence	17 131	17	48.0
	Progressives	8 530	14	23.9
1934	Independence	21 974	20	42.3
	Progressives	11 377	15	21.9
	Soc. Dem.	11 269	10	21.7
1937	Progressives	14 556	19	24.9
	Independence	24 132	17	41.3
	Soc. Dem.	11 084	8	19.0
1942(1)	Progressives	16 033	20	27.6
	Independence	22 975	17	39.5
	United Soc.	11 059	10	18.5
1942(2)	Independence	23 001	20	38.5
	Progressives	15 869	15	26.6
	United Soc.	11 059	10	18.5
1946	Independence	26 428	20	39.4
	Progressives	15 429	13	23.1
	United Soc.	13 049	10	19.5
	Soc. Dem.	11 914	9	17.8
1949	Independence	28 546	19	39.5
	Progressives	17 659	17	24.5
	United Soc.	14 077	9	19.5

	Votes per party		Seats	% of votes
1953	Independence	28738	21	37.1
	Progressives	16959	16	21.9
	United Soc.	12422	7	16.1
1956	Independence	35027	19	42.4
	Progressives	12925	17	15.6
	People's Un.	15859	8	19.2
	Soc. Dem.	15153	8	18.3
1959(1)	Independence	36029	20	42.5
	Progressives	23061	19	27.2
	People's Un.	12929	7	15.3
1959(2)	Independence	33800	24	39.7
	Progressives	21882	17	25.7
	People's Un.	13621	10	16.0
	Soc. Dem.	12909	9	15.2
1963	Independence	37021	24	41.4
	Progressives	25217	19	28.2
	People's Un.	14274	9	16.0
1967	Independence	36036	23	37.5
	Progressives	27029	18	28.1
	People's Un.	13403	9	13.9
	Soc. Dem.	15059	9	15.7
1971	Independence	38170	22	36.2
	Progressives	26645	17	25.3
	People's Un.	18055	10	17.1
	Soc. Dem.	11020	6	10.5
1974	Independence	48758	25	42.8
	People's Alliance	20922	11	18.3
	Soc. Dem.	10321	5	9.1
	Progressives	28388	17	24.9
	Liberal and Leftist Union	5244	2	4.6
1978	Independence	39973	20	32.7
	People's Alliance	27962	14	22.9

	Votes per party		*Seats*	*% of votes*
	Soc. Dem.	26912	14	22.0
	Progressives	20561	12	16.9
	Liberal and Leftist Union	na		3.5
1979	Independence	42957	21	33.6
	People's Alliance	24390	11	19.1
	Soc. Dem.	27078	10	21.2
	Progressives	30871	17	24.2
	Others	2433	1	1.9
1983	Independence	50251	23	38.7
	Progressives	24095	14	18.5
	People's Alliance	22490	10	17.3
	Soc. Dem.	15214	6	11.7
	Soc. Dem. Alliance	9489	4	7.3
	Others	8423	3	6.5
1987	Independence		18	27.2
	Progressives		13	18.9
	Soc. Dem.		10	15.2
	People's Alliance		8	13.3
	Citizens' Party		7	10.9
	Women's Alliance		6	10.1
	Others		1	4.4
1991	Independence Party		26	38.6
	Progressive Party		13	18.9
	Social Democratic Party		10	15.5
	People's Alliance		9	14.4
	Women's Alliance		5	8.3
	Others		–	4.3
1995	Independence Party		25	37.1
	Progressive Party		15	23.3
	People's Alliance		9	14.3
	Social Democratic Party		7	11.4
	Awakening of the Nation		4	7.2
	Women's Alliance		3	4.9

	Votes per party	Seats	% of votes
1999	Independence Party	27	40.7
(8 May)	People's Alliance	17	26.8
	Progressive Party	12	18.4
	Left–Green Alliance	6	9.1
	Liberal Party	2	4.2
		64	

IRELAND

Voting procedures. From 1918–1921, single-member constituencies, spot voting and plurality counting. From 1921, multi-member constituencies with preferential voting and quota counting. Suffrage for men of 21 and over, and women of 30 and over, until 1923 when the age limit for both was 21. From 1918–1923, university graduates and owners of businesses had extra votes.

	Electorate	Valid votes	Votes per party		Seats	% of electorate	% of votes
1918	1936673	1046541	Sinn Fein	496961	73	–	47.5
			Unionists	298726	26	–	28.5
			Nationalists	233690	6		22.3
1921	–	–	Sinn Fein	–	124		–
			Unionists	–	4		

(*Note*: This was not a normal election; no poll took place; all borough and county seats were taken by Sinn Fein and the Unionists were returned for Dublin University.)

1922	1026289	627623	Pro-Treaty	245336	58	–	39.1
	(first preference)		Anti-Treaty	134801	36	–	21.5
			Labour	132511	17		21.1

(*Note*: Pro- and Anti-Treaty parties were the result of the division of Sinn Fein.)

1923	1785436	1052495	Fine Gael	409184	63	22.9	38.9
			Fianna Fail	291191	44	16.3	27.7
			Labour	130659	16	7.3	12.4
1927(1)	1730426	1146460	Fine Gael	314711	46	18.2	27.5
			Fianna Fail	299476	44	17.3	26.1
			Labour	159046	23	9.2	13.9

	Electorate	Valid votes	Votes per party		Seats	*% of* electorate	*% of* votes
1927(2)	1728340	1170856	Fine Gael	453013	61	26.2	38.7
			Fianna Fail	411833	57	23.8	35.2
			Labour	111287	13	6.4	9.5
1932	1601933	1274026	Fianna Fail	566498	72	33.5	44.5
			Fine Gael	449506	56	26.6	35.3
			Independence	106466	12	6.3	8.4
			Labour	114163	9	6.7	9.0
1933	1724420	1386558	Fianna Fail	689054	76	40.0	49.7
			Fine Gael	422495	48	24.5	30.5
			Labour	88347	9	5.1	6.4
1937	1775055	1324449	Fianna Fail	599040	68	33.7	45.2
			Fine Gael	461171	48	26.0	34.8
			Labour	147728	15	8.3	11.2
1938	1697323	1286259	Fianna Fail	667996	76	39.4	51.9
			Fine Gael	428633	45	25.3	33.3
			Labour	140099	9	8.3	10.9
1943	1816142	1331709	Fianna Fail	557525	66	30.7	41.9
			Fine Gael	307499	32	16.9	23.1
			Labour	214743	17	11.8	16.1
1944	1776850	1217349	Fianna Fail	595259	75	33.5	48.9
			Fine Gael	249329	30	14.0	20.5
			Labour	140245	12	7.9	11.5
1948	1800210	1323443	Fianna Fail	553914	67	30.8	41.9
			Fine Gael	262393	31	14.6	19.8
			Labour	150229	19	8.3	11.4
1951	1785144	1331573	Fianna Fail	161212	68	34.5	46.3
			Fine Gael	342922	40	19.2	25.8
			Labour	151828	16	8.5	11.4
1954	1763209	1335202	Fianna Fail	578960	65	32.8	43.4
			Fine Gael	427031	50	24.2	32.0
			Labour	163982	18	9.3	12.3
1957	1738278	1227019	Fianna Fail	592994	78	34.1	48.3
			Fine Gael	326699	40	18.8	26.6
			Labour	111747	11	6.4	9.1

	Electorate	Valid votes	Votes per party		Seats	% of electorate	% of votes
1961	1 670 860	1 168 404	Fianna Fail	512 073	70	30.6	43.8
			Fine Gael	374 099	47	22.4	32.0
			Labour	139 822	16	8.4	12.0
1965	1 683 019	1 253 122	Fianna Fail	597 414	72	35.4	47.7
			Fine Gael	427 081	47	25.4	34.1
			Labour	192 740	22	11.5	15.4
1969	1 735 388	1 318 953	Fianna Fail	602 234	75	34.7	45.7
			Fine Gael	449 749	50	25.9	34.1
			Labour	224 498	18	12.9	17.0

In the five elections of 1973–1982, the seats won were as follows:

Party	1973	1977	1981	1982 (Feb)	1982 (Nov)
Fianna Fail	69	34	78	81	75
Fine Gael	54	43	65	66	70
Labour	19	17	15	15	16
Independents/Others	2	4	8	7	5

In the elections of 1987, 1989 and 1992 the seats won were as follows:

Party	1987	% of votes**	1989	% of votes	1992	% of votes
Fianna Fail	81	44.1	77	43.7	68	39.1
Fine Gael	51	27.1	55	29.6	45	245
Labour Party	12	6.5	15	8.0	33	19.3
Workers' Party***	4	3.8	7	5.6	4	2.8
Progressive Democrats	14	11.9	6	5.0	10	4.7
Others*	4	6.6	6	8.2	6	9.6

* Including in 1989 the first Green Party elected member.
** First preference votes.
*** Democratic Left in 1992.

In elections held on 6 Jun 1997 the results were:

	Seats	% vote
Fianna Fail	77	39.3
Fine Gael	54	27.9
Labour Party	17	10.4
Progressive Democrats	4	4.7
Democratic Left	4	2.5
Others*	10	15.1

* Including 2 Greens.

ITALY

The elections of 1919 and 1921 were fought on adult male suffrage and the *d'Hondt* system of proportional representation. The election of 1924 was not a free election because of Fascist intimidation. After 1945, the new constitution provided for a bicameral parliament, with a minimum voting age of 21. Deputies are chosen by proportional representation using the *Imperiali* system. Proportional representation was introduced into the lower house in 1994.

From 1900 to 1914, four elections were held (in 1900, 1904, 1909 and 1913). Each election was dominated by the combined Ministerial and Opposition Liberals (412 out of 508 seats in 1900, 415 in 1904, 382 in 1909 and 310 in 1913). The Socialist vote rose from 13 per cent (33 seats) in 1900 to 17.6 per cent (52 seats) in 1913. The best Republican performance was 6.2 per cent in 1900, the best Radical Party 11.7 per cent in 1913.

	Votes per party		Seats	% of votes
1919	Socialist	1 834 792	156	32.3
	Popular	1 167 354	100	20.5
	Centre coalition	904 195	96	15.9
	Democrats	622 310	60	10.9
1921	Socialist	1 631 435	123	24.7
	Popular	1 377 008	108	20.4
	Nat. Bloc.	1 260 007	105	19.1
	Lib. Dem.	684 855	68	10.4
1924	Fascist	4 671 550	375	65.3
	Popular	645 789	39	9.0

	Votes per party		Seats	% of votes
1946	Chris. Dem.	8101004	207	35.2
	Socialist	4758129	115	20.7
	Communist	4356686	104	18.9
1948	Chris. Dem.	12741299	305	48.5
	Communist[1] ⎫ Socialist ⎭	8137047	183	31.0
1953	Chris. Dem.	10864282	263	40.1
	Communist	6121922	143	22.6
	Socialist	3441305	75	12.7
	Monarchist	1855843	30	6.9
1958	Chris. Dem.	12520556	273	42.4
	Communist	6704763	140	22.7
	Socialist	4206777	84	14.2
1963	Chris. Dem.	11763418	260	38.3
	Communist	7763854	166	25.3
	Socialist	4251966	87	13.8
1968	Chris. Dem.	12441553	266	39.1
	Communist	8557404	177	26.9
	Socialist	4605832	91	14.5
1972	Chris. Dem.	12943675	267	38.8
	Communist	9085927	179	27.2
	Socialist	4925700	89	14.7
1976	Chris. Dem.	14211005	262	38.7
	Communists	12620509	228	34.4
	Socialists	3541383	57	9.6
	Social Democrats	1237483	15	3.4
	Republicans	1134648	14	3.1
	Liberals	478157	5	1.3
	Italian Social Movement	2243849	35	6.1
	Others	1248543	14	3.4
1979	Chris. Dem.	14007594	262	38.3
	Communists	11107883	201	30.4

[1] Under the name Democratic Popular Front.

	Votes per party		*Seats*	*% of votes*
	Socialists	3 586 256	62	9.8
	Italian Social Movement	1 924 251	30	5.3
	Social Democrats	1 403 873	20	3.8
	Republicans	1 106 766	16	3.0
	Liberals and Radicals	1 967 384	27	5.3
	Others	1 462 578	12	4.1
1983	Chris. Dem.	12 145 800	225	32.9
	Communists	11 028 158	198	29.9
	Socialists	4 222 487	73	11.4
	Italian Social Movement	2 511 722	42	6.8
	Republicans	1 872 536	29	5.1
	Social Democrats	1 507 431	23	4.1
	Liberals and Radicals	1 875 505	27	5.1
	Others	1 726 642	13	4.7
1987	Chris. Dem.	13 231 960	234	34.3
	Communists	10 249 690	177	26.6
	Socialists	5 501 980	94	14.3
	Italian Social Movement	2 282 212	35	5.9
	Republicans	1 428 358	21	3.7
	Social Democrats	1 140 086	17	3.0
	Liberals and Radicals	1 798 636	24	4.7
	Greens	969 534	13	2.5
	Others	1 970 598	15	5.0
1992	Christian Democrats		206	29.7
	Democratic Party of the Left		107	16.1
	Socialists (PSI)		92	13.6
	Italian Social Movement (MSI)		34	5.4
	Republicans (PRI)		27	4.4
	Social Democrats (PSDI)		16	2.7
	Liberals (PLI)		17	2.8
	Northern League		55	8.7
	Communists		35	5.6
	Greens		16	2.8

		Seats	% of votes
	La Rete	12	1.9
	Others	13	6.3
1994 (27–28 Mar)	Freedom Alliance	366	42.9
	Forze Italia		(21.0)
	National Alliance		(13.5)
	Northern League		(8.4)
	Progressive Alliance	213	34.4
	Democratic Party of the Left		(20.4)
	PRC (Refounded Communists)		(6.0)
	Greens		(2.7)
	Socialists, La Rete, AD		(5.3)
	Centre (Popular Party, Segni Pact)	46	15.7
	Others	5	7.0
1996 (21 Apr)	Olive Tree Alliance	284	41.2
	Freedom Alliance	246	37.3
	Northern League	59	
	Refounded Communists	35	8.6
	Minor Parties	6	

LATVIA

A Constituent Assembly in May 1920 established a parliament (*Saeima*) of 100 deputies to be elected every 3 years. Elections were held in 1922, 1925, 1928 and 1931. The system favoured a proliferation of parties: 22 in 1922; 27 in 1925; 25 in 1928 and 24 in 1931. The more numerous parties were, from right to left: Farmers' Union; Catholics; Democratic Centre; New Settlers; Right-wing Socialists; Social Democrats. The Communist Party was illegal, but ran as the Workers' Bloc in 1931, gaining 7 seats. The Social Democrats had 30 deputies in each election, except that of 1931, when they had 22. There were Jewish, Polish, Russian and German national minority parties, and also a fascist party, Thunder Cross (*Perkonkrusts*). On 15 May 1932 Ulmanis assumed dictatorial powers by dismissing the *Saeima* and prohibiting all party political activity.

The country was occupied by Soviet troops on 16 Jun 1940 and an election was held on 14 and 15 Jul 1940. The resultant People's *Saeima* voted unanimously for incorporation into the USSR.

The first elections in newly-independent Latvia took place on 5 and 6 Jun 1993, with 874 candidates from 23 parties.

	Seats	% of votes
Latvian Way	36	32.4
Latvian National Independence Movement[1]	15	13.3
Harmony for Latvia – Revival of the Economy	13	12.0
Latvian Farmers' Union	12	10.6
Equal Rights Movement	7	5.8
Fatherland and Freedom Union	6	5.4
Christian Democratic Union of Latvia	6	5.0
Democratic Centre Party[2]	5	4.8
Others		10.7
Total	100	

[1] Later renamed the Latvian National Conservative Party.
[2] Subsequently took name Democratic Party.

In parliamentary elections on 3 Oct 1998, the result was:

	Seats	% of votes
People's Party	24	21.2
Latvian Way (LC)	21	18.1
Conservative Union for Fatherland and Freedom/LNNK	17	14.1
National Harmony Party	16	14.6
Latvian Social Democratic Union	14	12.8
New Party	8	7.3
Others	–	11.9
	100	

LITHUANIA

On 22 Sep 1917 a congress of 214 Lithuanian delegates elected a 20-strong council (*Taryba*) which proclaimed independence and organized elections for a Constituent Assembly. These were held by universal suffrage on the proportional representation system on 15 May 1920. One representative stood for 15 000 inhabitants. There were 112 seats in the Constituent Assembly, distributed as follows: Christian Democrats, 59; Social Populist Democrats, 29; Social Democrats, 13; Jews, 6; Poles, 3; Independents, 2.

This enacted that a parliament (*Semias*) of 80 was to be elected every 3 years by universal suffrage on the proportional representation system, 1 deputy representing 25 000 electors.

At the elections of 10 Oct 1922 the results were: Christian Democrats (including the Farmers' Union and the Workers' Federation), 38; Social Populist Democrats, 19; Social Democrats, 11; Workers' Party, 5; Jews, 3; Poles, 2. A. Stulginskis was elected President.

A further election was held on 5 Jun 1923: Christian Democrats, 40; Social Populist Democrats, 16; Social Democrats, 8; Jews, 5; Poles, 5; Germans, 2; Russians, 2.

Elections 8 and 10 May 1926: Christian Democrats, 30; Social Populist Democrats, 22; Social Democrats, 15; Poles, 4; Jews, 3; Germans, 1; and from Memel (Klaipeda) Agrarians, 3; People's Party, 2.

By a *coup d'état* of 17 Dec 1926, A. Smetona assumed dictatorial powers as President, and parliamentary government lapsed.

Elections in newly-independent Lithuania took place on 25 Oct 1993 (with run-offs in 51 constituencies on 10 Nov). The former Communists (now the Lithuanian Democratic Labour Party) dominated the results.

	Seats
Democratic Labour Party	73
Sajudis	30
Christian Democratic Party	16
Social Democratic Party	8
Union of Poles	4
Independents and Others	10
	141

In elections in Oct and Nov 1996 the result was:

Homeland Union (party of Vytautas Landsbergis)	70
Democratic Labour Party (ex-Communists)	12
Christian Democratic Party	16
Social Democratic Party	12
Others	27
	137

The presidential elections of 21 Dec 1997 resulted in victory (on the second ballot on 4 Jan 1998) for Valdas Adamkus (with 50.4 per cent) over his opponent Arturas Paulauskas (49.6 per cent).

MACEDONIA

The first general election in independent Macedonia took place on 16 and 30 Oct 1994. The presidential election, easily won by Kiro Gligorov, was also held on 16 Oct. The general election was dominated by the 3-party Alliance for Macedonia (comprising the Social Democratic Alliance of Macedonia (58 seats), the Liberal Party (29 seats) and the Socialist Party of Macedonia (8 seats)). Of the remaining 25 seats in the 120-seat Assembly, the Party for Democratic Prosperity had 10 and the National Democratic Party 4.

In elections on 18 Oct 1998 (with the second round on 1 Nov) the results of the run-off ballot saw the defeat of the ruling Social Democrats.

	Seats	% vote
⎧ Internal Macedonian Revolutionary Organization (VMRO)	62	⎰ 28.1
⎩ Democratic Alternative Party (DA)		⎱ 10.1
Social Democrats	27	25.2
⎧ Party of Democratic Prosperity (ethnic Albanian)	25	19.3
⎩ National Democratic Party (ethnic Albanian)		
Unfilled (repeat elections held 15 Nov)	6	
	120	

MALTA

In the first election after independence (held in 1966), the Nationalists under Dr Borg Olivier won 28 seats, the Labour Party won 22. Thereafter the results were as follows:

	Votes per party		Seats	% of votes
1971	Malta Labour Party	85 448	28	50.8
	Nationalist Party	80 753	27	48.1
	Others	1 756	–	–
1976	Malta Labour Party	105 854	34	51.5
	Nationalist Party	99 551	31	48.5
	Independent	35	–	–
1981	Malta Labour Party	109 990	34	49.1
	Nationalist Party	114 132	31	50.9

	Votes per party		Seats	% of votes
1987	Nationalist Party	119 721	35	50.9
	Malta Labour Party	114 937	34	48.9
	Others	511	–	0.2
1992	Nationalist Party	127 932	34	51.8
	Malta Labour Party	114 911	31	46.5
	Others	4 296	–	1.7
1996	Malta Labour Party	132 497	31*	50.7
	Nationalist Party	124 864	34	47.8
	Others	3 863	–	1.5
1998	Nationalist Party	137 037	35	51.8
	Malta Labour Party	124 220	30	46.9
	Democratic Alternative	3 208	–	1.2
	Others	27	–	0.1
			65	100.0

* Eventual seat allocation to Labour was 35.

MOLDOVA

The first elections in independent Moldova were held on 27 Feb 1994. The outcome was a victory for the Agrarian Democratic Party.

	Seats	% of votes
Agrarian Democratic Party	56	43.2
Socialist Unity	28	22.0
Bloc of Peasants and Intellectuals	11	9.2
Popular Front Alliance	9	7.5
Others (including Social Democrats, Democratic Labour and Reform)	–	18.1

The parliamentary elections of Mar 1998 were dominated by the Moldovan Party of Communists (40 seats, 30.1 per cent) with the Democratic Convention of Moldova in second place (26 seats, 19.2 per cent) and the Movement for a Democratic and Prosperous Moldova third (24 seats, 18.2 per cent). Nearly a quarter of the vote went to a variety of smaller parties (including Social Democrats).

THE NETHERLANDS

Voting procedures. Direct proportional elections on the party list system. Elections to 100 seats, the rest allocated according to the greatest remainder vote. Suffrage for men over 25, until 1922 when it was extended to women the same age. In 1946, extended to all citizens 23 and over and in 1967 all citizens over 21.

Between 1900 and 1914, elections were held on 4 occasions (1901, 1905, 1909 and 1913). The period saw a steady rise in the Social Democratic Workers vote (from 9.5 per cent in 1901 to 18.5 per cent in 1913). The largest party in 1901 and 1905 was the Free Liberal League. The Catholic Party and the Anti-Revolutionary Party each won 25 seats in 1909. The Catholic Party won 25 seats again in 1913 with the Liberal Union taking 22.

		Votes per party	*Seats*	*% of votes*
1918	RKS	402 908	30	30.0
	SDAP	296 145	22	22.0
	PvV	202 972	15	15.1
	ARP	179 523	13	13.4
1922	RKS	874 745	32	29.9
	SDAP	567 769	20	19.4
	ARP	402 277	16	13.7
1925	RKS	883 333	30	28.6
	SDAP	706 689	24	22.9
	ARP	377 426	13	12.2
1929	RKS	1 001 589	30	29.6
	SDAP	804 714	24	23.9
	ARP	391 832	12	11.6
	CHU	354 548	11	10.5
1933	RKS	1 037 364	28	27.9
	SDAP	798 632	22	21.5
	ARP	499 892	14	13.4

	Votes per party		Seats	% of votes
1937	RKS	1170431	31	28.8
	SDAP	890661	23	22.0
	ARP	665501	17	16.4
1946	KV	1466582	32	30.8
	PvA	1347940	29	28.3
	ARP	614201	13	12.9
1948	KV	1531154	32	31.0
	PvA	1263058	27	25.6
	ARP	651612	13	13.2
1952	KV	1529508	30	28.7
	PvA	1545867	30	29.0
	ARP	603329	12	11.3
1956	PvA	1872209	50	32.7
	KV	1529508	49	31.7
	ARP	567535	15	9.9
1959	KV	1895914	49	31.6
	PvA	1821825	48	30.3
	VVD	732658	19	12.2
	ARP	563091	14	9.4
1963	KV	1993352	50	31.9
	PvA	1753084	43	28.0
	VVD	643839	16	10.3
	ARP	545836	13	8.7
	CHU	536801	13	8.6
1967	KV	1822904	42	26.5
	PvA	1620112	37	23.5
	VVD	738202	17	10.7
	ARP	681060	15	9.9
1971	KV	1379672	35	21.8
	PvA	1554280	39	24.6
	VVD	653370	16	10.3
	ARP	542742	13	8.6

	Votes per party		*Seats*	*% of votes*
1972	KV	1305401	27	17.7
	PvA	2021454	43	27.3
	VVD	1068375	22	14.4
	ARP	653609	14	8.8
1977	CDA	2652278	49	31.9
	PvdA	2813793	53	33.8
	VVD	1492689	28	17.9
	D-66	452423	8	5.4
	PSP	77972	1	0.9
	CPN	143481	2	1.7
	Others	684976	9	8.2
1981	CDA	2676525	48	30.8
	PvdA	2455424	44	28.3
	VVD	1504293	26	17.3
	D-66	959661	17	11.0
	PSP	184039	3	2.1
	CPN	178147	3	2.0
	Others	728298	9	8.5
1982	PvdA	2499562	47	30.4
	CDA	2141176	45	29.3
	VVD	1897986	36	23.0
	D-66	355830	6	4.3
	PSP	187150	3	2.3
	SGP	156782	3	1.9
	CPN	147510	3	1.8
	PPR	136095	2	1.6
	RPF	124018	2	1.5
	Others	313711	3	3.8
1986	CDA	3170081	54	34.6
	PvdA	3012268	52	33.3
	VVD	1595377	27	17.4
	D-66	561865	9	6.1
	SGP	159897	3	1.8

	Votes per party		Seats	% of votes
	PPR	115009	2	1.3
	PSP	110331	1	1.2
	GPV	88006	1	1.0
	Others	314501	1	3.3
1989	CDA	3140502	54	35.3
	PvdA	2835251	49	31.9
	VVD	1295402	22	14.6
	D-66	701934	12	7.9
	Greens	362304	6	4.1
	SGP	166082	3	1.9
	GPV	109637	2	1.2
	Others	166658	2	3.1
1994	PvdA		37	24.0
	CDA		34	22.2
	VVD		31	19.9
	D-66		24	15.5
	SGP		7	4.8
	AOV (Third Age)		6	3.6
	Green Links		5	3.5
	Extreme Right		3	2.5
	Extreme Left		2	1.3
	Others		1	2.7
1998 (May)	Democrats (PvdA)		45	29.0
	Liberals (VVD)		38	24.7
	Christian Democrats (CDA)		29	18.4
	Democrats '66 (D-66)		14	9.0
	Green Left		11	7.2
	Others		13	11.7

NORWAY

Voting procedures. Direct proportional elections in multi-member constituencies. Suffrage for men and women over 23 until 1949, when it was extended to men and women over 21.

Prior to 1918, elections were held in 1900, 1903, 1906, 1909, 1912 and 1915. The elections were dominated by the battle between Liberals and Conservatives (the Conservatives won only in 1903 and 1909). A major trend was the rise of Labour (from 3 per cent of the vote and no seats in 1900 to 32 per cent of the vote and 19 seats in 1915).

	Votes per party		*Seats*	*% of votes*
1918	Left	187657	51	28.3
	Right	201325	50	30.4
	Labour	209560	18	31.6
1921	Right	301372	57	33.3
	Left	181989	37	20.1
	Labour	192616	29	21.3
	Agrarian	18657	17	13.1
1924	Right	316846	54	32.5
	Left	180979	34	18.6
	Labour	179567	24	18.4
	Agrarian	131706	22	13.5
1927	Labour	388106	59	36.8
	Conservative	240091	30	24.0
	Liberal	172568	30	17.3
	Agrarian	149026	26	14.9
1930	Labour	374854	47	31.4
	Conservative	327731	41	21.1
	Liberal	241355	33	20.2
	Agrarian	190220	25	15.9
1933	Labour	500526	69	40.1
	Conservative	252506	30	20.2
	Liberal	213153	24	17.1
	Agrarian	173634	23	13.9
1936	Labour	618616	70	42.5
	Conservative	310324	36	21.3
	Liberal	232784	23	16.0
	Agrarian	168038	18	11.6

	Votes per party		Seats	% of votes
1945	Labour	609348	76	41.0
	Conservative	252608	25	27.0
	Liberal	204852	20	13.8
1949	Labour	803471	85	45.7
	Conservative	311819	23	17.7
	Liberal	235876	21	13.4
1953	Labour	830448	77	46.7
	Conservative	344067	27	18.8
	Liberal	177662	15	10.0
	Chr. People's	186627	14	10.5
	Agrarian	160583	14	9.0
1957	Labour	865675	78	48.3
	Conservative	338651	29	18.9
	Liberal	173525	15	9.7
	Agrarian	166757	15	9.3
1961	Labour	860526	74	46.8
	Conservative	368340	29	20.0
	Agrarian	170645	16	9.3
	Chr. People's	176896	15	9.6
1965	Labour	883320	68	43.1
	Conservative	432025	31	21.1
	Liberal	211853	18	10.4
	Agrarian	202396	18	9.9
1969	Labour	1000348	74	46.5
	Conservative	406209	13	18.8
	Liberal	202553	13	9.4
	Agrarian	194128	20	9.0
1973	Labour	759482	62	35.3
	Conservative	375782	29	17.5
	Centre (Agrarian)	237073	21	11.0
	Christian Democrats	261869	20	12.2
	Left Socialists	241816	16	11.2
	Liberals	76155	2	3.5
	Others	200966	5	9.3

	Votes per party		*Seats*	*% of votes*
1977	Labour	962728	76	42.4
	Conservative	560025	41	24.7
	Centre (Agrarian)	196005	12	8.6
	Christian Democrats	274516	22	12.1
	Left Socialists	102371	2	4.5
	Liberals	73371	2	3.2
	Others	80929	–	3.6
1981	Labour	896796	66	37.6
	Conservative	746614	53	31.3
	Centre	220827	10	9.3
	Christian Democrats	160224	16	6.7
	Left Socialists	116637	4	4.9
	Progress Party	107971	4	4.5
	Liberals	92266	2	3.9
	Others	40860	–	1.7
1985	Labour	1033650	71	41.2
	Conservative	755159	50	30.1
	Christian People's	208315	16	8.3
	Centre Party	169223	12	6.7
	Left Socialists	135191	6	5.4
	Progressives	92635	2	3.7
	Liberals	77919	–	3.1
	Others	39637	–	1.6
1989	Labour	907393	63	34.3
	Conservative	588682	37	22.2
	Progressives	345185	22	13.0
	Left Socialists	266782	17	10.1
	Christian People's	224852	14	8.5
	Centre Party	171269	11	6.5
	Liberals	84740	–	3.2
	Others	59701	1	2.2
1993	Labour	908724	67	36.9
	Centre Party	412187	32	16.7

	Votes per party		Seats	% of votes
	Conservatives	419373	28	17.0
	Left Socialists	194633	13	7.9
	Christian People's	193885	13	7.9
	Progress	154497	10	6.3
	Liberals	88985	1	3.6
	Others	89665	1	3.7
1997	Norwegian Labour Party		65	35.0
(16 Sep)	Fremskrittspartiet		25	15.3
	Conservatives (Høyre)		23	14.3
	Christian People's Party		25	13.7
	Centre Party		11	7.9
	Others		16	13.8

POLAND

J. Piłsudski proclaimed independence on 10 Nov 1918 and appointed governments on 18 Nov 1918 and 16 Jan 1919.

Elections to the Sejm (parliament) were held in non-occupied Poland on 26 Jan 1919 and supplemented by by-elections in Nov. There were 394 deputies from 14 parties including:

National Democrats and allies (dubbed 'Endecja' from the initials)	140	(of these 116 were National Democrats, *i.e.* 37% of all deputies)
Polish Peasant Party 'Liberation' (*i.e.* left-wing)	71	
Polish Peasant Party 'Piast' (*i.e.* right-wing)	46	
Polish Socialist Party	35	
National Workers' Party	32	
National minority parties	13	

A constitution was promulgated on 17 Mar 1921 by which a bicameral parliament was set up, to be elected by universal suffrage every 5 years by proportional representation, consisting of a Senate of 111 senators and the Sejm of 444 deputies.

At the elections of 5 and 12 Nov 1922 the electorate was 13 109 793 of whom 8 760 195 (67 per cent) voted. Representatives of 15 parties were elected to the Sejm, including:

Party	Votes	Seats	% of Votes
Christian League of National Union	2 551 000	169	29.1
Polish Peasant Party 'Piast'	1 150 000	70	13.1
Polish Peasant Party 'Liberation'	963 000	49	11.0
Polish Socialist Party	906 000	41	10.3
National Workers' Party	474 000	18	5.4
Polish Centre	260 000	6	3.0
Communist Party	121 000	2	1.4
National minority parties	1 963 000	86	22.4

On 14 May 1926 Piłsudski staged a *coup d'état* and issued a constitution in June which restricted the powers of the Sejm.

At the elections of 4 Mar 1928 the electorate was 15m. and 11 408 218 voted.

Party	Votes	Seats
Non-party pro-Piłsudski Bloc (BBWR)	2 399 032	130
Polish Peasant Party 'Liberation'		66
Polish Socialist Party	1 148 279	63
People's Party (SN; formerly National Democrats)	925 744	37
Polish Peasant Party 'Piast'		21
Christian Democratic Party		19
National Workers' Party		14
Communist Party (illegal, but running under the name 'Union of Town and Country Proletariat')	940 000	8
National minority parties		86

This Sejm was dissolved on 30 Aug 1930.

During the campaign before the elections of 16 and 23 Nov 1930 opposition politicians were imprisoned.

The electorate was 15 520 342, of whom 13 078 682 voted. 372 deputies were elected to the Sejm, and the number was made up to 444 by allotments according to proportional representation:

	Votes	Seats
Non-party pro-Piłsudski Bloc (BBWR)	5 292 725	247
People's Party (SN)	1 455 399	62
6-Party Centre-Left coalition	1 907 380	
Polish Peasant Party 'Liberation'		33
Polish Socialist Party		24
Christian Democrats		15
Polish Peasant Party 'Piast'		15
National Workers' Party		10
Communist Party		5
National minority parties		33

A new constitution was promulgated on 23 Apr 1935. The Sejm was reduced to 208 deputies, elected by universal suffrage at 24 years. The Senate was reduced to 96, of whom one-third were appointed by the President and the remainder elected by a college of 300 000. Methods of election were not changed but district electoral assemblies acquired a decisive role in the designation of candidates.

All political parties boycotted the elections of 8 and 15 Sep 1935. The electorate was 16 332 100, of whom according to the government's own figures only 45.9 per cent voted (7 512 102). 153 BBWR members were returned to the Sejm and 22 members of national minority groups.

President Móscicki dissolved Sejm and Senate on 22 Sep 1935.

All political parties abstained from the elections of 6 and 13 Nov 1938. The turnout was 67.4 per cent. Of the non-party Camp of National Unity (OZN) 161 members were returned to the Sejm.

The liberation of part of Poland from German occupation by Soviet forces enabled the Polish Committee of National Liberation (PKWN) to be set up on 21 Jul 1944, proclaiming itself the sole legal Polish executive power. It was composed of Communists, left-wing socialists, left-wing peasants and Democratic Party representatives. It became the provisional government on 31 Dec 1944. At the Yalta conference (Feb 1945), it was agreed that a Provisional Government of National Unity should be formed based on this government, and this was done on 28 Jun 1945. It contained Communists (PPR, *i.e.* Polish Workers' Party) and representatives of the Polish Socialist Party (PPS), and the Polish Peasant (PSL), Democratic (SD) and Christian Democratic Labour (SP) parties.

A referendum was held on 30 Jun 1946, at which the electorate was asked to approve (1) the abolition of the Senate, (2) basic nationalization and land reform, (3) the fixing of Poland's borders on the Baltic and the Oder-Neisse line. The turnout was 80.8 per cent (11 530 551), and affirmative answers were recorded as follows: (1) 68 per cent, (2) 77.2 per cent, (3) 91.4 per cent.

An electoral law of Sep 1946 disfranchised collaborators: approximately 1m. people lost their vote in this way.

During the elections of 19 Jan 1947 some 12.7m. votes were cast, of which 11 244 873 were valid (89.19 per cent of electorate voted). The Communists together with the Polish Socialist, Peasant and Democratic parties stood as the Democratic Bloc, polling 9m. votes (80.1 per cent of the vote) and gaining 392 seats in the Sejm. Other parties:

Party	Seats	% of Votes
Polish Peasant Party	27	10.3
Christian Labour Party (SP)	15	4.7
Peasant Party 'Liberation'	7	
Catholic independents	3	

On 19 Feb 1947 the Sejm passed an interim constitution, which became known as the 'Little Constitution'. A permanent constitution was passed on 22 Jul 1952. This gave the ground plan of the electoral provisions later extant, although these were liberalized by later amendments. The Sejm was elected every 4 years by all citizens over 18. Citizens could stand as candidates at 21. There was 1 deputy per 60 000 inhabitants. Only political and social organizations (trade unions, youth and cultural organizations) could nominate candidates, who had to be on the single list of the National Unity Front (FJN), which grouped three parties: Communist (PZPR), United Peasant (ZSL) and Democratic (SD).

The office of President was abolished. The Chairman of the Council of State would henceforth be head of state.

At the elections of 26 Oct 1952 the number of candidates was the same as the number of seats. The electorate was 16 305 891: votes cast, 15 495 815. The single list of National Front candidates gained 99.8 per cent of valid votes and took up seats in the Sejm:

Party	Seats
Communist Party (PZPR)	273
United Peasant Party (ZSL)	90
Democratic Party (SD)	25
Independents	37
	425

By an electoral law of 24 Oct 1956 the single list of candidates was allowed to include up to two-thirds more candidates than seats. All electors were to make their vote behind curtains. Negative votes were to be recorded by crossing out the candidates' names.

At the elections of 20 Jan 1957 there were 717 candidates (51 per cent of whom were Communists) for 459 seats. Turnout was 94.14 per cent (16892213 votes were cast from an electorate of 17944081). 280002 votes (1.6 per cent of votes) were made against National Front candidates. Seats:

Communists (PZPR)	239
United Peasant Party (ZSL)	118
Democratic Party (SD)	39
Independents (including 12 Catholics, 9 of whom from the Znak group)	63
	459

An electoral law of 22 Dec 1960 reduced the ratio of candidates to seats.

At the elections of 16 Apr 1961 there were 616 candidates for 460 seats. The turnout was 94.83 per cent. There were 292009 votes against the National Front list (1.57 per cent of votes).

Party	Seats
Communists (PZPR)	256
United Peasant Party (ZSL)	117
Democratic Party (SD)	39
Independents (including 5 Catholics of the Znak group)	48
	460

After the elections of 30 May 1965, 1 Jun 1969 and 19 Mar 1972 the parties' positions were the same.

Communists (PZPR)		255
United Peasant Party (ZSL)		117
Democratic Party (SD)		39
Independents (including 14 Catholics)		49
		460

	1965	1969	1972
Electorate	19 645 893	21 148 879	21 854 481
Turnout	96.62%	97.61%	97.94%
Votes against	226 324	161 569	–
National Front List	(1.15% of votes)	(0.78% of votes)	–

In elections held on 21 Mar 1976, 631 candidates contested the 460 seats. Of the 24 069 579 registered voters, 23 652 256 (98.27 per cent) cast their votes. Some 99.43 per cent voted for the official candidates of the National Unity Front.

In elections held on 23 Mar 1980, 646 candidates contested the 460 seats. Official figures stated that 98.87 per cent of the 25 098 816 total electorate voted. Of these 99.52 per cent voted for the list of National Unity Front candidates.

In elections for the Sejm held on 4 and 18 Jun 1989, it had been agreed at talks between government and opposition earlier in the year that Solidarity and other opposition groups would contest only 35 per cent of the seats. The outcome was:

Party	Seats
Polish United Workers' Party (PZPR)*	173
Solidarity	161
Catholics allied to PZPR	23
Others	103
	460

* Dissolved in Jan 1990 to become part of a social democratic grouping.

The first free presidential elections in Poland since the end of Communist rule were held on 25 Nov and 9 Dec 1990. The outcome of the second round was: Walesa, 74.25 per cent, Tyminski, 25.75 per cent. Mazowiecki was eliminated on the first ballot.

The following general elections have been held since 1990:

		Seats	% of votes
1991 (27 Oct)	Democratic Union	62	12.3
	Democratic Left Alliance (DLA)	60	12.0
	Catholic Action	49	8.7
	Polish Peasant Party (PPP)	48	8.7
	Confederation for an Independent Poland	46	7.5
	Centre Citizens' Alliance	44	8.7
	Liberal Democratic Congress	37	7.5
	Peasant Alliance	28	5.5
	Solidarity	27	5.0
	Polish Beer Lovers' Party	16	3.3
	Others	43	20.8
	Total	460	100.0
1993 (19 Sep)	Democratic Left Alliance (DLA)	171	20.4
	Polish Peasant Party (PPP)	132	15.4
	Democratic Union	74	10.6
	Union of Labour	41	7.3
	Confederation for an Independent Poland	22	5.8
	Non-Party Bloc for Reform	16	5.4
	Others	4*	–
1997 (21 Sep)	Solidarity Election Action (AWS)	201	33.8
	Democratic Left Alliance (SLD)	164	27.1
	Freedom Union (UW)	60	13.4
	Polish Peasant Party	27	7.3
	Movement for the Reconstruction of Poland	6	5.6
	Others	2	11.8

* Other parties to contest the election and poll over 4% included the Catholic Electoral Committee ('Homeland'), Solidarity, the Centre Alliance and the Liberal Democratic Congress.

DANZIG

Danzig was created a Free City by the Versailles Treaty of 28 June 1919, under a League of Nations High Commissioner and in customs union with Poland. It was incorporated into Germany during World War II, and into Poland (as Gdańsk) after it.

The constitution provided for a Senate of 20 plus a President and Vice-President elected by the People's Assembly for 4 years. The President was head of state: 1918, H. Sahm; 1931, E. Ziehm; 1933, H. Rauschning; 1934, A. Greiser.

The Assembly (*Volkstag*) of 120 (reduced to 72 in 1930) was elected by universal secret suffrage at 20 for 4-year terms on a proportional representational system.

Election 16 May 1920. Social Democrats, 37 seats; German Nationalists, 34; Centre (Catholics), 17; German Democrats, 10; Poles, 7; Populists, 6; National Liberals, 3; German Liberals, 3; Communists, 3.

Election 9 Nov 1923. Social Democrats, 30; German Nationalists, 26; Centre (Catholics), 15; Communists, 11; German Social Party, 7 (10301 votes; the first appearance of a racialist party); Populists, 6; German Democrats, 5; German Liberals, 5; Poles, 5; National Liberals, 4; Middle-class Federation, 2; Independents, 4.

Election 13 Nov 1927. Social Democrats, 42; German Nationalists, 25; Centre (Catholics), 18; Communists, 8; Populists, 5; National Liberals, 5; German Liberals, 4; Middle-class Federation, 3; Poles, 3; German Social Party, 1 (2130 votes); Nazis, 1 (1483 votes).

ELECTIONS

	16 Nov 1930		28 May 1933		7 Apr 1935	
	Votes	*Seats*	*Votes*	*Seats*	*Votes*	*Seats*
Social Democrats	49965	19	38703	13	37804	14
Nazis	32457	12	107335	38	128619	40
Centre (Catholics)	30232	11	31339	10	31576	11
German Nationalists	25938	10	13595	4	9822	3
Communists	20194	7	44766	5	7935	2
Poles	6377	2	6738	2	8311	2
Others		11				

The 1935 election was fought for a two-thirds majority to enable the Nazis to ask the League of Nations to revise the constitution. The Polish government and the opposition parties alleged terror and unlawful practices by the Nazis. The Danzig Court discovered some illegality, and reduced the Nazi vote and number of seats as first officially proclaimed. The final figures are given above.

By dissolutions and amalgamations the Nazis became supreme in the Assembly by 1939, except for the two Polish deputies. On 22 Mar 1939 it was declared that the elections then due were 'unnecessary' and would not be held.

PORTUGAL

On 19 Mar 1933, the *Estado Novo* constitution (providing for an authoritarian Republic on a corporative basis) was voted upon and adopted. This constitution provided for a President, to be elected for 7 years by direct suffrage by male Portuguese citizens, of age or emancipated, able to read or write, and those unable to read or write, being taxpayers to the state or administrative corporations for direct taxes, and Portuguese citizens, females, of age or emancipated, with a special, secondary school, or university diploma; and for a National Assembly (one chamber) of 90 deputies elected for 4 years by direct suffrage. In the 2 elections for the National Assembly (1934 and 1938) the only lists presented were those organized by the National Union, an association legally recognized, but without the character of a party, whose aim was to defend the principles contained in the constitution. The electoral law permitted, however, the presentation of more than one list of the deputies to be elected.

At the elections of 8 Nov 1953 the União Nacional (National Union) obtained all 120 seats; the 28 opposition candidates were defeated. At subsequent elections only government candidates stood for re-election.

On 25 Apr 1974, an almost bloodless *coup* took place in Portugal. The new military government promised a return of normal political life. After a troubled period, the first elections to a Constituent Assembly were held in Apr 1975. The outcome was:

	Votes per party	Seats	% of votes
Portuguese Socialist Party (PSP)	2 145 392	115	37.9
Portuguese Democratic Party (PDP)	1 494 575	80	26.4
Portuguese Communist Party (PCP)	709 639	30	12.5
Social Democratic Centre (CDS)	433 153	16	7.6
Portuguese Democratic Movement (MDP)	233 362	5	4.1
Portuguese Socialist Front (FSP)	66 161	–	1.2
Movement of the Socialist Left (MES)	57 682	–	1.0
Others	132 579	1	2.3

Elections for a legislative assembly were subsequently held in Apr 1976, the Socialists again emerging as the largest party.

Portuguese Socialist Party (PSP)	1 887 180	107	35.0
Portuguese Democratic Party (PPD)	1 296 432	73	24.0
Social Democratic Centre (CDS)	858 783	42	15.9
Portuguese Communist Party (PCP)	785 620	40	14.6
Popular Democratic Union (UDP)	91 383	1	1.7
Popular Socialist Front (FSP)	41 954		0.8

After a succession of political crises, Parliament was dissolved prematurely and elections took place on 2 Dec 1979.

Democratic Alliance	2 497 019	118	42.2
Socialists	1 621 950	73	27.4
Communists	1 121 224	47	19.0
Others	503 933	8	8.6

Under the new constitution, elections had still to be held in Oct 1980.

	Seats		% of votes
Democratic Alliance			47.1
PSD	82		
CDS	46	= 134	
PPM	6		
Republican and Socialist Front			28.0
PSP	66		
UEDS	4	= 74	
ASDI	4		
United People's Alliance			16.9
PCP	39		
MDP	2	= 41	
Popular Democratic Union	1		1.4

Elections were next held in 1983. The results were:

PSP	101	36.3
PSD	75	27.0
PCP	44	18.2
CDS	30	12.4
PPM	–	0.5
Pop. Dem. Un.	–	0.5
Others	–	5.1

The results of elections held in Portugal in Oct 1985 were:

	Seats	% of votes
PSD	88	29.9
PSP	57	20.8
PRD	45	18.0
APU	38	15.4
CDS	22	9.8
Others	–	6.1

The results of the Jul 1987 elections were:

	Seats	% of votes
PSD	148	50.2
PS	60	22.2
CDU	31	12.1
PRD	7	4.9
CDS	4	4.5
Others	–	6.1

The results of the Oct 1991 elections were:

	Seats	% of votes
PSD	135	50.6
PS	72	29.1
CDU	17	8.8
CDS	5	4.4
PSN	1	1.7
Others	–	5.4

The results of the Oct 1995 elections were:

	Seats	% of votes
PS	112	42.9
PSD	88	34.0
CDS	15	5.1
CDU	15	8.6
Others	–	9.4

The results of the Oct 1999 elections were:

	Seats	% of votes
Socialist Party (PS)	115	44.0
Social Democratic Party (PSD)	81	32.3

Marxists/Green Coalition (CDU)	17	9.0
Democratic Social Centre/ People's Party	15	8.4
Left Bloc	2	2.5
Others	–	3.8

ROMANIA

1919	Chamber of Deputies: 568 of which:	
	National Party of Transylvania	199
	Peasants	130
	National Liberals	120
	Nationalists and Democrats	27
	Conservative Democrats	16

In 1920 the number of deputies was reduced to 369 and conducted under proportional representation.

1920	People's Party	224
	Peasants	40
	National Party of Transylvania	30
	Socialists	19
	National Liberals	17
	Germans	8

1922	National Liberals	227
	Peasants and National Party of Transylvania	62
	People's Party	11
	Conservative Democrats	8
	Germans	8
	Social Democrats	1
	Jews	1

Opposition parties challenged validity of this election and withdrew.

A new constitution of 23 Mar 1923 reorganized the Senate to consist of 249 seats elected on a more restricted suffrage (over 40-year-olds and members of the ruling élite). The Chamber of Deputies was to be elected by universal secret suffrage at 21 years of age on a constituency basis.

By an electoral law of 1926 that party which obtained 40 per cent of the vote was awarded 50 per cent of the seats plus a proportionate share of the seats remaining.

Party	Number of votes	Seats gained	% of votes
1926 Electorate: 3 496 814, of which 75% voted.			
National Liberals	192 309	16	7
National Peasants	727 202	69	28
People's Party	1 306 100	292	52
Christian League of National Defence	124 778	10	5
1927 The electorate was 3 586 806, of which 77% voted.			
National Liberals	1 704 435	298	
Peasants		22	62
National Peasants	610 149	54	22
Hungarians	173 517	15	6
1928 The electorate was 3 671 352, of which 77.4% voted.			
National Peasants	2 228 922	348	78
National Liberals	185 939	13	7
People's Party	70 490	5	2
Peasants	70 506	5	2
Hungarians	172 699	16	6
1931 The electorate was 4 038 464, of which 72.5% voted.			
National Union	1 389 901	289	48
National Peasants	438 747	30	15
National Liberals (G. Brătianu)	173 586	12	6
People's Party	141 141	10	5
Hungarians	139 003	10	5
Christian League of National Defence	113 863	8	4
Peasant Party	100 682	7	3
Social Democrats	94 957	6	3

Party	Number of votes	Seats gained	% of votes
Peasant Democrats Union in alliance with League against Usury	80 570	6	3
Labour and Peasant Group	73 716	5	3
Jews	64 193	4	2

1932   The electorate was 4 220 731, of which 70.8% voted.

National Peasants	1 203 700	274	41
National Liberals (Duca)	407 023	28	14
National Liberals (Brătianu)	195 048	14	7
Peasants	170 860	12	6
Christian League of National Defence	159 071	11	5
Hungarians	141 894	14	5
National Agrarians	108 857	8	4
Social Democrats	101 068	7	3
Iron Guard	70 674	5	2
National Union	68 116	5	2
Jews	67 582	5	2
People's Party	64 525	4	2

1933   The electorate was 4 380 354, of which 68% voted.

National Liberals	1 518 864	300	51
National Peasants	414 685	29	14
Peasants	152 167	11	5
National Liberals (Brătianu)	147 665	10	5
Christian League of National Defence	133 205	9	5
National Agrarians	121 748	9	4
Hungarians	119 562	8	4
Radical Peasants	82 930	6	3
Agrarian Union	73 208	5	2

1937   66% of the electorate voted.

Government Party (National Liberals, etc.)	1 103 323	152	36
National Peasants	626 642	86	20

Party	Number of votes	Seats gained	% of votes
'All-for-Country' (*i.e.* Iron Guard)	478 378	66	16
Christian League of National Defence	281 167	39	9
Hungarians	136 139	19	4
National Liberals (Brātianu)	119 361	16	4
Radical Peasants	69 208	9	2

The government failed to get its necessary 40 per cent of the votes. King Carol II picked on the Christian League of National Defence to form a government. He dismissed this government on 10 Feb 1938 and instituted a royal dictatorship, called the Government of National Concentration.

A new constitution of 20 Feb 1938 reduced the electorate to some 2m. (voting was universal and secret at age 30) and established a Senate. Political parties were banned except for the royalist monolithic National Renaissance Front. A plebiscite of 24 Feb 1938, conducted by open voting, confirmed the new constitution by 4 283 395 to 5413 votes. Turnout (compulsory): 92 per cent. A corporatist parliament was returned at the election of 2 Jun 1939: 86 representatives of agrarian and labour interests, 86 of commerce and industry, 86 intelligentsia and 88 senators. Turnout was 85 per cent. There were twice as many candidates as seats.

An electoral law of 14 Jul 1946 abolished the Senate, enfranchised all at 21 and provided for a unicameral Assembly elected for 4-year terms.

At the election of 19 Nov 1946 the government bloc (National Democratic Front) obtained 71 per cent of the votes cast and 347 seats. The National Peasants gained 33, the National Liberals 3. The validity of the results has been challenged.

1947	Electorate: 7 859 212. Voted: 6 934 563 (88.9%).		
	National Democratic Front	(348)	(4 766 630)
	National Liberals	75	
	Social Democrats	75	
	Communists	73	
	Ploughmen's Front	70	
	National People's Party	26	
	Dissident National Peasants	20	
	Jews	2	
	Independents	7	

Party	Number of votes	Seats gained
Opposition parties	(1 361 536)	(66)
National Peasants	879 927	32
National Liberals	259 306	3
Democratic Peasants	156 775	2
Hungarian People's Union	569 651	29

The opposition parties protested at the falsification and terror used in these elections.

In Dec 1947 King Michael abdicated, and a People's Republic was proclaimed on the 30th. On 28 Mar 1948, an election was held for a new National Assembly to pass a new constitution.

The remnants of the Social Democrats were merged with the Communists to form the Workers' Party, which ran for election in the single-list monolithic National Democratic Front comprising also the Ploughmen's Front, the National Peasants and the Hungarian People's Union. Electorate 8 417 467. Voted: 7 663 675 (91 per cent turnout). Voted for National Democratic Front: 6 958 531 (90.8 per cent). The Front gained 405 of the 414 Assembly seats, the Liberals 7, the Democratic Peasants 1 with 1 Independent.

On 13 Apr 1948 a new constitution, of the Soviet type, was promulgated: vote at 18, stand at 23, universal secret suffrage.

A further constitution was instituted on 24 Sep 1949, in general outline the same as that of 1948. Deputies to the Grand National Assembly (*Marea Adunare Naţională*) were to represent 40 000 electors for 4-year terms.

1952   Electorate: 10.5m. Voted: 97%. For National Democratic Front: 98%.

1957   Electorate: 11.7m. Voted: 99.15%. For National Democratic Front: 99.88%.

At the elections of 5 Mar 1961, 7 Mar 1965 and 2 Mar 1969 a single list of candidates was presented, the number of candidates equalling the number of seats. At least 99 per cent of the voters turned out, at least 99 per cent of these voted for the National Democratic Front (Socialist Unity Front since 19 Nov 1968).

In elections held on 9 Mar 1975 for the first time 139 of the 349 seats were contested by more than one candidate (although all belonged to the Socialist Unity Front). According to official figures, 99.96 per cent of the 14 900 000 registered voters went to the polls.

In elections held on 9 Mar 1980, officially some 15 629 098 voters (99.99 per cent) of the total electorate voted. Of these, 98.52 per cent voted for official candidates.

In elections held on 17 Mar 1985, officially some 15 732 095 voters (99.99 per cent) of the total electorate voted. Of these 97.7 per cent voted for official candidates.

Following the revolution of Dec 1989 and the overthrow of the Ceauçescu régime, during the first half of 1990 Presidential elections were held and elections to the National Assembly.

Presidential Election

	Votes	% of votes
Ion Iliescu (Nat. Salv. Front)	12 232 498	85.1
Radu Campeanu (NLP)	1 529 188	10.2
Ion Ratiu (CDNPP)	617 007	4.3

Electorate, 17 200 722

Turnout 86.2%

National Assembly Elections May 1990

	Votes	Seats	% of votes
National Salvation Front	9 090 000	263	66.3
Hungarian Democratic Union of Romania	992 000	29	7.2
National Liberal Party	879 000	29	6.4
Ecological Movement	359 000	12	2.6
CDNPP (Christian Democrat National Peasants' Party)	351 000	12	2.6
Unity Alliance	300 000	9	2.2
Others	1 080 000	33	na

At the general election of Sep 1992 the outcome was:

	Seats	% of votes
Democratic National Salvation Front (DNSF)[1]	117	27.7
Democratic Convention of Romania Alliance	82	20.0
National Salvation Front	43	10.2

	Seats	*% of votes*
Romanian National Unity Party	30	7.7
Hungarian Democratic Union of Romania	27	7.5
Greater Romania Party	16	3.9
Socialist Labour Party (ex-Communists)	13	3.0
Ethnic Minorities (reserved seats)	13	na
Others	0	
Total	341	

[1] Became Party of Social Democracy of Romania in Jul 1993.

The presidential elections of Nov 1996 marked a watershed in the history of the country with the victory of the right-wing candidate Emil Constantinescu over the incumbent, former communist Ion Iliescu. Constantinescu took 54.4 per cent of the votes cast on a turnout of 75.9 per cent.

At elections held on 3 Nov 1996, the Democratic Convention of Romania (DCR) emerged as easily the largest single party in the Chamber of Deputies:

	Seats
Democratic Convention of Romania	122[1]
Party of Social Democracy of Romania	91
Social Democratic Union	53[2]
Hungarian Democratic Union of Romania	25
Greater Romania Party	19
Romanian National Unity Party	18

[1] A coalition, initially of 5 parties, of which the Christian Democratic National Peasants' Party of Romania secured 88 seats, the National Liberal Party 25.
[2] An alliance of the Democratic Party and the Romanian Social Democratic Party.

RUSSIA

No reliable statistics of voting in Tsarist Russia can be obtained. Various estimates have been made, however, of the relative strengths of different groups in the four Dumas. These are given below:

THE FIRST DUMA

The predominance of the large landowners and upper middle class was made certain by the electoral law of 11 Dec 1905. The actual elections (in Feb–Mar

1906) took place in an atmosphere of active police repression. The Bolsheviks boycotted the election (with obvious success in St Petersburg, Poland and the Baltic). The Kadets (Constitutional Democrats) easily emerged as the largest single party.

Composition of the First Duma

The Right (Monarchists, Octobrists, Industrialists, etc.)	44
The Autonomists (Polish League, Lithuanian Circle, Ukrainian Democrats, etc.)	44
Party of Democratic Reform	6
Kadets	179
Labour Group	94
Social Democratic Group	18
Cossack Group	1
Non-party	100

Composition of the Second Duma

The Reactionary Right	10
Octobrists	42
Polish League	46
Muslim Group	30
Party for Democratic Reform	1
Kadets	98
Labour Group	104
Popular Socialists	16
Socialist Revolutionaries	37
Social Democrats	65
Cossack Group	17
Non-party	50
	516

Composition of the Third Duma (First Session)

The Reactionary Right	49
Moderate Right Wing	69
Russian National Group	26
Alliance of 17 October	148
Polish/Lithuanian Group	7

Polish League	11
Progressives	25
Muslim Group	8
Kadets	53
Labour Group	14
Social Democrats	20
Non-party	16
	446

Composition of the Fourth Duma (First Session)

The Reactionary Right	64
Moderate Right	88
Centre Party	32
Alliance of 17 October	99
Polish/Lithuanian Group	6
Polish League	9
Progressives	47
Muslim Group	6
Kadets	58
Labour Group	10
Social Democrats	14
Non-party	5
	438

After the elections to the Fourth Duma, no further elections occurred until after the fall of the Tsarist régime. During 1917, the Provisional Government had been organizing elections to establish a Constituent Assembly. The Bolsheviks allowed these elections to take place on 25 Nov 1917. With universal suffrage, the electorate numbered 41 700 000. No reliable figures exist for the results, but the following table gives approximate figures.

Party	Votes cast	Delegates returned
	17 100 000 (Total)	429 (Total)
Bolsheviks	9 600 000	168
Mensheviks	1 400 000	18
Kadets	2 000 000	17
Monarchists	300 000	–
National Minorities	1 700 000	–

At the end of 1917, the Kadets were proscribed. The Constituent Assembly met on 18 Jan 1918. It was dissolved by the Bolsheviks a day later after rejecting (237 votes to 136) a Bolshevik motion to recognize the Congress of Soviets as the supreme government authority. For the position in the Soviet Union, *see* p. 309.

Following the collapse of the Soviet Union, the first free presidential elections in the history of Russia were held on 12 Jun 1991. The result was:

	Vote	% of votes
Boris Yeltsin	45 552 041	57.3
Nikolai Ryzhkov	13 395 335	16.9
Vladimir Zhirinovsky	6 211 007	7.8
Others (3)	8 148 357	10.3

The nationwide elections for Russia's Parliament were held on 12 Dec 1993. Duma seats gained (including, where blocs surpassed the 5 per cent threshold for proportional representation votes, seats thus gained with percentage votes cast) were as follows:

	Seats (total)	% of votes
Liberal Democrats (extreme Right)	59 (70)	22.8
Russia's Choice (Pro-Government)	40 (96)	15.4
Communists	32 (65)	12.4
Agrarian	21 (47)	7.9
Women's Party of Russia	21 (25)	8.1
Yavlinsky bloc (free market)	20 (33)	7.8
Democratic Party	14 (21)	5.5
Others	18 (30)	19.0
Independents	(30)	

Presidential elections were again held in Russia in Jun 1996, with Boris Yeltsin decisively emerging as the victor in the second round of voting on 3 Jul. The second-round voting figures were Yeltsin (40 100 000; 53.8 per cent), Zyuganov (the Communist candidate, 30 110 000; 40.3 per cent). Turnout was 68 per cent, with 3 600 000 voting against both candidates.

The third parliamentary elections since the fall of communism took place on 19 Dec 1999. The war in Chechnya meant that no polling took place in the north Caucasus region. The election was marked by unexpected support for the pro-government centre parties. Provisional results on a 57 per cent turnout of the 107 million electorate were:

	Seats
Communists	111
Unity Bloc	76
Union of the Right	29
Fatherland-All Russia (OVR)	62
Yabloko	22
LDPR (Zhirinovsky)	17
Others	133
	450

Following the resignation of Boris Yeltsin on 31 Dec 1999, presidential elections were rescheduled for 26 Mar 2000. The victor was Vladimir Putin.

SLOVAKIA

The first elections following independence on 1 Jan 1993 were held on 30 Sep and 1 Oct 1994. Approximately 76 per cent of the electorate of 3 900 000 voted in an election dominated by HZDS (Movement for a Democratic Slovakia) which won 61 of the 150 seats. Results were: the HZDS (61 with 35 per cent of the vote); the Common Choice Coalition (a left-wing grouping), 18 with 10.4 per cent; the Hungarian Coalition, 17 with 10.2 per cent; the Christian Democratic Movement, 17 with 10.1 per cent; the Democratic Union, 15 with 8.6 per cent; the Union of Slovak Workers (ZRS), 13 with 7.3 per cent; the Slovak National Party (SNS), 9 with 5.4 per cent.

Further elections took place on 25–26 Sep 1998. The outcome was:

Movement for a Democratic Slovakia (HZDS)	43	27.0
Slovak Democratic Coalition (SDK)	42	26.3
Party of the Democratic Left (SDL)	23	14.7
Party of the Hungarian Coalition (SMK)	15	9.1
Slovak National Party (SNS)	14	9.1
Party of Civic Understanding	13	8.0
Others	–	5.8

SLOVENIA

Following independence in 1991, presidential and general elections were held on 6 Dec 1992. In the presidential election, Milan Kučan was the easy victor with 63.9 per cent of the vote. The general election result was:

	Seats	% of votes
Liberal Democratic Party	22	23.3
Christian Democratic Party	15	14.5
Associated List (Left-Wing Coalition including former Communists)	14	13.6
National Party	12	9.9
People's Party	10	8.8
Democratic Party	6	5.0
Greens	5	3.7
Social Democratic Party	4	3.3
Others	–	–

A further election was held in Nov 1996:

	Seats	% of votes
Liberal Democracy of Slovenia*	25	27.0
Slovene People's Party**	19	19.4
Social Democratic Party**	16	16.1
Christian Democrats of Slovenia**	10	9.6
United List of Social Democrats	9	9.0
Democratic Party of Pensioners	5	4.3
Others	4	14.6

* Formed in Mar 1994 out of the Liberal Democratic Party, the Democratic Party and the Greens.
** The three parties fought as Slovenian Spring, winning 45 seats in all.

SPAIN

Elections held in Feb 1918 were followed by a 5-year period of political stability.

On 12 Sep 1923 Primo de Rivera took over the country in a *coup d'état*. In Sep 1927 the National Assembly met, members having been nominated by Primo de Rivera.

In Feb 1931 elections were announced but postponed because of a government crisis and elections under a provisional government were held for the constituent *Cortes*. Franchise minimum voting age reduced from 25 to 23 years. Eligibility for *Cortes* membership extended to women and priests. Electoral divisions revised to give one deputy for every 50 000 inhabitants to a *Cortes* which was a single chamber elected by direct popular vote.

	Party	Seats
Feb 1931	Socialists	116
	Radical Socialists	60
	Azana's Republican Action Party	30
	Radicals (following Lerroux)	90
	Progressives (following Zamona)	22
	Catalan Esquerra	43
	Casares Quirozaś Gallegan Nationalists	16
	Parties of the right of which only 19 were members of the Monarchist Party	60
Nov 1933	*Parties of the left centre* { Acción Republicana	8
	Socialists	58
	Remainder of pro-government parties	33
	Radicals (following Lerroux)	167
	Parties to the right	207
Feb 1936	Parties of the left	278
	Centre parties	55
	Parties of the right	134

Traditionally designated as the *Cortes* (courts), the Spanish parliament was revived by General Franco in 1942 as a unicameral body with very limited powers under the official name of Spanish Legislative Assembly (*Las Cortes Españolas*). Until 1967 it had no directly elected members but was made up of appointed and *ex officio* dignitaries, representatives of syndical (trade union) and professional and business associations, and 108 indirectly elected representatives from the 53 Spanish and African provinces and the two North African *presidios*. Under the Organic Law of 1967, its membership was expanded by the addition of 108 'family representatives' to be directly elected for a 4-year term by heads of families, married women and widows. The first elections of family representatives were held 10 Oct 1967.

In 1969, the membership of the *Cortes* was made up of the categories and approximate numbers listed below; however, since some members sat in more than one capacity, the total membership was somewhat less than the indicated 563. The succession law of 22 Jul 1969 was adopted by a vote of 491 in favour, 19 opposed, 9 abstaining, and 15 absent, making a total of 534.

High Officials	23
Appointed	25

Members of the National Council of the Movement		102
Representatives of cultural bodies		18
Representatives of professional associations		22
Syndical representatives		150
Municipal and provincial representatives		115
Family representatives		108
		563

	Party	Seats
1977	UCD	165
	PSOE	118
	PCE	20
	CD	16
	CU	11
	PNV	8
	Others	12
1979	UCD	168
	PSOE	121
	PCE	23
	CD	9
	CU	8
	PNV	7
	PSA	5
	Others	9

		Votes per party	Seats	% of votes
1982	PSOE/PSC-PSOE	10 127 392	202	48.7
	APAP-PDP	5 543 107	106	26.6
	UCD	1 425 093	12	6.8
	CU	772 726	12	3.7
	PNV	395 656	8	1.9
	PCE-PSUC	844 976	4	4.1
	CDS	600 842	2	2.9
	HB	210 601	2	1.0
	ERC	138 116	1	0.7

		Votes per party	Seats	% of votes
	EE	100326	1	0.5
	Others	648346		3.1
1986	PSOE	8887345	184	44.3
	CP	5245396	105	26.2
	CDS	1862856	19	9.3
	CiU	1012054	18	5.0
	IU	930223	7	4.6
	PNV	308991	6	1.5
	HB	231558	5	1.2
	EE	106937	2	0.5
	Others	1472380	4	7.4
1989	PSOE		175	39.6
	PP		106	25.8
	IU		18	9.1
	CDS		14	7.9
	CiU		18	5.0
	PNV		5	1.2
	HB		4	1.1
	PA		2	1.0
	Others		9	9.3
1993	PSOE		159	38.8
	PP		141	34.8
	United Left		18	9.6
	CiU		17	4.9
	PNV (Basques)		5	1.2
	Others		10	4.7
			350	
1996	PP		156	38.9
	PSOE		141	37.5
	United Left		21	10.6
	CiU		16	4.6
	PNV (Basques)		5	1.3
	Others		11	7.1
			350	

SWEDEN

Voting procedures. Election to the First Chamber indirect through electoral colleges. Direct election to the Second Chamber. Proportional representation. Suffrage – for the First Chamber, universal suffrage extended at age 27; for the Second, suffrage for men at 24. In 1927, the First Chamber suffrage extended to age 23, and to age 21 in 1941. In 1945 suffrage for the Second Chamber altered to universal suffrage at 21.

	*Votes per party**		*Seats*	*% of electorate*
1902	Social Democrats	6 000	4	3.5
	Liberals	93 000	107	51.2
	Conservatives	82 000	119	45.3
1905	Social Democrats	21 000	13	9.5
	Liberals	98 000	109	45.2
	Conservatives	98 000	108	45.3
1908	Social Democrats	45 000	34	14.6
	Liberals	144 000	105	46.8
	Conservatives	119 000	91	38.5
1911	Conservatives	189 000	65	31.2
	Liberals	243 000	101	40.2
	Social Democrats	172 000	64	28.5
1914 (Mar)	Conservatives	286 000	86	37.7
	Liberals	245 000	71	32.2
	Social Democrats	229 000	73	30.1
1914 (Sep)	Conservatives	267 000	86	36.5
	Liberals	196 000	57	26.9
	Social Democrats	266 000	87	36.4
1917	Högern (Con.)	181 333	59	16.1
	Agrarians/Centre	62 658	12	5.6
	Liberaler (Lib.)	202 936	62	18.0
	Social Dem.	288 020	97	25.6
	Others	1 037		0.1
1920	Högern (Con.)	183 019	70	15.3
	Agrarians/Centre	92 941	30	7.8

* Only votes for major parties given for early elections.

	Votes per party		Seats	% of electorate
	Liberaler (Lib.)	144946	48	12.2
	Social Dem.	237177	82	19.9
	Others	100		0.0
1921	Högern (Con.)	449302	62	13.9
	Agrarians/Centre	192269	21	6.0
	Liberaler (Lib.)	332765	41	10.3
	Social Dem.	687096	99	21.3
	Soc. and Comm.	80355	7	2.5
	Others	165		0.0
1924	Högern (Con.)	461257	65	13.8
	Agrarians/Centre	190396	23	5.7
	Liberaler (Lib.)	69627	5	2.0
	Frisinnade (Lib.)	228913	28	6.9
	Social Dem.	725407	104	21.7
	Soc. and Comm.	89902	5	2.7
	Others	84		0.0
1928	Högern (Con.)	692434	73	19.8
	Agrarians/Centre	263501	27	7.5
	Liberaler (Lib.)	70820	4	2.1
	Frisinnade (Lib.)	303995	28	8.7
	Social Dem.	873931	90	25.0
	Soc. and Comm.	151567	8	4.4
	Others	2563		0.1
1932	Högern (Con.)	585248	58	15.8
	Agrarians/Centre	351215	36	9.5
	Liberaler (Lib.)	48722	4	1.3
	Frisinnade (Lib.)	244577	20	6.6
	Social Dem.	1040689	104	28.0
	Socialist	132564	6	3.6
	Communist	74245	2	2.0
	Others	17846		0.5
1936	Högern (Con.)	512781	44	13.0
	Agrarians/Centre	418840	36	10.7

	Votes per party		Seats	% of electorate
	Folkpartiet (Lib.)	376161	27	9.6
	Social Dem.	1338120	112	34.0
	Socialist	127832	6	3.3
	Communist	96519	5	2.5
	Others	47500		1.2
1940	Högern (Con.)	518346	42	12.6
	Agrarians/Centre	344345	28	8.4
	Folkpartiet (Lib.)	344113	23	8.4
	Social Dem.	1546804	134	37.6
	Socialist	18430		0.4
	Communist	101424	3	2.5
1944	Högern (Con.)	488921	39	11.3
	Agrarians/Centre	421094	35	9.8
	Folkpartiet (Lib.)	398293	26	9.2
	Social Dem.	1436571	115	33.3
	Socialist	5279		0.1
	Communist	318466	15	7.6
	Others	17680		0.4
1948	Högern (Con.)	478786	23	10.2
	Agrarians/Centre	480421	30	10.2
	Folkpartiet (Lib.)	882437	57	18.7
	Social Dem.	1789459	112	38.0
	Communist	244826	8	5.2
	Others	3062		0.0
1952	Högern (Con.)	543825	31	11.3
	Agrarians/Centre	406183	26	8.5
	Folkpartiet (Lib.)	924819	58	19.2
	Social Dem.	1742284	110	36.3
	Communist	164194	5	3.4
	Others	2402		0.0
1956	Högern (Con.)	663693	42	13.6
	Agrarians/Centre	366612	19	7.5
	Folkpartiet (Lib.)	923564	58	18.9

	Votes per party		Seats	% of electorate
	Social Dem.	1 729 463	106	35.4
	Communist	194 016	6	4.0
	Others	1 982		0.0
1958	Högern (Con.)	750 332	45	15.0
	Agrarians/Centre	486 760	32	9.7
	Folkpartiet (Lib.)	700 019	38	14.0
	Social Dem.	1 776 667	111	35.6
	Communist	129 319	5	2.6
	Others	1 155		0.0
1960	Högern (Con.)	704 365	39	14.2
	Agrarians/Centre	579 007	34	11.6
	Folkpartiet (Lib.)	744 142	40	15.0
	Social Dem.	2 033 016	114	40.9
	Communist	190 560	5	3.8
1964	Högern (Con.)	582 609	33	11.4
	Agrarians/Centre	559 632	36	11.0
	Folkpartiet (Lib.)	720 733	43	14.1
	Social Dem.	2 006 923	113	39.4
	Communist	221 746	8	4.4
	Others	154 137		3.0
1968	Högern (Con.)	621 031	29	12.9
	Agrarians/Centre	757 215	37	15.7
	Folkpartiet (Lib.)	688 456	32	14.3
	Social Dem.	2 420 277	125	50.1
	Communist	145 172	3	3.0
	Others	197 228	7	4.1
1970	Högern (Con.)	573 812	41	11.5
	Agrarians/Centre	991 208	71	19.9
	Folkpartiet (Lib.)	806 667	58	16.2
	Social Dem.	2 256 369	163	45.3
	Communist	236 659	17	4.8
	Others	111 481		2.3

		Votes per party	Seats	% of electorate
1973	Social Democrats	2 247 727	156	43.6
	Communist Left	274 929	19	5.3
	Centre Party	737 584	51	14.3
	Moderates	1 295 246	90	25.1
	Liberals	486 028	34	9.4
	Minor Parties	117 325	–	2.3
1976	Social Democrats	2 320 818	152	42.9
	Communist Left	257 967	17	4.7
	Centre Party	845 580	55	15.6
	Moderates	1 307 927	86	24.1
	Liberals	600 249	39	11.0
	Minor Parties	90 790	–	1.7
1979	Social Democrats	2 356 234	154	43.5
	Communist Left	305 420	20	5.6
	Moderates	1 108 406	73	20.5
	Centre Party	984 589	64	18.2
	Liberals	577 063	38	10.6
	Minor Parties	86 855	–	1.6
1982	Social Democrats	2 533 250	166	45.6
	Communist Left	308 899	20	5.6
	Moderates	1 313 337	86	23.6
	Centre Party	859 618	56	15.5
	Liberals	327 770	21	5.9
	Minor Parties	211 670	–	3.8
1985	Social Democrats	2 487 551	159	44.7
	Communist Left	298 419	19	5.4
	Moderates	1 187 335	76	21.3
	Liberals	792 268	51	14.2
	Centre Party/KDS	691 258	44	12.4
	Others	110 191	–	2.0
1988	Social Democrats		156	43.6
	Communist Left		21	5.9
	Moderates		66	18.4
	Liberals		44	12.2

	Votes per party	*Seats*	*% of electorate*
	Centre Party	42	11.4
	Greens	20	5.5
	Others	–	3.0
1991	Social Democratic Labour	138	37.6
	Moderates	80	21.9
	Liberals	33	9.1
	Centre Party	31	8.5
	Christian Democrats	26	7.1
	New Democracy	25	6.7
	Left Party	16	4.6
	Green Party	–	3.4
	Others	–	1.2
1994	Social Democratic Labour	161	45.3
	Moderates	80	22.4
	Centre Party	27	7.7
	Liberals	26	7.2
	Left Party	22	6.2
	Green Party	18	5.0
	Christian Democrats	15	4.1
	New Democracy		1.2
	Others	–	1.1
1998 (20 Sep)	Social Democratic Labour Party (SDP)	131	36.6[1]
	Moderate Unity Party	82	22.7
	Left Party (ex-Communists)	43	12.0
	Christian Democrats	42	11.8
	Centre Party	18	5.1
	Liberal Party	17	4.7
	Green Party	16	4.5
	Others	–	2.6

[1] The worst result for the Social Democrats since World War II.

SWITZERLAND

A general election takes place by ballot every 4 years. Every citizen of the Republic who has entered on his 20th year is entitled to vote, and any voter, not a clergyman, may be elected as a deputy. Laws passed by both chambers may be submitted to direct popular vote, when 30000 citizens or 8 cantons demand it; the vote can be only 'Yes' or 'No'. This principle, called the referendum, is frequently acted on.

Women's suffrage, although advocated by the Federal Council and the Federal Assembly, was repeatedly rejected but at a referendum held on 7 Feb 1971 women's suffrage was carried.

The elections between 1900 and 1918 were dominated by the Radical Democrats. Seats won were as follows:

	1902	1905	1908	1911	1914	1917
Catholic Conservatives	34	34	34	38	38	42
Democrats	3	5	4	5	3	4
Liberal Conservatives	19	18	16	13	14	12
Radical Democrats	99	104	104	114	111	105
Social Democrats	7	2	7	17	19	22
Others	5	4	2	2	4	4
	167	167	167	189	189	189

		Votes per party	Seats	% of votes
1919	Liberal Democratic	28497	9	3.8
	Peasant and Middle Class	114537	31	15.3
	Catholic Conservative	156702	41	21.0
	Radical	215566	58	28.8
	Socialist	175292	41	23.5
	Others	59360	9	7.6
1922	Liberal Democratic	19041	10	4.0
	Peasant and Middle Class	118382	35	16.1
	Catholic Conservative	153836	44	20.9
	Radical	208144	58	28.3
	Socialist	170974	43	23.3
	Communist	13441	2	1.8
	Others	43605	6	5.6

		Votes per party	*Seats*	*% of votes*
1925	Liberal Democratic	30523	7	4.1
	Peasant and Middle Class	113512	31	15.3
	Catholic Conservative	155467	42	20.9
	Radical	206485	59	27.8
	Socialist	192208	49	25.8
	Communist	14837	3	2.0
	Others	34106	7	4.1
1928	Liberal Democratic	23752	6	2.9
	Peasant and Middle Class	126961	31	15.8
	Catholic Conservative	172516	46	21.4
	Radical	220135	58	27.4
	Socialist	220141	50	27.4
	Communist	14818	2	1.8
	Others	29149	5	3.3
1931	Liberal Democratic	24573	6	2.8
	Peasant and Middle Class	131809	30	15.3
	Catholic Conservative	184602	44	21.4
	Radical	232562	52	26.9
	Socialist	247946	49	28.7
	Communist	12778	2	1.5
	Others	32305	4	3.4
1935	Independent	37861	7	4.2
	Liberal Democratic	30476	7	3.3
	Peasant and Middle Class	100300	21	11.0
	Catholic Conservative	185052	42	20.3
	Radical	216664	48	23.7
	Socialist	255843	50	28.0
	Communist	12569	2	1.4
	Others	78810	10	8.1
1939	Independent	43735	9	7.1
	Liberal Democratic	10241	6	1.6
	Peasant and Middle Class	91182	22	14.7
	Catholic Conservative	105018	43	17.0
	Radical	128163	51	20.8

		Votes per party	Seats	% of votes
	Socialist	160377	45	25.9
	Communist	15962	4	2.6
	Others	69062	7	10.3
1943	Independent	48557	7	5.5
	Liberal Democratic	28434	8	3.2
	Peasant and Middle Class	101998	22	11.6
	Catholic Conservative	182916	43	20.8
	Radical	197746	43	22.5
	Socialist	251576	56	28.6
	Others	76449	11	7.8
1947	Independent	42428	9	4.4
	Liberal Democratic	30492	7	3.2
	Peasant and Middle Class	115976	21	12.1
	Catholic Conservative	203202	44	21.2
	Radical	220486	52	23.0
	Socialist	251625	48	26.2
	Communist	49353	7	5.1
	Others	53118	6	4.8
1951	Independent	49100	10	5.1
	Liberal Democratic	24813	5	2.6
	Peasant and Middle Class	120819	23	12.6
	Catholic Conservative	216616	48	22.5
	Radical	230687	51	24.0
	Socialist	249857	49	26.0
	Communist	25659	5	2.7
	Others	50438	5	4.5
1955	Independent	53450	10	5.5
	Liberal Democratic	21688	5	2.2
	Peasant and Middle Class	117847	22	12.1
	Catholic Conservative	226122	47	23.2
	Radical	227370	50	23.3
	Socialist	263664	53	27.0
	Communist	25060	4	2.6
	Others	46819	5	3.4

		Votes per party	Seats	% of votes
1959	Independent	54049	10	5.5
	Liberal Democratic	22934	5	2.3
	Peasant and Middle Class	113611	23	11.6
	Catholic Conservative	229088	47	23.3
	Radical	232557	51	23.7
	Socialist	259139	51	26.3
	Communist	26346	3	2.7
	Others	51281	6	4.1
1963	Independent	48224	10	5.0
	Liberal Democratic	21501	6	2.2
	Peasant and Middle Class	109202	22	11.4
	Catholic Conservative	225160	48	23.4
	Radical	230200	51	24.0
	Socialist	256063	53	26.6
	Communist	21088	4	2.2
	Others	49693	6	4.2
1967	Independent	89950	16	9.1
	Liberal Democratic	23208	6	2.3
	Peasant and Middle Class	109621	21	11.0
	Catholic Conservative	219184	45	22.1
	Radical	230095	49	23.2
	Socialist	233873	51	23.5
	Communist	28723	5	2.9
	Others	59194	7	3.6
1971	Independent	150684	13	7.6
	Liberal Democratic	43338	6	2.2
	Peasant and Middle Class	217909	23	11.0
	Catholic Conservative	402528	44	20.4
	Radical	431364	49	21.8
	Socialist	452194	46	22.9
	Communist	50834	5	2.6
	Republican Movement	88327	7	4.5
	Others	138417	7	5.3

		Seats	% of votes
1975	Social Democrats	55	25.4
	Radical Democrats	47	22.2
	Christian Democrats	46	20.6
	Swiss People's Party	21	10.1
	Independents Party	11	6.2
	Liberal Democrats	6	2.3
	Republican Movement	4	3.0
	Party of Labour (Communists)	4	2.2
	Others	6	8.0
1979	Social Democrats	51	24.4
	Radical Democrats	51	24.1
	Christian Democrats	44	21.5
	Swiss People's Party	23	11.6
	Independents Party	8	4.1
	Liberal Democrats	8	2.8
	Republican Movement	1	1.9
	Party of Labour (Communist)	3	1.7
	Others	11	7.9
1983	Radical Democrats	54	23.4
	Social Democrats	47	22.8
	Christian Democrats	42	20.2
	Swiss People's Party	23	11.1
	Independents Party	8	4.0
	Liberal Party	8	2.8
	Others	18	11.5
1987	Radical Democratic Party	51	22.9
	Christian Democratic People's Party	42	20.0
	Social Democrats	41	18.4
	Swiss People's Party	25	11.0
	Greens	9	4.8
	Liberal Party	9	2.7
	Independent Alliance	8	4.2
	Minor Parties	15	15.9

		Seats	*% of votes*
1991	Radical Democratic Party	44	
	Social Democratic Party	43	
	Christian-Democratic People's Party	37	
	Swiss People's Party	25	
	Greens	14	
	Liberals	10	
	Independent Alliance	9	
	Automobile Party	8	
	Minor Parties	10	
1995 (Oct)	Radical Democratic Party	45	
	Christian Democratic Party	34	
	Swiss Social Democratic Party	54	
	Swiss People's Party/ Democratic Centre Union	29	
	Others	38	
1999 (Oct)	Social Democratic Party (SPS-PSS)	51	22.5
	Swiss People's Party (SVP-UDC)	44	22.6
	Radical Democratic Party	43	19.9
	Christian Democratic People's Party	35	15.8
	Green Party of Switzerland	9	5.0
	Liberal Party of Switzerland	6	2.2
	Evangelical People's Party	3	1.8
	Others	9	10.2

TURKEY

No meaningful figures are available for the elections held in the old Ottoman Empire in 1908 and 1912. The first Turkish Grand National Assembly met in Ankara on 23 Apr 1920. In these circumstances, only indirect elections proved possible, every province putting forward 5 delegates. The Assembly consisted of 337 members, 232 of whom had been newly elected. Under the constitution of 20 Jan 1921, which the Assembly adopted and which legalized the organization it had set up, the deputies' term of office was set at 2 years.

In the 1920 elections Kemalists held 197 seats; Opposition, 118; Nonaligned, 122. In 1923, Grand National Assembly Party n.a.; Progressive Republican Party n.a.; Republican People's Party, 304.

The first Assembly was prorogued on 1 Apr 1923 after deciding that new elections should be held. On 19 Oct 1923, the Republic was proclaimed and the 1924 constitution extended the franchise to all men aged 18 or over. Candidates had to be at least 30 years old, and the deputies' term of office was lengthened to 4 years. A constitutional amendment adopted on 5 Jan 1934 extended the franchise to women, but raised the minimum voting age to 22. Elections continued to be indirect: voters chose an electoral college which then elected the Assembly. This practice was continued until 1946. The membership of the Assembly increased constantly until the adoption of the 1961 constitution, since it had been laid down that there should be one deputy per 40 000 citizens.

The first effective political party in the history of the Turkish Republic, the People's Party, was formed in Oct 1923; in Nov 1924 its name was changed to Republican People's Party. This party remained in power until 1950. The Free Republican Party, formed in 1930, had a brief existence. Then between 1930 and 1945 Turkey had a single-party régime. On 5 Jun 1945 the authorities allowed the formation of political parties without a preliminary permit, and as a consequence the elections held on 21 Jul 1946 were for the first time contested by more than one party. Voting was direct and public, electors were allowed to divide their votes between party lists of candidates (producing 'mixed' lists), but votes were counted in secret. To win, candidates needed to obtain the simple majority of the votes cast. Two changes were introduced in the elections held on 14 May 1950: voting became secret, and the counting of votes open. In 1957 mixed lists were banned, but electors were allowed to delete the names of individual candidates from the party lists of their choice. After 27 May 1960, the National Unity Committee first assumed all the powers vested in the Grand National Assembly under the 1924 constitution. This transfer of power, legalized by the provisional constitution of 12 Jun 1960, was followed on 13 Dec of the same year by a law setting up a Constituent Assembly, which was opened on 6 Jan 1961.

The constitution which this Assembly drew up governed the elections held on 15 Oct 1961 which produced a new Turkish Grand National Assembly. Article 55 of the constitution required voting to be free, direct, universal and secret, and the counting of votes to be open. However, the constitution did not define the system of representation which was to be used, and this was regulated by electoral laws. Proportional representation was introduced for the first time in the elections of 15 Oct 1961 and has been retained since, although the basic d'Hondt formula has been varied: first candidates had to obtain a minimum number of votes (known as the 'barrage') to qualify for consideration: then the country-wide pooling and redistribution of wasted votes ('the national residue') was introduced in time for the elections of 12 Oct 1965, but dropped together with the 'barrage' requirement before the 1969 elections.

		Votes per party	*Seats*
1950	Democratic Party	4242831	396
	Republican People's Party	3165096	68
	Nation Party	240209	1
	Independents	258698	7
1954	Republican People's Party	3161696	31
	Republican Nation Party	434085	5
	Democratic Party	5151550	505
	Peasant Party	57011	–
	Independents	137318	1
1957	Republican People's Party	3753136	178
	Republican Nation Party	652064	4
	Democratic Party	4372621	424
	Freedom Party	350497	4
	Independents	4944	–
1961	Justice Party	3527435	158
	Republican People's Party	3724752	173
	Republican Peasants and Nation Party, renamed Nationalist Action Party	1415390	54
	New Turkey Party	1391934	65
	Independents	81732	–
1965	Justice Party	4921235	240
	Republican People's Party	2675785	134
	Republican Peasants and Nation Party, renamed Nationalist Action Party	208696	11
	Nation Party	582704	31
	Turkish Workers' Party	276101	14
	New Turkey Party	346514	19
	Independents	296528	1
1969	Justice Party	4219712	256
	Republican People's Party	2487006	143

	Votes per party	*Seats*
Republican Peasants and Nation Party, renamed Nationalist Action Party	275091	1
Nation Party	292961	6
Turkish Workers' Party	243631	2
New Turkey Party	197929	6
Independents	511023	13
Unity Party	254695	8
Reliance Party, renamed National Reliance Party in 1971	597818	15

Senators are elected for six years, but one-third of the membership is re-elected every other year. Voting is free, equal, universal, direct and secret, and counting open. The Senate was first set up in 1961. That year and in 1964, a simple majority sufficed for the election of a senator; in 1966 and 1968 proportional representation (with 'national residue') was introduced.

		Votes per party	*Seats*
1961	Justice Party	3560675	71
	Republican People's Party	3734285	76
	Republican Peasants and Nation Party	1350892	16
	New Turkey Party	1401636	27
	Independents	39558	–
1964	Justice Party	1385655	31
	Republican People's Party	1125783	19
	Republican Peasants and Nation Party	88400	–
	New Turkey Party	96427	–
	Independents	64498	1
1966	Justice Party	1688316	35
	Republican People's Party	877066	13
	Republican Peasants and Nation Party	57367	1
	Nation Party	157115	1
	Turkish Workers' Party	116375	1
	New Turkey Party	70043	1
	Independents	980	–

		Votes per party	*Seats*
1968	Justice Party	1 656 802	38
	Republican People's Party	899 444	13
	Republican Peasants and Nation Party	66 232	–
	Reliance Party, renamed National Reliance Party	284 234	1
	Nation Party	200 737	1
	Turkish Workers' Party	157 062	–
	Independents	58 317	–

After a period of disguised military rule, Parliament reasserted its influence in 1973. In the elections of Oct 1973 there was a shock rebuff for Mr Demirel with major gains by Ecevit (much more in the Social Democrat mould).

	Votes per party		*Seats*	*% of votes*
1973	Republican People's Party	3 570 583	185	33.3
	Justice Party	3 179 897	149	29.8
	National Salvation Party	1 265 771	48	11.8
	National Action Party	362 208	3	3.4
	Democratic Party	1 275 502	45	11.9
	Republican Reliance Party	564 343	13	5.3
	Turkish Unity Party	121 759	1	1.1
	Others	365 595	6	3.4
1977	Republican People's Party	6 117 280	213	41.4
	Justice Party	5 457 649	189	36.9
	National Salvation Party	1 271 620	24	8.6
	National Action Party	942 606	16	6.4
	Republican Reliance Party	277 059	3	1.9
	Democratic Party	273 426	1	1.8
	Turkish Unity Party	58 319	–	0.4
	Others	387 855	4	2.6

On 10 Sep 1980, for the third time in 20 years, the military took control of Turkey. A general election took place on 6 Nov 1983. The result was:

Motherland Party	7 823 827	212	45.7
Populist Party	5 277 698	117	30.8
Nationalist Democracy Party	4 032 046	71	23.5

Recent election results have been as follows:

	Votes per party		Seats	% of votes
1987	Motherland Party	8 704 335	292	36.3
	Social Democratic Populist	5 931 000	99	24.7
	True Path	4 587 062	59	19.1
	Democratic Left	2 044 576	–	8.5
	Welfare Party	1 717 425	–	7.2
	Others*	987 231	–	4.1

* All polling less than 5% of the votes each.

		Seats	% of votes
1991 (Oct)	True Path Party	178	27.0
	Motherland Party	115	27.0
	Social Democratic Populist	88	na
	Welfare Party (Refah)	62	16.9
	Democratic Left Party	7	10.8
	Total	450	
1995 (Dec)	Welfare Party (Refah)	158	21.4
	True Path Party	135	19.2
	Motherland Party	132	19.7
	Democratic Left	76	14.6
	Republican Populist Party	49	10.7
	Others	0	14.4
	Total	550	
1999 (Apr)	Democratic Left Party (DSP)	136	22.3
	Nationalist Movement Party (MHP)	129	18.1
	Virtue Party (FP)	111	15.5
	Motherland Party (ANAP)	86	13.3
	True Path Party (DYP)	85	12.1
	Independents	3	0.9
	Others	–	17.8

UKRAINE

The first presidential elections in independent Ukraine, following the collapse of the Soviet Union, were on 1 Dec 1991. The easy victor was Leonid Kravchuk with 19 643 000 votes (61.6 per cent). His nearest rival was Vyacheslav Chornovil with 7 420 000 (23.3 per cent). The first general election, held in Mar/Apr 1994, resulted in 112 of the 450 seats left unfilled. Of the 338 seats, the Communist Party of the Ukraine had 86 seats followed by Rukh with 20 and the Peasants' Party with 18. No fewer than 170 Independents were returned.

In parliamentary elections held on 29 Mar 1998, the Communists were most successful. Of the total 413 seats, one source gave the KPU (Communists) 110 seats, Rukh 45, and the Socialist and Peasant Parties electoral bloc 33. No other party won over 30 seats, while there were over 100 Independents. In the presidential elections on 31 Oct 1999, Kuchma failed to win on the first round but was re-elected in the run-off ballot on 14 Nov.

USSR

In 1917 the Provisional Government had been organizing elections to establish a Constituent Assembly, and these the Bolsheviks allowed to take place on 25 Nov 1917. Suffrage was universal, and the electorate numbered 41.7m. Figures are uncertain and contradictory. *See* p. 285 for some reputable estimates.

The Kadets were proscribed at the end of 1917. The Constituent Assembly met on 18 Jan 1918, just over half the delegates being present. It was dissolved by the Bolsheviks the following day after rejecting by 237 votes to 136 a Bolshevik motion which would have recognized the Congress of Soviets to be the supreme government authority.

The Congress of Soviets was therefore the supreme organ of state power until it was replaced by the Supreme Soviet in 1937. There were altogether ten All-Russian Congresses until the formation of the USSR (30 Dec 1922) and eight All-Union Congresses thereafter.

Elections were indirect, from amongst the deputies in the hierarchy of soviets throughout the country. The latter were elected on a franchise restricted to workers, peasants and the armed forces. Deputies to town soviets were elected on a basis of 1 per 25 000 electors; to rural soviets on a basis of 1 per 125 000.

By 1922 all public opposition to the Communist Party had been brought to an end. Party allegiance in the early Congresses of Soviets (for the first two see above):

> 3rd (Jan 1918) Bolsheviks 61%
>
> 4th (Extraordinary) (Mar 1918) Bolsheviks 66%
>
> 5th (Jul 1918) Bolsheviks (now called Communists) 66%
>
> 6th (Nov 1918) Communists 90%
>
> 7th (Dec 1918) Communists 95%
>
> 8th (Dec 1920) Communists 95%

The 'Stalin' Constitution of 1936 replaced the Congresses of Soviets with the Supreme Soviet (*Verkhovnyi Sovet*). This had two chambers: the Soviet of the Union (*Sovet Soyuza*) and the Soviet of Nationalities (*Sovet Natsionalnostei*). Elections were held every 4 years. Suffrage universal at 18 years; candidates could stand at 23. The Soviet of the Union was elected on a basis of 1 deputy per 300 000 electors. Deputies to the Soviet of Nationalities were elected in the following proportions: 32 from each Federative Republic, 11 from each Autonomous Republic, 5 from each Autonomous Oblast (Province) and 1 from each National District.

Although it was constitutionally the supreme legislative body, the Supreme Soviet had no significance in the realm of policy-making: *de facto* supreme power was in the hands of the Communist Party. Candidates for election could be nominated only by recognized organizations: the Communist Party, trade unions, industrial co-operatives, agricultural collectives, youth organizations and cultural organizations. Candidates need not belong to the party, but they had to support its programme. On average, some 75 per cent of deputies were party members.

More than one candidate could be nominated, and there was no constitutional bar to more than one standing for election, but the practice was that one only of the nominees was selected to stand by local party officials, and the elector's choice was thus limited to voting for or against him.

The ballot was secret but so arranged that only a contrary vote actually required entry into the polling booth.

Elections were held in Dec 1937, Feb 1946, Mar 1950, Mar 1954, Mar 1958, Mar 1962, Jun 1966, Jun 1970, Jun 1974 and Mar 1979. In 1937, 91 113 153 votes were cast out of an electorate of 93 139 478, and subsequently the turnout had always exceeded 99 per cent. Less than 1 per cent of votes cast had been against candidates, and no candidate ever failed to be elected.

For elections in Russia following the collapse of the Soviet Union, *see* p. 286.

INDEPENDENT TERRITORIES (1918–1921)

Armenia, Azerbaijan and Georgia proclaimed independence jointly as the Transcaucasian Federative Republic on 22 Apr 1918; reconquered respectively 29 Nov 1920, 27 Apr 1920 and 18 Mar 1921.

The Transcaucasian Federative Republic was governed by a *Seim* of delegates based upon the elections to the Russian Constituent Assembly (dissolved on 18 Jan 1918): Mensheviks, 33; Musavat (Moslem Nationalists), 30; Dashnaktsutiun (Armenian Nationalists), 27; Moslem Socialists, 7; Socialist revolutionaries, 5; others 10.

The Federation collapsed upon the secession of Georgia on 26 May 1918, and each Republic became separately independent.

Armenia set up a National Council (*Khorhurd*) on 1 Aug 1918, the party composition of which was: Dashnaktsutiun, 18; Populist, 6; Moslems, 6; Mensheviks, 5; independents, 2; Bolsheviks, 1; Yezidis, 1; Russians, 1.

Azerbaijan set up a National Council composed as follows: Musavat (Moslem Nationalists) and Neutral Democratic Group (Sunni Moslems), 30; Socialists, 11; Moslem Union, 3. In Jun 1918 the Council was reformed under the insistence of the Turkish military commander to exclude socialists and give predominance to the conservative Moslem Union. In turn the British military commander after the surrender of the Turks objected to the Council as unrepresentative. A new Council was created in Dec 1918: Musavat, 38; Neutral Democratic Group, 7; Unity Party, 13; Socialists, 11; Dashnaktsutiun (Armenian Nationalists), 7; other Armenian parties, 4; Bolsheviks, 1; others, 15.

Georgia. In Feb 1919 the National Council held elections for a Constituent Assembly. Suffrage was universal and by proportional representation: 15 parties presented candidates for election, 505 477 votes were cast (some 60 per cent of the electorate). The Assembly had 130 deputies, distributed as follows:

	Votes cast	*Deputies in the Assembly*
Mensheviks	409 766	109
National Democrats	30 154	8
Social-Federalists	33 721	8
Social-Revolutionaries	21 453	5

UNITED KINGDOM

In 1911 the maximum duration of a parliament, which since 1715 had been seven years, was reduced to five years.

By 1918 virtually all men were enfranchised together with all women over 30 years of age who were householders or the wives of householders. Voting in more than two constituencies was prohibited. General elections which had hitherto been spread over 2 weeks and more were concentrated on a single day. Candidates were required to provide a deposit of £150 to be forfeit if they failed to secure one-eighth of the votes cast in their constituency. Seats were redistributed, for the first time on the basis of approximately equal electorates, and the House of Commons was increased to 707 members (this fell to 615 in 1922, with the independence of Southern Ireland).

The age of women voting was lowered to 21 in 1928 and they were given the vote on exactly the same basis as men.

In 1948 university seats and all plural voting were abolished. Machinery was set up for Permanent Boundary Commissions to redraw constituencies once in the life of every normal 5-year parliament, but because the first routine distribution of seats in 1954–1955 (which increased the House to 630 members) had caused so much annoyance and difficulty, an Act was passed in 1958 to reduce the frequency of redistribution to between 10 and 15 years.

		Votes	% share of total vote	Members
1900	Conservatives	1767958	50.3	402
	Liberals	1572323	45.0	184
	Irish Nationalist	91055	2.6	82
	Labour	62698	1.3	2
	Others	29448	0.8	–
				670
1906	Conservatives	2422071	43.4	157
	Liberals	2751057	49.4	400
	Irish Nationalist	35031	0.7	83
	Labour	321663	4.8	29
	Others	96269	1.7	1
				670
1910 (Jan)	Conservatives	3104407	46.8	273
	Liberals	2866157	43.5	275
	Irish Nationalist	126647	1.9	82
	Labour	505657	7.0	40
	Others	64532	0.8	–
				670
1910 (Dec)	Conservatives	2420169	46.6	273
	Liberals	2293869	44.2	271
	Irish Nationalist	131720	2.5	84
	Labour	371802	6.4	42
	Others	17678	0.3	–
				670
1918	Electors:	21392322	Turnout: 58.9%	
	Total votes cast	10766583	100.0	707
	Coalition Unionist	3504198	32.6	335
	Coalition Liberal	1455640	13.5	133
	Coalition Labour	161521	1.5	10

		Votes	*% share of* *total vote*	Members
	(Coalition)	(5 121 259)	(47.6)	(478)
	Conservative	370 375	3.4	23
	Irish Unionist	292 722	2.7	25
	Liberal	1 298 808	12.1	28
	Labour	2 385 472	22.2	63
	Irish Nationalist	238 477	2.2	7
	Sinn Fein	486 867	4.5	73
	Other	572 503	5.3	10
1922	Electors:	21 127 663	Turnout: 71.3%	
	Total votes cast	14 393 632	100.0	615
	Conservative	5 500 382	38.2	345
	National Liberal	1 673 240	11.6	62
	Liberal	2 516 187	17.5	54
	Labour	4 241 383	29.5	142
	Other	462 340	3.2	12
1923	Electors:	21 281 232	Turnout: 70.8%	
	Total votes cast	14 548 521	100.0	615
	Conservative	5 538 824	38.1	258
	Liberal	4 311 147	29.6	159
	Labour	4 438 508	30.5	191
	Other	260 042	1.8	7
1924	Electors:	21 731 320	Turnout: 76.6%	
	Total votes cast	16 640 279	100.0	615
	Conservative	8 039 598	48.3	419
	Liberal	2 928 747	17.6	40
	Labour	5 489 077	33.0	151
	Communist	55 346	0.3	1
	Other	126 511	0.8	4
1929	Electors:	28 850 870	Turnout: 76.1%	
	Total votes cast	22 648 375	100.0	615
	Conservative	8 656 473	38.2	260
	Liberal	5 308 510	23.4	59
	Labour	8 389 512	37.1	288
	Communist	50 614	0.3	–
	Other	243 266	1.0	8

		Votes	% share of total vote	Members
1931	Electors:	29 960 071	Turnout: 76.3%	
	Total votes cast	21 656 373	100.0	615
	Conservative	11 978 745	55.2	473
	National Liberal	341 370	1.6	13
	Liberal National	809 302	3.7	35
	Liberal	1 403 102	6.5	33
	(National government)	(14 532 519)	(67.0)	(554)
	Independent Liberal	106 106	0.5	4
	Labour	6 649 630	30.6	52
	Communist	74 824	0.3	–
	New Party	36 377	0.2	–
	Other	256 917	1.2	5
1935	Electors:	31 379 050	Turnout: 71.2%	
	Total votes cast	21 997 054	100.0	615
	Conservative	11 810 158	53.7	432
	Liberal	1 422 116	6.4	20
	Labour	8 325 491	37.9	154
	Independent Labour Party	139 577	0.7	4
	Communist	27 117	0.1	1
	Other	272 595	1.2	4
1945	Electors:	33 240 391	Turnout: 72.7%	
	Total votes cast	25 085 978	100.0	640
	Conservative	9 988 306	39.8	213
	Liberal	2 248 226	9.0	12
	Labour	11 995 152	47.8	393
	Communist	102 780	0.4	2
	Common Wealth	110 634	0.4	1
	Other	640 880	2.0	19
1950	Electors:	33 269 770	Turnout: 84.0%	
	Total votes cast	28 772 671	100.0	625
	Conservative	12 502 567	43.5	298
	Liberal	2 621 548	9.1	9
	Labour	13 266 592	46.1	315
	Communist	91 746	0.3	–
	Other	290 218	1.0	3

		Votes	% share of total vote	Members
1951	Electors:	34 645 573	Turnout: 82.5%	
	Total votes cast	28 595 668	100.0	625
	Conservative	13 717 538	48.0	321
	Liberal	730 556	2.5	6
	Labour	13 948 605	48.8	295
	Communist	21 640	0.1	–
	Other	177 329	0.6	3
1955	Electors:	34 858 263	Turnout: 76.7%	
	Total votes cast	26 760 493	100.0	630
	Conservative	13 286 569	49.7	344
	Liberal	722 405	2.7	6
	Labour	12 404 970	46.4	277
	Communist	33 144	0.1	–
	Other	313 410	1.1	3
1959	Electors:	35 397 080	Turnout: 78.8%	
	Total votes cast	27 859 241	100.0	630
	Conservative	13 749 830	49.4	365
	Liberal	1 638 571	5.9	6
	Labour	12 215 528	43.8	258
	Communist	30 897	0.1	–
	Other	224 405	0.8	1
1964	Electors:	35 892 572	Turnout: 77.1%	
	Total votes cast	27 655 374	100.0	630
	Conservative	12 001 396	43.4	304
	Liberal	3 092 878	11.2	9
	Labour	12 205 814	44.1	317
	Communist	45 932	0.2	–
	Other	302 982	1.1	–
1966	Electors:	35 964 684	Turnout: 75.8%	
	Total votes cast	27 263 606	100.0	630
	Conservative	11 418 433	41.9	253
	Liberal	2 327 533	8.6	12
	Labour	13 064 951	47.9	363
	Communist	62 040	0.2	–
	Other	390 649	1.4	2

		Votes	% share of total vote	Members
1970	Electors:	39384364	Turnout: 72%	
	Total votes cast	28344807	100.0	630
	Conservative	13144692	46.4	330
	Liberal	2117638	7.5	6
	Labour	12179166	42.9	287
	Communist	38431	0.1	–
	Other	864880	3.1	7
1974 (Feb)	Electors:	39798899	Turnout: 78.7%	
	Total votes cast	31333226	100.0	635
	Conservative	11868906	37.9	297
	Liberal	6063470	19.3	14
	Labour	11639243	37.1	301
	Communist	32741	0.1	–
	Plaid Cymru	171364	0.6	2
	SNP	632032	2.0	7
	National Front	76865	0.3	–
	Others (G.B.)	131059	0.4	2
	Others (N.I.)	717986	2.3	12
1974 (Oct)	Electors:	40072971	Turnout: 72.8%	
	Conservative	10464817	35.8	277
	Liberal	5346754	18.3	13
	Labour	11457079	39.2	319
	Communist	17426	0.1	–
	Plaid Cymru	166321	0.6	3
	SNP	839617	2.9	11
	National Front	113843	0.4	–
	Others (G.B.)	81227	0.3	–
	Others (N.I.)	702094	2.4	12
1979	Electors:	41093264	Turnout: 76.0%	
	Conservative	13697690	43.9	339
	Liberal	4313811	13.8	11
	Labour	11532148	36.9	269
	Communist	15938	0.1	–
	Plaid Cymru	132544	0.4	2
	SNP	504259	1.6	2

		Votes	% share of total vote	Members
	National Front	190747	0.6	–
	Ecology	38116	0.1	–
	WRP	13535	0.1	–
	Others (G.B.)	85338	0.3	–
	Others (N.I.)	695889	2.2	12
1983	Conservatives	13012602	42.4	397
	Liberal/SDP Alliance	7780577	25.4	23*
	Labour	8457124	27.6	209
	Plaid Cymru	125309	0.4	2
	SNP	331975	1.1	2
	Others (G.B.)	289033	1.0	–
	Others (N.I.)	674275	2.1	17

* SDP 6, Liberals 17.

		Votes	% share of total vote	Members
1987	Conservative	13763747	42.2	375
	Labour	10029270	30.8	229
	Liberal/SDP	7341275	22.6	22
	Plaid Cymru	123589	0.3	3
	SNP	416873	1.4	3
	Others (N.I.)	730152	2.3	17
	Others	151517	0.4	1
1992	Conservative	14092891	41.9	336
	Labour	11559735	34.4	271
	Lib. Dems.	5999384	17.8	20
	Plaid Cymru	154439	0.5	4
	SNP	629552	1.9	3
	Others (N.I.)	740485	2.4	17
	Others	436107	1.4	–
1997	Labour	13517911	43.2	418
	Conservative	9600940	30.7	165
	Lib. Dems.	5243440	16.8	46
	Plaid Cymru	161030	0.5	4
	SNP	622260	2.0	6
	Others (N.I.)	780920	2.5	18
	Others	1361701	4.3	2

YUGOSLAVIA

The 1920 elections were held on proportional principles by universal male suffrage; 65 per cent of electorate voted.

	Party	Seats	% of votes
1920	Democrats (a combination of S. Pribičevič's Habsburg Serbs and the Independent Radicals)	92	19.9
	Radicals	91	17.0
	Communists (became illegal 1921)	58	12.4
	Croat Peasants	50	14.3
	Serbian Agrarians	39	
	Moslems	32	
	Slovene Catholic People's Party	27	
	Social Democrats	10	
	Others	19	

The proportional system was modified in the 1923 election. 73 per cent of the electorate voted.

1923	Radicals	108	25.8
	Croat Peasants	70	21.8
	Democrats	51	
	Slovene Catholic People's Party	22	
	Moslems of Bosnia	18	
	Moslems of Macedonia	14	
	Serbian Agrarians	10	
	Germans	8	
	Social Democrats	2	
	Others	9	

At the 1925 elections 76.9 per cent of the electorate voted.

1925	Radicals	142
	Independent Democrats	22
	Croat Peasants	67
	Slovene Catholic People's Party	20
	Moslems	15

Party	Seats
Serbian Agrarians	5
Germans	5
Montenegrins	3
Others	34

At the 1927 elections 68 per cent of the electorate voted.

1927	Radicals	112
	Croat Peasants	61
	Democrats	59
	Independent Democrats	22
	Slovene Catholic People's Party	21
	Moslems	18
	Serbian Agrarians	9
	Germans	6
	Social Democrats	1
	Others	6

The *Vidovdan* constitution and the *Skupština* were abolished on 6 Jan 1929 by King Alexander, who set up a royal dictatorship which found permanent expression in the constitution of 3 Jun 1931. This instituted a bicameral legislature: a National Assembly elected every 4 years publicly by all males over 21, each deputy representing 50 000 inhabitants; and a Senate half appointed and half elected by regional colleges of electors. The powers of the *Skupština* were reduced. In an attempt to eliminate regionalism all parties centred about ethnic or religious particularities were declared illegal. The name of the kingdom was changed to Yugoslavia in a similar gesture against separatism. Proportional representation was abolished: any party which won a majority of votes would henceforth be allotted two-thirds of the seats in the *Skupština*.

At the elections of 8 Nov 1931 only the government list was presented; 65 per cent of the electorate voted.

In 1933 this electoral law was relaxed. The winning party was to receive three-fifths of the seats; and conditions for establishing countrywide lists of candidates were made easier.

On 9 Oct 1934 King Alexander was assassinated, and Prince Paul became Regent.

The elections of 25 May 1935 were public. The opposition parties (Croat Peasant, Independent Democrats, Democrats, Serbian Agrarians and Moslems) formed a united bloc; 73.7 per cent of the electorate voted.

	Votes	Seats
The Government	1 746 982	303
The Opposition	1 076 345	67

At the elections of 11 Dec 1938, 74.5 per cent of the electorate voted.

	Votes	Seats
The Government (Yugoslav Radical Union)	1 643 783	306
The Opposition	1 364 524	67

All opposition parties abstained from the elections to the Constituent Assembly of 11 Nov 1945 leaving only a single Popular Front list; 88 per cent of the electorate voted, 90 per cent for the Popular Front.

In 1950 an electoral law abolished the single list system, and candidates were nominated individually. In the election of 26 Mar 1950 the number of candidates was still the same as the number of seats: there was no contest. Popular Front candidates polled 93.25 per cent of the votes cast.

At the elections of 22 Nov 1953 the electorate for the Federal Council was 10 580 648: 527 candidates stood for 484 seats (Federal Council, 282; Council of Producers, 202, of whom 135 were industrial and 67 were agricultural); 89.4 per cent of the electorate voted.

At the elections of 23–26 Mar 1958, 307 candidates stood for the 301 seats of the Federal Council. The electorate was 11 331 727: 94 per cent of the electorate voted, 216 representatives were elected to the Council of Producers: 168 industrial, 48 agricultural.

By the constitution of 7 Apr 1963 Yugoslavia became a 'Socialist' instead of a 'People's' Republic. This constitution did away almost entirely with direct elections, replacing these by an electoral filtering system. The electoral emphasis moved from the formal act of voting to the nominating process in which citizens participated through their local government wards and workers through their workplace. The Council of Producers was abolished and replaced by 4 specialized councils (Administration; Culture; Economy; Welfare). The Federal Assembly of 670 was to be elected for 4-year terms. Every second year one-half of each council was renewed.

Elections were held on 25 May and 16 Jun 1963. The number of candidates was the same as the number of seats; 95.5 per cent of the electorate voted. Half the seats came up for renewal on 19 Mar and 19 Apr 1965, when a few constituencies had more than one candidate; 93.6 per cent of the electorate voted.

By a constitutional amendment in 1968 the Federal Council was abolished and divided into its two political components: (1) Social and Political Council, elected by citizens in local government wards: (2) Council of Nations, representing the republican legislatures.

At the elections of 12 Apr and 10 May 1969 for the Social and Political Council there were 179 candidates for the 120 seats; 87 per cent of the electorate voted. There were 624 candidates for the 360 seats of the 4 specialized councils.

The first elections to be held on the 'delegate' principle, as outlined in the new constitution, took place between Mar and May 1974. In early May elections were held to the two Chambers of the new Assembly of the Federation. At subsequent elections, until 1990, all candidates were either chosen or screened by the Socialist Alliance of the Working People of Yugoslavia, the official Communist organization.

During 1990, against a background of growing separatism and the collapse of Communism elsewhere in Eastern Europe, multi-party elections took place in the constituent republics of Yugoslavia. In Apr and May 1990, elections were held in Slovenia and Croatia. In Slovenia, the greatest number of seats in the Assembly was won by the Democratic Opposition of Slovenia (DEMOS), a centre–right coalition. In Croatia, an absolute majority was won by the Croatian Democratic Union (CDU), a nationalist movement. Elsewhere Communists retained power and in Serbia in Dec 1990 won 194 of the 250 seats (fighting under the new name of the Socialist Party).

Elections were held in 'rump' Yugoslavia (comprising Serbia and Montenegro) in Dec 1992, when the Socialist Party of Serbia won 47 seats (31.4 per cent), the Serbian Radical Party 34 seats (22.4 per cent) and the Democratic Movement of Serbia 20 seats (17.2 per cent) out of the 138 seats in the Chamber of Citizens. The elections of Nov 1996 were again dominated by the Socialist Coalition led by Slobodan Milosevic (with 50 per cent of the vote). The Zajedno ('Together') opposition alliance (including the Serbian Renewal Party) took 23 per cent and the Radical Party 18 per cent.

6
Political Parties

ALBANIA

During the Communist era, the ruling party was the Albanian Party of Labour (originally founded in 1941). It was the only recognized party in the state. Following anti-government demonstrations in Dec 1990, the ruling Party of Labour announced its abandonment of Stalinism, the legalization of political parties, and free elections to the People's Assembly. The following main parties have emerged:

DEMOCRATIC PARTY OF ALBANIA (DPA)
Formed in Dec 1990, the DPA advocates free-market economics within a parliamentary democratic system. The party won 29 seats in the People's Assembly in the 1997 elections.

SOCIALIST PARTY OF ALBANIA (SPA)
Formerly the Albanian Party of Labour, the party took the name Socialist Party of Albania in 1991 and is committed to democratic socialism and a free-market economy. The SPA won 101 seats in the 1997 People's Assembly elections which it dominated.

SOCIAL DEMOCRATIC PARTY (SDP)
The SDP was formed in 1990 and has a platform of gradual economic reform. The party won only eight seats in the 1997 general election.

UNION FOR HUMAN RIGHTS
Formed in 1992, the Union for Human Rights won 3 per cent of the vote for the People's Assembly in Mar 1992. It won four seats in 1997.

ALBANIAN REPUBLICAN PARTY (ARP)

The ARP, which was formed in 1991, took 3 per cent of the vote in the March 1992 general election. It won only one seat in 1997.

Among a profusion of other parties are the Albanian Green Party, the Albanian Liberal Party, the People's Party, the Independent Party, the Democratic Union of the Greek Minority, and the Albanian Women's Federation, all of which were formed in 1991. Other recent parties include the Civil Party (f.1998), Movement for Democracy (f.1997) and the Union of Social Democrats (f.1995) (a breakaway from the SDP).

ARMENIA

Political parties in Armenia have had a chequered history. During the first brief period of independence, 1918–1920, the Armenian Revolutionary Federation (ARF), founded in 1891, was the ruling party. Banned under Soviet rule, it has operated legally again since 1991. In the Soviet era, the ruling party was the Communist Party of Armenia (which dissolved itself in Sep 1991). The Armenian Pan-National Movement (APM), founded in 1989, emphasizes Armenian culture and sovereignty. In the 1995 election this was part of the Republican bloc, a coalition which included the Republican Party of Armenia, the Christian Democratic Union and the Liberal Democratic Union. The Unity Bloc won in 1999.

AUSTRIA

Up to the 1880s, political parties in the Habsburg Monarchy were really only informal groupings of parliamentary notables. There was virtually no constituency organization. The Liberals tended to represent the German-speaking urban middle class, whilst the Conservatives spoke for the nobility, the interests of agriculture and the non-German minorities. The main developments prior to 1918 were:

1882   Foundation of Georg von Schonerer's Pan-German League. Extremely anti-clerical and racialist, with a more militant defence of German-speaking interests. Essentially a dissident Liberal Party.

1887   Formation of the Catholic Social Union. Anti-Liberal (and anti-Semitic) with support from lower middle class in Vienna.

1889   Foundation of the Social Democratic Party.

1896   German People's Party founded.

1903   German Radical Party founded.

1905   German Agrarian Party founded.

1910   Union of the Liberal-National parties into the *Deutscher National-verband*.

SOCIAL DEMOCRATIC PARTY 1889

Socialist social and economic aims, supported political union with Germany. After World War II, changed its name to the *Austrian Socialist Party (SPÖ)*, no longer pan-German. The SPÖ obtained an absolute majority in parliament in 1970 under the leadership of Bruno Kreisky and remained in power for 13 years before losing its majority and forming a 'small coalition' with the FPÖ (*q.v.*). Its support is disproportionately concentrated in Vienna. It took the name Social Democratic Party in 1991.

CHRISTIAN SOCIALIST PARTY 1892

Conservative with strong clerical Roman Catholic influence. Politically divided with one section monarchist and the other pan-German. In 1945 it was reformed as the *Austrian People's Party (ÖVP)* with a conservative Christian-Democrat programme. The core of its support comes from the urban middle classes and farmers.

ALL-GERMANY PARTY 1917

Developed out of the German National Club and some sections of the old National Democratic Party. Politically centre, committed to union with Germany. Dissolved by World War II.

COMMUNIST PARTY (KPÖ) 1918

Communist programme included committal to strict neutrality. Major strength was in the trade unions. Opposed to EU membership.

AUSTRIAN PEOPLE'S PARTY 1945

A Christian Democratic Party which advocates a social market economy. Junior party in ruling coalition in 1990s.

AUSTRIAN LIBERAL PARTY (FPÖ) 1955

Partially succeeds the previous Independent League dissolved in 1956. Programme of moderate social reform and inter-Europe co-operation. It is structured on a federal basis, and regional parties enjoy a great deal of autonomy. The party first came to power in 1983 as the junior coalition partner of the SPÖ.

DEMOCRATIC PROGRESSIVE PARTY (DPF) 1965

UNITED GREENS OF AUSTRIA (VGÖ)/THE ALTERNATIVE LIST OF AUSTRIA (1982)

A more conservative and middle-class party than its German counterpart. First entered parliament in 1986 with nine members.

LIBERAL FORUM (1993)

Founded by former members of the FPÖ.

AUSTRIAN FREEDOM PARTY

The far-right party whose success in the 1999 elections upset the traditional political landscape. Founded in 1955 it adopted its present name in 1995.

BELARUS

Since independence the number and position of political parties has constantly changed. Among those dominating the 1995 elections were the Communist Party of Belarus (which had been suspended in 1991, re-legalized in 1993 and subsequently merged with the Party of Communists of Belarus) and the Agrarian Party. The centrist United Civic Party of Belarus (f.1990) came third. The Party of People's Accord won 8 seats. No other party (of the 25 or so groupings) won more than 2 seats. In 1998 there were 28 officially registered parties.

BELGIUM

Before the advent of the Belgian Labour Party, party politics were dominated by two parties: the Liberals, who formed a national party organization in 1846, and the Conservatives, whose national organization, dating from the 1860s, remained weak until 1921, when the Catholic Union (*Union Catholique Belge*) was established.

The Liberals lost ground after 1884 with the rise of the Belgian Labour Party and the extension of the franchise.

The Belgian Labour Party (*Parti Ouvrier Belge*) was founded in 1885 by César de Paepe, rapidly making progress in such cities as Brussels, Ghent, the Liège country and Hainaut province. The Daensists (*Christene Volkspartis*) were formed in 1894 by the Abbé Daens.

CATHOLIC PARTY

This, with the Liberal Party, was one of the main parties of the nineteenth century. It was divided on the French–Flemish language question, and had clearly defined left and right wings but was mainly conservative and clerical. It survived until 1945, when it was reformed as the *Christian Socialist Party (PSC)* which is now undenominational and has a Christian-Democrat moderate reform programme.

LIBERAL PARTY

The other main party of the nineteenth century, less influential since. It had a moderate social and religious policy. In 1961 it was succeeded by the *Party for Liberty and Progress (PLP)*. This is anti-federalist and concerned specially with farmers and industrial workers.

BELGIAN SOCIALIST PARTY (PSB) 1885

Founded as *Parti Ouvrier Belge*. Orthodox socialist programme. Split from the Flemish wing in 1979.

FRONT PARTY 1918

Founded to divide Belgium by setting up a separate Flemish state. Modern counterpart is the *People's Union (see below)*.

FRONT DEMOCRATIQUE DES FRANCOPHONES

Front composed of several small Walloon parties.

FLEMISH PARTY

The Vlaamske Blok was founded in 1979.

PEOPLE'S UNION (VOLKSUNIE)

Flemish Nationalist Party, founded in 1954, aiming at a Federal structure for the country.

ECOLOGIST PARTY

There are two Ecologist parties. *Agalev* is the Dutch-speaking environmental party, founded 1982; *Ecolo* is the environmental party for the French-speaking community.

NATIONAL FRONT 1988

An extreme right-wing nationalist party.

WALLOON PARTY (PW) 1985

An amalgamation of previous Walloon groupings. PW is a left-wing socialist party which advocates an independent Walloon state.

Other parties include the Feminist Humanist Party, which adopted this name in 1990 from the former United Feminist Party. ROSSEM (f.1991) is the ultra-liberal party advocating privatization of social security, abolition of the monarchy etc.

BOSNIA-HERCEGOVINA

In the very confused political situation of independent Bosnia, the following three major parties represent the main ethnic groupings:

PARTY OF DEMOCRATIC ACTION (PDA)

The leading Muslim nationalist party, led by Dr Alija Izetbegovič.

CROATIAN DEMOCRATIC UNION OF BOSNIA AND HERCEGOVINA (f.1990)

The Croat nationalist party, affiliated to the CDU in Croatia.

SERBIAN DEMOCRATIC PARTY OF BOSNIA AND HERCEGOVINA (f.1990)

The Serb nationalist party, allied to the SDP in Serbia.

Other parties include the Socialist Democratic Party (the former ruling League of Communists) and the secular Muslim Liberal Bosniak Organization (created in 1992 from a merger of the Liberal Party of Bosnia and the Muslim Bosniak Organization). Over 40 political parties were in existence in 1999.

BULGARIA

After independence, Bulgarian politics was dominated by the political groupings around Stambulov, Radoslavov and Tontchev. Among other groups active prior to 1914 were:

(1) *The Social Democratic Party* (founded 9 Aug 1891). By 1899, its membership was 800. In 1901, this total had risen to 2180 and by 1902 to 2507. An orthodox evolutionary party, its extremist left broke away in 1903, eventually forming the Communist Party in 1918.

(2) *The Democratic Party* was founded in 1895 by P. Karavelov. The governing party from Jan 1908 to Mar 1911.

(3) *The Radical Party*. Founded in 1906 by N. Tsanov, who broke away from the Democratic Party. It advocated radical tax reforms and protection of co-operative societies.

(4) *The Agrarians' Union*. Founded in 1899, and ably led by Stamboulisky. Secured a major increase in influence during the Balkan Wars. Its programme was heavily in favour of the protection of agriculture and allied industries. In 1919 a breakaway group, led by D. Dragyhev, organized a rival, more moderate faction.

From 1918 to 1945 the major parties were:

COMMUNIST PARTY 1918

Dominant party of the Fatherland Front organization which claimed 800000 members. Founded from a splinter group of the moderate left *Social Democratic Party* (1893). Renamed Bulgarian Socialist Party (1989).

AGRARIANS' UNION 1899

Founded to protect farming and related industries. Main body continued as Stamboulinsky's party when Dragyhev's party broke away in 1919 as a more moderate group, defending parliamentary methods in politics.

DEMOCRATIC PARTY 1895

Founded as a group to reconcile differing parties with a centre policy. In 1906 the *Radical Party* split off, in support of co-operatives, radical tax reforms and a federation of Balkan states.

NATIONAL LIBERAL PARTY 1920

United three small parties to rebuild post-war Bulgaria and gain a revision of the peace treaty. Stambulov's *National Liberal Party* broke away in 1925.

PARTY OF THE DEMOCRATIC ENTENTE 1923

Moderate reform party committed to peace and strengthening of the law and the economy.

After 1945 Bulgaria was effectively a one-party state until 1989. The Fatherland Front, which included the Bulgarian Communist Party and the Bulgarian Agrarian Party, attracted more than 99 per cent of the vote. Anti-government demonstrations in 1989 forced the Fatherland Front to relinquish sole governing power and to allow the formation of other parties. The first free elections in 58 years were held on 10 and 17 Jun 1990.

BULGARIAN AGRARIAN PARTY (BAP)

The BAP was founded in 1899 as a mass peasant party. Some members refused to co-operate with the Communists in the Fatherland Front of 1944 and formed an independent agrarian party, which effectively ceased to exist after the establishment of Communist rule in 1947.

BULGARIAN COMMUNIST PARTY (BCP)

Formed in 1891 as the Bulgarian Social Democratic Party, from which it split in 1919, it formed part of the broad-based Fatherland Front, which took power in 1946 with the backing of the USSR, and subsequently came to dominate the organization. In 1989, it changed its name to Bulgarian Socialist Party (*see* below).

BULGARIAN SOCIALIST PARTY (BSP)

The former Bulgarian Communist Party changed its name following anti-government demonstrations that led to constitutional reforms in 1989. In the Jun 1990 Assembly elections the BSP won 211 of the 400 seats. In 1997, fighting as the Democratic Left, it won 58 seats with 22 per cent of the vote.

UNION OF DEMOCRATIC FORCES (UDF)

The main opposition grouping, an alliance of 16 parties formed in 1989, the UDF included the Ecoglasnost Independent Association, Citizens' Initiative Movement and Bulgarian Workers' Social Democratic Party (United) among its component organizations. The UDF won 144 National Assembly seats in the 1990 elections. In 1997, it won 137 seats with 52.6 per cent of the vote.

Among other parties in what remains a fluid situation are the Agrarian Party (which had been absorbed in the Fatherland Front in 1946) and the Movement for Rights and Freedom (MRF), an ethnic Turkish minority party that took 23 seats in the 1990 elections. Over 80 political parties (some very small) existed at the end of the 1990s.

CROATIA

Since independence, political life has been dominated by the Croatian Democratic Union. In addition to the parties listed below, over 30 smaller groupings exist.

CROATIAN DEMOCRATIC UNION (CDU) (f.1989)

Nationalist party led by Franjo Tudjman. It dominated the presidential election of Aug 1992 and the 1995 general election (with 42 out of 80 seats) but lost its dominance in Jan 2000.

CROATIAN SOCIAL-LIBERAL PARTY (CSLP) (f.1989)

Second strongest party, led by Dražen Budisa. Part of the 1995 opposition electoral alliance.

SERBIAN PEOPLE'S PARTY (SPP)

The party of the ethnic Serbs in Croatia.

SOCIAL DEMOCRATIC PARTY – PARTY OF DEMOCRATIC REFORM OF CROATIA

The former ruling League of Communists; adopted present name in 1991.

CROATIAN PARTY OF RIGHTS

Right-wing, nationalist.

CYPRUS

Since the division of the island, political parties have polarized as follows:

GREEK

These include AKEL (Progressive Party of the Working People, successor to the Communist Party), the Democratic Party (f.1976, supports UN policy on Cyprus), the Democratic Rally (f.1976, opposition party) and the socialist EDEK (f.1969). The Liberal Party (f.1986) advocates solving the Cyprus problem by adhering to United Nations resolutions. ADISOK, formed 1990, also supports a settlement of the Cyprus problem based on UN resolutions. In 1996 the Free Democrats merged to form the United Democrats.

TURKISH

These include the socialist Republican Turkish Party (f.1970), the social democratic Democratic People's Party (f.1979), the Populist Party (f.1976) and the government National Unity Party (f.1976). The Social Democratic Party (f.1982) advocates a two-community Cyprus federation. The Northern Cyprus Socialist Party (f.1985) stands for complete independence for the Turkish area. There is also a right-wing New Dawn Party (f.1984).

The Democratic Struggle Party was an opposition alliance to contest the 1990 general election.

CZECHOSLOVAKIA

Note: From the Communist takeover until 1989 Czechoslovakia was effectively a one-party state. Free elections took place in 1990. On 31 Dec 1992 Czechoslovakia ceased to exist.

COMMUNIST PARTY OF CZECHOSLOVAKIA 1921

Incorporated extreme left elements of the former Czech Social Democratic Labour Party, a working-class and mainly anti-communist socialist party, and the Slovak Labour Party.

CZECH CATHOLIC PEOPLE'S PARTY 1918

Founded from three smaller Catholic parties, with mainly peasant support. The *Slovak Catholic People's Party* seceded from it in 1921.

CZECH NATIONAL DEMOCRATIC PARTY 1917

Developed from the Young Czech Party (liberals), the Radical Party (right-wing), the Moravian Progressive Party and the Realist Party. The bulk of membership of the last two seceded in 1925 to form the National Party of Labour.

The party represented big industrial and banking interests and the anti-Socialist bourgeoisie.

NATIONAL PARTY OF LABOUR 1925

Liberal intellectual support. Programme of moderate social reform, its socialist tendencies evolutionary and not revolutionary.

CZECH PEOPLE'S PARTY 1919

Christian party which supported the National Front government.

SLOVAK RECONSTRUCTION PARTY 1948

Developed from the former Slovak Democratic Party. Supported the National Front government.

CIVIC FORUM 1989

Party advocating a return to parliamentary democracy formed by human rights and opposition groups. In February 1991 the party split into two, with moderate and radical supporters.

PUBLIC AGAINST VIOLENCE 1989

The sister-party to Civic Forum in Slovakia.

CHRISTIAN DEMOCRATIC UNION 1989

Conservative coalition formed by the Czech and Slovak *Christian Democrats* and the *People's Party*.

CZECH REPUBLIC

Among the political parties in the newly-independent Czech Republic are:

CIVIC DEMOCRATIC PARTY (f.1991)

Liberal-Conservative Party, formed following a split in Civic Forum. It won 63 seats in the 1998 elections.

BOHEMIAN-MORAVIAN UNION OF THE CENTRE

Renamed in 1994 following merger of the Liberal Social Union and the Agrarian Party.

CZECH SOCIAL DEMOCRATIC PARTY

Originally founded 1878. Banned in 1948, and re-founded 1989. It won the most seats in 1998.

Other significant parties include the Christian Democratic Union, the extreme right-wing Association for the Republic (f.1989), the Free Democrats, the Liberal National Social Party, the reorganized Communist Party of Bohemia and Moravia (which won 24 seats and 11 per cent of the vote in 1998) and the Freedom Union.

DENMARK

The Liberal Party (*Venstre*) exercised a dominant control of the Folketing prior to the First World War, despite repeated secession to both right and left. Founded in 1870, it was split and reunited on several occasions. A traditional Liberal Party, its aims were free trade and a minimum of state control.

The historic opponents of the Liberals were the Right (*Hojre*). From 1875 to 1894, under the leadership of Estrup the main planks in the Conservative programme were the elevation of the Landsting (upper house) to equal authority with the Folketing and the strengthening of national defences. In 1916 the Right was formally constituted as the Conservative People's Party (*Konservative Folkeparti*). The period prior to 1914 also saw the emergence of the Social Democratic Party (*see below*).

LIBERAL-DEMOCRATIC PARTY 1870

Support mainly from farmers, and its main aim the dominance of the Folketing (second chamber) over Landsting (first chamber). Name changed to *Venstre*, a moderate liberal party with support no longer confined to farmers. Programme of free trade and a minimum of state interference.

SOCIAL DEMOCRATIC PARTY 1871

Non-communist socialist party supported mainly by industrial and farm workers. With a long history of strong support, it was still the largest party in the 1998 elections.

CONSERVATIVE PEOPLE'S PARTY 1916

Originally supported by propertied class and concerned to support the authority of the Landsting over the Folketing. Developed as a party of free initiative, maintaining private property, restricting state action to necessary economic and social intervention.

RADICAL LIBERAL PARTY 1905

The party was founded in 1905 as a result of a split in the Liberal Party. Its chief adherents were the small landed proprietors and certain intellectuals. It held office from 1909 to 1910, and again, with Zahle as Prime Minister, from

1913 to 1920. The main planks of its programme were social reform, reduction of armaments, and the establishment of small-holdings.

Other parties included the Retsforbund (Single Tax Party), founded 1919, the Communist Party (f.1919), the Left Socialists (f.1967), the Christian People's Party (f.1970), the left-wing Socialist People's Party (f.1959), the Progress Party (f.1972), the European Centre-Democrats (f.1974), and the Green Environmentalists' Party (f.1983). The anti-EU June Movement was founded in 1992.

ESTONIA

During the first period of independence (1918–1940) the main parties were:

CHRISTIAN PEOPLE'S PARTY 1918

Formed mainly to introduce religious teaching into the elementary and secondary schools. A centre party, slightly to the right.

REFORMIST LABOUR PARTY 1917

Left of centre, formed from the old Radical Socialist Party.

PEOPLE'S PARTY

Right of centre, developed from the old Democratic and Radical-Democratic parties.

ESTONIAN COMMUNIST PARTY 1920

The party declared its independence from the Communist Party of the Soviet Union in Mar 1990.

Since 1988, the following parties have emerged:

POPULAR FRONT OF ESTONIA 1988

Advocated an independent Estonian Republic and a multi-party parliamentary system.

ESTONIAN COALITION PARTY/RURAL UNION

The alliance which won 41 of the 101 seats in 1995. The Rural Union comprised four agrarian parties.

ESTONIAN NATIONAL INDEPENDENCE PARTY (ESRP) 1988

Supported complete Estonian independence from the USSR. Merged in 1995 as the Fatherland Union.

There are also, among many other parties, the *Estonian Christian Democratic Party* (f.1988), the *Estonian Democratic Labour Party* (f.1989), the *Estonian Green*

Party (f.1989), a royalist party and in 1999 four parties representing the Russian-speaking minority.

FINLAND

In the late nineteenth century, the main political party in Finland was the Finnish Nationalist Party. This later split into the Old Finns and the Young Finns. Other developments were:

1899   Foundation of the Finnish Labour Party.
1903   Finnish Labour Party renamed Social Democratic Party.
1906   Formation of the Swedish People's Party representing the Swedish minority.

Other parties contesting elections prior to 1918 were the Christian Labour Union and the Agrarian Union. The following parties flourished in the modern period:

SOCIAL DEMOCRATIC PARTY 1899

Constitutional socialist.

CENTRE PARTY 1906

Formed as the Agrarian Union, name changed in 1965. Centre with tendencies to the left, aims to support the interests of smallholders and small farmers.

FINNISH PEOPLE'S DEMOCRATIC LEAGUE 1944

Union of Communists and left-wing socialists, including the old Socialist Union Party. Advocated broad left platform. Declined in 1970s. Merged to form Left-Wing Alliance in 1990.

COMMUNIST PARTY 1918

Established in Moscow in 1917 before becoming active in Finland. It did not become legal in Finland until 1944.

NATIONAL COALITION PARTY 1918

Conservative, supporting private enterprise.

SWEDISH PEOPLE'S PARTY 1906

To protect the interests of the Swedish minority; divided politically, but mainly liberal.

FINNISH RURAL PARTY 1959

An anti-socialist party appealing to smaller farmers and owners of small businesses.

Among many other parties are the Finnish Pensioner's Party (formed in 1986); the Green League (formed in 1988); the Communist Workers' Party (formed in 1989); and the Constitutional Party of the Right (formed in 1973). The Left Alliance was formed in 1990 from, among others, the Finnish People's Democratic League (f.1944) and the Communist Party of Finland.

FRANCE

Despite the many upheavals in French politics, the development of clear-cut political parties in France was a slow process. Inside the parliament, deputies often belonged to more than one group whilst constituency organization at local level was hardly developed. By 1900, in addition to the Conservative Right and a variety of socialists, other parties contesting elections included *Action Française* (see below). Key events between 1900 and 1914 were the foundation of the Radical Socialist Party (1901), the foundation of the Socialist Party in 1905 (*see* p. 336) and the involvement of the Republican Union in the 1910 elections.

ACTION FRANÇAISE 1898

Right-wing, nationalist, monarchist, anti-democratic and originally anti-Semitic. Supported considerable autonomy for the provinces and a government of ministers responsible only to a king.

ACTION NATIONALE 1918

A combination of the former Action Liberale Populaire (Catholic), the Federation of Democratic Republicans and the Republican Federation. A centre party supporting indirect taxation, the free play of economic laws, decentralized administration and free enterprise.

DEMOCRATIC AND SOCIAL REPUBLICAN PARTY 1901

Founded as Republican Democratic Alliance. Favoured direct taxation, diplomatic relations with the Vatican, but a careful balance between clerical and anti-clerical influences and the separation of church and state.

GAUCHE RADICALE

Moderate socialist party, most active following 1918. Conciliatory in foreign policy.

FEDERATION OF RADICALS AND RADICAL SOCIALISTS POST-1918

Socialist reform party supporting state monopolies, the League of Nations and the full implementation of the Treaty of Versailles.

SOCIALIST PARTY 1905

Amalgamation of the Socialist Party of France (revolutionary) and the French Socialist Party (moderate evolutionary). The union split in 1920 and the resulting party was anti-communist, collectivist in theory but moderate in practice. Moved towards the eventual abolition of private property.

UNION OF DEMOCRATS FOR THE REPUBLIC

Development through several former parties with successive titles:
    Democratic Labour Union,
    Union for the New Republic,
    Democratic Union for the Fifth Republic,
    Union for the Defence of the Republic, and
the Gaullist Party, which actively supported continuation of Gaullist policy and a more independent role for France in the Western Alliance.

NATIONAL FEDERATION OF INDEPENDENT REPUBLICANS 1962

Liberal policy.

REPUBLICAN RADICAL AND RADICAL-SOCIALIST PARTY

Traditional centre party of the Third Republic. Extreme left-wing dissidents broke away in 1956, the remaining body continued with a liberal economic policy, support for NATO and European unity.

UNITED SOCIALIST PARTY 1960

Developed from the Independent Socialist Party, the Union of the Left Socialist Party and the Tribune of Communism dissident section.

DEMOCRATIC CENTRE

Formed from former sections of the Independent and Republican Movement parties. Centre-left policy, supported a united Europe and NATO.

Among the very many parties active in the post-de Gaulle years, there have been:

SOCIALIST PARTY (PS) 1971

Proposed planned economy, nationalization of key industries.
Subscribed to the United Left programme with the Communists until 1977.
Won major victory in 1997 elections.

COMMUNIST PARTY (PCF) 1920

Advocates democratic path to socialism.
Subscribed to United Left programme with Socialists until 1977.

RASSEMBLEMENT POUR LA REPUBLIQUE (RPR) 1976

A successor of the Gaullist UDR (Union of Democrats for the Republic) following the resignation of Jacques Chirac. Campaigned with UDF in 1988. A breakaway group late in 1999 emerged forming the Rassemblement Pour La France in Jan 2000.

UNION POUR LA DEMOCRATIE FRANÇAISE (UDF) 1978

Formed by Giscard d'Estaing to unite the non-Gaullist 'majority' candidates. It split after the 1998 regional elections, one splinter forming *La Droite*.

REPUBLICAN PARTY 1977

Name changed in 1997 to Démocratie Libérale.

RADICAL PARTY 1901

Forms part of the UDF (*see above*).

NATIONAL FRONT (FN) 1972

An extreme right-wing party led by Jean-Marie Le Pen. Virulently anti-immigrant. It split in the late 1990s.

THE GREENS 1972

Formerly the Ecologists, this environmental party was renamed in 1984.

MOUVEMENT GAULLISTE POPULAIRE 1982

AREV 1993
AREV (Alternative Rouge et Verte) was founded to replace the Parti Socialiste Unifié.

GERMANY

In the German Empire, the electoral stage was dominated up to 1900 by three main groups: the Centre Party (*Deutsche Zentrums-partei*), the National Liberals (the *Nationalliberale*) and a small but rapidly growing Social Democratic Party, formed in 1871. In 1877, the National Liberals split, with the Liberal Union (*Liberale Vereinigung*) breaking away over the tariff question. In addition there were some right-wing German national parties (*e.g.* the *Deutsche Reichs partei* and the *Deutsche-Konservative*) and the national minority parties of Poles, Danes and Alsatians, these latter first fighting elections after 1874. Prior to 1914 other developments included:

1884   Elections contested by the Free Thinking Party (*Freisinnige Partei*), a merger of the Progressive Party and the Liberal Union.

1892   The Free Thinking Party split in this year to form the Free Thinking People's Party (*Freisinnige Volks Partei*) and the Free Thinking Union (*Freisinnige Vereinigung*).

1898   Two farmers' parties, the Bavarian Farmers' League (*Bayerische Bauernbund*) and the Farmers' League (*Bund der Landwirte*) contested the elections.

1907   The Economic Union (*Wirtschafts Vereinigung*) formed.

1912   Progressive People's Party formed from a merger of the Free Thinking Union, the Free Thinking People's Party and the German People's Party.

During the period 1918 to 1945 the following parties were active:

GERMAN NATIONAL PEOPLE'S PARTY (DNVP) 1918

Conservative, formed from a union of the Free Conservative Party, the Economic Union, the Conservative Party and the Christian Socialists. Aimed at a restoration of German sovereignty and a revision of the Treaty of Versailles. Protection for home industries, anti-Communist, pro-Christian.

NATIONAL PARTY OF GERMAN MODERATES (RDM) 1920

Supported by and concerned for the industrial and commercial middle classes. Anti-Socialist and against state controls.

SOCIAL DEMOCRATIC PARTY OF GERMANY 1871

Republican, democratic. Unqualified support for peace and reconciliation after 1918. Repudiated nationalism, aimed at socialization of large-scale production.

GERMAN DEMOCRATIC PARTY 1918

Formed from the former Progressive People's Party of 1910 and the left wing of the National Liberal Party. Republican and moderate reformist.

GERMAN COMMUNIST PARTY 1919

Revolutionary Communist.

GERMAN CENTRE PARTY 1870

Catholic centre party committed to fulfilling Versailles treaty obligations with a view to reconciliation. Supported the Weimar constitution.

GERMAN PEOPLE'S PARTY 1918

Formed from the right wing of the former National Liberal Party, Protectionist in trade, nationalist and monarchist in politics.

NATIONAL SOCIALIST GERMAN WORKERS' PARTY 1925

Seceded from the German People's Party. Nationalist, supporting rearmament. Anti-Semitic. Protectionist in trade policy. Committed to expansion of German sovereignty in Europe. The party led by Adolf Hitler.

FEDERAL REPUBLIC OF GERMANY

{ CHRISTIAN-DEMOCRATIC UNION (CDU) 1945
{ CHRISTIAN SOCIAL UNION (CSU) – EQUIVALENT BAVARIAN PARTY 1945

United Catholic–Protestant action on Christian principles, supporting maintenance of private property and individual freedom. Moderate conservative. The dominant party in recent years under Helmut Kohl.

SOCIAL DEMOCRATIC PARTY OF GERMANY (SPD) 1945

Orthodox social-democrat policies, supporting a competitive economy, moderate social policy.

FREE DEMOCRATIC PARTY (FDP)

Liberal social policies. Long-time junior partner of the Christian Democrats.

NATIONAL DEMOCRATIC PARTY OF GERMANY (NPD) 1964

Right wing, nationalist.

DIE GRÜNEN (THE GREENS)

Founded 1980. A left-wing party concentrating on ecological issues, it was anti-NATO, anti-Warsaw Pact and favoured smaller economic units. Merged in 1993 with Bundnis 90 (f.1990) to form new Green Alliance (Alliance 90/The Greens). The party had the support of around 6 per cent of voters in the 1998 election.

REPUBLICAN PARTY 1983

Right-wing nationalist party.

PARTY OF DEMOCRATIC SOCIALISM (PDS) 1989

The successor party to the collapsed Communist Party. It gained increasing support in the east in the 1990s.

GERMAN DEMOCRATIC REPUBLIC

SOCIALIST UNITY PARTY OF GERMANY 1946

Founded as a union of the Social Democratic Party and the Communist Party. Communist policy. The party collapsed in 1989, becoming the Party of Democratic Socialism (*see* p. 339).

CHRISTIAN DEMOCRAT UNION OF GERMANY 1945

These and six others belonged to a National Front and issued a joint manifesto before elections.

CHRISTIAN DEMOCRATIC UNION (CDU) 1989

Sister-party of the West German conservative CDU.

GERMAN SOCIAL UNION (DSU) 1989

Formed by 12 centre-right and opposition groups as the sister-party of the Bavarian Christian Social Union.

DEMOCRATIC AWAKENING (DA) 1989

A Christian party.

SOCIAL DEMOCRATIC PARTY (SPD) (1989)

Sister-party of the West German SPD, reconstituted in 1989 following the collapse of the Socialist Unity Party in which it had been forcibly united with the Communists.

GREECE

Pre-1967 political parties included:

POPULAR PARTY 1920

Parliamentary methods, moderate socialist policies.

LIBERAL-CONSERVATIVE PARTY 1920s

Republican. Aimed at government through a state council.

REPUBLICAN UNION 1920s

Formerly the extreme left of the Liberal Party. Committed to increased industrial production and the welfare of industrial workers. Supported proportional representation.

COMMUNIST PARTY

Supported proportional representation, women's suffrage, confiscation of large properties. Anti-armament.

NATIONAL RADICAL UNION 1956

Concerned with stimulating production and economic stability. Moderate.

These and other parties were suspended in 1967 when all political parties ceased to function. Other parties recently formed and then suspended:

Union of Democratic Left – extreme left wing.
Progressive Agrarian Democratic Union – moderate.
Union of Populist Parties – right wing, monarchist.
Centre Union – liberal and progressive coalition.
Liberal Democratic Centre Party – breakaway group from the CU.

Since the restoration of democracy in Greece, the following major parties have emerged:

PANHELLENIC SOCIALIST MOVEMENT (PASOK) 1974

Left-wing, incorporating Democratic Defence and Panhellenic Liberation Movement resistance organizations. Led until his death by Andreas Papandreou, it favoured socialization of the means of production.

DEMOCRATIC CENTRE UNION (EDIK) 1974

A democratic socialist party which combined the Centre Union (f.1961) and the New Political Forces (f.1974).

COMMUNIST PARTY OF GREECE (KKE) 1918

The orthodox Moscow-dominated party. It was banned in 1947 and reappeared in 1974. It became part of the Left Coalition in 1989.

GREEK COMMUNIST PARTY (KKE-INTERIOR) 1968

A Marxist movement, independent of the 'Moscow-line'. It separated from the pro-Moscow Communist Party of Greece in 1968, and joined the Greek Left Party in 1987.

NEW DEMOCRACY 1974

A moderate pragmatic reform party founded by Karamanlis which took Greece into the EU.

DEMOCRATIC INITIATIVE PARTY 1987

A democratic socialist party supporting a mixed economy and the removal of foreign bases from Greece.

DEMOCRATIC REVIVAL 1985

A populist moderate centre-right party.

POLITICAL SPRING 1993

Formed by former foreign minister Antonis Samatas to 'break the mould' of Greek politics. It won ten seats in the 1993 election but none in 1996.

LEFT COALITION 1989

Alliance of Greek Left Party (f.1987) and Communist Party of Greece (Exterior).

Other parties include the Democratic Socialist Party (f.Mar 1979 by former EDIK activists), the right-wing Progressive Party (f.1979), the far-right Golden Dawn, and the Liberal Party (f.1981). These is also an Ecologist Alternative Party.

HUNGARY

Parties prior to and during the Communist era included:

PARTY OF NATIONAL UNITY 1921

Developed from the Party of Christian Small Landowners and Citizens. Conservative.

CHRISTIAN ECONOMY PARTY 1923

Formed from the former People's Party, Unionist Party, and Christian Socialists. Conservative and legitimist.

HUNGARIAN SOCIALIST WORKERS' PARTY 1956

The Communist Party and the Social Democratic Party merged to create the Working People's Party. The name was later changed. Moscow-oriented Communist. It became the Hungarian Socialist Party in 1989.

PATRIOTIC PEOPLE'S FRONT 1954

Replaced the former Hungarian Independent People's Front. Represented the mass organizations such as Trade Unions. Independent Communist.

Note: From the Communist takeover after World War II until 1989, Hungary was effectively a one-party state. The Hungarian Socialist Workers' Party dominated the Patriotic People's Front, of which all candidates had to be supporters. Hungary underwent fundamental political and constitutional changes in 1989. Political parties were legalized in Oct 1989. Free elections for the National Assembly were held on 25 Mar 1990, with a second round on 8 Apr 1990.

HUNGARIAN SOCIALIST PARTY 1989

Successor party to the Hungarian Socialist Workers' Party, advocating a mixed economy on Scandinavian lines. The second largest party in the 1998 elections.

HUNGARIAN DEMOCRATIC FORUM (HDF) 1988

Centre-right party legalized in 1989. It supported economic privatization and a negotiated withdrawal from the Warsaw Pact. Lost support after 1991 over slow pace of reform and disenchantment with the economy.

ALLIANCE OF FREE DEMOCRATS (SzDSz) 1989

Advocates rapid moves towards a market economy and privatization.

INDEPENDENT SMALLHOLDERS' PARTY (FKgP) 1988

Legalized in 1989, the party advocates privatization and the return of land confiscated in 1947 to its former owners.

CHRISTIAN DEMOCRATIC PEOPLE'S PARTY 1989

A centre party which split in 1997.

FEDERATION OF YOUNG DEMOCRATS 1988

Renamed in 1995 as the Federation of Young Democrats–Hungarian Civic Party.

SOCIAL DEMOCRATIC PARTY 1890, REVIVED 1989

Absorbed by the Communist Party in 1948 to form the Working People's Party, the Social Democrats became a legally organized separate party in 1989.

Other parties include the Agrarian Association and the Green Party (f.1989). Nationalist parties include the Movement for Hungarian Unity (f.1995) and the National Alliance for Hungary (f.1995). Representatives of national minorities are guaranteed one seat each in the National Assembly.

ICELAND

INDEPENDENCE PARTY (1929)

Amalgamation of Conservative (1924) and Liberal (1925) parties. Aimed at social reform within a capitalist framework and furtherance of national independence, through renunciation of the Act of Union with Denmark.

PROGRESSIVE PARTY 1916

Supports co-operatives, aims at educational and social reform.

SOCIAL DEMOCRATIC PARTY 1916

Moderate evolutionary socialist.

PEOPLE'S ALLIANCE 1956

Formed from sections of the Social Democrats and the Socialist Unity Party, and reorganized in 1968 as a socialist party.

CITIZENS' PARTY 1987

Shares the Independence Party's ideological position but puts stress on individual rights.

WOMEN'S ALLIANCE 1983

A feminist party emphasizing the rights of women and children, with a rotating parliamentary leadership.

AWAKENING OF THE NATION 1994

A breakaway by dissident members of the SDP.

IRELAND

CUMAN-NA-GAEDHEAL

Moderate party accepting partition and the Act of Settlement in 1921. Aimed for economic and social stability within the Empire. Became part of Fine Gael.

FIANNA FAIL 1926

Republican. Successor to those bodies not accepting the Act of Settlement. Neutralist.

FINE GAEL 1933

Formed by amalgamating Cuman-na-Gaedheal, the Centre Party and the National Guard Party. Centre.

LABOUR PARTY 1912

Formed as an organ of the Trades Unions, separated from them in 1930. Socialist.

SINN FEIN 1905

Formed to end British occupation, and then to end partition and achieve a Democratic Socialist Republic of all Ireland.

PROGRESSIVE DEMOCRATS 1985

The party – set up by former Fianna Fail members – advocates constitutional reform, a lessening of church influence in the state, and private enterprise.

GREEN PARTY

Formerly the Ecology Party.

WORKERS' PARTY 1905

Formerly Sinn Fein The Workers' Party. Seeks an All-Ireland Socialist State.

Among smaller parties are the Irish Republican Socialist Party (f.1974), the Communist Party of Ireland (f.1933), the Democratic Socialist Party (f.1982 out of the earlier Socialist Party), Republican Sinn Fein (f.1986) and Democratic Left (f.1992).

ITALY

In Italy, even by 1900, political parties had been extremely slow to develop. Politics centred around the groups attached to a particular individual. Although after 1870, deputies could usually be identified with the right (*Destra*) or left (*Sinistra*), such labels often meant little, whilst the deputies from the south could usually be 'bought' by the government. One of the historic parties was the Liberal Party, founded by Cavour in 1848 and an influential democratic force in the reunification of Italy. The impetus to the development of political parties came in 1892, with the formation of the Socialist Party (*Partito Socialista Italiano*, PSI). Other developments by 1914 were:

1898   Dissolution of the Italian Republican Party (originally founded in 1880 and reorganized in 1892) by order of Pelloux. It was subsequently reformed.

1904   The Vatican began to allow Catholics to vote for moderate candidates – but no national Catholic party formed until 1919, when the Popular Party (*Partito Popolare Italiano*) came into being.

1913   Splits in the Socialist ranks led to the elections being contested by Independent Socialists and by the Reformist Socialist Party.

Since 1914, among a myriad of political parties are the following:

CHRISTIAN DEMOCRAT PARTY 1943

Successor to the pre-Fascist Popular Party, Anti-Communist, moderate social policy. It is now the Popular Party (see p. 347).

ITALIAN COMMUNIST PARTY 1921

The largest in Western Europe. Advocated nationalization and land redistribution. Became the Democratic Party of the Left in February 1991.

ITALIAN SOCIALIST PARTY (PSI) 1966

Founded by a merger of the Italian Socialist Party and the Italian Democratic Socialist Party. The latter broke away in 1969. Centre left, adhering to the Second International.

UNITED SOCIALIST PARTY (PSU) 1969

Splinter from the Democratic Socialists.

ITALIAN SOCIAL MOVEMENT – NATIONAL RIGHT (MSI–DN) 1946

Extreme right, neo-fascist. Now absorbed by Alleanza Nazionale (*q.v.*) A splinter group, National Democracy, broke away in 1977.

UNITED PROLETARIAN ITALIAN SOCIALIST PARTY 1964

Further left than the Italian Socialist Party, from whom it broke away.

NATIONAL FASCIST PARTY 1919

Formed to resist Bolshevism by force. Policies developed as conservative, nationalist, militarist and imperialist. ('Fascismo' = absolute and dictatorial government.) The party of Benito Mussolini.

ITALIAN POPULAR PARTY 1919

Catholic independent party with social-democrat policies.
  (*All non-fascist parties were dissolved in 1926*)

UNITED PARTY 1922

Formed from a section of the old Socialist Party. Revolutionary socialist and reformist.

MASSIMALIST PARTY 1922

Hard-core theoretical socialists remaining after the United Party breakaway.

RADICAL PARTY (PR)

A party which concentrated on civil rights issues.

SOCIAL DEMOCRAT PARTY (PSDI) 1969

A breakaway from the former United Socialist Party, the PSDI stands to the right of the PSI.

GREEN PARTY 1987

Environmental and anti-nuclear party.

During the 1990s political parties in Italy were transformed as old parties (such as the Christian Democrats) became discredited and new alliances were forged. Among the new parties are:

FORZE ITALIA 1994

The right-wing party formed by Berlusconi to fight the 1994 elections. Anti-immigrant, pro-market forces and populist, it gathered much of the old Christian Democrat vote.

NORTHERN LEAGUE

This party represents the populist rising force of northern Italy. The party is anti-Rome, anti-Mafia, anti-immigrant and anti-tax. It is led by Umberto Bossi. Part of the short-lived 1994 Berlusconi alliance.

POPULAR PARTY

The successor to the discredited Christian Democrats. Right wing, conservative.

DEMOCRATIC PARTY OF THE LEFT

Formed in Feb 1991, this party was the successor to the former Italian Communist Party. Led by Achillo Occhetto, it sought to find a new identity after the collapse of communism in the Eastern bloc.

COMMUNIST REFOUNDATION

The hard-line core of the old Communist Party that refused to join the PDS when it abandoned Marxism in 1991. This party split in 1998 with the formation of the new Party of Italian Communists led by Armando Cossutta.

LA RETE

The Anti-Mafia Party founded originally in 1991 to contest regional elections in Sicily.

OLIVE TREE ALLIANCE

The Centre–Left Alliance which won power in the 1996 elections. Led by Romano Prodi.

ALLEANZA NAZIONALE (NATIONAL ALLIANCE)

The extreme right party formed in 1994 which absorbed the old neo-fascist Italian Social Movement in 1995. Led by Gianfranco Fini.

LATVIA

During the inter-war period, parties included:

SOCIAL DEMOCRATIC PARTY
Allied with the Jewish Bund. Moderate.

DEMOCRATIC CENTRE PARTY
Middle-class support, policy left of centre.

FARMERS' UNION
Left-of-centre party to support rural interests.

INDEPENDENT NATIONALISTS
Right-wing, support from the commercial and industrial class.

Following the ending of the Communist Party's monopoly of power in 1990 (and the subsequent ban on the Communist Party in Aug 1991) political parties have proliferated. The first elections (*see* p. 255) were dominated by Latvian Way. Latvian Way (f.1993) advocates a democratic state with a free market economy, private ownership of land, and closer links with the other Baltic states.

Other parties include the Latvian National Independence Movement (f.1988), the National Harmony Party (f.1993) and the rural centrist Latvian Farmers' Union. Following a split in the Communist Party of Latvia, the Democratic Labour Party of Latvia was formed in 1990. The Latvian Social Democratic Workers' Party, originally founded in 1904, was re-established in 1989. More recent parties include the Freedom Party (f.1997) and the New Party (f.1998) which advocates privatization.

LIECHTENSTEIN

PROGRESSIVE CITIZENS' PARTY

PATRIOTIC UNION 1936
Evolved from the People's Party.

CHRISTIAN-SOCIALIST PARTY 1962

FREE LIST (FL) 1985
An environmental party supporting social progress.

LITHUANIA

The groupings of political parties in inter-war Lithuania were as follows:

Christian Democrats	
Farmers' Union	} Extreme right.
Labour Federation	
Populist Party	
Nationalist Party	} Liberal.
Social Democrats	Left of centre.
Communist Party	Communist.
of Lithuania (f.1919)	

The period immediately prior to independence was dominated by Sajudis, the main nationalist movement (founded in 1988 as the Lithuanian Movement for Reconstruction). The period saw the refounding of many old parties (the Christian Democratic Party, originally founded in 1905, the Lithuanian Democratic Party, founded 1902, and the Lithuanian Social Democratic Party, founded 1896). The 1993 elections, however, were dominated by the former Communists (now the Lithuanian Democratic Labour Party). The Conservative Party was founded in 1993 from elements of Sajudis. Over 30 political parties were active in the late 1990s.

LUXEMBOURG

From 1868, when the first directly-elected parliament was introduced, the Liberals were the dominant party. They formed every administration until 1915. Major dates in the evolution of national party organizations were:

1896   Formation of the Socialist Party (*Parti Sociale Démocrate*).

1902   Formation of the orthodox left-wing Socialist Workers' Party.

1904   The *Ligue Liberale* formed, first national organization of the Liberals.

1914   Right wing (*Parti de la Droite*) established rival national organization.

CHRISTIAN SOCIALIST PARTY 1914

Dominant party in government since its foundation.

COMMUNIST PARTY 1921

THE GREENS

An environmental party supporting decentralization of power and increased aid to developing states. Originally formed in 1983 as the Green Alternative Party.

THE LEFT 1999

Déi Lénk (The Left) is a very recent creation with no formal leadership.

MACEDONIA

Among the parties to have emerged since independence are:

INTERNAL MACEDONIAN REVOLUTIONARY ORGANIZATION – DEMOCRATIC PARTY FOR MACEDONIAN NATIONAL UNITY (IMRO–DPMNU)

The main nationalist party, led by Ljučo Georgievski.

PARTY OF DEMOCRATIC PROSPERITY 1990

The predominantly ethnic Albanian and Muslim party. It split in 1994.

NATIONAL DEMOCRATIC PARTY 1990

Largely Albanian and Muslim. Now merged in Democratic Party of Albanians since July 1997.

SOCIAL DEMOCRATIC ALLIANCE OF MACEDONIA

Founded in 1943 as the League of Communists of Macedonia. Part of the 'Alliance for Macedonia' in the 1994 elections.

Many smaller parties have emerged, mainly on ethnic lines, including those representing Turks, Romanies, Croats etc. There are also growing nationalist parties.

MALTA

NATIONALIST PARTY 1880

Supports the European and Catholic tradition in Malta. Democratic conservative. Pro-Western and pro-EU. The party formerly led by Borg Olivier.

MALTA LABOUR PARTY 1920

Socialist. Foreign policy of non-alignment and security through the United Nations. Opposed to membership of EU. The party formerly led by Dom Mintoff.

PROGRESSIVE CONSTITUTIONAL PARTY 1953

Supported association with EU, close relations with Britain and NATO. The party once led by Mabel Strickland.

MALTA DEMOCRATIC PARTY (PDM) 1985

Supports human rights, environmental protection and decentralization of power.

COMMUNIST PARTY (1969)

Neutralist, Marxist Leninist.

DEMOCRATIC ALTERNATIVE (1989)

Founded as an environmentalist and human rights party.

MOLDOVA

The once dominant Communist Party of Moldova was banned in Aug 1991. In 1991 the National Alliance for Independence was formed, a coalition of 12 pro-independence parties. These included the Moldovan Democratic Movement, the National Christian Party, the Popular Front of Moldova and the Social Democratic Party. Other current parties include the Yedinstvo Movement (founded 1989, representing ethnic minorities in Moldova), the centrist Social Democratic Party of Moldova (f.1990) and the centre-right middle-class Reform Party (f.1993). The Christian Democratic Popular Front and also the Congress of Intelligentsia favour union with Romania. The Agrarian Democratic Party is a moderate party favouring economic and agricultural reform. The successor to the Communist Party of Moldova is the Socialist Party. Party alliances are constantly changing. The Democratic Convention of Moldova, a right-wing alliance, was formed in 1997. On the left, Popular Patriotic Forces was formed in 1997 from the Moldovan Party of Communists, the Socialist Party and the Yedinstvo (Unity) Movement.

THE NETHERLANDS

The main political parties began to develop party organization after the establishment of the Anti-Revolutionary Party in 1879. The main groupings were:

(1) *The Catholic State Party* (after 1897, the Catholic Electoral League). The Catholic State Party subscribed to the ruling and tenets of the Roman Catholic Church as expressed, in religious affairs, in the *Quanta Cura* Encyclical and, in social affairs, in the *Rerum Novarum* Encyclical. Including, as it did, Conservatives and Democrats, anti-militarists and Labour leaders, it was anything but homogeneous, and was repeatedly threatened with schism.

(2) *The Anti-Revolutionary Party* (ARP). Established in 1879 as a political organization of orthodox neo-Calvinistic Protestants. Strongly opposed to Liberalism and Socialism, it aims at founding a polity 'based on that traditional national character which the Reformation created and which William the Silent moulded'.

(3) *Christian Historical Union* (*Christelijk-Historische Unie*, CHU). Formed in 1908, from a variety of earlier local groupings; these included the Free

Anti-Revolutionaries (founded in 1894), the Christian Historical Electoral Union (founded 1896 and became Christian Historical Party in 1903) and the Friesian Christian Historical Party (originally established in 1898) as a result of the secession from the Anti-Revolutionary Party of its anti-democratic elements. The Christian Historicals constituted the more conservative Protestants, approximating on politico-religious questions to the Anti-Revolutionaries and on economic questions to the Liberals. The Union leaned towards Nationalism and Orangism, advocated a strong army and navy, and upheld the rights of the Dutch Reformed Church as the national church.

(4) *The Liberal Union* (Liberale Unie).

(5) *The Radicals.* Merged in 1901 as the Liberal Democratic League (*Urijzinnig-Democratische Bond*).

(6) *The Social Democratic Workers' Party.*

(7) *The Free Liberal League* (formed 1891), composed of Conservative dissenters from the Liberal Union.

(8) *The Social Democratic League.*

Developments after 1900 have included:

CATHOLIC PEOPLE'S PARTY (KVP) 1945

Democratic section seceding from the State Party. Present-day membership open to Protestants.

CHRISTIAN HISTORICAL UNION (CHU) 1908 (*see* p. 351)

RADICAL POLITICAL PARTY (PPR) 1968

Progressive, pro-environmental, anti-nuclear party. Co-operates with socialist groups.

PEOPLE'S PARTY FOR FREEDOM AND DEMOCRACY (VVD) 1948

Non-denominational. Liberal. Free enterprise and social security within one system.

SOCIAL DEMOCRATIC WORKERS' PARTY

Developed from the previous Socialist Party which it saw as anarchical and non-parliamentary. Moderate left. In 1946 the most active section broke away and formed the Labour Party (*q.v.*).

LABOUR PARTY (PvDA) 1946

A democratic socialist party, it took many members from the Social Democratic Workers' Party.

CHRISTIAN DEMOCRATIC APPEAL (CDA) 1980

Formed by the merger of the Anti-Revolutionary Party, the Christian Historical Union, and the Catholic People's Party.

EVANGELICAL POLITICAL FEDERATION (RPF) 1975

A Calvinist party with support from other Christians.

Among recent smaller parties are the Socialist Workers' Party (Trotskyist,
f.1974), the General Union of the Elderly (AOV), Union 55+ (also for the elderly),
the Liberal Democratic Party (founded 1994 out of Democrats '66), the extreme
right-wing Nederlands Blok, f.1992), the Green Party (f.1983) and the Green Left
(f.1991, arising from a merger of the old Communist Party, the Radical Party etc).

NORWAY

In the second half of the nineteenth century, the main party division lay
between the left (the *Venstre*, or Liberals) and the conservative right (the *Höyre*).
Generally, the left had the support of the radicals and the peasantry. From 1903
to 1913, the Conservatives fought under the title of *Samlingspartei* (Unionist
Party). From 1894, the Norwegian Labour Party (*Norske Arbeiderpartei*) began to
capture the working-class vote. By 1912, it was polling over 26 per cent of all
votes cast.

Other parties to contest elections were the Free-Thinking Left (*Frisinnide
Venstre*) after 1909, the Worker Democrats (after 1906) and the Agrarian League
(formed in 1915).

Parties since 1918 have included:

HØYRE 1884 (*see above*)

Conservative. Aimed at a property-owning democracy, private enterprise.

CENTRE PARTY 1920

Moderate democratic party. Formed as Farmers' Party, name changed in
1959.

CHRISTIAN DEMOCRATIC PARTY 1933

Traditional Christian Democrat Party.

LIBERAL PARTY (VENSTRE) 1884 (*see above*)

Moderate reform party.

WORKERS' PARTY (ARBEIDERPARTEI) 1887 (*see above*)

Orthodox evolutionary socialist.

SOCIALIST PEOPLE'S PARTY 1961

Broke away from Workers' Party, being farther to the left. Opposed nuclear weapons and the Atlantic alliance. Neutralist. Merged into the Socialist Left Party in 1975.

SOCIALIST LEFT PARTY 1975

A union of the group which had formed the Socialist Electoral League in 1973 *e.g.* the Socialist People's Party, the Democratic Socialists etc.

PROGRESS PARTY (FP) 1978

A right-wing party advocating reducing the welfare state, tax and immigration and increasing privatization. Led by Carl Hagen it attracted 15 per cent of the vote in the 1990s.

GREEN ENVIRONMENTAL PARTY 1988

An ecological grouping.

Other recent developments include the transformation of the Communist Party which merged with the Red Electoral Alliance in 1989 to become Local Candidates for the Environment and Solidarity. The Coastal Party secured its first representation in parliament in 1997. There is also a Pensioners' Party.

POLAND

Prior to the Communist takeover, the main parties included:

Polish People's Party	The right-wing, Catholic, alliance of Church and
National Christian Club	State, nationalist, anti-Communist and anti-
Christian Democrats	Socialist.

PEASANTS' UNION 1924

Aimed for the abolition of the senate and universal franchise for all.

UNION OF POLISH PEASANT PARTIES 1923

Radical, concerned for small farmers and labourers. Aimed for peasant proprietorship.

RADICAL PEASANTS' PARTY 1918

Bolshevik.

NATIONAL LABOUR PARTY 1905

Workers' reform party, nationalist.

POLISH SOCIALIST PARTY 1892

Orthodox socialist, evolutionary reform party.

The main parties under communism were:

POLISH UNITED WORKERS' PARTY 1948

Formed by merging the former Socialist Party and Workers' Party. Communist.

UNITED PEASANTS' PARTY 1949

Formed from merging the Peasant Party and the Polish Peasant Party. Communist, concerned for small farmers and rural workers.

The parties that helped produce the fall of communism were:

SOLIDARITY CITIZENS' COMMITTEE 1989

The political wing of the Solidarity trade union movement formed to contest elections.

POLISH PEASANT PARTY – SOLIDARITY 1989

The political wing of Solidarity in rural areas, formed to contest elections.

With the collapse of communism, a bewildering number of political parties have emerged (over 250 had registered by 1995). Lech Walesa's supporters were gathered round the Centre Alliance, a christian democratic party. The Polish Peasant Party replaced the United Peasants' Party, whilst Social Democracy of the Republic of Poland replaced the Polish United Workers' Party and was itself part of the Democratic Left Alliance. The power of the former Communists was reflected in the success of Aleksander Kwaśniewski in the 1995 presidential elections. Freedom Union was founded in 1994. Various right-wing parties formed the Patriotic Camp in 1995.

PORTUGAL

MONARCHIST PARTY

Formed to support the claims of former King Manuel or Prince Duarte Nuno.

CATHOLIC PARTY

Conservative.

NATIONALIST PARTY   pre-Salazar

Conservative policy, republican.

REPUBLICAN PARTY

Democratic policy, republican.

POPULAR NATIONAL ACTION

Formerly National Union, the ruling conservative party under the Salazar régime until the revolution.

After the military *coup* of 25 Apr 1974, the following main parties emerged in Portugal:

SOCIAL DEMOCRATIC PARTY (PSD) 1974

Policies similar to major European Social Democratic parties. A partner in the Democratic Alliance.

PORTUGUESE COMMUNIST PARTY (PCP) LEGALIZED 1974

Marxist-Leninist. Ultimate goal of a Socialist Portugal. Led for many years by Secretary-General Alvaro Cunhal. A partner in the United People's Alliance (*q.v.*). Now part of the CDU coalition.

DEMOCRATIC ALLIANCE (AD) 1979

An alliance of the Social Democratic Party (*q.v.*) and the Centre Democratic Party (*q.v.*) to fight the 1979 elections.

CENTRE DEMOCRATIC PARTY (CDP) 1974

Centrist Party, in Christian Democrat tradition. The party of Professor Freitas Do Amaral. Partner in the Democratic Alliance.

UNITED PEOPLE'S ALLIANCE (APU) 1979

An electoral alliance of two main groupings: the People's Democratic Movement (*q.v.*) and the Portuguese Communist Party (*q.v.*).

PEOPLE'S DEMOCRATIC MOVEMENT

A partner in the United People's Alliance led by Jose Tengarrinha.

SOCIALIST PARTY (PS) 1973

Democratic socialist. Affiliated to Socialist International. A successor to the earlier Portuguese Socialist Action. Led for many years by Dr Mario Soares.

PEOPLE'S MONARCHIST PARTY (PPM) 1974

An anti-nuclear environmentalist party which supports restoration of the monarchy.

DEMOCRATIC RENEWAL PARTY (PRD) 1985

A centre-left party.

An ecological party (*Partido Ecologista Os Verdes – PEV*) is part of the CDU coalition. The elderly are represented by the National Solidarity Party (f.1991). The Revolutionary Socialist Party (PSR) was formed in 1978 through a merger of two Trotskyist groups. The CDU is an electoral alliance which includes the Communists and Greens.

ROMANIA

For political parties and groupings contesting elections prior to 1939, *see* p. 277. The Romanian Nazis, the Iron Guard, polled well after 1935. After the Second World War, until the revolution of 1989, Romania was effectively a one-party state dominated by the Romanian Communist Party, technically part of the Socialist Unity Front. Founded in 1921, the party campaigned with others in a People's Democratic Front (PDF) after 1944. Following its union with the Social Democratic Party in 1947, it changed its name to the Romanian Workers' Party. Unsympathetic social democrats and other non-Communists were subsequently excluded from the PDF. The party was led by Nicolae Ceauçescu from 1965 to 1989. The Socialist Labour Party now claims the mantle of the former Communists.

Following the 1989 revolution, provisional power was taken by a 145-strong National Salvation Front which ruled by decree. Political parties were legalized, and in Feb 1990 the NSF offered to share power with other parties. Presidential and legislative elections were held in May 1990.

Parties since 1989 include:

NATIONAL SALVATION FRONT (NSF) (1989)

The party is a centre-left grouping founded to advance political democratization. The NSF formed a provisional government until the May 1990 elections, in which its presidential candidate, lon lliescu, was elected with 85.0 per cent of the vote. The NSF then won 263 out of the 387 National Assembly seats. The Front split in 1993.

NATIONAL LIBERAL PARTY (NLP) (1869)

Originally founded in 1869, banned in 1947 and revived in 1989. It advocates privatization of the economy and parliamentary democracy. The NLP won 29 National Assembly seats with 6.4 per cent of the popular vote in the 1990 elections. Its presidential candidate was the runner-up with 10 per cent of the vote.

HUNGARIAN DEMOCRATIC UNION OF ROMANIA (HDUR) (1989)

The party represents the interests of Romania's Hungarian minority population. The HDUR was elected to 29 seats with 7.2 per cent of the vote in the 1990 elections.

PARTY OF SOCIAL DEMOCRACY OF ROMANIA

Strongly represented in parliament, with 77 deputies in 1999. It formed from a split in the National Salvation Front in 1993.

SOCIALIST LABOUR PARTY (former Communists, *see* p. 357).

DEMOCRATIC CONVENTION OF ROMANIA (DCR) (1992)

An alliance of 15 centre-right political parties.

CHRISTIAN DEMOCRATIC NATIONAL PEASANTS' PARTY (CDNPP) (1990)

Formed in 1990 by a merger of the previously banned National Peasant Party and the Christian Democratic Party. It is a centre-right party supporting parliamentary democracy and a market economy. In 1999 it had 82 deputies.

Among other parties are the Romanian Ecological Movement, the Romanian Unity Alliance, the Agrarian Democratic Party (f.1990), the Romanian Ecological Party, and the Socialist Democratic Party of Romania. A monarchist party was formed in 1990. The Greater Romania Party had 19 deputies in 1999. Over 80 political parties had registered to contest elections by the late 1990s.

RUSSIA

For the emergence of political parties in Russia prior to the 1917 revolution, *see* section on elections (pp. 283–5).

During the era of the Soviet Union, from 1917 to 1991, the ruling party was the Communist Party of the Soviet Union (*see* p. 367). As the decline of the Soviet Union gathered momentum, a large number of non-Communist parties emerged in 1988–1991 (the most prominent of which was Democratic Russia) and more were formed following the collapse of Soviet communism in 1991. The early parties included:

DEMOCRATIC PARTY IN RUSSIA

Formed in 1990 by members of the Democratic Platform wing of the CPSU and the Moscow Society of Electors, the party was moderately conservative and advocated a united Russia.

PEOPLE'S PARTY OF FREE RUSSIA

Formed in 1990 as the Democratic Party of Communists of Russia as part of the former CPSU.

PEOPLE'S PARTY OF RUSSIA

A liberal democratic party formed in 1991.

REPUBLICAN PARTY OF THE RUSSIAN FEDERATION

Formed in 1990 from members of the Democratic Platform grouping in the CPSU, the party was committed to a mixed economy and the unity of Russia.

RUSSIAN CHRISTIAN-DEMOCRATIC MOVEMENT

Formed in 1990, the movement advocated the restoration of the monarchy and parliamentary democracy.

Among the many parties formed to contest the 1993 elections, or subsequently emerging and disappearing in the 1990s have been:

RUSSIAN COMMUNIST PARTY

A Russian Communist Party was formed in Jun 1990 but was outlawed following the *coup*. The party was re-legalized in Nov 1992. It is a left-wing party advocating a change to economic reforms, including more state protection for industry and slower privatization. Led by Gennadi Zyuganov. Its image has been revamped to allow some free market measures.

RUSSIA'S CHOICE

The main former pro-government, pro-Yeltsin party led by Yegor Gaidar, the architect of the Yeltsin economic reforms. It was committed to reduce state involvement in economic management. Liberal reformist.

MOVEMENT FOR DEMOCRATIC REFORM

Reformist party, led by Mayor of St Petersburg, Anatoly Sobchak.

OUR HOME IS RUSSIA

Centre-right bloc created with President Yeltsin's blessing. Led by Viktor Chernomyrdin. It became very unpopular.

PARTY OF UNITY AND ACCORD

Reformist. Led by Sergei Shakrai. It would give greater power to the regions.

YABLOKO (APPLE) BLOC

The Yavlinsky-led bloc emphasizes continuation of slower, more considered reforms. Led by Grigori Yavlinsky. It is a true liberal, reformist party. It has campaigned strongly against corruption.

LIBERAL DEMOCRATIC PARTY

Extreme right, nationalist and anti-Semite. Led by Vladimir Zhirinovsky. Polled well in 1993 elections.

AGRARIAN PARTY

Left-wing and anti-reform. Favours collective and state farms and wants strict controls on private land ownership. Support in rural areas.

CONGRESS OF RUSSIAN COMMUNITIES

Nationalist group which has emerged under popular General Aleksandr Lebed and Yuri Skokov. Lebed went on to form the Russian Popular Republican Party (*see* below).

WOMEN OF RUSSIA

Centre-left women's group formed mainly by former Communists. It supports moderate reforms. Led by Alevtina Fedulova.

DERZHAVA

Nationalist party with name meaning Great Power. Led by Aleksandr Rutskoi.

COMMUNISTS OF WORKING RUSSIA

Extreme left Stalinist Party.

RUSSIAN POPULAR REPUBLICAN PARTY (f.1996)

Formed in late Dec 1996 by Aleksandr Lebed as a 'third way' alternative to communism and 'the current democratic elite'.

Among new parties fighting the 1999 parliamentary elections were:

UNION OF RIGHT FORCES

A broadly pro-Kremlin coalition of reformers which contested the 1999 election. Supported by former Prime Minister Sergei Kiriyenko. Aligned with Unity (*see* below).

FATHERLAND–ALL RUSSIA ALLIANCE

Led by former Prime Minister Yevgeny Primakov, it emerged on a left-leaning platform to fight the 1999 elections. A centralised coalition of regional governors (and a vehicle of Moscow mayor Yuri Luzhkov), it polled relatively poorly in 1999.

UNITY

Established in Sep 1999, a regional-based party supported by the Kremlin (and by Vladimir Putov). It hoped to secure votes from the Fatherland–All Russia alliance. Led by Sergei Shoigu, its programme was vague, but it polled well in the Dec 1999 election.

SLOVAKIA

Since the independence of Slovakia, political parties have begun to take a distinct shape. The old Communist Party of Slovakia was replaced in 1991 by the Party of the Democratic Left. The Social Democratic Party of Slovakia was re-established in 1990. The Democratic Union of Slovakia was formed in 1994 by members of the Movement for a Democratic Slovakia (f.1991) and in 1995 it absorbed the National Democratic Party – New Alternative. Separate parties represent ethnic Hungarian interests (such as Coexistence, Hungarian Christian Democratic Movement, etc.).

Among developments in the late 1990s were the emergence in 1997 of the Slovak Democratic Coalition (including the Christian Democrats, Democrats, Greens and the Social Democratic Party) and the founding of the Party of the Hungarian Coalition in 1998.

SLOVENIA

Political parties in independent Slovenia have been subject to rapid change. The former League of Communists of Slovenia changed its name to become the Party of Democratic Reform in 1990. This became part of the United list of Social Democrats in 1993. The Socialist Party of Slovenia is the successor to the former Communist Socialist Alliance of Slovenia. The Liberal Democratic Party, a centre-left group, emerged from the former Union of Socialist Youth. In 1994 this merged with the Greens and other groups to become Liberal Democracy of Slovenia (LDS). Until its dissolution in Dec 1991 the Democratic Opposition of Slovenia (DEMOS) was an electoral alliance which included the Democratic Party of Slovenia (the first opposition party to the Communists), the Greens of Slovenia, the Liberal Party, Christian Democrats, etc. The Associated List of Social Democrats became a single party in 1993. Right-wing Nationalists include the Slovenian National Party (f.1991) and the Slovenian National Right (f.1993).

SPAIN

Prior to the Franco régime, the historic parties included:

CONSTITUTIONAL LIBERAL PARTY 1875

Advocated religious toleration, a bicameral system of government, a constitutional monarchy and universal suffrage. Split into left and right factions in 1903.

SOCIALIST PARTY (PSOE) 1879 (*see* p. 362)

REFORMIST PARTY 1913

Sovereignty to be vested in the people. Foreign policy of friendship with neighbouring states.

PATRIOTIC UNIONISTS 1924

'Religion, country, monarchy' – party formed and inspired by the Military Directory.

In the Franco régime, there was only one political party, the National Movement. Its adherents were better known as Falangists.

In the post-Franco era, a large number of political parties, both national and regional, emerged. By the late 1990s over 1000 political parties had been registered. They include:

POPULAR ALLIANCE (AP) 1976

Centrist party. Part of the Democratic Coalition (CD).

COMMUNIST PARTY OF SPAIN (PCE) 1922

A Euro-Communist party. Absorbed PCOE in 1986.

SOCIALIST PARTY (PSOE) 1879

Democratic Socialist. Affiliated to the Socialist International. A splinter group formed Democracia Socialista in 1989.

CENTRE DEMOCRATIC UNION (UCD) 1977

A coalition of several centre parties to fight elections.

DEMOCRATIC AND SOCIAL CENTRE (CDS) 1982

A centre-left party.

NATIONAL FRONT (FN) 1986

Extreme right-wing party.

POPULAR PARTY (PP) 1989

Formerly the Popular Alliance (AP). Victors in the 1996 election.

CONVERGÈNCIA i UNIO (CiU) 1979

An electoral alliance of Catalan parties.

GREEN PARTY (1984)

Los Verdes was formed as an anti-military, anti-nuclear energy party.

SWEDEN

In the late nineteenth century, the main party divisions in Sweden revolved round the tariff question – the Free Traders (*Frihardelssinade*) against the

Protectionist Right (*Protektionistiska Hôgermân*). The Swedish Social Democratic Party was originally formed in 1880. By 1914, it had secured 36 per cent of all votes cast. During the First World War, other parties to begin contesting elections were the Agrarian Party (*Bonde-fôrbundet*), the Farmers' Union and the Left Socialists. The Left Socialists provided the core of the Swedish Communist Party (established in 1921).

SOCIAL DEMOCRATIC LABOUR PARTY 1880

Socialist party, economical reform policy, supports United Nations. Except for 1976–1982, it has been in office or in coalition almost continuously. It remained the largest party in 1998 (the last election of the century).

PEOPLE'S PARTY 1902

Liberal. Advocates traditional liberal policies and a free-market economy.

MODERATE PARTY 1904

Conservative, free enterprise and private property.

LEFT PARTY 1990

Formed as the Left Social Democratic Party of Sweden in 1917, renamed the Communist Party in 1921. Changed its name to the Communist Party of the Left in 1967. Current name, Left Party (Vänsterpartiet), adopted in 1990.

CENTRE PARTY 1922

Formed from a coalition of two smaller moderate parties. Developed more progressive social policies. Strongly opposed to nuclear power.

CHRISTIAN DEMOCRATIC UNION 1964

Orthodox Christian Democrat policies.

SWEDISH WORKERS' COMMUNIST PARTY 1977

A breakaway group from the Communist Left Group (VPK), which it regarded as too Euro-Communist.

GREEN ECOLOGY PARTY (MpG) 1981

An environmental party. Relatively small membership (8000).

NEW DEMOCRACY 1991

A right-wing populist party.

SWITZERLAND

In the last decade of the nineteenth century, the later divisions in Swiss party politics began to appear. Hitherto, Swiss parties had been almost exclusively cantonal affairs. The first organized group was the Social Democratic Party (founded in 1888). The old left wing formed the Radical Democratic Party in 1894, whilst the right came together the same year as the Popular Catholic Party.

RADICAL DEMOCRATIC PARTY 1894

The heirs of the movement towards the confederation of 1848. Liberal policies, supports strong central, federal power.

CHRISTIAN DEMOCRATIC PEOPLE'S PARTY OF SWITZERLAND 1912

Formed by parties which had opposed centralization since 1848. Non-sectarian Christian; the most numerous parliamentary group in the Council of States.

SOCIAL DEMOCRATIC PARTY OF SWITZERLAND 1888

Socialist. Its influence dates mainly from the first proportional representation in 1919.

FARMERS', ARTISANS' AND CITIZENS' PARTY 1919

Seceded from the Radical Democrats. Mainly agrarian concerns, liberal social policies. Merged into Swiss People's Party, 1971.

LABOUR PARTY 1944

Communist and left-wing socialist; aims to co-ordinate all left-wing influences.

SWISS PEOPLE'S PARTY 1971

A union of the Democratic Party and the Farmers', Artisans' and Citizens' Party. Under Christoph Blocher it achieved second place in the 1999 elections.

REPUBLICAN MOVEMENT 1917

Founded to maintain Swiss independence. Opposed to UN or EU entry.

INDEPENDENT PARTY 1936

An opposition party, liberal in social policies. Now called the Independent Alliance.

LIBERAL PARTY 1977

A party which opposes moves towards centralization.

GREEN PARTY OF SWITZERLAND 1983

An environmental party.

AUTOMOBILE PARTY 1985

Founded to support motorists' rights. It won seven seats in the 1995 election.

TURKEY

Political parties were late to develop in Turkey and have always had a precarious, shifting existence. No political parties had emerged in time to contest the elections of 1876 or 1877. Under the despotism of Abdul Hamid, a number of illegal opposition groups were formed. Easily the most important was the Committee of Union and Progress. This party dominated the parliaments of the second constitutional period (1908–1920). Only one other party, the Liberals (Ahrar) contested the 1908 elections. The Liberals stood only in Istanbul and all were defeated. After 1913, the Committee of Union and Progress established a virtual dictatorship. In the May 1914 elections, the Committee was the only party to fight. It remained the only party until the 1918 armistice. It dissolved itself at its last party Congress on 14–19 Oct 1918.

Prior to 1980 (when the National Security Council banned all political parties), some of the more important parties had been:

REPUBLICAN PEOPLE'S PARTY 1923

Founded by Kemal Atatürk. Left of centre, favoured a combination of state and private enterprise. The party once led by Bulent Ecevit.

PROGRESSIVE REPUBLICANS 1924

Liberal policies, free trade programmes. Dissolved for 'being in league with reactionary groups'.

JUSTICE PARTY 1961

Private enterprise party. The party once led by Süleyman Demirel.

NATIONAL SALVATION PARTY 1972

Right-wing Islamic. The replacement party for the National Order Party (*q.v.*).

RELIANCE PARTY 1967

Broke away from the Republican People's Party. Belief in political democracy. Policies left of centre. Merged 1973 with the Republican Party.

NATIONAL ORDER PARTY 1969

Extreme right wing, aimed for the abolition of the Senate. Dissolved 1971, but resurrected 1979.

TURKISH SOCIALIST WORKERS' PARTY 1974

Left-wing socialist. Supported nationalization, withdrawal from NATO.

Political parties were allowed to reform from May 1983. They have included:

MOTHERLAND PARTY (ANAP) 1983

Advocated a market economy, support for the European Union and closer relations with the Islamic world. Merged in 1986 with the Free Democratic Party.

TRUE PATH PARTY (DYP) 1983

A centre-right party which replaced the Justice Party (*q.v.*). The party of Tansu Çiller. Originally founded 1961, banned 1981 and re-founded.

SOCIAL DEMOCRATIC POPULIST PARTY (SDP) 1985

A centre-left party formed by the merger of the Populist Party and the Social Democratic Party. Merged with Republican People's Party in 1995.

DEMOCRATIC LEFT PARTY (DSP) 1985

Centre-left party supported by former members of the Republican People's Party.

REPUBLICAN PEOPLE'S PARTY (CHP)

The old CHP, dissolved in 1981, was reorganized in 1992. Merged with Social Democratic Populist Party in 1995.

NATIONALIST ACTION PARTY (MHP)

Founded in 1983 from the old Conservative Party.

REFAH (WELFARE PARTY)

The Islamic fundamentalist party founded in 1983. Supported closer Islamic ties with its neighbours, opposed to EU entry. Gained electoral successes in mid-1990s. Replaced by Fazilet (*see* p. 367).

NEW DEMOCRACY MOVEMENT (YDH)

Founded 1994 to support a political solution to Kurdish conflict and greater emphasis on human rights.

FAZILET (VIRTUE PARTY) 1997

Turkey's large Islamist party, the successor to Refah, but banned in Mar 1999.

Note: More relaxed guidelines for the establishment of political parties led to a proliferation of parties in the 1990s (*e.g.* FAZILET (*see* above), a Liberal Democratic Party etc.).

UKRAINE

During the period prior to the collapse of the Soviet Union, the only legal political party was the Communist Party of the Ukraine. Its monopoly of power was abolished in 1990 and it was banned after the Aug 1991 *coup* attempt. Earlier, the nationalist movement Rukh (the People's Movement for Restructuring) was formed in 1988 and in 1993 it became a fully-fledged political party (People's Movement of Ukraine). Over 30 other political parties have registered, from the far-right National Fascist Party to the extreme left socialist Party of Ukraine. The old Communist Party was allowed to contest the 1994 elections and went on to dominate the polls, with the Rukh second but a long way behind.

USSR

From 1917 to 1991 the ruling party was the Communist Party of the Soviet Union. The Russian Social Democratic Labour Party was founded in 1898. Lenin's Bolsheviks broke away in 1903 becoming a separate party in 1912. The Bolsheviks seized power during the Oct 1917 Revolution. The Bolsheviks became the Russian Communist Party in 1917, the All-Union Communist Party of Bolsheviks in 1925 and the Communist Party of the Soviet Union in 1952. The CPSU's last general secretary, Mikhail Gorbachev, resigned from the party following the abortive Aug 1991 *coup* mounted by party conservatives. *See* also p. 358.

UNITED KINGDOM

Prior to 1900, British politics was dominated by two parties: Conservative and Liberal. The Labour Party emerged after 1900. A strong Irish Nationalist Party was influential at Westminster.

CONSERVATIVE AND UNIONIST PARTY 1886

Formed by merger of the original Tory Party, renamed Conservative, with Liberals who did not accept Home Rule for Ireland. Policy imperialist and pro-tectionist. Traditional policy free enterprise, EU membership, and strongly for privatization. Increasingly right wing and Euro-sceptic under William Hague (leader after 1997).

LABOUR PARTY 1900

Formed as a federation of trades unions and similar organizations. Socialist economic and social policies, support for UN in foreign relations, formerly opposed EC membership. Modernization began under leadership of Neil Kinnock and John Smith. Currently (under Tony Blair) has become a centrist party, distancing itself from trade unions and socialism, under the 'New Labour' image.

LIBERAL PARTY 1832

Formed from amalgamation of the old Whig Party, the Radical Party and the Reformers. Originally aimed at free trade, Home Rule for Ireland, reform of the House of Lords and moderate social reform and land reform. Supported the League of Nations and later the United Nations. Supported entry into EC. Fought 1983 election in alliance with Social Democratic Party (*q.v.*). Now the Social and Liberal Democratic Party. Secured 46 seats in 1997, its highest total since 1929.

SOCIAL DEMOCRATIC PARTY 1981

Launched 26 Mar 1981 by Labour moderates opposed to left-wing movement in the Labour Party. Its four leading figures were Roy Jenkins, David Owen, William Rodgers and Shirley Williams. It merged in 1988 with the Liberal Party to form the Social and Liberal Democrats (*q.v.*).

CO-OPERATIVE PARTY 1917

Sponsored Labour and Co-operative candidates through a formal agreement of 1926, in which Co-operative parties became eligible for affiliation to Labour parties, and a further agreement of 1946 whereby Co-operative candidates were to run as Co-operative and Labour candidates.

INDEPENDENT LABOUR PARTY 1893

Originally affiliated to the Labour Party until policy differences grew and the parties split in 1932. Its members gradually returned to the Labour Party after 1946.

WELSH NATIONALIST PARTY (PLAID CYMRU) 1925

Campaigns for greater independence for Wales. Now the main opposition in the Welsh Assembly.

SCOTTISH NATIONAL PARTY 1928

Formed as the National Party of Scotland. Merged with the Scottish Party in 1933. Campaigns for independence for Scotland. Now the main opposition in the Scottish Parliament.

COMMUNIST PARTY OF GREAT BRITAIN 1920

Not represented in parliament since 1950. After adjusting to the fall of communism in Eastern Europe has become Democratic Left.

ECOLOGY PARTY 1973

The environmentalist party. Now the Green Party (since 1985) (*q.v.*).

NATIONAL FRONT 1974

A nationalist, anti-immigration extreme right grouping.

SOCIAL AND LIBERAL DEMOCRATS (LIBERAL DEMOCRATS) 1988

Formed by the merger of the Liberal Party (*q.v.*) and the Social Democratic Party.

GREEN PARTY 1985

Formerly the Ecology Party. It has no representation in Parliament, but secured more votes than the Liberal Democrats in the 1989 European Elections, but its influence has since somewhat declined, and it is not represented at Westminster (although it has won seats in EU elections).

REFERENDUM PARTY

Campaigned on single issue of a referendum on the EU. Led by Sir James Goldsmith.

SOCIALIST LABOUR PARTY 1996

Left-wing socialist party led by Arthur Scargill.

UK INDEPENDENCE PARTY

An anti-federalist anti-EU grouping founded by an LSE academic, Alan Sked. Since 1999 represented in the European Parliament (but not at Westminster).

YUGOSLAVIA

National Radical Party	– monarchist, centralist and nationalist	
Slovenian People's Party	– anti-centralist, demanding autonomy for different groups	
National Democratic Party	– split from the Radicals, centralists but ready to grant autonomy as a concession in some cases	pre-1945
Peasants' Party	– originally republican, by 1925 veering towards monarchy: supported co-operatives and agrarian reform	

LEAGUE OF COMMUNISTS OF YUGOSLAVIA

The only effective party until 1989.

After 1989, over 250 parties emerged. Among early groups were:

ASSOCIATION FOR A YUGOSLAV DEMOCRATIC INITIATIVE 1989

Formed as a national opposition party to the League of Communists of Yugoslavia.

RADICAL PARTY 1881, RE-ESTABLISHED 1990

Advocated retaining federal control over the economy, defence, foreign policy and security.

SOCIAL DEMOCRATIC ALLIANCE OF YUGOSLAVIA 1990

Supported preserving the Yugoslav federation with greater equality.

WORKERS' PARTY OF YUGOSLAVIA 1990

Advocated retaining the federal system, but stressed Serbian interests.

YUGOSLAV DEMOCRATIC PARTY 1990

Supported the federal system, but with election of a single national President in free elections.

YUGOSLAV GREEN PARTY 1990

An environmental party which was open to all nationalities and creeds in the state.

With the disintegration of Yugoslavia, 'rump' Yugoslavia (*i.e.* Serbia and Montenegro) has seen the former dominant League of Communists become the Socialist Party of Serbia. The People's Assembly Party (f.1992 as the Democratic Movement of Serbia) is a multi-party coalition. The Democratic Party is a nationalist party, the Serbian Radical Party is an extreme nationalist party advocating a 'Greater Serbia'. It is headed by Vojislav Seselj. The Serbian Renewal Movement (SPO), a major opposition party, is led by Vuk Draskovic.

7
Justice

ALBANIA

Prior to 1992, under the Communist régime, there was a revised Penal Code in Oct 1977 followed by a Labour Code and a Code of Penal Procedure in 1980, a Civil Code with a Code of Civil Procedure in 1982 and a Family Code in 1982. Justice was administered by the People's Courts and minor crimes were tried by tribunals. Judges of the Supreme Court were elected by the People's Assembly for four-year terms.

A new criminal code was introduced in Jun 1995. The administration of justice is presided over by the *Council of Justice*, chaired by the President of the Republic, which appoints judges to courts. A Ministry of Justice was re-established in 1990 and a Bar Council set up. In Nov 1993 the number of capital offences was reduced from 13 to 6 and the death penalty was abolished for women.

ANDORRA

Justice is administered by the High Council of Justice, comprising five members appointed for single six-year terms. The independence of judges is constitutionally guaranteed. Judicial power is exercised in civil matters in the first instance by Magistrates' Courts and a Judge's Court. Criminal justice is administered by the *Corts*, consisting of the judge of appeal, two *rahonadors* elected by the General Council of the Valleys, a general attorney and an attorney nominated for five years alternately by each of the co-princes.

AUSTRIA

The Austrian legal system provides for three supreme courts, all of them located in Vienna: the Constitutional Court (*Verfassungsgerichtshof*), the Administrative

Court (*Verwaltungsgerichtshof*) and the Supreme Court (*Oberster Gerichtshof*), the latter being the highest court for all judicial matters.

At the next level below the Supreme Court, 4 High State Courts (*Oberlandesgerichte*) are instituted which have merely appellate competence. Beneath them 16 State Courts of Justice (*Landes-und Kreisgerichte*) are competent for civil and criminal justice both in first instance for major cases and as courts of appeal for those petty matters for which, at the lowest level, 187 District Courts (*Bezirksgerichte*) are installed as courts of first instance, again in civil and penal matters. With the exception of the District Courts, all courts of justice with competence for penal matters have an office of the public prosecution at their side.

AUSTRIA–HUNGARY

In Austria the ordinary judicial authorities were: (i) The Supreme Court of Justice and Court of Cassation (*Oberste Gerichts-und Kassationshof*) in Vienna; (ii) the higher provincial courts (*Oberlandesgerichte*); (iii) the provincial and district courts (*Landes-und Kreisgerichte*), and, in connection with these, the jury courts (*Geschworenengerichte*); (iv) the county courts (*Bezirksgerichte*). Of these, the third and fourth groups were courts of first instance; the second group consisted of courts of second instance. Courts of first instance acted as courts of inquiry and had summary jurisdiction. Courts of second instance were courts of appeal from the lower courts, and had the supervision of the criminal courts in their jurisdiction. The jury courts tried certain cases where severe penalties were involved, political offences, and press offences. The county courts exercised criminal jurisdiction in the counties and co-operated in preliminary proceedings regarding crime. There existed also special courts for commercial, revenue, military, shipping and other matters.

In case of conflict between different authorities the Imperial Court (*Reichsgerichte*) in Vienna had power to decide. Private persons could in certain cases appeal against the decisions of magistrates to the High Court for Administrative Affairs.

For Hungary with Fiume the judicial authorities were: [the Royal] Court (*Kuria*) in Budapest, and the Supreme Court of Justice in Zagreb, of the highest instance in all civil and criminal matters.

BELGIUM

Judges are appointed for life. There is a court of cassation, 5 courts of appeal, and assize courts for political and criminal cases. There are 27 judicial districts, each with a court of first instance. In each of the 222 cantons is a justice and judge of the peace. There are, besides, various special tribunals. There is trial by jury in assize courts. The death penalty, which had been in abeyance for 45 years, was formally abolished in 1991. The Gendarmerie ceased to be part of the army in Jan 1992.

BULGARIA

The Constitution of 1947 provided for the election (and recall) of the judges by the people and, for the Supreme Court, by the National Assembly, but in 1982 this was amended so that all judges are elected and recalled by the National Assembly. The lower courts include laymen ('assessors') as well as jurists. There are a Supreme Court, 28 provincial (including Sofia) courts and 105 (formerly 103) people's courts.

In Jun 1961, 'Comrades' Courts' were set up for the trial of minor offenders by their fellow-workers. The maximum term of imprisonment is 20 (formerly 15) years. 'Exceptionally dangerous crimes' carry the death penalty.

From 1992 the Prosecutor-General and judges were elected by the Supreme Judicial Council.

CYPRUS

The administration of justice is exercised by a separate and independent judiciary. There is a Supreme Court of the Republic, the Assize Courts and the District Courts.

The Supreme Court is composed of 13 judges, one of whom is the President of the Court. The Supreme Court adjudicates exclusively and finally (a) on all constitutional and administrative law matters, including any recourses that any law or decision of the House of Representatives, or the budget, is discriminatory against either of the two communities; (b) on any conflict of competence between state organs in the Republic; (c) questions of the unconstitutionality of any law, or on any question of interpretation of the constitution in case of ambiguity; and (d) on recourses for annulment of administrative acts, decisions or omissions.

All judicial power in civil and criminal matters is also exercised by the Supreme Court and its subordinate Courts. The Supreme Court is the highest appellate Court in the Republic and has jurisdiction to hear and determine all appeals from any Court.

There are six Assize Courts and six District Courts, one for each district. The Assize Courts have unlimited criminal jurisdiction and power to order compensation up to £C3000. The District Courts exercise original civil and criminal jurisdiction, the extent of which varies with the composition of the Bench.

There is a Supreme Council of Judicature, consisting of the President and Judges of the Supreme Court entrusted with the appointment, promotion, transfers, termination of appointment and disciplinary control over all judicial officers, other than Judges of the Supreme Court.

The Attorney-General is head of the independent Law Office and legal adviser to the President and his Ministers.

CZECHOSLOVAKIA

The criminal and criminal procedure codes dated from 1 Jan 1962, as amended in Apr 1973. There was a Federal Supreme Court and federal military courts, with judges elected by the Federal Assembly. Both republics had Supreme Courts and a network of regional and district courts whose professional judges were elected by the republican National Councils. Lay judges were elected by regional or district local authorities. Local authorities and social organizations could participate in the decision-making of the courts.

CZECH REPUBLIC

The post-Communist judicial system became law in Jul 1991. This provides for 4 types of courts: civil, criminal, commercial and administrative. Commercial courts arbitrate in disputes arising from business activities. Administrative courts examine the legality of the decisions of state institutions when appealed by citizens. In addition, there are military courts which operate under the jurisdiction of the Ministry of Defence. There is a Supreme Court, and a hierarchy of courts under the Ministry of Justice at Republic, region, and district level. District courts are courts of first instance. Cases are usually decided by a Senate comprising a judge and 2 associate judges, though occasionally by a single judge. (Associate judges are citizens in good standing over the age of 25 who are elected for 4-year terms.) Regional courts are courts of first instance in more serious cases and also courts of appeal for district courts. Cases are usually decided by a Senate of 2 judges and 3 associate judges, although again occasionally by a single judge. There is also a Supreme Administrative Court. The Supreme Court interprets law as a guide to other courts and functions also as a court of appeal.

Judges are appointed for life by the National Council. The death penalty has been abolished.

DENMARK

The lowest courts of justice are organized in 82 tribunals (*byretter*), where minor cases are dealt with by a single judge. The tribunal at Copenhagen has one

President and 44 other judges and Aarhus has one President and 15 other judges; the other tribunals have 1 to 11. Cases of greater consequence are dealt with by the 2 superior courts (*Landsretterne*); these courts are also courts of appeal for the above-named minor cases. Of superior courts there are two: *Østre Landsret* in Copenhagen with a President and 61 other judges, *Vestre Landsret* in Viborg with a President and 38 other judges. From these an appeal lies to the Supreme Court (*Højesteret*) in Copenhagen, composed of 17 judges. Judges under 65 years of age can be removed only by judicial sentence.

ESTONIA

A post-Soviet criminal code was introduced in 1992. The death penalty was abolished 1998. There is a three-tier court system with the State Court and both city and district courts. The latter act as courts of appeal. The State Court is the final court of appeal, and also functions as a constitutional court. There are also administrative courts for petty offences. Judges are appointed for life. City and district judges are appointed by the President; State Court judges are elected by parliament.

FINLAND

The lowest court of justice is the District Court. In most civil cases a District Court has a quorum with three legally-qualified members present. In criminal cases as well as in some cases related to family law the District Court has a quorum with a chair and three lay judges present. In the preliminary preparation of a civil case and in a criminal case concerning a minor offence a District Court is composed of the chair only. From the District Court an appeal lies to the courts of appeal (*Hovioikeus*) in Turku, Vaasa, Kuopio, Helsinki, Kouvola and Rovaniemi. The Supreme Court (*Korkein oikeus*) sits in Helsinki. Appeals from the decisions of administrative authorities are in the final instance decided by the Supreme Administrative Court (*Korkein hallintooikeus*), also in Helsinki. Judges can be removed only by judicial sentence.

Two functionaries, the *Oikeuskansleri* or Chancellor of Justice, and the *Oikeusasiamies* (ombudsman), or Solicitor-General, exercise control over the administration of justice. The former acts also as counsel and public prosecutor for the government; while the latter, who is appointed by the parliament, exerts a general control over all courts of law and public administration.

FRANCE

The system of justice is divided into two jurisdictions: the judicial, and the administrative.

Within the judicial jurisdiction are common law courts including 473 lower courts (*tribunaux d'instance*, including 11 in overseas departments), 186 higher courts (*tribunaux de grande instance*, including 5 *tribunaux de première instance* in the overseas territories), 454 police courts (*tribunaux de police*, including 11 in overseas departments).

The *tribunaux d'instance* are presided over by a single judge. The *tribunaux de grande instance* usually have a collegiate composition, although they may be presided over by a single judge in some civil cases. The police courts, presided over by a judge on duty in the *tribunal d'instance*, deal with petty offences (*contraventions*); correctional chambers (*chambres correctionelles*, of which there is at least one in each *tribunal de grande instance*) deal with graver offences (*délits*), including cases involving imprisonment up to 5 years. Correctional chambers consist of 3 judges of a *tribunal de grande instance* (a single judge in some cases). Sometimes in cases of *délit*, and in all cases of more serious *crimes*, a preliminary inquiry is made in secrecy by one of 569 examining magistrates (*juges d'instruction*), who either dismisses the case or sends it for trial before a public prosecutor.

Within the judicial jurisdiction were (1999) various specialized courts, including 227 commercial courts (*tribunaux de commerce*), composed of trades-men and manufacturers elected for 2 years initially and then for 4 years; 271 conciliation boards (*conseils de prud'hommes*), composed of an equal number of employers and employees elected for 5 years to deal with labour disputes; 437 courts for settling rural landholding disputes (*tribunaux paritaires des baux ruraux*, including 11 in overseas departments); and 116 social security courts (*tribunaux des affaires de sécurité sociale*).

When the decisions of any of these courts are susceptible of appeal, the case goes to one of the 35 courts of appeal (*cours d'appel*) each composed of a President and a variable number of members. There were (1999) 104 courts of assize (*cours d'assises*), each composed of a President who is a member of the court of appeal, and 2 other magistrates, and assisted by a lay jury of 9 members. These try crimes involving imprisonment of over 5 years. The decisions of the courts of appeal and the courts of assize are final. However, the Court of Cassation (*Cour de cassation*) has discretion to verify if the law has been correctly inter-preted and if the rules of procedure have been followed exactly. The Court of Cassation may annul any judgment, following which the cases must be retried by a court of appeal or a court of assize.

The administrative jurisdiction exists to resolve conflicts arising between citi-zens and central and local government authorities. It consists of 34 adminis-trative courts (*tribunaux administratifs*, including 7 in overseas departments and territories) and 5 administrative courts of appeal (*cours administratives d'appel*). The Council of State is the final court of appeal in administrative cases, though it may also act as a court of first instance.

Cases of doubt as to whether the judicial or administrative jurisdiction is competent in any case are resolved by a *Tribunal de conflits* composed in equal measure of members of the Court of Cassation and the Council of State.

On 24 Jan 1973 the first Ombudsman (*médiateur*) was appointed for a six-year period.

Capital punishment was abolished in Aug 1981, and a revised penal code came into force on 1 Mar 1994, replacing the *Code Napoléon* of 1810.

Penal institutions consist of: (1) *maisons d'arrêt*, where persons awaiting trial as well as those condemned to short periods of imprisonment are kept; (2) punishment institutions – (a) central prisons (*maisons centrales*) for those sentenced to long imprisonment, and (b) detention centres for offenders showing promise of rehabilitation; (3) hospitals for the sick. Special attention is being paid to classified treatment and the rehabilitation and vocational re-education of prisoners including work in open-air and semi-free establishments. There are three penal institutions for women.

Juvenile delinquents go before special judges in 137 (11 in overseas departments and territories) juvenile courts (*tribunaux pour enfants*); they are sent to public or private institutions of supervision and re-education.

GERMANY

A uniform system of law courts existed throughout Germany, though, with the exception of the *Reichsgericht*, all courts were directly subject to the state in which they exercised jurisdiction, and not to the central government.

After Apr 1935 all courts became organs of central government. The Nazi concept of justice was defined as 'Right is that which is useful to the nation.'

The lowest courts of first instance were the *Amtsgerichte*, competent to try petty civil and criminal cases, with the exception of capital cases which fell within the jurisdiction of the Court of Assizes, or the *Reichsgericht*. Cases relating to property in which the amount involved did not exceed 500 marks were usually tried by a single judge. In the trial of more serious criminal cases the judge was assisted by two assessors (laymen), to whom on the request of the public prosecutor a professional magistrate might further be added (*Schoffengericht*). The *Amtsgerichte* dealt also with guardianships, estates and official records. The *Landgerichte* contained both civil and criminal chambers. The former, consisting of 3 judges, were competent to deal in first instance with all civil cases in as far as they had not been referred to the *Amtsgerichte*, especially with divorces, and also exercised a revisory jurisdiction over the *Amtsgerichte*. For trying commercial cases there were further commercial chambers, consisting of 1 judge and 2 laymen. The criminal chamber heard appeals from the *Amtsgerichte* in criminal cases; if the appeal was from the decision of a single magistrate it was heard by 1 judge with 2 lay assessors (small chamber); if from a decision of the *Schoffengericht*, by 3 judges and 2 laymen (large chamber). For the trial of capital cases, the *Landgerichte* were transformed into *Schwurgerichte*, consisting of 3 judges and 6 laymen. The *Amtsgerichte* and *Landgerichte* had as superior court the *Oberlandesgerichte*. There were 27 such courts in Germany. The *Oberlandesgerichte* contained criminal and civil senates consisting of three judges. They exercised appellate jurisdiction over the *Landgerichte* in civil cases, and over the 'small chambers' (and in some cases over the 'large chambers') in criminal cases. The supreme court was the *Reichsgericht*, which sat at Leipzig. This court exercised an appellate jurisdiction over all inferior courts, and also an original and final jurisdiction in cases of treason.

A law promulgated in Jul 1935 established the novel principle in criminal law that the courts should punish offences not punishable under the Criminal Code if they were deserving of punishment 'according to the underlying idea of a penal code or according to healthy public sentiment'.

Special courts existed for all civil disputes arising from the relationship between employers and employed. Qualified judges were appointed to these judicial bodies and they were attended by representatives of employers and employed.

There were 206 Sterilization Courts, composed of 1 judge and 2 medical men, in 1934, and 56 344 persons were sterilized.

FEDERAL REPUBLIC OF GERMANY

Justice is administered by the Federal Courts and by the courts of the Länder. In criminal procedures, civil cases and procedures of non-contentious jurisdiction the courts on the Land level are the local courts (*Amtsgerichte*), the regional courts (*Landgerichte*) and the courts of appeal (*Oberlandesgerichte*). On the Federal level decisions regarding these matters are taken by the Federal Constitutional Court (*Bundesverfassungsgericht*) elected by the Bundestag and Bundesrat. The Länder also have constitutional courts. In labour law disputes the courts of the first and second instance are the labour courts and the Land labour courts and in the third instance, the Federal Labour Court (*Bundesarbeitgericht*). Disputes about public law in matters of social security, unemployment insurance, maintenance of war victims and similar cases are dealt with in the first and second instances by the social courts and the Land social courts and in the third instance by the Federal Social Court (*Bundessozialgericht*). In most tax matters the finance courts of the Länder are competent and in the second instance, the Federal Finance Court (*Bundesfinanzhof*). Other controversies of public law in non-constitutional matters are decided in the first and second instance by the administrative and the higher administrative courts (*Oberverwaltungsgerichte*) of the Länder, and in the third instance by the Federal Administrative Court (*Bundesverwaltungsgericht*).

For inquiry into maritime accidents the admiralty courts (*Seeämter*) are competent on the Land level and in the second instance the Federal Admiralty Court (*Bundesoberseeamt*).

The death sentence has been abolished.

Under the Unification Treaty signed 31 Aug 1990, the Basic Law of the Federal Republic of Germany was applied to the five new Länder of Brandenburg, Mecklenburg-Western Pomerania, Saxony, Saxony-Anhalt and Thuringia.

GERMAN DEMOCRATIC REPUBLIC

The judicial system of the German Democratic Republic was instituted following World War II. The principles on which the judicial system functioned were embodied in the constitution. Judges were elected by the people's representative bodies or by the citizens directly. State Prosecuting Counsels were nominated by the Prosecutor-General. Jurisdiction was exercised by the Supreme Court, by the *Bezirke* Courts and by the *Kreis* Courts. All courts decided on the appointment of one presiding and two assistant magistrates. The Assistant Magistrates in the First instance were jurors (lay magistrates from all classes of society); the Labour Law Tribunal of the Supreme Court appointed two official judges and three lay magistrates.

Judges were independent and subject only to the constitution and the Legislature. A Judge could be recalled only if he had committed a breach of the law, grossly neglected his duties or been convicted by a court.

Lay magistrates were elected for a period of four years after nomination by the democratic parties and organizations. Magistrates of the *Kreis* Courts were directly elected by the people; Magistrates of the *Bezirke* Courts, by the *Bezirkstag*; Magistrates of the Labour Law Tribunal of the Supreme Court, by the *Volkshammer*. All were equally authorized Judges.

Attached to the *Volkshammer* was a Constitutional and Legislature Commission in which all parties were represented according to their numbers. In addition there were on the Commission three members of the Supreme Court as well as three State Law Teachers who might not be members of the *Volkshammer*. All members of the Constitutional and Legislature Commission were appointed by the *Volkshammer*.

On 14 Jan 1968 the whole judicial and penal system was reformed; the most important reform being the introduction of a new criminal code to replace the German Criminal Code of 1871.

GIBRALTAR

The judicial system is based entirely on the English system. There is a Magistrates' Court, a Court of First Instance (the equivalent of the English County Court), a Supreme Court with criminal and civil jurisdiction, and a Court of Appeal. The final appeal lies with the Judicial Committee of the Privy Council in London. In the Supreme Court, criminal cases are tried by jury. In addition, there is a Juvenile Court, and a Coroner's Court. There is no death penalty in Gibraltar.

GREECE

Under the 1975 Constitution, judges are appointed for life by the President of the Republic, after consultation with the judicial council. Judges enjoy personal and functional independence. There are three divisions of the courts – administrative, civil and criminal – and they must not give decisions which are contrary to the Constitution. Final jurisdiction lies with a Special Supreme Tribunal. Some laws, passed before the 1975 Constitution came into force, and which are not contrary to it, remain in force.

HUNGARY

The administration of justice is the responsibility of the Procurator-General, who is elected by parliament for a term of 6 years. There were (1999) 111 local courts, 20 labour law courts, 20 county courts, 6 district courts and a Supreme Court. Criminal proceedings are dealt with by district courts through 3-member councils and by county courts and the Supreme Court in 5-member councils. A new Civil Code was adopted in 1978 and a new Criminal Code in 1979.

Regional courts act only as courts of first instance; county courts as either courts of first instance or of appeal. The Supreme Court acts normally as an appeal court, but may act as a court of first instance in cases submitted to it by the Public Prosecutor. All courts, when acting as courts of first instance, consist of one professional judge and two lay assessors, and, as courts of appeal, of three professional judges. Local government Executive Committees may try petty offences.

Regional or county judges and assessors are elected by the district or county councils, all members of the Supreme Court by Parliament. There are also military courts of the first instance. Military cases of the second instance go before the Supreme Court.

Judges are appointed for life, subject to removal for disciplinary reasons.

The death penalty was abolished in 1990.

The office of Ombudsman was established in 1993, elected by parliament for a six-year term, renewable once.

ICELAND

The courts consist of courts of first instance, exercising jurisdiction on a district level, and the Supreme Court, a national court of appeal. There were 33 judicial districts in 1990. Each had one court of ordinary jurisdiction for civil cases and another for criminal cases, as well as a Sheriff's Court, a Probate Court and a Court of Auctions. However, one district, being divided for purposes of criminal law and law enforcement, had an additional Criminal Court and Sheriff's Court, making 34 in all. The urban districts also had a Maritime and Commercial Court. Other special courts are of less importance.

There are no intermediate courts of appeal, but these existed on a regional level prior to 1920, at which time the Supreme Court was established in its current form.

Appeal to the Supreme Court could be made from all other courts except the High Court of State, the decisions of which were not subject to judicial review. The Labour Court and the Ecclesiastical Court also constituted an exception. As to the Labour Court, only questions of procedure could be appealed to the Supreme Court. As regards the Ecclesiastical Court, its decisions were subject to appeal to the Synodal Court, which thus replaced the Supreme Court as the court of last resort.

Generally, unanimity of opinion in a court of more than one judge was not required for a valid decision, the issue being conclusively decided by a majority of votes. Dissenting opinions would be recorded and published in the same manner as the majority opinion. Juries are not used within the judicial system.

New laws were enacted in 1992 on practically all aspects of legal procedure. Traditionally Icelandic procedural law has been similar to that of Denmark and Norway, but in some respects Icelandic legal procedure now has no exact correlation in the Nordic countries.

There are two judicial instances, the lower instance being formed by the 8 district courts, and the Supreme Court being the superior instance and the only appeal court, thus transferring jurisdiction from the provincial magistrates to the district courts and separating the judiciary from the prosecution. The principle that a case may pass through these two instances is, however, subject to three exceptions. Firstly, certain cases concerning labour disputes and the interpretation of collective labour agreements are subject to the jurisdiction of the Labour Court. Secondly, the special Court of Impeachment, whose judgments are not subject to appeal, has jurisdiction in cases concerning criminal violations committed in public office by ministers of the government. Thirdly, in cases of damages claimed on account of tortious acts in judicial office the Supreme Court is the first and only instance.

IRELAND

The Constitution provides that justice shall be administered in public in Courts established by law by judges appointed by the President on the advice of the government. The jurisdiction and organization of the Courts are dealt with in the Courts (Establishment and Constitution) Act, 1961 and the Courts (Supplemental Provisions) Acts, 1961–1991. The Courts consist of Courts of First Instance and a Court of Final Appeal, called the Supreme Court. The Courts of First Instance are the High Court with full original jurisdiction and the Circuit and the District Courts with local and limited jurisdiction. A judge may not be removed from office except for stated misbehaviour or incapacity and then only on resolutions passed by both Houses of the *Oireachtas*. Judges of the Supreme, High and Circuit Courts are appointed from among practising barristers. Judges of the District Court (called District Justices) may be appointed from among practising barristers or practising solicitors.

The Supreme Court, which consisted (1999) of the Chief Justice (who is *ex officio* an additional judge of the High Court) and seven ordinary judges, has appellate jurisdiction from all decisions of the High Court. The President may, after consultation with the Council of State, refer a Bill, which has been passed by both Houses of the *Oireachtas* (other than a money bill and certain other bills), to the Supreme Court for a decision on the question as to whether such Bill or any provision thereof is repugnant to the Constitution.

The High Court, which consists of a President (who is *ex officio* an additional Judge of the Supreme Court) and 23 ordinary judges, has full original jurisdiction in and power to determine all matters and questions, whether of law or fact, civil or criminal. In all cases in which questions arise concerning the validity of any law having regard to the provisions of the Constitution, the High Court alone exercises original jurisdiction. The High Court on Circuit acts as an appeal court from the Circuit Court.

The Court of Criminal Appeal consists of the Chief Justice or an ordinary judge of the Supreme Court, together with either two ordinary judges of the High Court or the President and one ordinary judge of the High Court. It deals with appeals by persons convicted on indictment where the appellant obtains a certificate from the trial judge that the case is a fit one for appeal, or, in case such certificate is refused, where the court itself, on appeal from such refusal, grants leave to appeal. The decision of the Court of Criminal Appeal is final, unless that court or the Director of Public Prosecutions certifies that the decision involves a point of law of exceptional public importance, in which case an appeal is taken to the Supreme Court.

The High Court exercising criminal jurisdiction is known as the Central Criminal Court. It consists of a judge or judges of the High Court, nominated by the President of the High Court. The Court sits in Dublin and tries criminal cases which are outside the jurisdiction of the Circuit Court or which may be sent forward to it for trial from the Circuit Court on the application of the Director of Public Prosecutions.

The Offences against the State Act, 1939 provides for the establishment of Special Criminal Courts. A Special Criminal Court sits without a jury. The rules of evidence that apply in proceedings before a Special Criminal Court are the same as those applicable in trials in the Central Criminal Court.

The Circuit Court consists of a President (who is *ex officio* an additional judge of the High Court) and 25 ordinary judges. The country is divided into 8 circuits for the purposes of the Circuit Court. The Circuit Court acts as an appeal court from the District Court.

The District Court, which consists of a President and 50 ordinary judges, has summary jurisdiction in a large number of criminal cases where the offence is not of a serious nature.

All criminal cases, except those of a minor nature, and those tried in the Special Criminal Court, are tried by a judge and a jury of 12. A majority vote of the jury (10 must agree) is necessary to determine a verdict.

ITALY

Italy has 1 court of cassation, in Rome, and was divided for the administration of justice into 28 appeal court districts in 1999, subdivided into 164 tribunal districts, and these again in *mandamenti* each with its own magistracy (*Pretura*), 617 in all. There are also 90 first degree assize courts and 28 assize courts of appeal. For civil business, besides the magistracy above mentioned, *Conciliatori* have jurisdiction in petty plaints.

LATVIA

The new criminal code came into force in 1998. Judges are appointed for life. There is a Supreme Court, regional and district courts and administrative courts. The death penalty is retained, but has been subject to a moratorium since Oct 1996.

LIECHTENSTEIN

The principality has its own civil and penal codes. The lowest court is the county court, *Landgericht*, presided over by one judge, which decides minor civil cases and summary criminal offences. The criminal court, *Kriminalgericht*, with a bench of five judges is for major crimes. Another court of mixed juris-diction is the court of assizes (with three judges) for misdemeanours. Juvenile cases are treated in the Juvenile Court (with a bench of three judges). The superior court, *Obergericht*, and Supreme Court, *Oberster Gerichtshof*, are courts of appeal for civil and criminal cases (both with benches of five judges). An administrative court of appeal from government actions and the State Court determines the constitutionality of laws.

The death penalty was abolished in 1989.

LITHUANIA

In 1999 the Court system in Lithuania comprised the Constitutional Court, the Supreme Court, the Court of Appeal, circuit courts and district courts, made up of elected judges and assessors. In Dec 1998 parliament amended the Criminal Code and abolished the death penalty. The three-tier system of administrative courts consisting of the Administrative Cases Department at the Court of Appeal, the Higher Administrative Court and five county admin-istrative courts started functioning from May 1999.

Trial by jury was still under consideration and no decision had been made by end Dec 1999.

LUXEMBOURG

The courts are entrusted by the Constitution with the exercise of judicial power. The Constitution applies to them the principle of the separation of powers by making them independent in performing their functions, restricting their sphere of activity, defining their limits of jurisdiction and providing for a number of procedural guarantees.

The courts of the Justices of the Peace are the lowest; they are at Luxembourg City, Esch-sur-Alzette and Diekirch. They deal with minor civil, commercial and criminal cases. There are two judicial districts of Luxembourg and Diekirch. The district courts deal with civil, commercial and criminal cases. The Superior Court of Justice includes both a court of appeal, hearing decisions made by district courts, and a *Cour de Cassation*. The Court of Assizes, which fell within the jurisdiction of the Superior Court, heard criminal cases, but was abolished in 1987. There is no jury system. A defendant is acquitted if fewer than four of the six judges find them guilty.

The High Court of Justice sits in Luxembourg. It consists of a Supreme Court of Appeal and a Court of Appeal. The Court of Appeal is subdivided in six cham-bers each sitting with three magistrates. The Court of Appeal deals with judg-ments passed in the first instance by district courts. The Supreme Court of Appeal consists of one chamber which sits with five magistrates *i.e.* the President of the Court, two councillors from the Appeal Court and two judges chosen among councillors who never dealt with the case at any time previously. It deals primarily with decisions made by the Court of Appeal, the Military Court and with judgments passed without appeal by district courts or by Justices of the Peace. No decision or judgment may be brought before the Supreme Court of Appeal except for violations of the law, action ultra vires or procedural offences, either substantial or barred under pain of being declared void. Matters of social administration such as social insurance are dealt with by special tribunals. The administration of the judiciary and the supervision of judicial police investigations is the responsibility of the *Procureur général*.

Judges are appointed for life by the Grand Ducal order, and are not removable except by judicial sentence.

Capital punishment was abolished in 1979.

MACEDONIA
Former Yugoslavia

Courts are autonomous and independent. Judges are tenured and elected for life on the proposal of the *Judicial Council*, whose members are themselves elected for renewable 6-year terms. The highest court is the Supreme Court. There are 28 courts of first instance and 3 higher courts.

MALTA

Civil law has generally evolved from Roman law. Public law and some commercial and maritime affairs are influenced by English law.

There is a Constitutional Court, a Court of Appeal and a Criminal Court of Appeal, together with a Civil Court, a Criminal Court, a Commercial Court and from 1990 a three-tier system of Magistrates' Courts.

MONACO

There are the following courts: *Tribunal Supreme, Cour de Révision, Cour d'Appel*, a Correctional Tribunal, a Work Tribunal, a Tribunal of the First Instance, two Arbitration Commissions for Rents (one commercial, one domestic), courts for Work-related Accidents, and Supervision, a *Juge de Paix*, and a Police Tribunal. There is no death penalty.

THE NETHERLANDS

Justice is administered by the High Court of the Netherlands (Court of Cassation), by 5 courts of justice (Courts of Appeal), by 19 district courts and by 63 cantonal courts; trial by jury is unknown. The Cantonal Court, which deals with minor offences, comprises a single judge; more serious cases are tried by the district courts, formed as a rule by three judges (in some cases one judge is sufficient); the courts of appeal are constituted of three, and the High Court of five, judges. All judges are appointed for life by the Sovereign (the judges of the High Court from a list prepared by the Second Chamber of the States-General). They can be removed only by a decision of the High Court.

Juvenile courts were set up in 1922. The juvenile court is formed by a single judge especially appointed to try children's civil cases, at the same time charged with the administration of justice for criminal actions committed by young persons who are between 12 and 18 (in special cases up to 21) years old, unless imprisonment of 6 months or more ought to be inflicted; such cases are tried by 3 judges.

NORWAY

The judicature is common to civil and criminal cases; the same professional judges preside over both cases. These judges are as such state officials. The participation of lay judges and jurors, both summoned for the individual case, varies according to the kind of court and kind of case.

The ordinary Court of First Instance, the District or City Courts (*Herredsrett* and *Byrett*) is in criminal cases composed of 1 professional judge and 2 lay judges, chosen by ballot from a panel elected by the district council. In civil cases 2 lay judges may participate. The ordinary Court of First Instance is in general competent in all kinds of cases, with the exception of criminal cases where the maximum penalty prescribed in the Criminal Code for the offence in question exceeds 6 years' imprisonment. Altogether there are 96 District and City Courts.

In every community there is a Conciliation Board (*Forliksråd*) composed of three lay persons elected by the district council. A civil lawsuit usually begins with mediation in the council which can also pronounce judgment in certain cases.

The ordinary Courts of Second Instance, High Courts (*Lagmannsrett*), of which there are five, are composed of three professional judges. Additionally, in civil cases two or four lay judges may be summoned. In serious criminal cases which are being brought before the High Court in the first instance, a jury of ten lay persons is summoned to determine whether the defendant is guilty according to the charge. In other criminal cases the court is composed of two professional judges and three lay judges (*Meddomsrett*). In civil cases, the Court of Second Instance is an ordinary court of appeal. In criminal cases in which the lower court does not have judicial authority, it is itself the court of first instance. In other criminal cases it is an appeal court as far as the appeal is based on an attack against the lower court's assessment of the facts when determining the guilt of the defendant. An appeal based on any other alleged mistakes is brought directly before the Supreme Court.

The Supreme Court (*Høyesterett*) is the court of last resort. There are eighteen Supreme Court judges. Each individual case is heard by five judges. Some major cases are determined in plenary session. The Supreme Court may in general examine every aspect of the case and the handling of it by the lower courts. However, in criminal cases the Court may not overrule the lower court's assessment of the facts as far as the guilt of the defendant is concerned.

The Court of Impeachment (*Riksretten*) is composed of five judges of the Supreme Court and ten members of parliament.

All serious offences are prosecuted by the state. The public prosecution authority (*påtalemyndigheten*) consists of the Director-General of Public Prosecutions, 18 district attorneys (*statsadvokater*) and legally qualified officers of the ordinary police force. Counsel for the defence is in general provided for by the state.

POLAND

The legal system was reorganized in 1950. A new penal code was adopted in 1969. Espionage and treason carry the severest penalties. For minor crimes there is more provision for probation sentences and fines. Previous jurisprudence was based on a penal code of 1932 supplemented by the Concise Penal Code of 1946.

In 1955 the death penalty was suspended for five years. No executions have taken place since 1988.

There existed (1999) the following courts: 1 Supreme Court, 1 high administrative court, 10 appeal courts, 44 voivodship courts, 288 district courts, 66 family consultative centres and 34 juvenile courts. Judges and lay assessors are appointed. Judges for higher courts are appointed by the President of the Republic from candidatures proposed by the National Council of the Judiciary. Assessors are nominated by the Minister of Justice. Judges have life tenure. An ombudsman's office was established in 1987.

Family courts (now consultative centres) were established in 1977 for cases involving divorce and domestic relations, but divorce suits were transferred to ordinary courts in 1990.

PORTUGAL

Portuguese law distinguishes civil (including commercial) and penal, labour, administrative and fiscal law, each branch having its lower courts, courts of appeal and the Supreme Court.

There are four judicial districts (Lisbon, Porto, Coimbra and Evora) divided into 47 circuits. In 1993 there were 346 common courts, including 300 of the first instance (63 specialized). There were also 29 administration and fiscal courts. There are 4 courts of appeal (*Tribunal de Relação*) at Lisbon, Coimbra, Evora and Porto, and a Supreme Court in Lisbon (*Supremo Tribunal de Justiça*).

Capital punishment was totally abolished under the 1976 Constitution. It was abolished for political crimes in 1852, common law crimes in 1867 and common law crimes in overseas territories in 1870.

ROMANIA

Justice is administered by the Supreme Court, the 41 county courts, 81 courts of first instance and 15 courts of appeal. Lay assessors (elected for 4 years) participate in most court trials, collaborating with the judges. In 1991 there were 1547 judges. The Procurator-General exercises 'supreme supervisory power to ensure the observance of the law' by all authorities, central and local, and all citizens. The Procurator's Office and its organs are independent of any organs of justice or administration, and only responsible to the Grand National Assembly (which appoints the Procurator-General for 4 years) and between its sessions, to the State Council. The Ministry of the Interior is responsible for ordinary police work. State security is the responsibility of the State Security Council. The death penalty was abolished in Jan 1990 and is forbidden by the 1991 constitution.

RUSSIA

The Supreme Court is the highest judicial body on civil, criminal and administrative law. The Supreme Arbitration Court deals with economic cases. The KGB, and the Federal Security Bureau which succeeded it, were replaced in Dec 1992 by the Federal Counter-Intelligence Service.

A new civil code was introduced in 1993 to replace the former Soviet code. It guarantees the inviolability of private property and includes provisions for the freedom of movement of capital and goods. The death penalty is retained for 5 crimes against the person. It is not applied to minors, women and men over 65. Twelve-member juries were introduced in a number of courts after Nov 1993.

SAN MARINO

Judges are appointed permanently by the Great and General Council; they may not be San Marino citizens. Petty civil cases are dealt with by a justice of the peace; legal commissioners deal with more serious civil cases and all criminal cases and appeals lie to them from the justice of the peace. Appeals against the legal commissioners lie to an appeals judge, and the Council of the Twelve functions as a court of third instance.

SERBIA

The judges were appointed by the King, but according to the constitution could not be removed against their will; however, when the constitution was suspended on 9 May 1894, their irremovability ceased. There were (1892) 22 courts of first instance, a court of appeal, a court of cassation, and a tribunal of commerce.

SLOVAKIA

The post-Communist judicial system was established by a federal law of Jul 1991. This provided for a unified system of 4 types of court: civil, criminal, commercial and administrative. Commercial courts arbitrate in disputes arising from business activities. Administrative courts examine the legality of the decisions of state institutions when appealed by citizens. In addition, there are military courts which operate under the jurisdiction of the Ministry of Defence. There is a Supreme Court, and a hierarchy of courts under the Ministry of Justice at republic, region and district level. District courts are courts of first instance. Cases are usually decided by Senates comprising a judge and 2 associate judges, though occasionally by a single judge. (Associate judges are citizens in good standing over the age of 25 who are elected for 4-year terms.)

Regional courts are courts of first instance in more serious cases and also courts of appeal for district courts. Cases are usually decided by a Senate of two judges and three associate judges, although again occasionally by a single judge. The Supreme Court interprets law as a guide to other courts and functions also as a court of appeal. Decisions are made by Senates of three judges. The judges of the Supreme Court are nominated by the President; other judges are appointed by the National Council.

SLOVENIA

There are 11 courts of first instance, 4 higher courts and a supreme court.

SPAIN

Justice is administered by *Tribunales* and *Juzgados* (Tribunals and Courts), which conjointly form the *Poder Judicial* (Judicial Power). Judges and magistrates cannot be removed, suspended or transferred except as set forth by law. The constitution of 1978 has established a new organ, the *Consejo General del Poder Judicial* (General Council of the Judicial Power), formed by 1 President and 20 magistrates, judges, attorneys and lawyers, governing the Judicial Power in full independence from the other 2 powers of the State, the Legislative (Cortes) and the Executive (President of the Government and his Cabinet). Its President is that of the *Tribunal Supremo*.

The Judicature is composed of the *Tribunal Supremo* (Supreme High Court); 17 *Audiencias Territoriales* (Division High Courts); 52 *Audiencias Provinciales* (Provincial High Courts); *Juzgados de Primera Instancia* (Courts of First Instance), *Juzgados de Distrito* (District Courts) and *Juzgados Municipales y de paz* (Municipal and Peace Courts, Courts of Lowest Jurisdiction held by Justices of the Peace).

The *Tribunal Supremo* consists of a President (appointed by the monarch, on proposal from the *Consejo General de Poder Judicial*) and various judges distributed among seven chambers; one for trying civil matters, three for administrative purposes, one for criminal trials, one for social matters and one for military cases. The *Tribunal Supremo* has disciplinary faculties; is court of cassation in all criminal trials; for administrative purposes decides in first and second instance disputes arising between private individuals and the state, and in social matters makes final decisions.

The jury system consisting of nine members became operative in Nov 1995 in criminal cases. First trials under a jury system began in May 1996.

The death penalty was abolished in 1978 by the Constitution (Art. 15). Divorce was allowed from Jul 1981 and abortion since Aug 1985. A new penal code came in force in May 1996 replacing the code of 1848. It provides for a maximum of 30 years' imprisonment in specified exceptional cases, with a normal maximum of 20 years. New offences include money laundering, misleading publicity, sexual harassment, damage to the environment, defamation in the press, sexual, racial, political or religious discrimination and incitement to genocide.

A new juvenile criminal law of 1995 lays emphasis on rehabilitation.

The *Audiencia Nacional* deals with terrorism, monetary offences and drug-trafficking where more than one province is involved. Its President is appointed by the General Council of the Judicial Power.

There is an Ombudsman (*Defensor del Pueblo*).

SWEDEN

The administration of justice is independent. The Attorney-General (appointed by the government) and three Ombudsmen exercise a check on judicial affairs administration.

There is a 3-tier hierarchy of courts: The Supreme Court, 6 intermediate courts of appeal, and 97 district courts. Of the district courts 27 also serve as real estate courts and 6 as water rights courts.

District courts are courts of first instance and deal with both civil and criminal cases. Petty cases are tried by one judge. Civil and criminal cases are tried as a rule by three to four judges or in minor cases by one judge. Disputes of greater consequence relating to the Marriage Code or the Code relating to Parenthood and Guardianship are tried by a judge and a jury of three–four lay assessors. More serious criminal cases are tried by a judge and jury of five members (lay assessors) in felony cases, and three members in misdemeanour cases. The cases in courts of appeal are generally tried by four or five judges, but the same cases, which are tried with a judge and jury in the first instance, are tried by three or four judges and a jury of two–three members.

Those with low incomes can receive free legal aid out of public funds. In criminal cases a suspected person has the right to a defence counsel, paid out of public funds.

The Attorney-General and the Judicial Commissioner for the Judiciary and Civil Administration (Ombudsman) supervise the application in the public sector of acts of parliament and regulations. The Attorney-General is the government's legal adviser and also the Public Prosecutor.

SWITZERLAND

The Federal Tribunal (*Bundes-Gericht*), which sits at Lausanne consists of 30 judges, with 15 supplementary judges, and 15 temporary supplementary judges elected by the Federal Assembly for 6 years and eligible for re-election; the President and Vice-President serve for 2 years and cannot be re-elected. The Tribunal has original and final jurisdiction in suits between the Confederation and cantons; between cantons and cantons; between the Confederation or cantons and corporations or individuals; between parties who refer their cases to it in such suits as the constitution or legislation of cantons places within its authority; and in many classes of railway suits. It is a court of appeal against decisions of other federal authorities, and of cantonal authorities applying federal laws. The Tribunal comprises 2 courts of public law, 2 civil courts, a chamber of bankruptcy, a chamber of prosecution, a court of criminal appeal, a court of extraordinary appeal, a federal criminal court and a criminal chamber for cases of treason (sitting very rarely).

On 3 Jul 1938 the Swiss electorate accepted a new federal penal code, to take the place of the separate cantonal penal codes. The new code, which abolished capital punishment, came into force on 1 Jan 1942.

A Federal Insurance Court sits at Lucerne and its judges are elected for six years by the Federal Assembly.

By federal law of 5 Oct 1950 several articles of the penal code concerning crimes against the independence of the state have been amended with a view to reinforcing the security of the state.

TURKEY

The unified legal system consists of: (1) justices of the peace (single judges with limited but summary penal and civil jurisdiction); (2) courts of first instance (single judges, dealing with cases outside the jurisdiction of (3) and (4); (3) central criminal courts (a President and two judges, dealing with cases where the crime is punishable by imprisonment over five years); (4) commercial courts (three judges); and (5) state security courts (a President and four judges, two of the latter being military).

The Council of State is the highest administration tribunal; it consists of 5 chambers. Its 31 judges are nominated from among high-ranking personalities in politics, economy, law, the army, etc. The Military Court of Cassation in Ankara is the highest military tribunal.

The Civil Code and the Code of Obligations have been adapted from the corresponding Swiss codes. The Penal Code is largely based upon the Italian Penal Code, and the Code of Civil Procedure closely resembles that of the Canton of Neuchâtel, Switzerland. The Commercial Code is based on the German.

UNION OF SOVIET SOCIALIST REPUBLICS (USSR)

The basis of the judiciary system was the same throughout the Soviet Union, but the constituent republics had the right to introduce modifications and to make their own rules for the application of the code of laws. The Supreme Court of the USSR was the chief court and supervising organ for all constituent republics and was elected by the Supreme Soviet of the USSR for five years. Supreme Courts of the Union and Autonomous Republics were elected by the Supreme Soviets of these republics, and Territorial, Regional and Area Courts by the respective Soviets, each for a term of five years. At the lowest level were the People's Courts, which were elected directly by the population.

Court proceedings were conducted in the local language with full interpreting facilities as required. All cases were heard in public, unless otherwise provided for by law, and the accused was guaranteed the right of defence.

Laws establishing common principles of criminal legislation, criminal responsibility for state and military crimes, judicial and criminal procedure and military tribunals were adopted by the Supreme Soviet on 25 Dec 1958 for the courts both of the USSR and the constituent Republics.

The Law Courts were divided into People's Courts and higher courts. The People's Courts consisted of the People's Judges and 2 Assessors, and their function was to examine, at the first instance, most of the civil and criminal cases, except the more important ones, some of which were tried at the Regional Court, and those of the highest importance at the Supreme Court. People's Judges and rota-lists of Assessors were elected directly by the citizens of each constituency: Judges for 5 years, Assessors for $2\frac{1}{2}$; they had to be over 25 years of age.

The Procurator-General of the USSR was appointed for five years by the Supreme Soviet. All procurators of the republics, autonomous republics and autonomous regions were appointed by the Procurator-General of the USSR for a term of five years. The procurators supervised the correct application of the law by all state organs, and had special responsibility for the observance of the law in places of detention. The procurators of the Union republics were subordinate to the Procurator-General of the USSR, whose duty was to see that acts of all institutions of the USSR were legal, that the law was correctly interpreted and uniformly applied.

Capital punishment was abolished on 26 May 1947, but was restored on 12 Jan 1950 for treason, espionage and sabotage; on 7 May 1954 for certain categories of murder; in Dec 1958 for terrorism and banditry; on 7 May 1961 for embezzlement of public property, counterfeiting and attacks on prison warders and, in particular circumstances, for attacks on the police and public order volunteers and for rape (15 Feb 1962), and for accepting bribes (20 Feb 1962). However, females and men who had reached 60 by the time of sentence were exempt.

In view of criminal abuses extending over many years, discovered in the security system, the powers of administrative trial and exile previously vested in the security authorities (MVD) were abolished in 1953; accelerated procedures for trial on charges of high treason, espionage, wrecking, etc., by the Supreme Court were abolished in 1955; and extensive powers of protection of persons under arrest or serving prison terms were vested in the Procurator-General's Office (1955). Supervisory commissions, composed of representatives of trade unions, youth organizations and local authorities, were set up in 1956 to inspect places of detention.

Further reforms of the civil and criminal codes were decreed on 25 Dec 1958. Thereby the age of criminal responsibility was raised from 14 to 16 years; deportation, banishment and deprivation of citizenship were abolished; a presumption of innocence was not accepted, but the burden of proof of guilt had been placed upon the prosecutor; secret trials and the charge of 'enemy of the people' were also abolished. Articles 70 and 100 of the Criminal Code, which dealt with 'anti-Soviet agitation and propaganda' and 'crimes against the system of administration' respectively, were, however, widely used against political dissidents but were abolished by 1990.

UNITED KINGDOM

Although the United Kingdom is a unitary state, it does not have a single body of law applicable universally within its limits. Scotland has its own distinctive legal system and law courts, and although a single parliament exists for Great Britain since 1707, common opinions on broader issues, and a common final court of appeal in civil cases have resulted in substantial identity on many points, differences in legal procedure and practice remain. In Northern Ireland on the other hand, the structure of the courts and legal procedure and practice have closely resembled those of England and Wales for centuries but, as Northern Ireland had its own parliament with defined powers (as well as being represented in the parliament at Westminster), its enacted law derives in certain spheres from a different source and may differ in substance from that which operates in England and Wales. However, a large volume of modern legislation, particularly in the social field, applies throughout the United Kingdom. A feature common to all systems of law in the United Kingdom (which differentiates them from some continental systems) is that there is no complete code, although the Law Commission is working on the codification of certain branches of law. The sources of law in all the systems include legislation and unwritten or 'common' law.

Legislation includes some 3000 Acts of Parliament and delegated or subordinate legislation made by ministers and others under powers conferred by parliament, Acts of Parliament being absolutely binding on all courts of the United Kingdom, and taking precedence over any other source of law. The common law of England originated in the customs of the realm and was built up by decisions of the courts. A supplementary system of law, known as 'equity', came into being during the Middle Ages to provide and enforce more effective protection for existing legal rights. It was administered by a separate court and later became a separate body of legal rules. In 1875 the courts of equity were fused with the courts of common law, so that all courts now apply both systems but, where they conflict, equity prevails. In Scotland the basic common law, which largely depends on the canon law of Rome, helped by continental commentators, is embodied in the writings of certain seventeenth-, eighteenth- and early nineteenth-century lawyers who, between them, described systematically almost the whole field of private and criminal law as existing in their times. Broadly speaking, the principles enunciated by these lawyers, together with the many judicial decisions which have followed and developed from those principles, form the body of Scots non-statutory law. Scotland has never had a separate system of equity – equitable principles having always permeated the ordinary rules of law. A feature common to the legal systems of the United Kingdom is the distinction made between the criminal law and the civil law. Criminal law is concerned with wrongs against the community as a whole; civil law is concerned with the rights, duties and obligations of individual members of the community between themselves.

YUGOSLAVIA

In the Socialist Federal Republic of Yugoslavia there were county tribunals, district courts, the Supreme Court of the Autonomous Province of Vojvodina, Supreme Courts of the constituent republics and the Supreme Court of the Socialist Federal Republic of Yugoslavia. In county tribunals and district courts the judicial functions were exercised by professional judges and by law assessors constituted into collegia. There were no assessors at the supreme courts.

All judges were elected by the social–political communities in their jurisdiction. The judges exercised their functions in accordance with the legal provisions enacted since the liberation of the country.

The constituent republics enacted their own criminal legislation, but offences concerning state security and the administration were dealt with at federal level.

FORMER YUGOSLAVIA
Serbia and Montenegro

The Federal Republic of Yugoslavia (Serbia and Montenegro) had (1999) 2 supreme courts, 32 district courts and 153 communal courts, with 1982 judges and 7621 lay assessors. There were 18 economic courts with 237 judges.

8

Defence and Treaties

PRINCIPAL EUROPEAN ARMED CONFLICTS SINCE 1900

ITALO–TURKISH WAR. *September 1911–1912*

On 29 Sep 1911 Italy declared war on the Ottoman Empire, with the aim of seizing Cyrenaica and Tripoli (modern Libya) to which they had long advanced claims. By November they had defeated the Turks in North Africa and in May 1912 occupied the Dodecanese islands in the Aegean. Italian finances suffered severely in the war, but the Ottoman Empire recognized their gains by the Treaty of Ouchy in October.

FIRST BALKAN WAR. *October 1912–1913*

Alliance of Balkan states (Bulgaria, Greece, Montenegro and Serbia) against Turkey. War began 1 Oct 1912. Ended by Treaty of London 30 May 1913. Turkey withdrew from most of her Balkan territory, on the understanding that a new and independent Albania would be created.

SECOND BALKAN WAR. *June–August 1913*

Friction between victors of First Balkan war. Bulgaria attacked Serbia and Greece 29 Jun 1913. They themselves were invaded by the Romanians and Turks and rapidly defeated. Settlement at the Treaty of Bucharest 10 Aug 1913; Turkey concluded peace treaties with Bulgaria 29 Sep 1913 and with Greece 14 Nov 1913.

WORLD WAR I (EUROPE). *July 1914–November 1918*

On 28 Jul 1914 Austria–Hungary declared war on Serbia. Austria was supported by her ally Germany, but they were faced by the 'Entente' powers, Russia, France and Britain. In late 1914 the Germans failed to capture Paris and the war settled into the deadlock of trench warfare. In 1915 the Entente tried to break the deadlock by expeditions to the Dardanelles and Salonika in south-east Europe, and by inducing Italy to attack Austria. In 1916 both sides launched grand offensives on the Western Front, the Germans against Verdun and the Allies on the Somme, but despite enormous casualties the deadlock continued. At sea the British and Germans fought the drawn battle of Jutland. In 1917 both sides were given hope – the Germans by the Russian Revolution (which eventually removed Russia from the war) and the Allies by the USA's entry into the war. The next year proved decisive. Germany agreed to an armistice in November. Her allies, Austria and the Ottoman Empire, had already given up the fight.

RUSSIAN CIVIL WAR. *June 1918–November 1920*

Civil War between Soviet Communists and White Russian forces, with intervention by outside powers on behalf of the anti-Communists. The first landing of British forces took place at Murmansk in Jun 1918, and further French and British troops landed at Archangel in Aug 1918; Japan and the United States also sent troops. The Civil War effectively ended when White Russian forces under General Wrangel evacuated the Crimea in Nov 1920.

RUSSO–POLISH WAR. *April 1919–October 1920*

Invasion by Polish forces of territory occupied by the Soviet Union as the German army withdrew at the end of World War I, in the hope of establishing a Soviet–Polish frontier which would give Poland possession of all the areas it traditionally claimed. After a Soviet counter-attack had been defeated, an armistice was signed on 12 Oct 1920, and a settlement was reached in the treaty of Riga (18 Mar 1921).

GRECO–TURKISH WAR. *January 1921–October 1922*

Greek invasion of Asian Turkey (Anatolia). This was repelled by the Turkish republican forces, and the Armistice of Mudanya (11 Oct 1922) ended the fighting. By the Treaty of Lausanne (24 Jul 1923), Greece renounced any claim to territory in Asia Minor, whilst Turkey surrendered all claims to territories of the Ottoman empire occupied by non-Turks.

SPANISH CIVIL WAR. *July 1936–March 1939*

A revolt by military leaders in Spanish Morocco against the civilian government led to general civil war. Unofficial military assistance was given by Germany, Italy, Portugal and the USSR; in all, 40 000 foreign volunteers including 2000 British, fought in the International Brigade on the republican side. The civil war ended when General Franco's Nationalist forces entered Madrid on 28 Mar 1939.

WORLD WAR II (EUROPE). *September 1939–May 1945*

German forces invaded Poland on 1 Sep 1939, which led Britain and France to declare war on Germany on 3 Sep. The Germans invaded the Low Countries on 10 May 1940, and France was compelled to sign an armistice on 22 Jun, the British army being evacuated from Dunkirk. Italy declared war on Britain and France on 10 Jun 1940. Breaking the Nazi–Soviet Pact of Aug 1939, Hitler invaded Russia on 22 Jun 1941. Allied forces drove Italian and German armies out of North Africa and invaded Italy in 1943. The invasion of Normandy was launched on 6 Jun 1944, and Germany was forced to accept unconditional surrender on 7 May 1945.

RUSSO–FINNISH WAR. *November 1939–March 1940*

Soviet forces invaded Finland following Finnish rejection of demands for territorial concessions. The war was ended by the Treaty of Moscow (12 Mar 1940), in which the Finns surrendered to Russia the south-eastern part of the country.

GREEK CIVIL WAR. *1946–1949*

Civil war between Communist partisan forces and the civilian government. The likelihood of a Communist victory was reduced by the break between Yugoslavia and the Communist bloc in 1948, which led to the closing of one stretch of Greece's northern frontier to the rebels. The Greek Communist broadcasting station announced the end of open hostilities on 16 Oct 1949.

GERMAN DEMOCRATIC REPUBLIC UPRISING. *June 1953*

Demonstrations in East Berlin and other cities of the German Democratic Republic against Russian domination began on 17 Jun 1953, but were suppressed by Soviet armed forces.

HUNGARIAN UPRISING. *October 1956*

Student demonstrations on 23 Oct 1956 led to a general uprising against the civil government and Soviet occupying power. On 27 Oct Soviet troops were forced to evacuate Budapest, but reinforcements arrived to surround the capital, and after ten days' fighting the uprising was suppressed.

INVASION OF CZECHOSLOVAKIA. *August 1968*

During the night of 20–21 Aug, Soviet troops and Warsaw Pact forces from Poland, Hungary, German Democratic Republic and Bulgaria occupied Prague and other leading cities to reverse the liberalizing reforms of the Czechoslovakian government. Though the Czechoslovakian armed forces were ordered to offer no resistance, there were extensive civilian demonstrations against the occupying forces.

TURKISH INVASION OF CYPRUS. *July–August 1974*

On 15 Jul 1974 a *coup* was staged by men of the Greek ruling junta for the overthrow of President Makarios and fighting between Greek and Turkish Cypriots led to a Turkish invasion of Cyprus on 20 Jul. A cease-fire on 22 Jul was followed by peace talks between Britain, Greece and Turkey at Geneva, but there was renewed fighting 14–16 Aug. Turkey was left in control of the northern two-fifths of the island.

YUGOSLAVIAN CIVIL WAR (SERBO–CROAT WAR). *1991–1995*

Declarations of independence by the former Yugoslav Republics of Slovenia and Croatia led to clashes on Slovenian borders from Jul 1991, followed by heavy fighting on Croatian territory between Croatian militia and Serbian irregulars (chetniks) backed by the Yugoslav Federal Army. Main centres of fighting were eastern and central Croatia and the Adriatic coast around Dubrovnik. Yugoslavia officially ceased to exist in Jan 1992 and Slovenia and Croatia were recognized as independent states.

On 29 Feb 1992, Muslim leaders in Bosnia–Hercegovina declared independence. Bosnian Serbs and the Serbian leadership in Belgrade rejected this, and war began on 6 Apr with the opening of the siege of the capital Sarajevo; Serbs were accused of 'ethnic cleansing' to secure territorial domination, and a UN trade embargo was imposed on Serbia on 31 May. Peace talks in Geneva, mediated by Lord Owen and Cyrus Vance, began on 26 Aug. On 16 Nov a UN naval blockade was mounted against Serbia and Montenegro. Fighting continued as a further peace conference was held in Geneva on 22–23 Jan 1993. Serbs attacked Muslim enclaves at Srebenica and Goradze. Numerous peace talks collapsed. In 1995 Croatia launched major offensives and an uneasy peace accord was signed at Dayton (Ohio).

RUSSIA-CHECHNYA WARS. *1994–1996, 1999 – continuing*

Russian troops were ordered into Chechnya in Dec 1994 to end the rebel Republic's bid for independence. Fighting ensued for 21 months as Russian troops failed to subdue the population. The fighting was the worst on Russian soil since the Second World War, with Grozny, the Chechnya capital, razed to the ground. The Russian army suffered a major loss of face. On 31 Aug 1996 Russia and Chechnya signed a peace deal, freezing the issue of independence for 5 years.

However, partly provoked by Chechen support for guerrillas in the adjacent Caucasus region of Dagestan, and partly because of terrorist bomb outrages in Russia itself, a renewed Russian offensive was launched against Chechnya in Sep 1999. Massive Russian aerial bombardment was followed by a major ground offensive against Grozny launched on 25 Dec 1999.

THE KOSOVO CONFLICT. *1998–1999*

The autonomous status of Kosovo (within Yugoslavia, but largely inhabited by Kosovar Albanians) was abolished in 1989 and Albanian cultural institutions suppressed. Ethnic Albanians declared a Republic. From Jul to Sep 1998 the Kosovo Liberation Army expanded its control to 40 per cent of Kosovo. Serb forces launched a massive and brutal counter-offensive, with hundreds of thousands of refugees fleeing. NATO air strikes were authorized on 12 Oct 1998 and Milosevic backed down. The crisis resumed in 1999. On 24 Mar 1999 NATO launched its air campaign against Yugoslavia. After numerous NATO bombing errors, and with Milosevic refusing to capitulate, it was only the assembly of a NATO ground invasion force which forced the Serb parliament to accept a peace deal on 3 Jun 1999.

PRINCIPAL ARMED CONFLICTS (OUTSIDE EUROPE) IN WHICH EUROPEAN POWERS PARTICIPATED 1900–2000

BOXER REBELLION (CHINA). *June 1900–September 1901*

The outbreak of rebellion against foreigners in China, provoked by the expansion of European commerce and territorial acquisitions in China by Germany, Russia and Britain. Major Boxer disturbances occurred in Peking and the provinces of Shensi and Manchuria. It was suppressed by forces from the major European powers as well as the United States and Japan.

RUSSO–JAPANESE WAR. *February 1904–September 1905*

Japan launched a surprise attack on the Russian Far East in Port Arthur on 4 Feb 1904. The Russians suffered major military reverses, culminating at the battle of Mukden. The main Russian fleet was defeated at Tsushima in May 1905. Although the war was ended by the Treaty of Portsmouth (New Hampshire), the military reverses provided a major catalyst of revolutionary activity in Russia.

ABYSSINIAN WAR. *October 1935–July 1936*

Italy invaded Abyssinia on 3 Oct 1935. Addis Ababa was captured on 5 May 1936, and the Emperor Haile Selassie was forced into exile in Britain. The League of Nations imposed sanctions on Italy, but these proved ineffective; they were lifted in Jul 1936.

WORLD WAR II (ASIA). *December 1941–August 1945*

Japan attacked the American base at Pearl Harbor on 7 Dec 1941, and within six months the Japanese were masters of South-east Asia and Burma. The Allied counter-offensive culminated in the dropping of the first atomic bombs on Hiroshima and Nagasaki in Aug 1945. On 15 Aug 1945 the Emperor of Japan broadcast to the nation to cease fighting. The principal European powers involved in the conflict were Britain and the Netherlands; the Soviet Union also declared war on Japan on 8 Aug 1945.

FIRST VIETNAM WAR. *December 1946–July 1954*

The war between the French colonial government and Communist forces led by Ho Chi Minh began with attacks on French garrisons by Vietminh troops throughout Vietnam on 19 Dec 1946. The French army was defeated at Dien Bien Phu in May 1954, and the war was ended by the Geneva Agreement of 21 Jul 1954, which divided Vietnam into the area north of the 17th parallel and an independent South Vietnam.

MALAYAN EMERGENCY. *July 1948–July 1960*

Insurgency by Communist forces, eventually suppressed by British and Malayan troops. The State of Emergency was ended on 31 Jul 1960. British troops were also involved in the 'confrontation' with Indonesia after the creation of the Malaysia Federation on 16 Sep 1963. An agreement was reached ending confrontation on 1 Jun 1966.

KOREAN WAR. *June 1950–July 1953*

The invasion of South Korea by North Korea on 25 Jun 1950 led to intervention by United Nations forces following an emergency session of the Security Council. The advance of the United Nations forces into North Korea on 1 Oct 1950 led to the entry of the Chinese into the war. An armistice was signed at Panmunjom on 27 Jul 1953. The European powers which contributed to the United Nations force were Britain, France, Turkey, Belgium, Luxembourg, the Netherlands and Greece.

ALGERIAN REVOLUTIONARY WAR. *October 1954–March 1962*

The uprising by the FLN (Front de Libération Nationale) against the French colonial government began during the night of 31 Oct–1 Nov 1954. A cease-fire agreement was signed on 18 Mar 1962, and after a referendum the independence of Algeria was recognized on 3 Jul 1962.

SUEZ WAR. *October–November 1956*

The Israeli army attacked Egypt on 29 Oct 1956. The rejection of a British and French ultimatum by Egypt resulted in a combined British and French attack on Egypt on 31 Oct. Hostilities ended at midnight on 6–7 Nov following the call for a cease-fire by the United Nations.

PORTUGAL'S WARS IN AFRICA. *1961–1975*

The struggle for independence against colonial rule in Portugal's African colonies began with an uprising in Angola in 1961 and spread to Guinea-Bissau and Mozambique. The conflicts put a growing strain on Portugal and by 1974 her forces had suffered some 11000 dead and 30000 wounded. Following the overthrow of the Portuguese government by a *coup d'état* in Apr 1974, independence was rapidly granted to Angola (11 Nov 1975), Guinea-Bissau (10 Sep 1974) and Mozambique (25 Jun 1975).

SOVIET INVASION OF AFGHANISTAN. *December 1979*

The instability of the Soviet-backed régime and growing resistance to its reforms led to a full-scale Russian invasion of Afghanistan on 27 Dec 1979. A new government under Babrak Karmal was installed, but a considerable Soviet military presence had to be maintained in the country to combat the Mujaheddin guerrillas. All Soviet troops were withdrawn by 15 Feb 1989.

FALKLANDS CONFLICT. *April–June 1982*

On 2 Apr 1982 Argentinian forces invaded East Falkland to assert Argentina's longstanding claim to sovereignty over the Falkland Islands. The first warships of the British Task Force sailed for the South Atlantic three days later. British troops established a beachhead at San Carlos on East Falkland on 21 May and Argentinian forces surrendered on 14 Jun.

THE GULF WAR. *August 1990–February 1991*

On 2 Aug 1990, Kuwait was invaded by Iraqi forces. US naval forces were sent to the Gulf and troops to Saudi Arabia. On 8 Aug 1990 Iraq announced the annexation of Kuwait. Britain joined the Allied forces in Operation 'Desert Storm' to repel the Iraqis from Kuwait. On 26 Feb 1991 Kuwait City was liberated by the Allies but Saddam Hussein retained power in Iraq.

WORLD WAR I EUROPEAN BELLIGERENTS

	Population (in millions)	Total mobilized (in thousands)	Soldiers killed or died of wounds (in thousands)
Austria–Hungary	47	7800	1200
Belgium	7	267	14
Britain	41	8904	908
Bulgaria	4	560	87
France	39	8410	1363
Germany	63	11000	1774
Italy	33	5615	560
Romania	7	750	336
Russia	150	12000	1700

WORLD WAR I EUROPEAN BELLIGERENTS (*continued*)

	Population (in millions)	Total mobilized (in thousands)	Soldiers killed or died of wounds (in thousands)
Serbia	3	707	45
Turkey	26	2850	325

Source: Quincy Wright, *A Study of War*, The University of Chicago Press, 1942: second edition, 1965.

WORLD WAR I – DECLARATIONS OF WAR (EUROPEAN POWERS AND THE UNITED STATES) BY COUNTRY

Austria–Hungary declared war on:	Serbia 28 July 1914; Russia 6 Aug 1914; Montenegro 9 Aug 1914; Belgium 22 Aug 1914; Portugal 15 Mar 1916
Britain declared war on:	Germany 4 Aug 1914; Austria–Hungary 12 Aug 1914; Turkey 5 Nov 1914; Bulgaria 15 Oct 1915
Bulgaria declared war on:	Romania 1 Sep 1916
France declared war on:	Austria–Hungary 13 Aug 1914; Turkey 5 Nov 1914; Bulgaria 16 Oct 1915
Germany declared war on:	Russia 1 Aug 1914; France 3 Aug 1914; Belgium 4 Aug 1914; Portugal 9 Mar 1916; Romania 28 Aug 1916
Greece declared war on:	Austria–Hungary, Bulgaria, Germany and Turkey 2 July 1917
Italy declared war on:	Austria–Hungary 23 May 1915; Turkey 21 Aug 1915; Bulgaria 19 Oct 1915; Germany 27 Aug 1916
Montenegro declared war on:	Austria–Hungary 5 Aug 1914; Germany 9 Aug 1914; Bulgaria 15 Oct 1915
Romania declared war on:	Austria–Hungary 27 Aug 1916
Russia declared war on:	Turkey 1 Nov 1914; Bulgaria 19 Oct 1915
Serbia declared war on:	Germany 6 Aug 1914; Turkey 2 Nov 1914; Bulgaria 16 Oct 1915
Turkey declared war on:	Romania 30 Aug 1916
United States declared war on:	Germany 6 Apr 1917; Austria–Hungary 7 Dec 1917

WORLD WAR II PRINCIPAL EUROPEAN BELLIGERENTS

	Population (in millions)	Total mobilized (in thousands)	Soldiers killed or died of wounds (in thousands)	Civilians killed (in thousands)
Belgium	8	625	8	101
Britain	48	5 896	557	61
Bulgaria	7	450	10	..
Czechoslovakia	15	150	10	490
Denmark	4	25	4	..
Finland	4	500	79	..
France	39	5 000	202	108
Germany	71	10 200	3 250	500
Greece	6	414	73	400
Hungary	9	350	147	..
Italy	44	3 100	149	783
Netherlands	9	410	7	242
Norway	3	75	2	2
Poland	35	1 000	64	2000
Romania	14	1 136	520	–
Soviet Union	175	22 000	7500	7500
Yugoslavia	15	3 741	410	1275

Source: Quincy Wright, *A Study of War*, The University of Chicago Press, 1942: second edition, 1965.

PEACE TREATIES ARISING FROM WORLD WAR I 1918–1923

TREATY OF BREST-LITOVSK. *3 March 1918*

The Soviet Union surrendered the Baltic Provinces and Russian Poland to the Central Powers, recognized the independence of Finland and the Ukraine, and ceded to Turkey the districts of Kars, Ardahan and Batum. The Treaty was formally invalidated by the Armistice in the West on 11 Nov 1918.

TREATY OF VERSAILLES. *28 June 1919*

The peace treaty between Germany and the Allied Powers. Germany surrendered territory to Belgium, Denmark, Poland and Czechoslovakia; Alsace-Lorraine was ceded to France. Germany also surrendered all her overseas territories. The Rhineland was declared a demilitarized zone, with Allied occupation for 15 years from when the Treaty came into effect on 10 Jan 1920. Severe restrictions were placed on the German Armed Forces; the army was limited to 100000 men. The union of Germany and Austria was forbidden. The Treaty declared Germany's responsibility for causing the war, and made Germany liable for the payment of Reparations. The Treaty also contained the Covenant of the League of Nations.

TREATY OF ST GERMAIN. *10 September 1919*

The peace treaty between the Austrian Republic and the Allied Powers. By the settlement Austria lost territory to Italy, Yugoslavia, Czechoslovakia, Poland and Romania. Hungary was recognized as an independent state, and the union of Austria and Germany was forbidden. The Austrian army was limited to 30000 men, and the Republic was made liable for the payment of Reparations.

TREATY OF NEUILLY. *17 November 1919*

The peace treaty between Bulgaria and the Allied Powers. Bulgaria lost Western Thrace to Greece, and territory to Yugoslavia. The Bulgarian army was limited to 20000 men, and Bulgaria was made liable for Reparations.

TREATY OF TRIANON. *4 June 1920*

The peace treaty between Hungary and the Allied Powers. Hungary surrendered territory to Romania, Czechoslovakia, Yugoslavia, Poland, Italy and the Austrian Republic, to a total of about two-thirds of its pre-war lands. The Hungarian army was limited to 35000 and Hungary was made liable for Reparations.

TREATY OF SÈVRES. *10 August 1920*

The peace treaty made with Ottoman Turkey, but never ratified by the Turks.

TREATY OF LAUSANNE. *24 July 1923*

Treaty made necessary by Turkey's refusal to accept the treaty of Sèvres. Turkey surrendered its claims to territories of the Ottoman Empire occupied by non-Turks, whilst retaining Constantinople and Eastern Thrace in Europe. The Greeks surrendered Smyrna, but were confirmed in possession of all the Aegean Islands except Imbros and Tenedos which were returned to Turkey. Turkey recognized the annexation of Cyprus by Britain and of the Dodecanese by Italy. The Bosphorus and the Dardanelles were declared to be demilitarized. (By the Montreux Convention of 20 Jul 1936 Turkey was permitted to re-fortify the Straits.)

TREATIES, AGREEMENTS AND ALLIANCES BETWEEN EUROPEAN COUNTRIES SINCE 1900

6 Oct 1900	London	Britain and Germany
20 Dec 1900	Rome	Austria–Hungary and Italy
Dec–Nov 1902	Rome	France and Italy
7 Sep 1901	Peking	Germany, Austria–Hungary, Belgium, Spain, United States, France, Britain, Italy, Japan, the Netherlands, Russia and China
4–17 Apr 1902	Bucharest	Austria–Hungary and Romania (with accession of Germany and Italy)
1 Jun 1902	Berlin	Austria–Hungary and Germany
28 Jun 1902	Berlin	Austria–Hungary, Germany and Italy
31 Mar 1904	Sofia	Bulgaria and Serbia
8 Apr 1904	London	Britain and France
2–15 Oct 1904	St Petersburg	Austria–Hungary and Russia
3 Oct 1904	Paris	France and Spain
7 Apr 1906	Algeciras	Britain, Austria–Hungary, Belgium, France, Germany, Italy, Morocco, Portugal, the Netherlands, Russia, Spain, Sweden and United States
31 Aug 1907	St Petersburg	Britain and Russia
9 Feb 1909	Berlin	France and Germany
30 Nov–15 Dec 1909	Vienna–Rome	Austria–Hungary and Italy
4 Nov 1911	Berlin	France and Germany
29 Feb 1912	Sofia	Bulgaria and Serbia
29 Apr 1912	Varna	Bulgaria and Serbia
16–29 May 1912	Sofia	Bulgaria and Greece
16 Jul 1912	Paris	France and Russia
12 Sep–6 Oct 1912	Lucerne	Serbia and Montenegro
22 Sep 1912	Sofia	Greece and Bulgaria
15 Oct 1912	Ouchy	Italy and Turkey
28 Oct 1912	Paris	France and Italy
5 Dec 1912	Vienna	Austria–Hungary, Germany and Italy

5 Feb 1913	Bucharest	Austria–Hungary and Romania (with accession of Germany and Italy)
22 Apr–5 May 1913	Athens	Greece and Serbia
1–14 May 1913	Salonika	Greece and Serbia
19 May–1 Jun 1913	Salonika	Greece and Serbia
30 May 1913	London	Turkey and Balkan allies
28 Jul–10 Aug 1913	Bucharest	Bulgaria, Romania, Greece, Montenegro and Serbia
2 Aug 1913	Vienna	Austria–Hungary, Germany and Italy
29 Sep 1913	Constantinople	Turkey and Bulgaria
14 Nov 1913	Athens	Turkey and Greece
15 Jun 1914	London	Britain and Germany
12 Aug 1914	Lisbon	Britain and Portugal
5 Sep 1914	London	Britain, France and Russia (accessions: Japan and Italy)
3 Mar 1918	Treaty of Brest-Litovsk	Russia and the Central Powers
28 Jun 1919	Treaty of Versailles	Germany and the Allied Powers
10 Sep 1919	Treaty of St Germain	Austrian Republic and the Allied Powers
27 Nov 1919	Treaty of Neuilly	Bulgaria and the Allied Powers
4 Jun 1920	Treaty of Trianon	Hungary and the Allied Powers
Aug 1920	Franco–Belgian Military Convention	
10 Aug 1920	Treaty of Sèvres	Turkey and the Allied Powers (not ratified by Turkey)
19 Feb 1921	Franco–Polish Treaty	
3 Mar 1921	Polish–Romanian Treaty	
18 Mar 1921	Treaty of Riga	Poland and the Soviet Union
16 Apr 1922	Treaty of Rapallo	Russia and Germany
31 Aug 1922	Little Entente	Czechoslovakia, Yugoslavia and Romania
24 Jul 1923	Treaty of Lausanne	

1 Dec 1925	Locarno Treaties	France, Belgium, Germany; guaranteed by Britain and Italy
24 Apr 1926	Soviet–German Neutrality Pact	
15 Jul 1932	Polish–Soviet Treaty	
26 Jan 1934	Polish–German Pact	
2 May 1935	Franco–Russian Alliance	
20 Jul 1936	Montreux Convention	Turkey permitted to re-fortify the Straits
25 Nov 1936	Anti-Comintern Pact	Germany and Japan; signed by Italy 6 Nov 1937
2 Jan 1937	Anglo–Italian Gentleman's Agreement	
29 Sep 1938	Munich Agreement	Britain, France, Germany, Italy
22 May 1939	Pact of Steel	Germany and Italy
23 Aug 1939	Nazi–Soviet Pact	
25 Aug 1939	Polish–British Treaty	
19 Oct 1939	British–French–Turkish Agreement	
12 Mar 1940	Treaty of Moscow	Ended war between Finland and Soviet Union
27 Sep 1940	Tripartite Pact	Germany, Italy, Japan
26 May 1942	Anglo–Soviet Treaty	
12 Dec 1943	Soviet–Czech Pact	
10 Dec 1944	Franco–Soviet Treaty	
21 Apr 1945	Soviet–Polish Pact	
4 Mar 1947	Dunkirk Treaty	Britain and France
10 Mar 1947	Polish–Czech Pact	
16 Dec 1947	Bulgarian–Albanian Pact	
16 Jan 1948	Bulgarian–Romanian Pact	
24 Jan 1948	Hungarian–Romanian Pact	
4 Feb 1948	Soviet–Romanian Pact	
18 Feb 1948	Soviet–Hungarian Pact	
17 Mar 1948	Brussels Treaty	Britain, France, Benelux
18 Mar 1948	Soviet–Bulgarian Pact	

5 Apr	1948	Soviet–Finnish Pact	
23 Apr	1948	Bulgarian–Czech Pact	
9 Jun	1948	Polish–Hungarian Pact	
18 Jun	1948	Bulgarian–Hungarian Pact	
21 Jul	1948	Romanian–Czech Pact	
21 Jan	1949	Polish–Romanian Pact	
4 Apr	1949	North Atlantic Treaty	See p. 14.
16 Apr	1949	Hungarian–Czech Pact	
9 Aug	1954	Balkan Pact	Greece, Turkey, Yugoslavia
24 Feb	1955	Baghdad Pact	Turkey and Iraq; Britain 5 Apr 1955; Pakistan 23 Sep 1955
5 May	1955	London and Paris Agreements	
13 May	1955	Warsaw Pact	See p. 31.
15 May	1955	Austrian State Treaty	
22 Jan	1963	Franco–Federal German Treaty	
27 Nov	1963	Soviet–Czech Pact	
12 Jun	1964	Soviet–Democratic German Pact	
8 Apr	1965	Soviet–Polish Pact	
1 Mar	1967	Polish–Czech Treaty	
15 Mar	1967	Polish–Democratic German Treaty	
17 Mar	1967	Democratic German–Czech Treaty	
13 May	1967	Soviet–Bulgarian Pact	
18 May	1967	Hungarian–Democratic German Pact	
6 Apr	1967	Polish–Bulgarian Pact	
7 Sep	1967	Soviet–Hungarian Pact	
7 Sep	1967	Bulgarian–Democratic German Pact	
26 Apr	1968	Bulgarian–Czech Pact	
16 May	1968	Polish–Hungarian Pact	
10 Jul	1969	Bulgarian–Hungarian Pact	
20 Mar	1970	Soviet–Czech Pact	
7 Jul	1970	Soviet–Romanian Pact	

12 Aug	1970	Soviet–Federal German Treaty	
12 Nov	1970	Polish–Romanian Treaty	
7 Dec	1970	Polish–Federal German Treaty	
26 Mar	1972	British–Maltese Agreement	Seven-year agreement on bases
21 Dec	1972	Federal German– Democratic German Treaty	Normalization of relations
11 Dec	1973	Czech–Federal German Treaty	
14 Jun	1975	Portuguese–Romanian Treaty	
7 Oct	1975	Soviet–Democratic German Treaty	
10 Nov	1975	Treaty of Osimo	
24 Mar	1977	Democratic German– Hungarian Treaty	
28 May	1977	Democratic German–Polish Treaty	
14 Sep	1977	Democratic German– Bulgarian Treaty	
3 Oct	1977	Democratic German–Czech Treaty	
20 Jun	1983	Soviet–Finnish Treaty	Renewed for 20 years
12 Jun	1985	Portugal, Spain, EC	Treaty of Accession
15 Nov	1985	Anglo–Irish Agreement	
1 Feb	1986	Single European Act	Creation of Single European Market in EU
14 Apr	1988	USSR–Afghanistan	Geneva Accord ending war
2 Dec	1989	USSR–Vatican	Re-establish diplomatic relations
Feb	1990	Hungary–Vatican	Re-establish diplomatic relations
27 Feb	1990	USSR–Czechoslovakia	Agreement on troop withdrawal
10 Mar	1990	USSR–Hungary	Agreement on troop withdrawal
19 Jun	1990	Schengen Agreement	Abolition of borders within EC states

12 Sep	1990	German Final Settlement Treaty	Union of two Germanies, end of allied role in Germany
19 Nov	1990	Conventional Forces in Europe Treaty	
6 Sep	1991	USSR–Baltic States	Independence of Estonia, Latvia and Lithuania recognized
18 Oct	1991	USSR–Israel	Diplomatic relations established
11 Dec	1991	Treaty of Maastricht	Agreement on future development of European Union (ratified later by individual countries)
7 Feb	1992	Russia–France	Treaty of Solidarity
21 Jul	1992	Russia–Moldova	Settlement of Transdniestra question
3 Aug	1992	Russia–Ukraine	Division of Black Sea fleet
Sep	1992	Russia–Lithuania	Agreement on troop withdrawals
Apr	1993	Russia–Latvia	Agreement on troop withdrawals
21 Nov	1995	Dayton Accord	Warring parties agreement to end war in Bosnia-Hercegovina (Bosnia, Croatia, Yugoslavia)
16 Mar	1996	Hungary–Slovakia	Bilateral agreement on outstanding issues (followed by Hungarian–Romanian agreement)
Dec	1996	Russia–China	Troop reductions along 2700-mile frontier
May	1997	Russia–NATO	Permanent Joint Council established under NATO–Russia Founding Act as a venue for consultation
Jul	1997	Ukraine–NATO	Partnership agreement between signatories
5 Dec	1998	Anglo–French Agreement	Agreement on future EU defence policy concluded at St Malo
2 Dec	1999	Anglo–Irish Treaty	Implementation of Good Friday Agreement of 10 Apr 1998
8 Dec	1999	Russia–Belarus	Treaty to pave way for joint tax system from 2001 and currency union from 2005

OUTLINE OF PRINCIPAL EUROPEAN DEFENCE TREATIES AND AGREEMENTS SINCE 1918

FRANCO–BELGIAN MILITARY CONVENTION. *August 1920*

The abrogation of treaties for the neutralization of Belgium was confirmed in a treaty signed by Britain, France and Belgium on 22 May 1926. Belgium announced its return to neutrality in Oct 1936 after the remilitarization of the Rhineland (7 Mar 1936), thereby preventing the vital co-ordination of strategic planning with France prior to World War II.

FRANCO–POLISH TREATY. *19 February 1921*

Provided for mutual defence against unprovoked aggression. Poland concluded a similar treaty with Romania on 3 Mar 1921.

TREATY OF RAPALLO. *16 April 1922*

Germany and Soviet Russia re-established diplomatic relations, renounced financial claims on either side, and pledged economic co-operation. The Treaty was reaffirmed by the German–Soviet Neutrality Pact of 24 Apr 1926.

THE LITTLE ENTENTE. *31 August 1922*

Bilateral agreements between Yugoslavia, Czechoslovakia and Romania were consolidated into a single treaty in Aug 1922, and further strengthened in May 1929. The object of the Little Entente was the maintenance of the *status quo* in Central Europe.

LOCARNO TREATIES. *1 December 1925*

The signatories, France, Germany and Belgium, recognized the inviolability of the Franco–German and Belgo–German frontier, and the existence of the demilitarized zone of the Rhineland; this was guaranteed by Britain and Italy. Franco–Polish and Franco–Czech Treaties of Mutual Guarantee were also signed, and action under these treaties was not to be regarded as aggression against Germany. The treaty was violated on 7 Mar 1936 when Hitler sent troops into the Rhineland.

POLISH–SOVIET TREATY. *25 July 1932*

A non-aggression treaty, valid for five years. It was prolonged for ten years in Dec 1934 after the signing of a Polish–German Treaty.

POLISH–GERMAN TREATY. *26 January 1934*

A non-aggression treaty, valid for ten years; repudiated by Hitler on 28 Apr 1939.

FRANCO–RUSSIAN ALLIANCE. *2 May 1935*

Provided for mutual aid in the event of unprovoked aggression.

ANGLO–GERMAN NAVAL AGREEMENT. *18 June 1935*

Limited the German navy to 35 per cent of the British, with submarines at 45 per cent or equality in the event of danger from Russia.

ANTI-COMINTERN PACT. 25 *November 1936*

Signed by Germany and Japan to oppose the spread of communism. Italy joined the Pact on 6 Nov 1937.

ANGLO–ITALIAN 'GENTLEMAN'S AGREEMENT'. *2 January 1937*

An agreement to maintain the *status quo* in the Mediterranean.

MUNICH AGREEMENT. *29 September 1938*

An agreement reached by Britain, France, Italy and Germany, by which territorial concessions were to be made to Germany, Poland and Hungary at the expense of Czechoslovakia. The rump of Czechoslovakia was to be guaranteed against unprovoked aggression, but German control was extended to the rest of Czechoslovakia in Mar 1939.

THE PACT OF STEEL. *22 May 1939*

The formal treaty of alliance between Italy and Germany. Prior to this Mussolini had announced the existence of the 'Rome–Berlin Axis' in a speech at Milan on 1 Nov 1936.

NAZI–SOVIET PACT. *23 August 1939*

The Soviet Union agreed to remain neutral if Germany was involved in a war. The Pact was broken when Hitler invaded Russia on 22 Jun 1941.

BRITISH–POLISH TREATY. *25 August 1939*

A mutual assistance treaty, subsequent to the Franco–British guarantee against aggression given to Poland on 31 Mar 1939.

BRITISH–FRENCH–TURKISH AGREEMENT. *19 October 1939*

A mutual assistance treaty. Turkey, however, remained neutral until 1 Mar 1945, and signed a treaty of non-aggression with Germany in Jun 1941.

TRIPARTITE PACT. *27 September 1940*

Germany, Italy and Japan undertook to assist each other if one of them was attacked by a power not already in the war. The Pact was signed by Hungary, Romania, Slovakia, Bulgaria and Yugoslavia 1940–1941.

ANGLO–SOVIET TREATY. *26 May 1942*

A treaty of alliance and mutual assistance, valid for 20 years. The treaty was abrogated by the Soviet Union on 7 May 1955 as a result of the ratification of the London and Paris Agreements by the British government.

FRANCO–SOVIET TREATY. *10 December 1944*

A treaty of alliance and mutual assistance, valid for 20 years. The treaty was abrogated by the Soviet Union on 7 May 1955 as a result of the ratification of the London and Paris Agreements by the French government.

DUNKIRK TREATY. *4 March 1947*

Treaty of alliance between Britain and France, valid for 50 years.

BRUSSELS TREATY. *17 March 1948*

An agreement signed by France, Britain and the Benelux countries for mutual aid in military, economic and social matters.

NORTH ATLANTIC TREATY. *4 April 1949*

Collective Security treaty signed by Belgium, Britain, Canada, Denmark, France, Iceland, Italy, Luxembourg, the Netherlands, Norway, Portugal and the United States. Greece and Turkey joined NATO in Feb 1952, and the Federal Republic of Germany joined in May 1955. *See also* p. 14.

BALKAN PACT. *9 August 1954*

A treaty of alliance, political co-operation and mutual assistance signed by Greece, Turkey and Yugoslavia, and valid for 20 years.

BAGHDAD PACT. *24 February 1955*

A mutual assistance treaty signed by Turkey and Iraq. Britain joined the Pact on 5 Apr 1955, and Pakistan on 23 Sep 1955.

LONDON AND PARIS AGREEMENTS. *5 May 1955*

The occupation régime in West Germany was ended, and the German Federal Republic attained full sovereignty and independence. The Federal

Republic became a member of NATO, and of the Western European Union, the expanded Brussels Treaty Organization which came into being on 5 May.

WARSAW PACT. *13 May 1955*

A treaty of friendship, co-operation and mutual assistance signed by the Soviet Union, Poland, Czechoslovakia, German Democratic Republic, Hungary, Romania, Bulgaria and Albania. The treaty also provided for the creation of a unified command for all the countries.

AUSTRIAN STATE TREATY. *15 May 1955*

Signed by the Soviet Union, Britain, France and the United States, the treaty re-established Austria as a sovereign, independent and neutral state.

FRANCO–WEST GERMAN TREATY. *22 January 1963*

Treaty of co-operation, providing for co-ordination of the two countries' policies in foreign affairs, defence, information and cultural affairs.

SOVIET–FEDERAL GERMANY TREATY. *12 August 1970*

A treaty renouncing the use of force.

POLISH–FEDERAL GERMAN TREATY. *7 December 1970*

An agreement that the existing boundary line on the Oder and the West Neisse constitutes the western frontier of Poland, and renouncing the use of force for the settlement of disputes.

TREATY OF OSIMO. *10 November 1975*

A treaty between Italy and Yugoslavia in which the two countries accepted border changes around Trieste slightly in favour of Italy, that national minorities were to be protected and there was to be greater economic co-operation.

CONVENTIONAL FORCES IN EUROPE TREATY. *19 November 1990*

A non-aggression treaty which aimed to reduce conventional weapons in Europe by almost a third, signed in Paris by 16 NATO members (Belgium, Canada, Denmark, France, the Federal Republic of Germany, Greece, Iceland, Italy, Luxembourg, Netherlands, Norway, Portugal, Spain, Turkey, UK and USA) and 6 Warsaw Pact members (Bulgaria, Czech and Slovak Federal Republic, Hungary, Poland, Romania and USSR).

TREATY OF MAASTRICHT. *11 December 1991*

The agreement on the future development of the European Union. It was ratified later by individual countries (after considerable opposition in such countries as Britain).

FOUNDING ACT. *May 1997*

Agreement on future co-operation between the NATO alliance and Russia in a post-Communist Europe.

9
Dependencies

BELGIUM

Congo, formerly Belgian Congo, then Congo (Kinshasa), then Zaïre and from 1997 the Democratic Republic of the Congo. Until the middle of the nineteenth century the territory drained by the Congo River was practically unknown. When Stanley reached the mouth of the Congo in 1877, King Leopold II of the Belgians recognized the immense possibilities of the Congo Basin and took the lead in exploring and exploiting it. The Berlin Conference of 1884–1885 recognized King Leopold II as the sovereign head of the Congo Free State.

The annexation of the state to Belgium was provided for by the treaty of 28 Nov 1907, which was approved by the chambers of the Belgian Legislature in Aug and Sep and by the King on 18 Oct 1908. The law of 18 Oct 1908, called the Colonial Charter (last amended in 1959), provided for the government of the Belgian Congo, until the country became independent on 30 Jun 1960.

The departure of the Belgian administrators, teachers, doctors, etc. on the day of independence left a vacuum which speedily resulted in complete chaos. Neither Joseph Kasavubu, the leader of the Abako Party, who on 24 Jun 1960 had been elected head of state, nor Patrice Lumumba, leader of the Congo National Movement, who was the Prime Minister of an all-party coalition government, could establish his authority. Personal, tribal and regional rivalries led to the breakaway of Katanga province under premier Moïse Tshombe. Lumumba found his main support in the Oriental and Kivu provinces. Early in July the *Force Publique* mutinied and removed all Belgian officers. Lumumba called for intervention by the UN as well as the USSR. The Secretary-General dispatched a military force of about 20000, composed of contingents from African and Asian countries. Lumumba was kidnapped by Katanga tribesmen and, in early Feb 1961, murdered; his place was taken by Antoine Gizenga, who set up a government in Stanleyville.

On 15 Aug 1961 the UN recognized the government of Cyrille Adoula as the central government. UN forces, chiefly Irish and Ethiopians, in mid-September invaded Katanga.

On 15 Jan 1962 the forces of Gizenga in Stanleyville surrendered to those of the central government, and on 16 Jan Adoula dismissed Gizenga. UN forces, chiefly Ethiopians and Indians, again invaded Katanga in Dec 1962 and by the end of Jan 1963 had occupied all key towns; Tshombe left the country. The UN troops left the Congo by 30 Jun 1964.

The Gizenga faction started a fresh rebellion and after the capture of Albertville (19 Jun) and Stanleyville (5 Aug) proclaimed a People's Republic on 7 Sep 1964. Government troops, Belgian paratroopers and a mercenary contingent captured Stanleyville on 24 Nov after the rebels had massacred thousands of black and white civilians. The last rebel strongholds were captured at the end of Apr 1965.

DENMARK

The Faroe Islands (Faerøerne). The islands were first colonized in the ninth century and were Norwegian possessions until 1380 and subsequently belonged to Denmark. They were occupied by British troops in World War II. In Sep 1946 they voted for independence from Denmark but now return two members to the *Folketing*. Home rule was granted in 1948.

Greenland (Grønland). From 1261 to 1953 Greenland was a Danish colony. On 5 Jun 1953 Greenland became an integral part of the Danish Realm with the same rights as other counties in Denmark, returning two members to the *Folketing*, and with a democratically elected council (*landsråd*). A Danish–American agreement for the common defence of Greenland was signed on 27 Apr 1951.

Iceland (Island). The first settlers came to Iceland in 874. Between 930 and 1264 Iceland was an independent Republic, but by the 'Old Treaty' of 1263 the country recognized the rule of the King of Norway. In 1381 Iceland, together with Norway, came under the rule of the Danish kings, but when Norway was separated from Denmark in 1814, Iceland remained under the rule of Denmark. Since 1 Dec 1918 it has been acknowledged as a sovereign state. It was united with Denmark only through the common sovereign until it was proclaimed an independent Republic on 17 Jun 1944.

FRANCE

The French Community (La Communauté). The constitution of the Fifth Republic, promulgated on 6 Oct 1958, 'offers to the overseas territories which manifest their will to adhere to it new institutions based on the common ideal of liberty, equality and fraternity and conceived with a view to their democratic evolution'. The territories were offered three solutions: they could keep their status; they could become overseas *départements*; they could become, singly or in groups, member states of the Community (Art. 76).

According to the amendment of the constitution adopted on 4 Jun 1960, member states of the Community could become independent and sovereign republics without ceasing to belong to the community. The 12 African and Malagasy members availed themselves of this *loi constitutionnelle* and became independent by the transfer of 'common powers' (*compétences communes*).

The territorial structure of the Community and affiliated states was as follows:

I. FRENCH REPUBLIC

    A. Metropolitan Departments.

    B. Overseas Departments:
    (i) Martinique; (ii) Guadeloupe; (iii) Réunion; (iv) Guiana.

    C. Overseas Territories:
    (i) French Polynesia; (ii) New Caledonia; (iii) French Territory of the Afars and the Issas; (iv) Comoro Archipelago; (v) Saint-Pierre and Miquelon; (vi) Southern and Antarctic Territories; (vii) Wallis and Futuna Islands.

II. MEMBER STATES

    1. French Republic; 2. Central African Republic; 3. Republic of Congo; 4. Republic of Gabon; 5. Madagascar; 6. Republic of Senegal; 7. Republic of Chad.

These countries concluded formal 'Community participation agreements'.

III. 'Special relations' or 'special links' were established by agreements between France and the other Franc zone countries and the following states:
1. Republic of Ivory Coast; 2. Republic of Dahomey; 3. Republic of Upper Volta; 4. Islamic Republic of Mauritania; 5. Republic of Niger; 6. Federal Republic of Cameroun.

IV. Co-operation in certain fields was established by special agreements between France and the Republic of Mali.

V. Co-operation was established between France and the Togo Republic by a convention signed on 10 Jul 1963.

VI. The states listed under II, 2–7, III, 1–3, 5 and 6, and V are the members of the organization *Commune Africaine et Malgache*.

VII. Other regional organizations:

1. The Customs and Economic Union of Central Africa, comprising the Central African Republic, Congo, Gabon, Chad and Cameroun; the common external tariff, effective from 1 Jul 1962, did not apply to the countries listed under II and III;

2. The entente of Ivory Coast, Dahomey, Upper Volta, Niger;

3. The customs union of Senegal, Mali, Ivory Coast, Dahomey, Upper Volta, Niger and Mauritania;

4. The West African monetary union of Senegal, Mauritania, Ivory Coast, Upper Volta, Niger, Dahomey and Togo.

VIII. Relations between France and Algeria (comprising the former Algerian and Sahara Departments) are governed by the Évian agreements of 19 Mar 1962 and subsequent agreements.

IX. The Anglo–French Condominium of the New Hebrides is administered according to the London Protocol of 6 Aug 1914.

Guinea opted out of the Community in 1958.

Algeria. Algeria was annexed by France in 1885 and became a department of France. French policy was to integrate Algeria completely into France itself but this was not acceptable to the French settlers, *colons*.

On 1 Nov 1954 the National Liberation Front (FLN), founded 5 Aug 1951, went over to open warfare against the French administration and armed forces. In Sep 1958 a free Algerian government was formed in Cairo with Ferhat Abbas as provisional President.

A referendum was held in Metropolitan France and Algeria on 6–8 Jan 1961 to decide on Algerian self-determination as proposed by President de Gaulle. His proposals were approved by 15 200 073 against 4 996 474 votes in Metropolitan France, and by 1 749 969 against 767 546 votes in Algeria. In Metropolitan France 20.2 m. out of 27.2 m. registered voters went to the polls; in Algeria 2.5 m. out of 4.5 m. registered voters.

Long delayed by the terrorism, in Metropolitan France as well as Algeria, of a secret organization (OAS) led by anti-Gaullist officers, a cease-fire agreement was concluded between the French government and the representatives of the Algerian Nationalists on 18 Mar 1962; but OAS terror acts continued for some months. On 7 Apr a provisional executive of 12 members was set up, under the chairmanship of Abderrhaman Farès.

On 8 Apr 1962 a referendum in Metropolitan France approved the Algerian settlement with 17 505 473 (90.7 per cent), against 1 794 553 (9.3 per cent) and 1 102 477 invalid votes; 6 580 772 voters abstained. On 1 Jul 1962, 5 975 581 Algerians voted in favour of, 16 534 against, the settlement.

Morocco. From 1912 to 1956 Morocco was divided into a French protectorate (established by the Treaty of Fez concluded between France and the Sultan on

30 Mar 1912), a Spanish protectorate (established by the Franco–Spanish convention of 27 Nov 1912) and the international zone of Tangier (set up by France, Spain and Britain on 18 Dec 1923).

On 2 Mar 1956 France and the Sultan terminated the Treaty of Fez; on 7 Apr 1956 Spain relinquished her protectorate, and on 29 Oct 1956 France, Spain, Britain, Italy, USA, Belgium, the Netherlands, Sweden and Portugal abolished the international status of the Tangier Zone.

Indo-China (Cambodia). Attacked on either side by the Vietnamese and the Thai from the fifteenth century on, Cambodia was saved from annihilation by the establishment of a French protectorate in 1863. Thailand eventually recognized the protectorate and renounced all claims to suzerainty in exchange for Cambodia's north-western provinces of Battambang and Siem Reap, which were, however, returned under a Franco–Thai convention of 1907, confirmed in the Franco–Thai treaty of 1937. In 1904 the province of Stung Treng, formerly administered as part of Laos, was attached to Cambodia.

A nationalist movement began in the 1930s, and anti-French feeling strengthened in 1940–1941, when the French submitted to Japanese demands for bases in Cambodia and allowed Thailand to annex Cambodian territory. On 9 Mar 1945 the Japanese suppressed the French administration and the treaties between France and Cambodia were denounced by King Norodom Sihanouk, who proclaimed Cambodia's independence. British troops occupied Phnom Penh in Oct 1945, and the re-establishment of French authority was followed by a Franco–Cambodian *modus vivendi* of 7 Jan 1946, which promised a constitution embodying a constitutional monarchy. Elections for a National Consultative Assembly were held on 1 Sep 1946, and a Franco–Thai agreement of 17 Nov 1946 ensured the return to Cambodia of the provinces annexed by Thailand in 1941.

In 1949 Cambodia was granted independence as an Associate State of the French Union. The transfer of the French military powers to the Cambodian government on 9 Nov 1953 is considered in Cambodia as the attainment of sovereign independence. In Jan 1955 Cambodia became financially and economically independent, both of France and the other two former Associate States of French Indo-China, Vietnam and Laos.

Laos. In 1893 Laos became a French protectorate and in 1907 acquired its present frontiers. In 1945 French authority was suppressed by the Japanese. When the Japanese withdrew in 1945 an independence movement known as *Lao Issara* (Free Laos) set up a government under Prince Phetsarath, the Viceroy of Luang Prabang. This government collapsed with the return of the French in 1946 and the leaders of the movement fled to Thailand.

Under a new constitution of 1947 Laos became a constitutional monarchy under the Luang Prabang dynasty, and in 1949 became an independent sovereign state within the French Union.

Vietnam. French interest in Vietnam started in the late sixteenth century with the arrival of French and Portuguese missionaries. The most notable of these was Alexander of Rhodes, who, in the following century, romanized Vietnamese writing. At the end of the eighteenth century a French bishop and several soldiers of fortune helped to establish the Emperor Gia-Long (with whom Louis XVI had signed a treaty in 1787) as ruler of a unified Vietnam, known then as the Empire of Annam.

An expedition sent by Napoleon III in 1858 to avenge the death of some French missionaries led in 1862 to the cession to France of part of Cochin-China, and thence, by a series of treaties between 1874 and 1884, to the establishment of French protectorates over Tonkin and Annam, and to the formation of the French colony of Cochin-China. By a Sino–French treaty of 1885 the Empire of Annam (including Tonkin) ceased to be a tributary to China. Cambodia had become a French protectorate in 1863, and in 1899, after the extension of French protection to Laos in 1893, the Indo-Chinese Union was proclaimed.

In 1940 Vietnam was occupied by the Japanese and used as a military base for the invasion of Malaya. During the occupation there was considerable underground activity among nationalist, revolutionary and Communist organizations. In 1941 a nominally nationalist coalition of such organizations, known as the Vietminh League, was founded by the Communists.

On 9 Mar 1945 the Japanese interned the French authorities and proclaimed the 'independence' of Indo-China. In Aug 1945 they allowed the Vietminh movement to seize power, dethrone Bao Dai, the Emperor of Annam, and establish a Republic known as Vietnam, including Tonkin, Annam and Cochin-China with Hanoi as capital. In Sep 1945 the French re-established themselves in Cochin-China and on 6 Mar 1946, after a cease-fire in the sporadic fighting between the French forces and the Vietminh had been arranged, a preliminary convention was signed in Hanoi between the French High Commissioner and President Ho Chi Minh by which France recognized 'the Democratic Republic of Vietnam' as a 'Free State within the Indo-Chinese Federation'. Subsequent conferences convened in the same year at Dalat and Fontainebleau to draft a definitive agreement broke down chiefly over the question of whether or not Cochin-China should be included in the new Republic. On 19 Dec 1946 Vietminh forces made a surprise attack on Hanoi, the signal for hostilities which were to last for nearly eight years.

An agreement signed by the Emperor Bao Dai on behalf of Vietnam on 8 Mar 1949 recognized the independence of Vietnam within the French Union, and certain sovereign powers were forthwith transferred to Vietnam. Others remained partly under French control until Sep 1954. The remainder, connected with services in which Cambodia, France, Laos and Vietnam had a common interest, were regulated by the Pau conventions of Dec 1950. These conventions were abrogated by the Paris agreements of 29 Dec 1954, which completed the transfer of sovereignty to Vietnam. Supreme authority in the military field remained with the French until the departure of the last French C.-in-C. in Apr 1956. Treaties of independence and association were initiated by representatives of the French and Vietnamese governments on 4 Jun 1954.

Gabon. In 1958 became an autonomous Republic within the French Community, gaining full independence in 1960.

In 1974 **Mayotte** voted against becoming independent with the rest of the Comoro Archipelago (an Overseas Territory). **Comoros** therefore became an independent state on 6 Jul 1975; Mayotte remained a dependency, and in 1976 was given the status of *collectivité territoriale* – an intermediate status between Overseas Territory and Overseas Department.

In Jul 1976 **Saint-Pierre and Miquelon**, an Overseas Territory, became an Overseas Department and in 1985 became a *collectivité territoriale*.

On 27 Jun 1977 the French Territory of the Afars and Issas, an Overseas Territory, became independent as the Republic of **Djibouti**.

Greater powers of self-government were granted in 1982 to the following Overseas Departments: French Guiana, Guadeloupe, Martinique and Réunion.

At 31 Dec 1999 the remaining Overseas Territories were: French Polynesia, New Caledonia, Southern and Antarctic Territories, and Wallis and Futuna Islands.

ITALY

Ethiopia (Abyssinia). In 1936 Ethiopia was conquered by the Italians, who were in turn defeated by the Allied forces in 1941 when the Emperor returned.

The former Italian colony of Eritrea, from 1941 under British military administration, was in accordance with a resolution of the General Assembly of the United Nations, dated 2 Dec 1950, handed over to Ethiopia on 15 Sep 1952. Eritrea thereby became an autonomous unit within the federation of Ethiopia and Eritrea, under the Ethiopian Crown. This federation became a unitary state on 14 Nov 1962 when Eritrea was fully integrated with Ethiopia but became an independent sovereign state on 24 May 1993 after a prolonged armed struggle.

Somalia. The Somali Republic came into being on 1 Jul 1960 as a result of the merger of the British Somaliland Protectorate, which became independent on 26 Jun 1960, and the Italian Trusteeship Territory of Somalia.

THE NETHERLANDS

Netherlands Antilles (De Nederlandse Antillen). Since Dec 1954, the Netherlands Antilles have been fully autonomous in internal affairs, and constitutionally equal with the Netherlands and Suriname. The Sovereign of the Kingdom of the Netherlands is head of the government of the Netherlands Antilles and is represented by a governor. On 1 Jan 1986 Aruba was constitutionally separated from the Netherlands Antilles and full independence was envisaged after a ten-year period.

Netherlands East Indies. From 1602 the Netherlands East India Company conquered the Netherlands East Indies, and ruled them until the dissolution of the company in 1798. Thereafter the Netherlands government ruled the colony from 1816 to 1945.

Complete and unconditional sovereignty was transferred to the Republic of the United States of Indonesia on 27 Dec 1949, except for the western part of New Guinea, the status of which was to be determined through negotiations between Indonesia and the Netherlands within one year after the transfer of sovereignty. A union was created to regulate the relationship between the two countries. A settlement of the New Guinea (West Irian) question was, however, delayed until 15 Aug 1962, when, through the good offices of the UN, an agreement was concluded for the transfer of the territory to Indonesia on 1 May 1963.

Suriname (Dutch Guiana). At the peace of Breda (1667) between Great Britain and the United Netherlands, Suriname was assigned to the Netherlands in exchange for the colony of New Netherlands in North America, and this was confirmed by the Treaty of Westminster of Feb 1674. Since then Suriname has been twice in British possession, 1799–1802 (when it was restored to the Batavian Republic at the peace of Amiens) and 1804–1816, when it was returned to the Kingdom of the Netherlands according to the convention of London of 13 Aug 1814, confirmed at the peace of Paris of 20 Nov 1815. Suriname became fully independent on 25 Nov 1975.

NORWAY

Svalbard. The main islands of the archipelago are Spitsbergen (formerly Vestspitsbergen), Nordaustlandet, Edgeøya, Barentsøya, Prins Karls Forland, Bjørnøya, Hopen, Kong Karls Land, Kvitøya, and many small islands.

The archipelago was probably discovered by Norsemen in 1194 and rediscovered by the Dutch navigator Barents in 1596. In the seventeenth century the very lucrative whale-hunting caused rival Dutch, British and Danish–

Norwegian claims to sovereignty and quarrels about the hunting-places. But when in the eighteenth century the whale-hunting ended, the question of the sovereignty of Svalbard lost its actuality; it was again raised in the twentieth century, owing to the discovery and exploitation of coalfields. By a treaty, signed on 9 Feb 1920 in Paris, Norway's sovereignty over the archipelago was recognized. On 14 Aug 1925 the archipelago was officially incorporated in Norway.

Jan Mayen. The island was possibly discovered by Henry Hudson in 1608, and it was first named Hudson's Tutches (Touches). It was again and again rediscovered and renamed. Its present name derives from the Dutch whaling captain Jan Jacobsz May, who indisputably discovered the island in 1614. It was uninhabited, but occasionally visited by seal hunters and trappers, until 1921 when Norway established a radio and meteorological station. On 8 May 1929 Jan Mayen was officially proclaimed as incorporated in the Kingdom of Norway. Its relation to Norway was finally settled by law on 27 Feb 1930.

Bouvet Island, Bouvetøya. This uninhabited island was discovered in 1739 by a French naval officer, Jean Baptiste Lozier Bouvet, but no flag was hoisted until, in 1825, Capt. Norris raised the Union Jack. In 1928 Britain waived its claim to the island in favour of Norway, which in Dec 1927 had occupied it. A law of 27 Feb 1930 declared Bouvetøya a Norwegian dependency.

Peter I Island, Peter I øy. This uninhabited island was sighted in 1821 by the Russian explorer, Admiral von Bellingshausen. The first landing was made in 1929 by a Norwegian expedition which hoisted the Norwegian flag. On 1 May 1931 Peter I Island was placed under Norwegian sovereignty, and on 24 Mar 1933 it was incorporated in Norway as a dependency.

Queen Maud Land, Dronning Maud Land. On 14 Jan 1939 the Norwegian cabinet placed that part of the Antarctic Continent from the border of Falkland Islands dependencies in the west to the border of the Australian Antarctic Dependency in the east (between 20°W. and 45°E.) under Norwegian sovereignty. The territory had been explored only by Norwegians and hitherto been ownerless. Since 1949 expeditions from various countries have explored the area. In 1957 Dronning Maud Land was given the status of a Norwegian dependency.

PORTUGAL

On 11 Jun 1951 the status of the Portuguese overseas possessions was changed from 'colonies' to 'overseas territories'. Each one had a governor and enjoyed financial and administrative autonomy. Their budgets were under approval of the Minister for the Overseas Territories. They were not allowed to contract public loans in foreign countries. Under the Organic Law for Overseas Territories, of May 1972, the overseas provinces were given greater autonomy 'without affecting the unity of the nation'. Angola and Mozambique were designated states instead of overseas provinces.

On 6 Sep 1961 all Africans were given full Portuguese citizenship, thereby achieving the same status as the inhabitants of Portuguese India and the other provinces.

All customs duties between Portugal and the overseas provinces were abolished with effect from 1 Jan 1964.

Cape Verde Islands. The Cape Verde Islands were discovered in 1460 by Diogo Gomes, the first settlers arriving in 1462. In 1587 its administration was unified under a governor. The territory consists of ten islands and five islets which were administered by a governor, whose seat was at Praia, the capital. The islands are divided into two groups, named Barlavento (windward) and Sotavento (leeward), the prevailing wind being north-east. The former is constituted by the islands of São Vicente, Santo Antão, São Nicolau, Santa Luzia, Sal and Boa Vista, and the small islands named Branco and Raso. The latter is constituted by the islands of Santiago, Maio, Fogo and Brava, and the small islands named Rei and Rombo. São Vicente was an oiling station which supplied all navigation to South America. The total area is 4033 sq. km (1557 sq. miles). The islands became independent on 5 Jul 1975 as the Republic of Cape Verde.

Portuguese Guinea. Portuguese Guinea, on the coast of Guinea, was discovered in 1446 by Nuno Tristão. It became a separate colony in 1879. It is bounded by the limits fixed by the convention of 12 May 1886 with France, and is bounded by Senegal in the north and by Guinea in the east and south. It includes the adjacent archipelago of Bijagoz, with the island of Bolama. The capital is, since 1942, Bissau. Area is 36 125 sq. km (13 948 sq. miles). The dependency became an independent state, as Guinea-Bissau, on 10 Sep 1974.

São Tomé e Principe. The islands of S. Tomé and Principe, which are about 125 miles off the coast of Africa, in the Gulf of Guinea, were discovered in 1471 by Pedro Escobar and João Gomes, and after 1522 constituted a province under a governor. The province also included the islands of Pedras Tinhosas and Rolas; the fort of St Jean Baptiste d'Ajudã on the coast was annexed by the Dahomey Republic on 1 Aug 1961. Area of the islands 964 sq. km (372 sq. miles). The islands became independent on 12 Jul 1975.

Angola. Angola, with a coastline of over 1000 miles, is separated from the Congo by the boundaries assigned by the convention of 12 May 1886; from Zaïre by those fixed by the convention of 22 Jul 1927; from Rhodesia in accordance with the convention of 11 Jun 1891, and from South-West Africa in accordance with that of 30 Dec 1886. The Congo region was discovered by the Portuguese in 1482, and the first settlers arrived there in 1491. Luanda was founded in 1575. It was taken by the Dutch in 1641 and occupied by them until 1648. The area is 1246700 sq. km (481351 sq. miles). By a decree of 20 Oct 1954 it is divided into 13 districts. The important towns are S. Paulo de Luanda (capital), Benguela, Moçâmedes, Lobito, Sá da Bandeira, Malange and Huambo (Novo Lisboa), the future capital. Angola became independent on 11 Nov 1975.

Mozambique. Mozambique was discovered by Vasco da Gama's fleet on 1 Mar 1498, and was first colonized in 1505. The frontier with British Central and South Africa was fixed between Great Britain and Portugal in Jun 1891. The border with Tanganyika, according to agreements of 1886 and 1890, ran from Cape Delgado at 10°40'S. Lat. until it meets the course of the Rovuma, which it follows to the point of its confluence with the 'Msinje, the boundary thence to Lake Nyasa being the parallel of latitude of this point. The Treaty of Versailles, 1919, allotted to Portugal the original Portuguese territory south of the Rovuma, known as the 'Kionga Triangle' (formerly part of German East Africa).

Mozambique, with an area of 784961 sq. km (303070 sq. miles) was administered by Portugal in 1942; the state took over the territory of Manica and Sofala, which was incorporated as a fourth district of the province, with Beira as its capital. Lourenço Marques is the capital of the province. As established by decree of 20 Oct 1954, the province was divided into nine districts: Lourenço Marques, Gazai Inhambane, Manica and Sofala, Tete, Zambézia, Mozambique, Cabo Delgado, Niassa.

There was a government council composed of officials and elected representatives of the commercial, industrial and agricultural classes, and also an executive council. Mozambique became independent on 25 Jul 1975.

Macao. Macao, in China, situated on a peninsula of the same name at the mouth of the Canton River, which came into possession of the Portuguese in 1557, forms with the two small adjacent islands of Taipa and Colôane a province (1961–1974), divided into two wards, each having its own administrator. The boundaries have not yet been definitely agreed upon; Portugal held the territory in virtue of the treaty with China of 1 Dec 1887. The area of the province is 16 sq. km (6 sq. miles). In 1987, in agreement with China, Macao became a Chinese territory under Portuguese administration. Macao was returned to China in 1999.

Timor. Portuguese Timor was under Portuguese administration from 1586. It consisted of the eastern portion of the island of that name in the Malay Archipelago, with the territory of Ambeno and the neighbouring islands of Pulo Cambing and Pulo Jako, a total area of 14 925 sq. km. By a treaty of Apr 1859, ratified 18 Aug 1860, the island was divided between Portugal and Holland; by convention of 1 Oct 1904, ratified in 1908, the boundaries were straightened and settled. The territory, formerly administratively joined to Macao, was in 1896 (confirmed in 1926) made an independent province. On 7 Dec 1975, during a civil war, the province was invaded by Indonesian forces. On 17 Jul 1976 it became an Indonesian province and was renamed Loro Sae. A referendum was held on 30 Aug 1999 and 78.5 per cent voted for independence for East Timor. Violence occurred after the vote was announced and UN forces arrived on 20 Sep. Indonesian troops and police were withdrawn on 27 Sep. The border between East and West Timor was agreed on 23 Nov.

Portuguese India (Estado da India), was under Portuguese rule 1505–1961. It consisted of Goa, containing the capital, Goa, together with the islands of Angediva, São Jorge and Morcegos, on the Malabar coast; Damão, with the territories of Dadrá and Nagar-Haveli, on the Gulf of Cambis; and Diu, with the continental territories of Gogola and Simbor, on the coast of Gujarat.

Indian troops invaded Goa, Damão and Diu without declaration of war on 18–19 Dec 1961 and forcibly incorporated the Portuguese territory in the Indian Union.

SPAIN

In Jan 1958 the territory of 'Spanish West Africa' was divided into the provinces of Ifni and Spanish Sahara; both were under the jurisdiction of the commanding officer of the Canary Islands. The province of Ifni was returned to Morocco on 30 Jun 1969.

The Province of Spanish Sahara consisted of two districts: Sekia El Hamra (82 000 sq. km) and Rio de Oro (184 000 sq. km). Area 266 000 sq. km (102 680 sq. miles). The population consisted of some 10 000 Spanish civilians, about 15 000 Spanish soldiers and perhaps 30 000–50 000 nomadic Saharans. The capital is El Aaiún. The strip between 27°40′N. and Wad Draa was ceded by Spain to Morocco on 10 Apr 1958. Strong pressure was brought, in 1970, by Morocco, Mauritania and Algeria for a referendum to be conducted by Spain in the province. In 1975, Spain, Morocco and Mauritania reached agreement on the transfer of power over Western Sahara to Morocco and Mauritania. The Spanish province ceased to exist on 31 Dec 1975, and the country was partitioned by Morocco and Mauritania. In Aug 1979 Mauritania withdrew from the territory it took over in 1976 and it was reorganized into a fourth province by Morocco. A Saharan nationalist party, the *Frente Polisario*, claims the independence of the country and has renamed it the Saharan Arab Democratic Republic.

Equatorial Guinea (Territorios Espãnoles del Golfo de Guinea). The territory was ceded to Spain by Portugal in 1777. Spain leased it to Britain in 1827, and began to administer it in 1855, as a colony. In 1959 it was turned into two provinces, comparable to the Spanish metropolitan provinces, and called Fernando Po and Rio Muni. In 1964 a degree of self-government was achieved. Independence followed on 12 Oct 1968 as a federation of two provinces and a unitary state was established on 4 Aug 1973.

UNITED KINGDOM

Until Jul 1925 the affairs of all the British Empire, apart from the United Kingdom and India, were dealt with by the Colonial Office. From that date a new secretaryship of state, for Dominion Affairs, became responsible for the relations between the United Kingdom and all the independent members of the Commonwealth.

In Jul 1947 the designations of the Secretary of State for Dominion Affairs and the Dominions Office were altered to 'Secretary of State for Commonwealth Relations' and 'Commonwealth Relations Office'. The following month, on the independence of India and Pakistan, the India Office ceased to exist and the staff were transferred to the Commonwealth Relations Office, which then became responsible for relations with India and Pakistan.

The Colonial Office was merged with the Commonwealth Relations Office on 1 Aug 1966 to form the Commonwealth Office, and the post of Secretary of State for Commonwealth Relations became Secretary of State for Commonwealth Affairs. The post of Secretary of State for the Colonies was retained until 6 Jan 1967. The Commonwealth Office was merged with the Foreign Office on 17 Oct 1968.

The Secretary of State for Foreign and Commonwealth Affairs became responsible for relations with the independent members of the Commonwealth, with the Associated States, and for the administration of the UK Overseas Territories, in addition to his responsibilities for relations with foreign countries.

On 18 Apr 1949, when the Republic of Ireland Act 1948 came into force, Southern Ireland ceased to be a member of the Commonwealth.

The Imperial Conference of 1926 defined Great Britain and the Dominions, as they were then called, as 'autonomous communities within the British Empire, equal in status, in no way subordinate one to another in any aspect of their domestic or foreign affairs, though united by a common allegiance to the Crown, and freely associated as members of the British Commonwealth of

Nations'. On 11 Dec 1931 the Statute of Westminster, which by legal enact-
ment recognized the status of the Dominions as defined in 1926, became law.
Each of the Dominions, which then included Canada, Australia, New Zealand,
South Africa and Newfoundland (which in 1949 became a Canadian Province)
had signified approval of the provisions of the Statute.

India and Pakistan became independent on 15 Aug 1947; Ceylon (now Sri
Lanka) on 4 Feb 1948; Ghana (formerly the Gold Coast) on 6 Mar 1957; the
Federation of Malaya on 31 Aug 1957 (renamed the Federation of Malaysia on
16 Sep 1963, including from that date North Borneo, Sarawak and Singapore
until 9 Aug 1965 when Singapore became a separate independent state); Cyprus
on 16 Aug 1960; Nigeria on 1 Oct 1960; Sierra Leone on 27 Apr 1961; Tanganyika on 9 Dec 1961 (renamed United Republic of Tanzania on 26 Apr 1964
when she joined with Zanzibar, which had become independent on 10 Dec
1963); Jamaica on 6 Aug 1962; Trinidad and Tobago on 31 Aug 1962; Uganda
on 9 Oct 1962; Western Samoa on 1 Jan 1962; Kenya on 12 Dec 1963; Malawi
(formerly Nyasaland) on 6 Jul 1964; Malta on 21 Sep 1964; Zambia (formerly
Northern Rhodesia) on 24 Oct 1964; The Gambia on 18 Feb 1965; Maldives on
26 Jul 1965; Guyana (formerly British Guiana) on 26 May 1966; Botswana (formerly Bechuanaland) on 30 Sep 1966; Lesotho (formerly Basutoland) on 4 Oct
1966; Barbados on 30 Nov 1966; Mauritius on 12 Mar 1968; Swaziland on 6
Sep 1968; Nauru on 31 Jan 1968; Tonga on 4 Jun 1970; Fiji on 10 Oct 1970;
Bangladesh on 4 Feb 1972; Bahamas on 10 Jul 1973; Papua New Guinea on 16
Sep 1975; Seychelles on 29 Jun 1976; Solomon Islands on 7 Jul 1978; Tuvalu
on 1 Oct 1978; Kiribati on 12 Jul 1979; Zimbabwe on 18 Apr 1980; Vanuatu
on 30 Jul 1980; Belize on 21 Sep 1981; Brunei on 31 Dec 1983.

On 4 Jan 1948 Burma became an independent Republic outside the
Commonwealth.

South Africa withdrew from the Commonwealth on becoming a Republic on
31 May 1961, but was re-admitted on 1 Jun 1994.

To cater for the special circumstances of small states (Nauru, Tuvalu, St
Vincent and the Grenadines, Maldives) a 'special membership' of the Commonwealth has been devised in close consultation with their governments.
Territories dependent on the United Kingdom comprise dependent territories
(properly so-called), a protectorate, a protected state and a Condominium. A
dependent territory is a territory belonging by settlement, conquest or annexation to the British Crown. A protectorate is a territory not formally annexed
but in which, by treaty, grant and other lawful means the Crown has power
and jurisdiction. A protected state is a territory under a ruler which enjoys Her
Majesty's protection, over whose foreign affairs she exercises control, but in
respect of whose internal affairs she does not exercise jurisdiction.

United Kingdom Overseas Territories (formerly British Dependent Territories)
administered through the Foreign and Commonwealth Office comprise in the

Indian Ocean: British Indian Ocean Territory; in the Mediterranean: Gibraltar; in the Atlantic Ocean: Bermuda, Falkland Islands and dependencies, South Georgia and South Sandwich Islands, British Antarctic Territory, St Helena and dependencies of Ascension and Tristan da Cunha; in the Caribbean: Montserrat, British Virgin Islands, Cayman Islands, Turks and Caicos Islands, Anguilla; and in the Western Pacific: Pitcairn. Hong Kong returned to China in 1997.

The islands of Antigua, St Christopher-Nevis-Anguilla, Dominica, Grenada and St Lucia had entered a new form of relationship with Britain in 1967, as associated states. St Vincent became an associated state in 1969. Each had control of its own internal affairs, with the right to amend the constitution and the right to end the associated status if it so wished. Grenada became independent on 7 Feb 1974, Dominica on 3 Nov 1978, St Lucia on 22 Feb 1979, St Vincent and the Grenadines on 27 Oct 1979, Antigua and Barbuda on 1 Nov 1981 and St Christopher-Nevis on 19 Sep 1983. The island of Anguilla, although technically a part of the State of St Christopher-Nevis-Anguilla, through the Anguilla Act of 1971 and the Anguilla (Administration) Order 1971, came under the direct administration of the United Kingdom and by the Anguilla Act 1980 *de jure* a separate dependency of the United Kingdom. Provision is thereby made for Her Majesty's Commissioner to administer the island in consultation with the Anguilla council.

While constitutional responsibility to parliament for the government of the Overseas territories rests with the Secretary of State for Foreign and Commonwealth Affairs, the administration of the territories is carried out by the governments of the territories themselves.

A protected state is a territory under a ruler which enjoys Her Majesty's protection, over whose foreign affairs she exercises control but in respect of whose internal affairs she does not exercise jurisdiction. Brunei was a protected state. Under the 1959 Agreement, as amended Nov 1971 the UK remained responsible for the external affairs of Brunei, while Brunei had full responsibility for all internal matters. The two governments were to consult together about measures to be taken separately and jointly in the event of any external threat to the State of Brunei. Under a treaty signed 7 Jan 1979 Brunei became a fully sovereign and independent state on 31 Dec 1983.

The following territories were dependencies or protectorates of Britain, and did not become members of the Commonwealth when they became independent:

Aden, held by Britain as a colony since 1839, and its associated territory as a protectorate, became independent on 30 Nov 1967 (as the Southern Yemen People's Republic) and later changed its name to the People's Democratic Republic of Yemen.

Bahrain had been under British protection by treaty since 1882, and became independent on 15 Aug 1971.

British Somaliland had been under British protection since 1887, and became independent on 26 Jun 1960; on 1 Jul 1960 it joined the former Italian Trusteeship Territory of Somalia as the Somali Republic.

Burma was annexed, by provinces, to British India between 1824 and 1886; the Indian Province of Burma was formed in 1852. Burma was separated from India in 1937 and became independent on 4 Jan 1948.

Egypt became a British protectorate in 1914, having been occupied in 1882. The protectorate ended on 28 Feb 1922 and Egypt became an independent kingdom.

Iraq came under British control in 1916 when it was part of the Ottoman Empire allied with Germany during World War I. It became a kingdom under British mandate in 1921 and an independent state on 3 Oct 1932.

Palestine was administered by Britain under a League of Nations mandate, 1922–1948.

Sudan was an Anglo–Egyptian Condominium from 1899 until independence on 1 Jan 1956.

Transjordan was administered by Britain under a League of Nations mandate 1922–1928, and full independence as a kingdom (Jordan) was achieved on 22 Mar 1946.

10
Population[1,2]

ALBANIA

	Population	Area	Density
1924	831 877	27 529	30.2
1930	1 003 124	27 529	36.4
1947	1 150 000	28 748	40.0
1960	1 626 315	28 748	56.6
1967	1 964 730	28 748	68.3
1970	2 135 600	28 748	74.2
1980	2 734 000	28 748	95.1
1990	3 262 000	28 748	113.5
1995	3 412 000	28 748	118.7
2000	3 490 000	28 748	121.4

ANDORRA

	Population	Area	Density
1963	5 000	468	10.7
1977	30 700	468	65.6
1984	41 627	468	88.9
1993	61 599	468	134.4
1996	72 766	468	155.5
2000	80 000	468	170.9

[1] Area in sq. km.
[2] 2000 UN estimates.

ARMENIA

	Population	*Area*	*Density*
1995	3 548 000	29 743	119.3
2000	3 660 000	29 743	123.1

AUSTRIA

	Population	*Area*	*Density*
1910	7 529 935	101 010	74.5
1920	6 428 336	83 792	76.7
1923	6 534 481	83 835	77.9
1934	6 760 233	83 835	80.6
1951	6 933 905	83 850	82.7
1961	7 073 807	83 850	84.4
1971	7 456 403	83 850	88.9
1981	7 555 338	83 853	90.0
1990	7 623 000	83 857	90.9
1995	8 063 000	83 857	96.2
2000	8 290 000	83 857	98.8

AUSTRIAN EMPIRE[1]

	Population
1900	25 921 671
1910	28 571 934

[1] Exclusive of Bosnia and Hercegovina.

BELARUS

	Population	*Area*	*Density*
1995	10 332 000	207 595	49.8
2000	10 280 000	207 595	49.5

BELGIUM

	Population	*Area*	*Density*
1900	6 694 000	29 456	227.3
1910	7 423 784	29 456	252.0

BELGIUM (*continued*)

	Population	Area	Density
1920	7 465 782	30 437	245.3
1930	8 092 004	30 437	265.9
1940	8 294 674	30 497	272.0
1947	8 512 195	30 497	279.1
1961	9 189 741	30 513	301.2
1970	9 690 991	30 513	317.6
1980	9 863 374	30 519	323.2
1990	9 958 000	30 519	326.3
1995	10 064 000	30 528	329.7
2000	10 260 000	30 528	336.1

BOSNIA–HERCEGOVINA

	Population	Area	Density
1995	3 459 000	51 129	67.6
2000	4 340 000	51 129	84.9

BULGARIA

	Population	Area	Density
1910	4 337 516	87 146	49.8
1921	4 909 700	103 188	47.6
1926	5 478 741	103 188	53.1
1934	6 077 939	103 146	58.9
1946	7 022 206	110 841	63.3
1956	7 629 254	110 911	68.8
1965	8 227 866	110 911	74.2
1970	8 467 300	110 911	76.3
1975	8 727 771	110 911	78.5
1981	8 890 002	110 911	80.2
1990	8 987 400	110 994	81.1
1995	8 351 000	110 994	75.2
2000	8 310 000	110 994	74.9

CROATIA

	Population	Area	Density
1995	4 495 000	56 691	79.5
2000	4 480 000	56 610	79.1

CYPRUS

	Population	Area	Density
1931	347 959	9251	37.6
1946	450 114	9251	48.7
1956	528 879	9251	57.2
1960	573 566	9251	62.0
1970	633 000	9251	68.4
1981	637 100	9251	68.9
1990	568 000	5896	96.3
1995	651 000	5896	110.4
1998	673 000	5896	114.1
1990[1]	171 000	3355	50.9
1995[1]	155 000	3355	46.2
1998[1]	188 000	3355	56.0

[1] Turkish Republic of Northern Cyprus.

CZECHOSLOVAKIA

	Population	Area	Density
1921	13 613 172	140 490	96.9
1930	14 729 536	140 490	104.8
1947	12 164 661	127 827	95.2
1961	13 745 577	127 870	107.5
1970	14 445 301	127 870	112.9
1980	15 276 799	127 871	119.0
1990	15 664 000	127 899	122.5

CZECH REPUBLIC

	Population	Area	Density
1995	10345644	78864	131.2
2000	10290000	78866	130.5

DENMARK

	Population	Area	Density
1901	2450000	40357	60.7
1911	2775076	40357	68.8
1921	3289195	44403	74.1
1930	3550656	42931	82.7
1935	3706349	42931	86.3
1950	4281275	42931	99.7
1960	4585256	43069	106.5
1971	4950048	43069	115.0
1981	5123989	43080	119.0
1991	5146000	43093	119.4
1995	5223000	43094	121.2
2000	5320000	43094	123.5

ESTONIA

	Population	Area	Density
1922	1110538	47549	23.4
1934	1126413	47549	23.7
1939	1134000	47549	23.8

Independence was regained in 1991.

	Population	Area	Density
1995	1487000	45227	35.1
2000	1420000	45227	31.4

FINLAND

	Population	Area	Density
1900	2 655 900	343 209	7.7
1910	3 115 197	343 209	9.1
1920	3 364 807	343 209	9.8
1930	3 667 067	343 405	10.7
1942	3 887 217	343 405	11.3
1950	4 029 803	305 475	13.2
1960	4 446 222	305 475	14.6
1970	4 707 000	305 475	15.4
1980	4 787 778	305 475	15.7
1990	4 978 000	305 475	16.3
1995	5 101 000	305 475	16.7
2000	5 180 000	305 475	17.0

FRANCE

	Population	Area	Density
1911 (excluding Alsace-Lorraine)	39 601 509	536 464	73.8
1921 (including) Alsace-Lorraine)	39 209 518	550 986	71.1
1931	41 834 923	550 986	76.0
1946	40 506 639	550 986	73.5
1954	42 777 174	551 601	77.6
1962	46 519 997	551 601	84.3
1968	49 778 540	551 601	90.2
1972	51 500 000	551 601	93.3
1975	52 655 802	551 601	97.0
1982	54 334 871	551 601	98.5
1990	56 615 100	543 965	104.1
1995	58 172 000	543 965	106.9
2000	59 060 000	543 965	108.5

GEORGIA

	Population	Area	Density
1995	5 514 000	69 492	79.3
2000	5 420 000	69 492	78.4

GERMANY (to 1940 and from 1990)

	Population	Area	Density
1910 (including Alsace-Lorraine)	64 925 993	540 740	120.1
1925 (after reduction at Versailles)	62 410 619	468 728	133.1
1933 (including Waldeck and Saarland)	66 030 491	470 600	140.3
1939 (including Austria and Sudetenland)	79 576 758	583 265	136.4
1990	79 112 831	357 041	221.6
1995	81 912 000	357 022	229.4
2000	82 690 000	357 022	231.6

FEDERAL REPUBLIC OF GERMANY (WEST)

	Population	Area	Density
1950	47 695 672	245 317	194.4
1971	61 502 500	248 593	247.4
1982	61 713 000	248 687	248.2
1989	62 679 035	248 706	252.0

GERMAN DEMOCRATIC REPUBLIC

	Population	Area	Density
1947	19 102 000	108 173	176.6
1950	17 313 734	108 173	160.1

GERMAN DEMOCRATIC REPUBLIC (*continued*)

	Population	Area	Density
1964	17003655	108173	157.2
1971	17042363	108178	157.5
1980	16737200	108177	154.0
1989	16433796	108333	151.7

GIBRALTAR

	Population	Area	Density
1911	19586	6.5	3013.0
1921	17160	6.5	2640.0
1931	17613	6.5	2709.0
1951	23232	6.5	3574.0
1961	24075	6.5	3704.0
1968	26007	6.5	4001.0
1970	26833	6.5	4127.0
1981	28719	6.5	4418.3
1990	30861	6.5	4747.8
1993	28051	6.5	4315.5
1997	27086	6.5	4167.1
2000	29000	6.5	4461.5

GREECE

	Population	Area	Density
1913	4821300	108606	44.4
1920	5536375	108606	51.0
1928	6204684	130199	47.7
1940	7347002	132561	55.4
1951	7403599	132727	55.8
1961	8388553	131944	63.6
1971	8745084	131944	66.3
1981	9740417	131986	73.8
1990	10038000	131957	76.1

GREECE (*continued*)

	Population	*Area*	*Density*
1995	10 496 000	131 957	79.5
2000	10 600 000	131 957	80.3

HUNGARY

	Population	*Area*	*Density*
1910 (including Croatia and Slavonia)	20 886 787	324 773	64.3
1920	7 980 143	92 916	85.9
1931	8 688 349	92 916	93.5
1941	14 670 000	92 916	157.9
1960	9 961 044	93 030	107.0
1970	10 314 152	93 030	110.9
1980	10 709 550	93 032	115.1
1990	10 374 823	93 032	111.5
1995	10 231 000	93 032	109.9
2000	9 810 000	93 032	105.4

ICELAND

	Population	*Area*	*Density*
1901	78 000	102 968	0.76
1910	85 183	102 968	0.83
1920	94 679	102 846	0.92
1930	108 870	102 846	1.05
1940	121 618	102 846	1.18
1950	144 263	102 846	1.40
1960	177 292	102 819	1.72
1971	207 174	102 819	2.01
1981	231 958	102 819	2.27
1990	256 000	102 819	2.49
1995	269 000	102 819	2.62
2000	282 000	102 819	2.74

IRELAND

	Population	*Area*	*Density*
1901	4459000	83013	53.7
1911	4390800	83013	52.9
1921	3096000	68893	44.9
1936	2968420	68893	43.1
1946	2955107	68893	42.9
1956	2898264	68893	42.1
1961	2818341	68893	40.9
1971	2971230	68893	43.1
1981	3443405	68895	50.0
1991	3494000	68895	50.1
1995	3590000	68895	51.1
2000	3710000	68895	53.9

ITALY

	Population	*Area*	*Density*
1901	32475000	286324	113.4
1911	35441918	286324	123.8
1921	37143102	305573	121.5
1931	40309621	310057	130.0
1936	42024584	310189	135.4
1951	46737629	301023	155.3
1961	50463762	301225	167.5
1970	54418831	301225	180.7
1981	56243935	301245	187.0
1991	57590000	301245	191.2
1995	57386000	301245	190.5
2000	57460000	301245	190.7

LATVIA

	Population	*Area*	*Density*
1920	1503193	51945	38.9
1935	1950502	51945	37.5

LATVIA (*continued*)

	Population	*Area*	*Density*
1939	1 994 506	51 945	38.4

Independence was regained in 1991.

	Population	*Area*	*Density*
1995	2 515 000	64 610	38.9
2000	2 400 000	64 610	37.1

LIECHTENSTEIN

	Population	*Area*	*Density*
1930	10 213	160	63.8
1960	16 628	160	103.9
1970	21 350	160	133.4
1981	26 130	160	163.3
1990	28 700	160	179.4
1995	30 900	160	193.1
2000	33 000	160	206.3

LITHUANIA

	Population	*Area*	*Density*
1923	2 168 971	59 463	36.5
1940	2 879 070	66 119	43.5

Independence was regained in 1991.

	Population	*Area*	*Density*
1995	3 700 000	65 301	56.7
2000	3 690 000	65 301	56.5

LUXEMBOURG

	Population	*Area*	*Density*
1900	236 000	2586	91.3
1916	263 824	2586	102.0
1950	298 578	2586	115.4
1970	339 848	2586	131.4

LUXEMBOURG (*continued*)

	Population	Area	Density
1980	365 100	2586	141.2
1990	379 000	2586	146.6
1995	409 000	2586	158.2
2000	430 000	2586	166.3

MACEDONIA
(Former Yugoslavia)

	Population	Area	Density
1995	2 104 000	25 713	81.8
2000	2 230 000	25 713	86.7

MALTA

	Population	Area	Density
1911	211 864	305.6	693.3
1921	213 024	305.6	697.1
1931	244 002	316.0	772.2
1948	306 996	316.0	971.5
1957	319 620	316.0	1011.4
1967	314 216	316.0	994.4
1971	322 072	316.0	1019.2
1981	319 936	316.0	1012.5
1991	357 000	316.0	1129.8
1995	370 000	316.0	1171.0
2000	378 000	316.0	1196.2

MOLDOVA

	Population	Area	Density
1995	4 350 000	33 700	129.1
2000	4 460 000	33 700	132.3

THE NETHERLANDS

	Population	*Area*	*Density*
1911	6022452	32758	183.8
1920	6865314	32587	210.7
1930	7935565	32580	243.6
1938	8728569	32924	265.1
1947	9625499	33328	288.8
1960	11556008	33612	343.8
1970	13119430	33686	389.4
1980	14091014	33938	415.0
1990	14934000	33937	440.1
1995	15487000	33939	456.3
2000	15870000	33889	468.3

NORWAY

	Population	*Area*	*Density*
1900	2240000	321496	7.0
1910	2391782	321496	7.4
1920	2649775	323658	8.2
1930	2814194	322683	8.7
1946	3156950	323917	9.7
1950	3278546	323917	10.1
1960	3591234	323917	11.1
1970	3866468	323878	12.6
1980	4091340	323895	12.6
1990	4246000	323878	13.1
1995	4360000	323878	13.5
2000	4410000	323878	13.6

POLAND

	Population	*Area*	*Density*
1900	25106000	380266	66.0
1921	27092025	380266	71.2

POLAND

	Population	*Area*	*Density*
1931	31948027	388396	82.3
1950	24976926	311732	80.1
1960	29776000	312700	95.2
1970	32670000	312700	104.5
1980	35380000	312683	113.1
1990	38064000	312683	121.7
1995	38641000	312683	123.6
2000	38730000	312683	123.9

PORTUGAL

	Population	*Area*	*Density*
1900	5423000	89329	60.7
1911	5958000	89329	66.7
1920	6032991	89329	67.5
1930	6360347	89329	71.2
1940	7722152	89329	86.4
1950	8441312	91709	92.0
1960	8889392	91641	97.0
1970	8668267	91641	94.5
1981	9833014	91631	107.3
1991	10421000	92389	112.8
1995	9906000	91831	107.9
2000	9790000	91831	106.6

ROMANIA

	Population	*Area*	*Density*
1912	7235000	. . .	. . .
1920	17393149	316710	54.9
1930	18025037	316710	56.9
1941	13551756	195198	69.4
1948	15872624	237428	66.9

ROMANIA (*continued*)

	Population	Area	Density
1956	17 489 794	237 428	73.7
1966	19 103 163	237 428	80.5
1970	20 140 000	237 428	84.8
1975	21 559 910	237 428	89.9
1980	22 200 000	237 428	92.5
1990	23 265 000	237 428	98.0
1995	22 693 000	237 428	95.5
2000	22 500 000	237 428	94.8

RUSSIA

	Population	Area	Density
1913	159 200 000	. . .	. . .
1995	147 168 000	17 075 400	8.6
2000	146 200 000	17 075 400	8.6

SAN MARINO

	Population	Area	Density
1963	17 000	61	278.7
1974	19 168	61	314.2
1980	21 300	61	349.2
1990	23 000	61	375.9
1995	24 900	61	406.9
2000	26 800	61	439.3

SLOVAKIA

	Population	Area	Density
1995	5 355 000	49 036	109.2
2000	5 370 000	49 036	109.5

SLOVENIA

	Population	Area	Density
1995	1 971 000	20 256	97.3
2000	1 990 000	20 256	98.2

SPAIN

	Population	Area	Density
1900	18 594 000	504 488	36.9
1910	19 588 688	504 488	38.8
1920	21 303 162	504 488	42.2
1930	23 563 867	509 212	46.3
1940	25 877 971	492 229	52.5
1950	27 976 755	503 061	55.6
1960	30 430 698	503 545	60.4
1970	33 823 918	503 545	67.1
1981	37 746 260	504 750	74.0
1990	39 618 000	504 750	78.5
1995	39 188 000	504 750	77.6
2000	39 800 000	504 750	78.8

SWEDEN

	Population	Area	Density
1900	5 137 000	447 749	11.5
1910	5 522 403	447 749	12.3
1920	5 904 489	448 161	13.2
1930	6 141 571	448 992	13.7
1940	6 370 538	449 101	14.2
1950	7 041 829	449 206	15.7
1960	7 495 129	449 793	16.7
1965	7 766 424	449 793	17.3
1970	9 076 903	449 793	20.1
1975	8 208 442	411 615	20.2
1980	8 320 438	411 615	20.2

SWEDEN (*continued*)

	Population	Area	Density
1990	8 529 000	410 929	20.8
1995	8 826 000	410 929	21.5
2000	8 900 000	410 929	21.7

SWITZERLAND

	Population	Area	Density
1900	2 315 000	41 378	55.9
1910	3 741 971	41 378	90.4
1920	3 880 320	41 378	93.8
1930	4 066 400	41 288	98.5
1941	4 265 703	41 288	103.3
1950	4 714 992	41 288	114.2
1960	5 429 061	41 288	131.5
1970	6 269 783	41 288	151.8
1980	6 365 960	41 288	154.0
1990	6 756 000	41 288	163.6
1995	7 039 000	41 288	170.5
2000	7 410 000	41 288	179.5

TURKEY

	Population	Area	Density
1927	13 648 270	762 537	17.9
1935	16 158 018	762 537	21.2
1940	17 820 950	762 537	23.4
1950	20 936 524	767 119	27.3
1960	27 754 820	767 119	36.2
1965	31 391 421	767 119	40.9
1970	35 666 549	767 119	46.5
1980	44 736 957	767 119	58.3
1990	56 941 000	767 119	73.0
1995	62 526 000	767 119	80.2
2000	65 730 000	767 119	85.6

UKRAINE

	Population	Area	Density
1995	52 003 000	603 700	86.1
2000	50 800 000	603 700	84.1

USSR

	Population	Area	Density
1920	135 710 423	24 900 000	5.4
1926	147 013 609	21 300 000	6.9
1939	170 467 186	21 200 000	8.0
1959	208 826 000	22 400 000	9.3
1970	241 748 000	22 400 000	10.8
1980	264 500 000	22 400 000	11.8
1990	290 122 000	22 275 000	13.0

UNITED KINGDOM

	Population	Area	Density
1901	41 459 000	243 363	170.3
1911	45 222 000	243 363	185.8
1921	43 176 521	243 363	177.8
1931	44 937 444	243 363	185.1
1951	49 012 362	243 363	201.4
1961	51 435 567	243 363	211.4
1971	55 347 000	243 363	227.8
1981	55 775 650	243 363	229.2
1991	57 333 000	244 110	235.7
1995	58 586 000	244 110	240.0
2000	59 450 000	244 110	243.5

YUGOSLAVIA

	Population	Area	Density
1921	12 017 323	248 987	48.3
1931	13 934 039	247 495	56.3

YUGOSLAVIA (*continued*)

	Population	*Area*	*Density*
1953	16 927 275	256 393	66.0
1961	18 549 291	255 804	72.5
1970	20 529 000	255 804	80.3
1981	22 424 711	255 804	87.7
1990	24 107 000	255 804	94.2
1995[1]	10 555 000	102 173	103.3
2000[1]	10 500 000	102 173	102.8

[1] Serbia and Montenegro.

EUROPEAN CAPITALS AND POPULATIONS

Country	*Capital*	*Population (thousands)*	
Albania	Tirana		243 (1990)
Andorra	Andorra la Vella		22 (1997)
Armenia	Yerevan		1283 (1991)
Austria	Vienna	1675 (1897)	1540 (1991)
Belarus	Minsk	91 (1897)	1695 (1995)
Belgium	Brussels	599 (1899)	948 (1996)
Bosnia-Hercegovina	Sarajevo		360 (1997)
Bulgaria	Sofia	68 (1900)	1117 (1996)
Croatia	Zagreb		868 (1991)
Cyprus	Nicosia		186[1] (1994)
Czech Republic	Prague	202 (1897)	1210 (1996)
Denmark	Copenhagen	401 (1897)	1346 (1994)
Estonia	Tallinn		435 (1996)
Finland	Helsinki	91 (1900)	532 (1997)
France	Paris	2714 (1897)	2152 (1990)
Georgia	Tbilisi	161 (1900)	1253 (1997)
Germany	Berlin	1889 (1900)	3470 (1995)
Greece	Athens	111 (1900)	772 (1991)
Hungary	Budapest	732 (1900)	1885 (1997)
Iceland	Reykjavik		105 (1996)

Country	Capital	Population (thousands)	
Ireland	Dublin	373 (1900)	481 (1996)
Italy	Rome	463 (1897)	2654 (1996)
Latvia	Riga	256 (1900)	827 (1996)
Liechtenstein	Vaduz		5 (1997)
Lithuania	Vilnius		573 (1996)
Luxembourg	Luxembourg		76 (1995)
Malta	Valletta		9 (1996)
Moldova	Chișinău		658 (1993)
The Netherlands	The Hague	212 (1900)	443 (1996)
Norway	Oslo (Christiania)	228 (1900)	494 (1997)
Poland	Warsaw	638 (1900)	1638 (1996)
Portugal	Lisbon	356 (1900)	663 (1991)
Romania	Bucharest	732 (1900)	2080 (1994)
Russia	Moscow[2]	989 (1897)	8400 (1996)
San Marino	San Marino		2 (1997)
Slovakia	Bratislava		452 (1996)
Slovenia	Ljubljana		270 (1995)
Spain	Madrid	540 (1900)	2867 (1996)
Sweden	Stockholm	301 (1900)	718 (1997)
Switzerland	Bern		127 (1996)
Turkey	Ankara		2838 (1995)
Ukraine	Kiev	247 (1900)	2630 (1996)
United Kingdom	London[3]	6586 (1900)	7074 (1996)
Yugoslavia	Belgrade	69 (1900)	1168 (1991)

[1] Republic of Cyprus only.
[2] St Petersburg then capital 1267 (1897).
[3] Greater London.

LIFE EXPECTANCY (1999)

	Male	Female
Albania	70	76
Andorra	76	82
Armenia	68	75
Austria	73	79

	Male	*Female*
Belarus	66	76
Belgium	72	79
Bosnia-Hercegovina	51	61
Bulgaria	69	75
Croatia	66	75
Cyprus	75	79
Denmark	72	78
Estonia	65	75
Finland	72	79
France	73	81
Georgia	69	76
Germany	73	79
Gibraltar	73	80
Greece	75	80
Hungary	65	74
Iceland	77	81
Ireland	70	76
Italy	73	79
Latvia	64	75
Liechtenstein	67	80
Lithuania	63	75
Luxembourg	73	79
Macedonia	70	74
Malta	73	78
Moldova	68	72
Netherlands	74	80
Norway	74	80
Poland	67	76
Portugal	71	78
Romania	69	75
Russia	64	71
San Marino	77	85
Slovakia	69	75
Slovenia	69	77
Spain	73	81

	Male	*Female*
Sweden	75	81
Switzerland	75	81
Turkey	69	73
Ukraine	66	75
United Kingdom	74	79
Yugoslavia[1]	70	75

[1] Serbia and Montenegro.

11
New Countries
A Guide to the New States of the Post-Communist Era

ARMENIA

Republic of Armenia (Hayastani Hanrapetut'yun) is bounded in the north by Georgia, in the east by Azerbaijan and in the south and west by Turkey and Iran. Capital: Yerevan. In a referendum in 1991, 99 per cent of the electorate voted for independence from the USSR, which was declared on 21 Sep 1991. In Dec 1991 it became a member of the Commonwealth of Independent States (CIS).

BELARUS

Republic of Belarus (Respublika Belarus) is bounded in west by Poland, north by Latvia and Lithuania, east by Russia and south by Ukraine. Capital: Minsk. Belarus issued a declaration of state sovereignty on 27 Jul 1990 and on 25 Aug 1991 adopted a declaration of independence from the USSR. In Dec 1991 it became a member of the Commonwealth of Independent States (CIS).

BOSNIA–HERCEGOVINA

Republic of Bosnia and Hercegovina (Republika Bosna i Hercigovina) is bounded in the north and west by Croatia and in the east and south-east by Yugoslavia (Serbia and Montenegro). Capital: Sarajevo. On 15 Oct 1991 the National Assembly adopted a memorandum on sovereignty, against the wishes of the Serb Democratic Party. A referendum for independence was held 29 Feb–1 Mar 1992. The turnout was 63 per cent, largely boycotted by the Serbian population: there were 99.78 per cent in favour. Bosnia-Hercegovina declared itself independent on 5 Apr 1992 and was recognized as an independent state by EU and USA on 2 Apr 1992. Fighting broke out between Serb, Croat and Muslim communities. UN-sponsored cease-fires were repeatedly violated. On

10 Apr 1994 NATO air strikes were used. On 21 Nov 1995 the prime ministers of Bosnia, Croatia and Yugoslavia signed an agreement at Dayton, Ohio, USA to end hostilities. The terms were that (i) Bosnia would include a Serb state containing 49 per cent of Bosnia territory and a Muslim–Croat Federation; (ii) a central government would represent all ethnic groups and deal with foreign, monetary and citizenship issues; and (iii) free elections would be held.

CROATIA

Republic of Croatia (Republika Hrvatska) is bounded in the north by Slovenia and Hungary and in the east by Yugoslavia and Bosnia-Hercegovina. Capital: Zagreb. In a referendum on 19 May 1991, 94.17 per cent of the population on a turnout of 82.97 per cent voted for independence. Independence was declared in Jun 1991 and fighting broke out between Croatia and Serbia and continued until Jan 1992 when a cease-fire was declared.

CZECH REPUBLIC

The Czech Republic (Česká Republika) is bounded in the west by Germany, north by Poland, east by Slovakia and south by Austria. Capital: Prague. On 25 Nov 1992 the Czechoslovakian Federal Assembly voted for the dissolution of the Czech and Slovak Federal Republics and to form two sovereign states. This came into effect on 1 Jan 1993.

GEORGIA

Republic of Georgia (Sakartvelos Respublika) is bounded in the west by the Black Sea and south by Turkey, Armenia and Azerbaijan. Capital: Tbilisi. Following a referendum, 98.9 per cent of the population voted for independence based on the Treaty of Independence of 26 May 1918. Independence was declared on 9 Apr 1991. In Jan 1992 there was an armed insurrection and the President was deposed. Georgia became a member of the Commonwealth of Independent States (CIS) by presidential decree on 22 Oct 1993 and this was ratified by parliament on 1 Mar 1994. South Ossetia, formerly an autonomous region, lost its autonomy on 11 Dec 1990. Fighting broke out between Georgian forces and those Ossetians who wished to unite with North Ossetia (part of the Russian Federation). In 1997 some 8500 Russian troops and 2100 peace-keeping forces were stationed in 3 military bases. The UN had 117 observers from 23 countries.

MACEDONIA
Former Yugoslavia

Republic of Macedonia (Republika Makedonija, member of the United Nations as 'Former Yugoslavia Republic of Macedonia' which was acceptable to Greece) is bounded in the north by Yugoslavia, in the east by Bulgaria, in the south by Greece and in the west by Albania. Capital: Skopje. Macedonia declared its independence on 20 Nov 1992.

MOLDOVA

Republic of Moldova (Republica Moldova) is bounded in the east and south by the Ukraine and in the west by Romania. Formerly Moldavia. Capital: Chişinău. Sovereignty was declared in Jun 1990 and independence in Aug 1991. In Dec 1991, Moldova became a member of the Commonwealth of Independent States (CIS). The majority of the Romanian population wished to rejoin Romania. After some fighting the Russian and Ukrainian populations declared their independence from Moldova in Dec 1991 as the Transdneister Republic. The Moldovan government refused to recognize the Republic and war continued during the early part of 1992 when a Russian CIS peace-keeping force was deployed.

RUSSIA

The Russian Federation (Rossiiskaya Federtsiya) is bounded in the north by the Arctic Ocean and the Barents Sea; in the west by Norway, the Gulf of Finland, Finland, Estonia, Latvia, Belarus and Ukraine; in the south by Georgia, Azerbaijan, the Black Sea, the Caspian Sea, Kazakhstan, China, Mongolia and North Korea; and in the east by the North Pacific and the Bering Strait. Capital: Moscow. The Federation consists of 89 members: 21 Republics, 10 Autonomous Areas (*okrug*), 49 Regions (*oblast*), 6 Autonomous Territories (*krai*), 2 cities with federal status (Moscow and St Petersburg) and one autonomous Jewish region, Birobijan.

With the break-up of the USSR in Dec 1991 Russia became one of the founding members of the Commonwealth of Independent States (CIS).

SLOVAKIA

The Slovak Republic (Slovenska Republika) is bounded in the north-west by the Czech Republic, north by Poland, east by the Ukraine, south by Hungary and south-west by Austria. Capital: Bratislava. On 25 Nov 1992 the Czechoslovakian Federal Assembly voted for the dissolution of the Czech and Slovak Federal

Republics, and to form two sovereign states. This came into effect on 1 Jan 1993.

SLOVENIA

Republic of Slovenia (Republika Slovenija) is bounded in the north by Austria, in the north-east by Hungary, in the south-east by Croatia and in the west by Italy. Capital: Ljubljana. A declaration of sovereignty was declared by the Assembly on 2 Jul 1990. A referendum held on 23 Dec 1990 gave 88.5 per cent voting for independence and this was declared on 26 Dec 1990. Federal Yugoslav troops moved into Slovenia on 27 Jun 1990 to 'secure Yugoslavia's external borders' but after a 10-day war, withdrew in July. Recognition as an independent state came from the Federal Republic of Germany 23 Dec 1991 and the European Union on 15 Jan 1992.

UKRAINE

Ukraine (Ukrayina) is bounded in the east by Russia; the north by Belarus; the west by Poland, Slovakia, Hungary, Romania and Moldova; and the south by the Black Sea and the Sea of Azov. Capital: Kiev (Kyyiv). On 5 Dec 1991 the Supreme Soviet unanimously repudiated the 1922 Treaty of Union and declared Ukraine an independent state. This followed a referendum held 1 Dec 1991 when 90 per cent of the electorate voted for independence. Ukraine was a founder-member of the Commonwealth of Independent States (CIS) in Dec 1991.

YUGOSLAVIA
Serbia and Montenegro

Federal Republic of Yugoslavia (Savezna Republika Jugoslavija) is bounded in the north by Hungary; north-east by Romania; east by Bulgaria; south by Macedonia and Albania; and west by the Adriatic Sea, Bosnia-Hercegovina and Croatia. Capital: Belgrade. On 27 Apr 1992 Serbia and Montenegro announced the formation of a Federal Republic of Yugoslavia constituted by themselves as the legal successor to the former Socialist Federal Republic of Yugoslavia (SFRY), but on 22 Sep 1992 the United Nations stated that the new Republic could not automatically assume the seat of the former SFRY.

Glossary of Terms

Action Française French nationalist, monarchist, anti-Semitic political organization founded in 1899 by Charles Maurras (1868–1952) which backed the Vichy régime and was banned after the 1944 Liberation.

Agadir Crisis Diplomatic and military crisis in 1911 caused by arrival of German warship *Panther* in Moroccan port of Agadir. Supposedly sent to protect German residents, the main aim was to gain colonial concessions from the French elsewhere in Africa in exchange for recognition of the French interest in Morocco.

Agrogorod (Russ. 'agro-town') Agricultural organization proposed by Nikita Khrushchev (1894–1971) under which farmers would live in flats and work on centrally-grouped private plots. A version was attempted in the Ukraine in the period 1959–1965.

Anschluss (Germ. 'union') Amalgamation of Germany and Austria forbidden by Versailles Treaty created on 13 Mar 1938 with entry of German troops after spurious request to maintain order by pro-Nazi Austrian Chancellor Seyss-Inquart.

Apparatchik Full-time paid officials working in the Soviet Communist party *apparat* (party machine).

Appeasement Diplomatic attempt to avoid war by conceding demands, notably Anglo-French acquiescence in Hitler's seizure of the Rhineland (1936), Austria (1938) and the Czech Sudetenland (1938). Abandoned when Germany absorbed the remainder of Czechoslovakia in Mar 1939.

Arrondissement In France, a subdivision of the larger political and administrative unit, the *département*.

Ausgleich (Germ. compromise) Agreement reached between the Austrian government and moderate Hungarian politicians in 1867 which transformed the Austrian Empire into the Dual Monarchy of Austria–Hungary. The system remained in operation until 1918.

Austro-Marxism Revisionist Marxist trend which emerged in Austria in 1907. Its main figures were Max Adler, Otto Bauer and Rudolf Hilferding.

Autarchy Attempt by a state – *e.g.* pre-World War II Germany – to attain economic self-sufficiency by reducing imports and increasing home production.

Axis Term used by Mussolini on 1 Nov 1939 to describe alliance of Germany and Italy, extended in World War II to include Bulgaria, Hungary, Japan, Romania, and Slovakia.

Ballila Youth wing of the Italian Fascist Party.

Baltic States Term used for Estonia, Latvia and Lithuania, formerly part of the Soviet Union from 1940 to 1991. The Soviet Union had seized them in 1940 as part of the 1939 Nazi–Soviet Pact.

Barbarossa, Operation Code name for the 22 Jun 1941 German invasion of the USSR.

Basic Law Post-war constitution which came into force in 1949 in West Germany.

Benelux Customs union of Belgium, Netherlands and Luxembourg agreed by treaty of 3 Feb 1958, coming into effect on 1 Nov 1960.

Black Hand Popular name of the Serbian secret society (*Ujedinjenje ili Smrt*) formed in Belgrade in May 1911. Led by Colonel Dragutin Dimitrievič, the society's main aim was the unifying of Serb minorities in Austria–Hungary and the Ottoman Empire with the independent state of Serbia.

Blackshirts   Initially term for Italian Fascists because of their uniform; extended in 1930s to include German Schutzstaffeln (SS) and Mosley's British Union of Fascists.

Black Tuesday   (Russia) The day (11 Oct 1994) when the rouble collapsed to 3926 to the dollar. The crash caused panic in Moscow's financial institutions and led to the removal of the Finance Minister Sergei Dubinin and the governor of the Central Bank. It fell to even lower levels in Jan 1995 because of the Chechen conflict, before stabilizing later.

Blank Cheque   The verbal reply given on 5 Jul 1914 in response to a letter from Emperor Francis Joseph of Austria by Kaiser Wilhelm II to Count Hoyos, an Austrian Foreign Ministry official, guaranteeing German support if Austria attacked Serbia.

Blitzkrieg   (Germ. 'lightning war') Military tactic of heavy air bombardment followed by rapid armoured advance, effectively used in Poland (1939) and Western Europe (1940).

Bloody Sunday   Term used of the massacre in St Petersburg on Sunday 22 Jan 1905. A procession of workers and their families led by Father George Gapon was fired on by troops guarding the Winter Palace in St Petersburg. Over one hundred people were killed and several hundred wounded, an event which helped to spark off the 1905 Russian Revolution.

Bolshevik   (Russ. 'larger') Militant majority under Lenin which emerged from a split in the Russian Social Democratic Party in 1903 (the Mensheviks made up the minority) and which seized power in October 1917.

Bosnian Serbs   The Serb population in Bosnia–Hercegovina who proclaimed the independent *Republika Srbska* during the civil war (*see* p. 399). Their leader was Radovan Karadzic.

Brezhnev Doctrine   The ideological basis of the Warsaw Pact invasion of Czechoslovakia in August 1968. Leonid Brezhnev pronounced a doctrine of 'limited sovereignty' denying East European states the right to diverge widely from the Soviet model, and asserting the legitimacy of intervention.

Bundesrat   West German federal council elected by members of the ten state (Länder) governments and which had restricted veto powers on Bundestag legislation. Joined in 1990 by the five former East German Länder.

Bundestag   German Federal Parliament established on 23 May 1949 and elected for a four-year fixed term. Prior to 1990, East Germany had its own parliament.

Bundeswehr   Armed forces of the Federal Republic of Germany (West Germany prior to 1990).

Cadres   Communist Party members with specific responsibility for organizing and politically educating the working class.

CAP   Common Agricultural Policy, the mechanism for organizing European Community farming and primary production and for distributing agricultural subsidies.

Caudillo, EL   (Sp. 'the leader') Title taken in 1937 by General Francisco Franco (1892–1975), the leader of the successful right-wing rising against the Spanish Republic.

Central Powers   Initially members of the Triple Alliance created by Bismarck in 1882, namely Germany, Austria–Hungary and Italy. As Italy remained neutral in the First World War, the term was applied to Germany, Austria–Hungary, their ally Turkey and later also Bulgaria.

Cetnik   *See* Chetnik.

CGT Confédération Générale du Travail. The largest French trade union federation, formed in 1906 on a non-political syndicalist platform.

Charter '77 Charter demanding recognition by Czechoslovak government of 1975 Helsinki human rights declaration; signed by many Czechs despite harassment and victimization.

Cheka Secret political police established in Russia to defend régime internally through terror following Bolshevik seizure of power in Oct 1917.

Chetnik Originally anti-Turkish Serbian nationalist guerrillas; in World War II initially active in anti-German resistance but their anti-communism encouraged some to collaborate with German and Italian forces.

Christmas Revolution Term applied to the popular uprising in Romania in Dec 1989 against the Ceauçescu dictatorship. Sometimes called the 'winter revolution'.

Cohabitation Term used to describe the political situation in France following the 1986 parliamentary election when the socialist President Mitterrand and the conservative government went on to tolerate and work alongside each other.

Cold War Post-World War II tension between capitalist states – led by the USA – and Communist states – led by the USSR – which thawed following Gorbachev's emergence as Soviet leader in 1985 and appeared effectively over with East European communism's collapse in 1989–1990.

Colons French colonial settlers, particularly in Algeria.

Cominform Communist Information Bureau formed in Feb 1947 to organize Communist activity in Europe, dissolved by Khrushchev in Apr 1956 as conciliatory gesture to the West.

Comintern Communist International formed in Mar 1919 to co-ordinate international revolutionary Communist activity but which developed into an arm of Soviet foreign policy. Dissolved in May 1943 by Stalin to allay Western allies' fears.

Commissar Head of a government department in the USSR; political commissars in the Red Army had responsibility for ideological education.

Conducator Title taken by Nicolae Ceauçescu (1918–1989), dictator of Romania from 1967 until his overthrow and execution on 25 Dec 1989.

Crocodile Group A group established by members of the European Parliament in 1980, named after the restaurant in Strasbourg at which they met. The group, whose leading figure was the Italian federalist Altiero Spinelli, proposed radical reform of the European Community (EC), advocated moves towards political union, and led to the European Parliament's production of a draft Treaty on European Union.

Curzon Line The frontier between the former Soviet Union and Poland after 1945, originally proposed in negotiations in 1920 led by British foreign minister Lord Curzon. Although rejected by Poland when first suggested, the frontier was imposed by Germany and the Soviet Union following their 1939 attack on Poland and accepted at the end of World War II.

D-Day The Allied invasion of Normandy, launched 6 Jun 1944.

Destalinization Criticism of Stalin's policies and attempt at reform following his death in 1953. Khrushchev denounced his 'cult of personality' and 1930s purges at the 1956 20th Party Congress; Stalin's role was increasingly attacked in post-glasnost USSR.

Deutsche Arbeiterfront (Germ. 'German Labour Front') Nazi organization formed in Nov 1933 replacing banned trade unions to unite all workers and employers in national rather than class interest.

Deuxième Bureau (Fr. 'Second Bureau') French military intelligence.

Dirigisme   Post-World War II French policy of state intervention in the free enterprise economy without centralized socialist planning.

Dissidents   Term formerly used paticularly in the context of Russia, Communist Eastern Europe and China to refer to those who refused to conform to the politics and beliefs of the society in which they lived. They have frequently been imprisoned and persecuted. Among the most famous were Alexander Solzhenitsyn, the Nobel Prize-winning novelist, expelled from Russia in 1974. In 1980 the most prominent Soviet dissident, Andrei Sakharov, was sentenced to internal exile in Gorky. The advent of Mikhail Gorbachev to the Soviet leadership produced rapid concessions on the treatment of dissidents. Notable dissidents in other Eastern bloc countries have included members of the Charter '77 group in Czechoslovakia, including the playwright and politician Vaclav Havel.

Drang nach Osten   (Germ. 'thrust to the east') Historic German wish to expand into Eastern Europe.

Dual Alliance   Also known as the Dual Entente. An alliance between Russia and France which lasted from 1893 until the Bolshevik Revolution of Oct 1917.

Duce IL   (It. 'the leader') Title of Benito Mussolini (1883–1945), Italian Prime Minister from Oct 22, outright fascist dictator from 1926.

Duma   Russian parliament established by the Tsar in 1905 in response to demands which emanated from the abortive revolution of 1905.

Eastern Bloc   Pre-1990 Communist states of Eastern Europe: Bulgaria, Czechoslovakia, East Germany, Hungary, Poland, USSR, and which also included – despite their differences – Albania, Romania and Yugoslavia.

Eastern Front   Battle lines between Germany and Russia in World Wars I and II.

Eastern Question   The title given to the various problems of international, and especially European, relations created by the gradual decline of the Ottoman Empire in the late nineteenth and early twentieth centuries.

EFTA   *see* p. 27.

Einsatzgruppen   (Germ. 'special service squads') Forces attached to German army to repress population in World War II occupied territories; responsible for killing of Jews, Communists, and anti-Nazi resistance members.

ELAS   National People's Army of Liberation formed by Communists in Greece following Apr 1941 German occupation. After liberation fought unsuccessful civil war against Western-backed monarchists, changing name to Democratic Army of Greece.

Enosis   (Gk. 'to unite') Greek Cypriot movement seeking union of Cyprus and Greece.

Entente Cordiale   (Fr. cordial agreement) Term first used in the 1840s to describe the special relationship between Britain and France. Revived in the Anglo–French Entente of 8 Apr 1904 and a similar agreement with Russia in Aug 1907.

EOKA   (Gk. Ethniki Orgánosis Kypriakoú Agnósos, 'National Organization of Cypriot Struggle') Anti-British Greek Cypriot guerrilla force founded by George Grivas (1898–1974) active from 1955–1959; remained in existence following 1960 Cypriot independence seeking union with Greece.

Épuration   Purge of collaborators conducted in 1944–1945 after liberation of France; 767 were legally executed following trial but 30000 were believed killed.

Ersatz   (Germ. 'substitute') Goods produced in wartime to replace unobtainable items, *e.g.* coffee made from acorns.

Estado Novo   The 'new state' in Portugal, the fascist régime established in 1926 and which was for long ruled after 1932 by António de Oliveira Salazar.

ETA Separatist terrorist movement seeking to re-establish Basque Republic of Euzkadi (*q.v.*) which existed in Northern Spain from Oct 1936–Jun 1938. Its political wing, Herri Batasuna, was founded in 1978.

Ethnic cleansing Euphemism which emerged in the break-up of the former Yugoslavia in 1992 to describe attempts to remove minority ethnic groups by persuading communities to flee through threats and near-genocidal violence. Most often used to describe Serb actions against the Muslim community in Bosnia.

Eurocommunism West European Communist parties' attempt to distance themselves from USSR and to seek power through parliamentary democracy and within own national traditions.

Europe des Patries (Fr. 'Europe of the nation states') The expression which denotes a European Community which does not move to complete economic and political union but which allows a continuing pursuit of individual national interests. First used by French politician Michel Debré in 1959, the expression was primarily associated with President de Gaulle and later Margaret Thatcher.

European Nuclear Disarmament (END) Movement formed in 1980 initially to agitate for a nuclear-free Europe, going on to seek an end to US and Soviet power in Europe.

Eurosceptic Term for opponents of greater European unity via the European Union (former EEC and European Community) brought to a head in Britain in Conservative Party debates in the 1990s over the Maastricht Treaty.

Euzkadi Autonomous state in Northern Spain established by Basques in Oct 1936; cultural and political suppression followed its occupation by Franco's forces in Jun 1938.

Falange The only political party permitted in Franco's Spain.

February Strike Communist-organized general strike in Amsterdam on 25 Feb 1941 in protest against transportation of 425 Jews to concentration camps, provoking German imposition of a state of siege.

Festung Europa (Germ. 'fortification of Europe') Hitler's World War II plans to create a Reich impregnable to Allied invasion.

Fifth Republic French Republic established under influence of Gen. Charles de Gaulle (1890–1970, President 1958–1969), with a strong presidency and a weak legislature.

Final Solution Nazi euphemism for their genocidal plans to destroy the Jews.

Finlandization Agreement under a 1948 treaty of friendship between the Soviet Union and Finland by which, effectively in return for its independence, Finland pledged to defend the Soviet Union if any power attempted invasion through Finland. The term is thus applied to any neighbour of a major power which effectively becomes a client state.

Force de frappe French strategic nuclear strike force.

Fourteen Points A peace programme put forward by President Woodrow Wilson to the US Congress on 8 Jan 1918 and accepted as the basis for an armistice by Germany and Austria–Hungary. Later it was alleged that the Allied powers had violated the principles embodied in the Fourteen Points, especially in relation to the prohibition of Anschluss, the union of Germany with Austria.

Fourth International Communist organization formed in 1934 by Leon Trotsky (1879–1940) because of his antagonism towards the Stalin-dominated Third International (Comintern).

Fourth Republic The French Republic from 1946 to 1958.

Franc fort The policy of successive French governments of preserving a 'strong' currency, *i.e.* maintaining the value of the franc.

Francistes   Blue-shirted French fascist movement formed by Marcel Duchard in 1934, initially financed by Italy and then by Nazi World War II occupation forces.

Free French   Forces Françaises Libres, World War II anti-German and anti-Vichy forces led by a French National Committee under Gen. Charles de Gaulle (1890–1970); renamed Forces Françaises Combatantes (Fighting French Forces) in Jul 1942.

Führer   (Germ. 'leader') Title taken by Hitler following appointment as German Chancellor in Jan 1933.

Gastarbeiter   (Germ. 'guestworker') Overseas labour, predominantly Greek, Turkish and Moroccan, recruited to meet the needs of West German industry in the 1960s and 1970s.

GATT   General Agreement on Tariffs and Trade, a United Nations agency formed in 1948 to weaken national tariff barriers and encourage international trade.

Gauleiter   Nazi official responsible for economic, political and civil defence organization in his Gau, a Nazi administrative area.

Gaullists   Political followers in France of Gen. Charles de Gaulle (1890–1970, President 1958–1969), mainly organized in the Rassemblement du Peuple Français (1947–1955) and the Union pour la Nouvelle République (formed 1958).

Generalissimo   Italian and Spanish title for the supreme commander of a military and naval force. Used especially to refer to Spanish dictator Franco.

Gestapo   (Germ. 'Geheime Staats Polizei') Nazi secret police force established on 26 Apr 1933 to arrest and murder opponents, expanding and becoming a wing of the SS (*q.v.*) under Heinrich Himmler (1900–1945).

Glasnost   (Russ. 'openness') Soviet political and intellectual liberalization following appointment of Mikhail Gorbachev as Communist Party Secretary in 1985, encouraging a questioning which ultimately weakened Party authority.

Gosplan   Soviet State Planning Commission created centrally to control Stalin's economic programmes from 1924 to 1953.

Grand Coalition   West German government from 26 Nov 1966 to 27 Sep 1969 with Christian Democrat Kurt Kiesinger as Chancellor and Social Democrat Willy Brandt as deputy and foreign minister, formed to face developing economic problems.

Grundgesetz   The post-war constitution (*i.e.* the Basic Law) of (originally) West Germany. It came into force in 1949.

Gulag   The forced labour camps of the former Soviet Union, established by Stalin in 1930. Their infamous record (of perhaps 8 million deaths) was immortalized by Aleksandr Solzhenitsyn in *The Gulag Archipelago*.

Habsburgs   The house of Habsburg-Lorraine, an Austrian royal dynasty which ruled from 1282 to 1918. The murder of the heir to the Austrian Habsburg throne in 1914, Francis Ferdinand, led to the outbreak of the First World War, and the last Emperor, Charles I, was forced to abdicate in 1918.

Hallstein Doctrine   The West German assertion in 1955 of its refusal to recognize East Germany, together with a declaration that it would resent any other state doing so. The purpose was to maintain the isolation of the GDR, which Bonn maintained was not a legally constituted state but a barrier to German reunification. Named after one of Chancellor Adenauer's senior foreign policy advisors.

Herrenvolk   (Germ. 'master race') Allegedly racially superior Aryans in Nazi ideology.

Historic compromise   Term used to describe the support given by the Italian Communist Party (PCI) to the governing Christian Democrats after 1976. The support marked the end of more than a generation of Communist exclusion from the governing coalitions of modern Italy and reflected the need to form a strong base with which to deal with growing problems of inflation and terrorism.

Hohenzollern German royal dynasty which provided the three German emperors, 1871–1918. Originally the Prussian royal house, the monarchy was finally brought to an end by the abdication of Kaiser Wilhelm II in Nov 1918.

Holocaust Nazi genocide against the Jewish race through murder in concentration camps during World War II.

Immobilisme The paralysis that marred the politics of the French Third Republic (1870–1940) and Fifth Republic (1946–1958), largely as a result of constantly shifting coalitions that led to weak government. The problem was said to have arisen from a combination of a weak presidency, a strong National Assembly and proportional representation.

Internal market Ultimate objective of the Treaty of Rome to establish a full common market in Europe. The internal market was effectively established in Jan 1993 but obstacles remained in the form of border controls which prevented the free movement of labour.

International Brigades Left-wing and Communist volunteers from many countries who fought for the Spanish Republic in the 1936–1939 Civil War.

Iron Curtain Post-war dividing line through Central Europe between Communist and non-Communist states which collapsed in 1989–1990.

Irredentism Demand by a country for the return of territory formerly in its possession; from nineteenth-century Italia Irredenta party.

July Conspiracy Abortive plot to murder Hitler in Jul 1944.

Kadets (Russ. Konstitutsionnye Demokraty, 'Constitutional Democrats') Russian liberal party formed after 1905 Revolution which proposed a democratic Republic after 1917 Revolution; banned by the Bolsheviks in 1918.

Kaiser (Germ. Caesar, *i.e.* Emperor) Title assumed by the Prussian King Wilhelm I following the unification of Germany and the creation of the German Empire. Wilhelm accepted the crown of a united Germany in Dec 1870.

Kapp Putsch Attempted overthrow of Weimar Republic in Mar 1920 by journalist Wolfgang Kapp (1868–1922) with right-wing support; failed after general strike and because army officers refused backing.

KGB (Russ. Komitet Gosudarstvennoe Bezopasnosti, 'Committee of State Security') Soviet secret police founded in Mar 1954 with responsibility for internal security, espionage and counter-espionage.

Kolkhoz Collective farms in the former Soviet Union. The term originated with the collectivization of agriculture in the USSR during the 1928–1933 Five Year Plan when all individual farms and smallholdings were combined into the kolkhoz system.

Komsomol (Russ. Kommunisticheski Soyuz Molodezki, 'Communist Union of Youth') Communist Party of the Soviet Union's youth wing.

Kraków Declaration Declaration made by Czechoslovakia, Hungary and Poland on 5–6 Oct 1991 pledging attempt to integrate their forces into NATO and to join the European Community.

Kremlin (Russ. 'citadel') Soviet government centre in Moscow; by extension the Soviet government itself.

Kulak (Russ. 'tight-fisted person') Relatively prosperous peasants; millions were deported or murdered because of their opposition to Soviet agricultural collectivization between 1928 and 1932.

Länder   States in the Weimar Republic from 1919–1933; the title was restored in the post-World War II Federal Republic of Germany.

Landtag   Legislatures in the states (Länder) of Austria and the Federal Republic of Germany.

League of Nations   *See* p. 6.

Little Entente   *See* p. 412.

Lublin Committee   The Soviet-backed Polish Committee of National Liberation established in the city of Lublin on 25 Jul 1944 as the core of a Communist government for the country, recognized by the USSR in Dec 1944 as the provisional government. The committee joined with the London-based Polish government in exile to form a Polish Provisional Government of National Unity in Jul 1945.

Lustration   A term (deriving from the Latin for sacrificial purification) used in the former Czechoslovakia and other East European states to describe the exposure of collaborators with the secret police of the previous Communist régimes, a central part of decommunisation.

Maginot Line   French defensive fortifications against Germany reaching from Luxembourg to the Swiss border, constructed 1929–1934, named after War Minister André Maginot (1877–1932). The Maginot Line was circumvented by the German offensive of 1940.

Maquis   World War II French anti-German resistance.

Marshall Plan   United States Plan for the economic reconstruction of Europe, named after Secretary of State General George C. Marshall. The Organization for European Economic Cooperation was established to administer the aid in Apr 1948.

May Events   The events of May 1968 when French students, demonstrating against education cuts in Paris, precipitated a political crisis in France. The strikes and riots went on into June, but the government eventually defused the situation by promising educational reform, and wage increases to the workers.

Mein Kampf   (Germ. 'My Struggle') Book written in prison in 1923 by Adolf Hitler (1889–1945) setting out his political programme of German expansion, anti-communism and anti-Semitism.

Menshevik   (Russ. 'the minority') Moderate wing emerging from the 1903 split in the Russian Social Democratic Party; outlawed by the Bolsheviks in 1922.

Messina Conference   Meeting in Jun 1955 of the foreign ministers of Belgium, France, Italy, Luxembourg, the Netherlands and West Germany at which agreement was reached to work towards the formation of a European Economic Community (EEC). Britain refused to attend. The conference was followed in 1957 by the Treaty of Rome.

Moroccan Crisis   A European crisis precipitated by German attempts to break up the Anglo–French Entente of 1904. Wilhelm II's landing at Tangier and his expression of German support for Moroccan independence led to acrimonious relations between Germany and France. The Algeçiras Conference of Jan–Apr 1906 recognized French predominance in Morocco and represented a defeat for the German stand.

National schism   Term for the bitter division between Constantine I, King of Greece, and his leading minister, Venizelos, over which side Greece should support in the First World War.

NATO   *See* p. 14.

Nazi   (Germ. Nationalsozialistische Deutsche Arbeiter Partei, German National Socialist Workers' Party) Member of the party formed in Oct 1920, led by Adolf Hitler (1889–1945) who became Chancellor in Jan 1933 and ruled until his suicide in Apr 1945.

NEP New Economic Policy; relative liberalization of Bolshevik policy introduced in Mar 1921 allowing growth of small businesses, limited private agriculture, and freer internal trade.

New Order World War II Nazi plans for a Europe united under German control.

Night of the Long Knives Murder of the Nazi SA leaders, many of their followers, and other potential political rivals, on 29–30 Jun 1934, ordered by Hitler on grounds that the SA was plotting against his régime. This action consolidated Hitler's power.

November criminals Abusive term current in Germany from 1918 to 1945, blaming politicians who negotiated Germany's surrender in 1918 for the nation's defeat.

Nuremberg Rallies Mass propaganda Nazi rallies organized at the Party's Nuremberg congresses from 1933–1938.

October Revolution Bolshevik overthrow of Provisional Government and seizure of power on 6–7 Nov 1917 led by Vladimir Lenin (1870–1924). (Under the old Julian calendar then in operation in Russia, the month was October.)

OGPU Soviet counter-revolutionary security police formed in 1922 as GPU (State Political Administration), renamed OGPU (Unified State Political Administration) in 1923. Replaced by the NKVD in 1934.

Ostpolitik (Germ. 'eastern policy') German Federal Republic policy from 1970s of improving relations with East European Communist states, recognizing German Democratic Republic, and acknowledging post-war boundaries.

Outremer (Fr. 'overseas') France's overseas colonies from the seventeenth to twentieth centuries.

OVRA Italian Fascist secret police formed in 1927.

Pact of Steel Military alliance concluded between Germany and Italy in Berlin on 22 May 1939.

Panslavism The name given to the various movements for closer union of peoples speaking Slavic languages in the nineteenth and early twentieth centuries.

Panzer German expression for an armoured fighting vehicle, extended to describe an armoured division.

Partisans Guerrilla groups fighting behind enemy lines, *e.g.* in World War II German-occupied Russia, Albania, Greece, Slovakia and Yugoslavia.

Perestroika (Russ. 'restructuring') Attempt at radical reform of Soviet economy introduced by Mikhail Gorbachev, Communist Party leader from 1985, involving increasing replacement of central control by market forces.

Phoney War Period of military inactivity on the Western Front between the declaration of war on Germany in Sep 1939 and the German advance of Apr 1940.

Pogrom (Russ. 'destruction') Organized massacre in Russia, particularly involving attacks on Jews, the first of which was authorized by the Tsarist authorities in 1881.

Politburo The leading Party committee in Communist controlled states.

Popular Front Communist tactic of allying with socialists and liberals to confront common fascist enemy in the 1930s. Popular Front governments were formed in France and Spain.

Poujadist Supporter of the Union de Défence des Commercants et Artisans, militant right-wing party active in France from 1954–1958, formed by Pierre Poujade.

Prague Spring Czechoslovak liberalization after the appointment of Alexander Dubček as Communist Party Secretary on 5 Jan 1968 and the adoption of a reform programme on 5 Apr. Warsaw Pact invasion ended the experiment on 20–21 Aug.

Provisional government The government of Russia between Mar and Oct 1917. Brought to power after the deposition of the monarchy, the Provisional government was made up of members of the Duma (*q.v.*) but had to share power in Petrograd with the Workers' and Soldiers' Soviet.

Putsch   (Germ. 'revolt') Overthrow of a government by conspiracy, *e.g.* the failed right-wing attempt led by Wolfgang Kapp in 1920 to oust the Weimar Republic.

Quai d'Orsay   The embankment in Paris where the French Foreign Office is situated.

Quisling   Collaborator with an occupying power, from Vidkun Quisling (1887–1945), a Norwegian Nazi who led a German puppet government during the 1940–1945 occupation.

Rapacki Plan   Proposal by Polish Foreign Minister Adam Rapacki on 2 Oct 1957 to ban nuclear weapons production and deployment in Czechoslovakia, Poland, East and West Germany; rejected by the West because the USSR would have retained conventional superiority.

Red Brigades   Italian 1970s left-wing terrorist group which kidnapped and murdered former Prime Minister Aldo Moro in 1976; a core remained active into the 1980s.

Refuseniks   Predominantly Jewish Soviet citizens refused permission to emigrate from the USSR by the authorities.

Reich   (Germ. 'empire') The First Reich was the medieval Holy Roman Empire; the Second from German unification in 1871 until the 1918 defeat; the Third the period of Nazi rule from 1933 to 1945.

Reichsbanner   The Reichsbanner Schwarz-Rot-Gold (the Weimar Republic's colours), mainly Social Democratic unarmed force formed in May 1924 to defend the Weimar Republic. Outlawed by Hitler in 1933.

Reichstag   German parliament building in Berlin from 1871 until its destruction by arson in Feb 1933.

Rentenmark   German currency introduced in 1923 by Chancellor Gustav Stresemann (1878–1929) to restore financial confidence following massive inflation and the French occupation of the Ruhr.

Reparations   Compensation for war damage demanded by victors from a defeated power, most notably the post-World War I figure of £6600 million (largely unpaid) imposed on Germany in Apr 1921.

Resistance   Armed opponents of German occupation in World War II Europe, particularly in France, who attacked enemy installations and personnel.

Revisionist   Term applied by orthodox Marxists to one who attempts to reassess the basic tenets of revolutionary socialism. Originating in Germany in the 1890s and 1900s, its chief exponents were Edouard Bernstein and Karl Kautsky. Regarded as heresy in the Soviet Union.

Romanov   The family name of the Russian royal house whose dynasty was ended by the deposition of Tsar Nicholas II in 1917 after the Russian Revolution.

SA   (Germ. Sturmabteilung, 'storm-troopers') Brownshirted Nazi private army founded in 1920–1921; 400000-strong by 1933. SA 'socialist' tendencies provoked Hitler into killing its leaders and weakening its influence in 1934.

Sajudis   The Lithuanian nationalist movement which declared Lithuania independent in 1990.

Samizdat   Dissident literature criticizing the Communist régime in the Soviet Union circulated secretly by its opponents.

Saneamento   Portuguese term, meaning cleansing, for the purging of officials and supporters of the old régime following the coup of Apr 1974.

Schlieffen Plan   German military plan for offensive action named after Chief of German General Staff, Count Alfred von Schlieffen, and first produced in 1905. In spite

88

of constant revision, the plan was the basis for the German attack in the west in Aug 1914.

Scrap of Paper   German Chancellor Bethmann-Hollweg's description of the 1839 Treaty of London, a five-power guarantee of Belgian neutrality which Germany violated by invasion on 4 Aug 1914, provoking a British declaration of war. He told the British ambassador that 'just for a scrap of paper, Great Britain is going to make war on a kindred nation which desires nothing better than to be friends with her.'

Second Economy   Term used in the Communist era for the 'black economy' of the Soviet Union and Eastern Europe. It embraced not only black market transactions, but currency speculation, corruption and independent enterprises condoned by the state.

Second Front   Allied invasion of Western Europe demanded by Stalin from 1941 to relieve German pressure on Soviet Union; opened with Anglo–American landings in Normandy on 6 Jun 1944.

Second International   Formed in Paris in 1889 and based on membership of national parties and trade unions, the Second International was a loose federation which held periodic international congresses. It stood for parliamentary democracy and thus rejected anarchist ideas, but also reaffirmed the commitment to Marxist ideas of the class struggle.

Second Reich   The German Empire 1871–1918 also known as the *Kaiserreich*; the period after German unification when Wilhelm I, King of Prussia was offered the throne of the Empire. The last Kaiser, Wilhelm II was forced to abdicate after the German army refused to support him at the end of the First World War.

Securitate   Romanian secret police during dictatorship of Nicolae Ceauçescu (1918– 1989).

SHAPE   Supreme Headquarters, Allied Powers in Europe; headquarters of the North Atlantic Treaty Organization, initially at Fontainebleau, then from 1966 in Brussels.

Show Trial   Political trials held for propaganda effect with generally pre-determined verdict, the most notorious of which were held during Stalin's 1930s purges and in post-war Eastern Europe.

Siegfried Line   German defensive line on Western Front in 1918; then the fortifications built by Germany against the French Maginot Line in the 1930s.

Sigurime   The security police in Albania during the Communist era.

Singing Revolution   Term applied to the Estonian demands for independence from the Soviet Union. It was a revolution in which no shots were fired and no blood was shed. The protests began in Jun 1988 with demands for the release of two political prisoners, Mart Niklus and Enn Tarto.

Social charter   The European Union (EU) Charter of Social Rights of Workers, setting out a pattern for a European labour law. Largely the work of Jacques Delors and his colleagues. Opposed by right-wing Conservatives, especially in Britain.

Social fascist   Abusive Communist epithet in early 1930s to describe Labour and Social Democratic competitors for working-class support.

Solidarity   Widely supported Polish free trade union formed on 8 Sep 1980; banned under martial law in Dec 1981. Formed government in 1989 with Tadeusz Mazowiecki as Prime Minister but appeared close to split over presidential candidate in 1990. Its leader, Lech Walesa, was eventually elected President.

Sottogoverno (Lit. 'quiet government')   The term used of the extended web of patronage in post-war Italian political life.

Soviet   (Russ. 'council') Workers' and soldiers' councils which emerged in the 1905 and 1917 Russian revolutions.

Sovkhoz (Russ. sovetskoe khozyaistvo, 'soviet farm') State-owned farm in the USSR.

Spartacists German radical socialists – named after Spartacus, the leader of a Roman slave revolt – led by Rosa Luxemburg and Karl Liebknecht who formed the German Communist Party in 1918.

'Splendid Isolation' Phrase used to describe Britain's diplomatic position in the latter part of the nineteenth century and, more generally, during the nineteenth century as a whole when Britain stood aside from entanglement in European alliances.

SS (Germ. Schutz Staffeln, 'guards detachment') Hitler's black uniformed bodyguard formed in 1928, led by Heinrich Himmler (1900–1945), which by 1936 controlled Germany's police force, guarded concentration camps, and created an elite military Waffen SS in 1939.

Stasi The name of the security police under the former Communist régime in East Germany. They were disbanded in the revolution of 1989.

State capitalism Term used by Vladimir Lenin (1870–1924) to describe the combination of central economic control and compromise with private financial interests in 1918 to preserve Bolshevik rule. More latterly a description of pre-1990 East European régimes.

Stormtroopers *See* SA.

Straits Question The issue of rights of passage through the Dardanelles and the Bosphorus which was disputed between the Great Powers and Turkey at several points in the nineteenth and twentieth centuries.

Subsidiarity The EU principle that, where possible, policy should be conducted at the lowest possible level of government. Only when this was impossible should a higher level of government become involved. It was defined in the 1991 Treaty on European Union.

Third Reich Period of Nazi power in Germany from 1933–1945, following upon the First Reich of the medieval Holy Roman Empire and the Second Reich from unification in 1871 until the defeat in 1918.

Third Republic Persistently weak French Republic from 1870 to 1946, but which effectively collapsed when Germany invaded in 1940, after having had 108 governments in 70 years.

Treuhandstalt The agency which organized the privatization of more than 8000 state enterprises in the former German Democratic Republic. Established in Mar 1990, its work was completed by the mid-1990s. Its head, Detlev Rohwedder, was assassinated by terrorists in Mar 1991.

Tripartism Name given to the joint governments of Christian Democrats, Socialists and Communists formed in France and Italy in the immediate aftermath of the Second World War. Tripartism lasted in Italy and also France only until 1947.

Triple Alliance Alliance formed between Germany, Austria–Hungary and Italy in 1882.

Triple Entente Agreement between Britain, France and Russia to resolve their outstanding colonial differences; it became a military alliance in 1914.

Trizonia Combined zones of American, British and French occupation in immediate post-World War II West Germany.

Trotskyist Follower of Leon Trotsky (1879–1940) who believed Stalin had betrayed the Russian Revolution and called for renewed socialist world revolution; briefly fashionable among student activists in the 1960s and 1970s.

Union Sacrée (Fr. Sacred Union) Government formed in France at the outbreak of the First World War which included, for the first time and as a symbol of national unity, two Socialists among its members.

Ustase   Croatian nationalist terrorist organization formed in 1929 which assassinated King Alexander of Yugoslavia in 1934 and formed a collaborationist Croatian state during the World War II Axis occupation.

Vatican 2   Year-long Roman Catholic Church Council called by Pope John XXIII which sat from 11 Oct 1962; sought friendlier relations with non-Catholic churches and appeared to promise a degree of liberalization.

Velvet Chancellors   First post-war Chancellors of the Federal Republic of Germany (West Germany), notably Konrad Adenauer (1876–1967), Chancellor from 1949 to 1963.

Velvet Divorce   The division on 1 Jan 1993 of Czechoslovakia into the separate states of the Czech Republic and Slovakia. So called because of the apparent amicable nature of the separation, but also an ironic reference to the 1989 Velvet Revolution (see below) which overthrew Communist rule.

Velvet Revolution   Term used for the revolution which ended the Communist régime in Czechoslovakia in 1989.

Victorious February   Term used (by the left) to describe the Communist takeover of Czechoslovakia in Feb 1948.

Volkshammer   Parliament in East Berlin until 1990 of the German Democratic Republic (East Germany).

Waffen SS   World War II elite military wing of the German SS, finally 40 divisions strong, made up of 'Aryans' from Germany and occupied European countries.

Walloons   French-speaking minority in industrial southern Belgium, making up 45 per cent of the population. The Mouvement Populaire Walloon seeks autonomy.

War Communism   Bolshevik policy from 1918–1921 to preserve régime in Russian Civil War, included seizure of agricultural produce, nationalization of industry, and harsh labour discipline.

War Guilt Clause   Art. 231 of the 1919 Versailles Treaty by which Germany acknowledged responsibility for World War I and which provided a legal basis for Allied reparations demands.

Warsaw Pact   *See* p. 31.

Weimar   Democratic German Republic from 1919–1933, named after the town in which a National Constituent Assembly met in Feb 1919 and drew up a constitution in Jul 1919.

Weltpolitik (Germ. lit. world politics)   A new trend in German foreign policy at the end of the nineteenth century. The Kaiser Wilhelm II determined to transform Germany into a first-rank global power. Ultranationalistic pressure combined with social and economic forces to support new interest in colonial expansion, the scramble for territory in China and Africa, and the establishment of a powerful navy.

White Russians   Anti-Bolshevik monarchist forces in the 1917–1921 Russian civil war, many of whom went into exile following the Red Army victory.

Winter War   War fought from 30 Nov 1939 to 12 Mar 1940 following the Soviet invasion of Finland.

Wirtschaftswunder   Term for the rapid recovery of the West German economy after the Second World War. The 'economic miracle', stimulated by the foreign aid received through the Marshall Plan (*see* p. 466) was associated with the economic policies of Ludwig Erhard.

Yalta Conference   The crucial conference of 4–11 Feb 1945 between Roosevelt, Churchill and Stalin which agreed the basic political structure of post-war Europe. There were to be East/West spheres of influence; a divided, disarmed and occupied Germany and Berlin following unconditional surrender; a 'Declaration on Liberated

Europe' guaranteeing democratic institutions in liberated states; and reaffirmation of the Atlantic and UN Charters. The US was later criticized for effectively placing Eastern Europe under Soviet control.

Yezhovschina   Stalinist purges in the 1930s, term coming from the head of the Soviet secret police. N.I. Yezhov (1894–1939).

Young Plan   Proposal by American businessman Owen D. Young (1874–1962) to reduce German war reparations by 75 per cent and extend payment period to 1988. Accepted by Germany in 1929 but Hitler abandoned payments in 1933.

Young Turks   Liberal reform movement among young army officers in the Ottoman Empire, active between 1903 and 1909.

Zimmermann Telegram   Coded message of 19 Jan 1917 from the German foreign minister, Arthur Zimmermann, to the German minister in Mexico, urging the conclusion of a German–Mexican alliance in the event of a declaration of war on Germany by America when Germany resumed unrestricted submarine warfare against shipping on 1 Feb.

Index